Adaptive Resilience

How to Thrive in a Digital Era

Maria Santacaterina

WILEY

Registered Offices
John Wiley & Sons, Inc., 111 River Street, Hoboken, NJ 07030, USA

John Wiley & Sons Ltd, The Atrium, Southern Gate, Chichester, West Sussex, PO19 8SQ, UK

For details of our global editorial offices, customer services, and more information about Wiley products visit us at www.wiley.com.

Wiley also publishes its books in a variety of electronic formats and by print-on-demand. Some content that appears in standard print versions of this book may not be available in other formats.

Library of Congress Cataloging-in-Publication Data

ISBN 9781119898184 (Cloth)
ISBN 9781119898191 (ePub)
ISBN 9781119898207 (ePDF)

Cover Design: Wiley
Cover Image: ©MF3d/Getty Images

Set in 11/14pts and Avenir LT Std by Straive, Chennai, India

SKY10054227_082923

To my family.

This book is dedicated to the leaders who strive to create new horizons to benefit present and future generations.

Contents

Preface

'Try to learn something about everything and everything about something.'[1]

These past three years have been particularly challenging for nearly everyone living on planet Earth, with the exception of the few, for whom financial concerns are not incidental to their daily lives. The global pandemic has shaken liberal democracies to their core, called into question the inequities of the capitalist system; and left war-torn, grief-stricken populations grappling to find new meaning in their lives.

Chief Executive Officers and the Boards of Directors are under increasing pressure to resolve the most intractable societal problems. They have sought to stabilise increasingly 'fragile' systems to ensure business continuity, whilst confronted with faltering business models, concerns over health in the workforce, safety and security issues, severe supply-chain disruption and climate change. Recent legislation is set to further regulate the functioning of Socio-Technical Systems and Artificial Intelligence, an all too pervasive part of our 'reality.'

This may at first glance appear overwhelming. However, human beings are remarkably *adaptive* and *resilient*.

We are at a new 'tipping point,' in the midst of a great transition without clear sight of our desired outcomes. It seems we are in a mad race for a destination that is as yet unknown. We do not have a clear vision and consequently the strategy as to how we will reach our new destination appears nebulous. However, this is an intrinsic part of the process of change. The so-called Exponential Age of Technology or the Fourth Industrial Revolution in the 21st century, is the moment 'to learn something about everything and everything about something,' lest you be left behind.

What concerns me, and I imagine many Business Leaders, is how we shall interact successfully with emergent technologies, and where this will take us on our future path of evolution. How shall we re-imagine our digital future for the benefit of Humanity and the Planet? Our quest to find meaning in the present and future reality shall be the subject matter of this book. A message to the unborn child, that through our uniqueness, consciousness, intelligence, curiosity, creativity and courage, we may still recognise what it means to be a 'human being,' distinct from *other inanimate forms* of 'Artificial Intelligence,' with the continuing evolution of *homo sapiens*.

As human beings, we have the unique ability to explore the past for lessons learned, while envisioning the future in the realm of the imagination. In contrast, 'Artificial Intelligence,' a subset of which is the confusingly named 'machine learning,' cannot compute nor fully discern the multifaceted dimensions of our 'reality.' We should not undervalue the power of the human mind, nor assume partially understanding the structure of some of the processes occurring within the human brain, sufficiently explain the *full* complexity of the same. Cognitive and perceptive abilities in human beings have developed over millennia and the intricacies of the same are not yet understood. In contrast, computers are only just beginning to learn; they serve to imitate some of the structures of the human brain and fail to replicate the complexity of human thought and actions.

Huxley, in his 'Romanes Lecture' in 1893, refers to ethical considerations as emanating from the 'cultured reflection' human beings have developed over time to form a sense of justice. This is, in turn, denoted by '*action from right motive*,' which he goes on to qualify further as '*the positive constituent of innocence and the very heart of goodness.*'[2]

To an extent, this still constitutes our notion of ethics today, and it is from the evolution of culture that societal norms develop. However, this essential notion of '*goodness*' has not necessarily been translated into the Socio-Technical Systems,[3] which operate in society across many sectors and run a large part of our lives today. From financial services to government institutions, business and manufacturing, as citizens, we are effectively entangled in a complex dynamic web of systems, which make up the greater whole. However, algorithms are structured using formal logic, a narrow set of mathematical rules to determine 'binary choices:' option A as an *intended* outcome, as opposed to option B, the less desirable *unintended* outcome. These computational processes rely on computable data being fed into the system; they are not yet *general* enough to take in the nuances of the human form of natural language and a highly complex *changing* reality. Often disproportionate and non-transparent algorithms and data sets lead to 'black box' or *unexplainable* outcomes, leaving potentially adverse effects on individual citizens unmitigated and residual risks undisclosed.

The fact that we are sometimes unable to explain how the algorithm has reached a given output adds an element of danger, depending on the context in which the particular model is being used. It begs the question as to whether we should continue to pursue current research to create 'Artificial super intelligence' to surpass our own capacities, if we are then putting ourselves in a situation where we cannot arrest the systems.[4] In the commercial sphere, we are surrounded by 'noise,' and it is not an easy task to extricate biases or errors embedded in the *data* being collected, which is used to train these *systems*. Since personal data about human beings is being collected indiscriminately, the potential for autonomous systems to cause harm is extremely high. Had we thought about the *ethical* values *a priori*, about what is *truly desirable*, we may have averted the worst outcomes. Just because we can use technology to assist a given task, doesn't mean we *should*.

The difficulty being that to reconcile '*the course of evolution into harmony with even the elementary requirements of the ethical ideal of the just and the good*,' has proven an elusive goal for millennia; as Huxley so eloquently puts it *both* for the '*ancient sage whether Indian or Greek*.'[5] Thus, in many of our modern theories and assumptions, we have conveniently ignored the '*messy*' nature of human morality, which is not so readily and neatly tied up into pure mathematical logic. We have chosen instead to look through an overly simplistic *lens*, constituting a somewhat imperfect and rather incomplete view of the reality; for instance, in economics, which underpins the thinking in modern businesses and governments that are inclined to take decisions based on the available and likely flawed data.

However, we need to take a much more nuanced view of emerging complexities in the reality, and strive to create innovative solutions to resolve structural and systemic problems that have thus far hindered progress. We need to prepare for *surprising* events and build a new capability, systematically, consciously and deliberately to ensure the future success of the Enterprise and the survival of our species. I call this capability Adaptive Resilience™ and we will explore what this means in nine dimensions, from Vision through to Evolution.

I hope you will enjoy the journey and that this book will spark the reader's curiosity and eventually inspire a *new way of thinking*. If we seek to *transform* our present reality, we need to change our thinking. It is within our reach to create a better world, though new *solutions* to our 'wicked problems' cannot be found through disparate actions or wilfully blinkered views of emergent complexities in the reality before us. Our world is constantly changing. It *continuously* evolves and transforms itself *synergistically* with the laws of nature and the universe, which we do not *fully* understand. We can envision an *alternative* future, provided we acknowledge the value of human relationships, our *interdependencies* and *interconnectedness* with the natural world. A world that *consciously* turns away from fear, anger, and *negative* self-interest can move towards a more positive growth trajectory. Celebrating the uniqueness of our human consciousness and ingenuity together with the infinite possibilities we are capable of discovering and exploring, for the benefit of *all* humanity and our planet.

> 'All nature is but art, unknown to thee;
> All chance, direction, which thou canst not see;
> All discord, harmony not understood;
> All partial evil, universal good;
> And spite of pride, in erring reason's spite
> One truth is clear: whatever is, is right.'[6]

London, 6 February 2023

Introduction

Adaptive Resilience™ is the ability to flourish as a human being in an artificially connected world, notwithstanding the impact of unforeseen events. We human beings are complex adaptive systems *par excellence*. We have an innate ability to adapt ourselves to changes in our environment. We are wired for survival and we are more successful in our quest when we seek to excel and thrive in social groups. As hunter-gatherers, our ancestors gradually learned to provide shelter, find food and eventually share stories in their communities through the use of a common language. No matter the hostility of the environment or competition with rival social groups, they found ways to adapt, and built up resilience by learning from experiences. Our basic needs have not changed. We need shelter, food and water to survive. However, our environment is radically altered and irrevocably so. In each of the following chapters we look through different lenses, seeking to understand the volatility, uncertainty, complexity and ambiguity in our modern world. In particular, taking a humanistic and holistic view of how business should respond to the so-called 'wicked' societal problems, which may present existential challenges. The ethical choices we make today will prove critical for the health and wellbeing of present and future generations, as well as of the planet itself.

The *Fourth Industrial Revolution,*[1] defined as the emergence of 'technology enabled platforms that combine both demand and supply to disrupt existing industry structures,' ushered in a new era of accelerating change. Boundaries between the physical, digital and biological world are no longer clearly defined. Arguably, we have leap-frogged more than a decade of technological progress in the last two years alone. Researchers claim the global pandemic has compressed the amount of time needed for radical technological change. The barrier is no longer technology. It is more about the lack of preparedness in society. While expectations of the Fifth Industrial Revolution are fast advancing new forms of interaction between humans and machines, the emerging possibilities require more careful consideration. We need to 'see' more clearly the ethical nature of the relationships between human beings and complex 'artificially intelligent' systems. Openly and consciously deliberate the nature of desirable outcomes, both for humanity and the planet. Substantive advances in digital technologies and the rapid proliferation of complex Socio-Technical Systems have fostered profound changes in society. The socio-economic, political and cultural landscape has been radically altered, impacting populations globally. Some claim the exponential *rate of growth* in the technology has itself accelerated exponentially;[2] encompassing every industrial sector and every aspect of our daily lives. This level of change is unprecedented in human history.

So, *how* can we thrive in the digital era?

Adaptive Resilience™ is a new business capability, which needs to be built deliberately in every organisation, both at an individual and at the collective level across the Enterprise ecosystem and thereby extended to society as a whole. Understanding the level of exposure to critical risks, inherent vulnerabilities in the business model, structural and systemic fragilities, and the potential for unexpected financial losses is business critical. However, this cannot be achieved without providing support at the granular level. Every individual will require holistic support to bounce back from adversity, in order for the whole organisation to respond to change with increasing resilience, whilst adapting to novel situations as they emerge. Failure to adequately prepare and respond appropriately to emerging changes whether internal or external in a timely fashion will place the organisation at high risk of extinction. Thus, organisations need to focus on strengthening their ability to withstand arbitrary shocks and proactively learn to overcome them with ease; after the shock passes, they must emerge stronger. It is a condition *sine qua non* for survival.

At the collective level, Adaptive Resilience™ must become part of a shared consciousness, embedded in the fabric of the Enterprise, pursued through its Vision, Strategy, and Culture. Oriented towards Growth, Innovation, and Transformation as part of a process, both of continuous learning and improvement. Ultimately, 'good' Governance, Sustainability and Evolution of the Enterprise must ensure its longevity and foster prosperity for all humanity both in the immediate present and in the future. It is a proactive endeavour, which cannot afford routine or repetition, boredom or disaffection; but should instead act as a catalyst for 'good' change and extend a beacon of hope. Trust, is the 'ultimate cause' that holds business and society together.

The urgency of building Adaptive Resilience™ within the fabric of the Enterprise has never been greater. Thinking of it this way could be helpful:

Adaptive Resilience™ is a new muscle, which needs to be nourished and *intentionally* exercised on a daily basis; as we all know with fitness, it takes time, effort and commitment to build.

Business cannot exist in a vacuum. It is an integral part and arguably the beating heart of society, with the power to transform its constructs and improve the quality of people's lives. Enabled by powerful new technologies, the Enterprise has a formidable opportunity to become a force for good. It is the conduit and the driving force of positive change in society. We cannot expect that governments have the necessary entrepreneurial capabilities to enact true innovation. But, that is not necessarily the role of government, since their duties and responsibilities have been defined differently. Perhaps the time has come to clarify anew the right balance between governments, industries, businesses and citizens. Chief Executive Officers of large corporations are called upon to demonstrate leadership, drive innovation, and inform government policies. However, effective policies can only be made reliably if there is a clear separation of powers and multiple diverse stakeholders are invited to the decision-making table, ranging from large businesses to small and medium sized businesses and single business owners, in recognition of the structural changes occurring in the world economy. Government should focus on creating the right environment for new investment opportunities and infrastructure to support innovation and economic growth. It should also provide safety and security for its citizens and behave in a responsible and ethical manner. Equally, it should be held to account by individual citizens, in the same way that business must seek its legitimacy within society as a whole, while earning and sustaining citizens' trust over the long-term, one member at a time.[3]

In an increasingly interconnected world, the 'surface area of attack' has substantially increased. Multiple concomitant threats create a cascading effect and undermine business continuity. Cyber 'warfare' is no longer a state affair, since cyberattacks affect public and private sector businesses with a degree of regularity, increasing financial pressures, as darker storm clouds gather. Previously familiar boundaries have become blurred, replaced by unforeseeable externalities. Short-term thinking and the pursuit of short-term goals are no longer viable options. The forces of change, amplified through the 'network effect,' necessitate new ways of thinking and more flexible approaches to overcome the challenges of the emerging reality. A small change in one part of the system can extend across the whole ecosystem at lightning-fast speed. Existing vulnerabilities become exacerbated and destabilise the hierarchical structures while exposing fundamental systemic weaknesses. 'Business as usual' has evaporated. Businesses large and small must instead proactively prepare for and aim to consistently anticipate *unknowable* future shocks. The appropriate level of responsiveness constitutes a level of preparedness for the 'unknown unknown.' And therein lies the paradox. However, consistent coordinated actions throughout the Enterprise ecosystem build adaptive capacity and resilience as internal and external situations evolve. We need to move from 'just-in-time' responses to thorough preparation for 'just-in-case' scenarios at the point of failure.

Prior to the Covid-19 global pandemic, companies and governments had been adjusting to increased risks, natural disasters, cyberattacks, technological disruption, loss of confidence and public distrust, partly fomented by media outlets. However, the unexpected outbreak of SARS-CoV-2 coronavirus late in the autumn of 2019 forced radical change. The virus knew no borders: its fast transmission rates and mutations had caught the world off guard.[4] Consequently, the world economy came to a grinding halt. Governments imposed partial or complete lockdowns for extended periods of time, including full border closures. The virus appeared out of control and severe restrictions on civil liberties seemed the only way to contain the spread. Governments attempted to justify their actions by suggesting they were being 'led by the science.' Businesses were forced to close; healthcare systems were at breaking point, and a degree of social unrest ensued.

We were *all* woefully ill prepared. But *should* we have been?

Notwithstanding the lack of preparedness, the response to the pandemic and the immediate aftermath was exemplary of human resourcefulness, intelligence and collaboration. Adaptive Resilience™ is, in essence, our unique human ability to sense, probe and respond appropriately when novel situations *suddenly* appear on the horizon. There are many lessons to be drawn from the coronavirus outbreak. One lesson learned the hardest way possible was that decoupling public health from the economy and environmental policy is a dangerous miscalculation. It is clear from scientific research that the natural equilibrium in the Earth's ecosystems has been severely disrupted, causing an increased risk of pathogen contamination from animals to human beings, due to significant biodiversity and habitat loss.[5] We cannot continue with the current level of pollution, and particularly fossil fuel combustion, without compromising our chances of survival long term. Since human health is inextricably linked with climate change, we must be prepared to change our ways and remain open to seeking new pathways for growth.

The aim must be to proactively redress the imbalances caused by human activities, better understand Nature's innate resilience, and explore new possibilities of working with nature *not* against it.

There is an urgent moral question which must be answered. Scientists had been modelling threats of this nature for decades, and yet policy makers dismissed their concerns. Lives were lost and there is no monetary value that can ever compensate for an avoidable single life lost. A person's life is simply worth more than the roll of a dice. Healthcare professionals were placed at unnecessary risk, since vital basic equipment such as PPE (personal protective equipment) was scarce, as were hospital beds and respiratory equipment. All humanity faced the same threat and it became apparent there were insufficient vaccines for everyone, in the first batches produced. And yet the claim made was that nobody is safe until everyone is vaccinated. But, shouldn't we be attacking the root causes of such incidences, instead of just scratching the surface with apposite remedies? Although some countries are transitioning from pandemic to endemic, the threat persists and the legacy impacts of coronavirus on the world population are of an order of magnitude greater. Covid-19 exposed both the extensive nature and scale of the global distribution problem, inherent supply chain fragilities, institutional failures and crucially the disproportionate impact on developing nations.

Globalisation has not fostered the necessary transitions towards a more equitable, prosperous future. The inherent vulnerabilities of the financial system pose a threat to the Global System as a whole. Urgent action is required to change the trajectory.

There are no shortcuts that can be taken to foster human development. We simply cannot allow the myopic pursuit of short-term gains to persist. While investment in new technology has been consistently high, investments in human development have been 'patchy,' and there are noticeable gaps in human capabilities.[6] Profits are vital for business, but they are the consequence of 'good' actions, not the end itself. Just as machines do not produce useful artefacts by themselves, without skilful human intervention, profits alone do not foster improved productivity. Moreover, profits that can be sustained, an order of magnitude greater will ensue, given the *right* focus.

'Economics and Ethics *naturally* come into rather *intimate relations* with each other since both recognisably deal with the problem of *value*.'[7]

We have a problem of distribution and of *real* value creation that is so often narrowly defined by monetary value alone. The definition of *value* in the modern world has been too closely linked with the financial markets. Whereas there is an intrinsic need for business to deliver products and services that better serve human *ideals*, the needs of *all* their stakeholders, employees, customers, communities, suppliers, shareholders, society as a whole and the environment. Ethics, purpose and the reflection of human values are 'not amenable to scientific description or logical manipulation.' Ethics-based principles and moral values are more akin to 'sympathetic interpretation' than 'intellectual cognition.' Emotions drive human behaviour, while reason provides the context and 'culture history' that may better explain the human condition. Economics as a science relies on basic assumptions calculated using mathematical logic, whereas 'human conduct' and 'consciousness' cannot be reduced to the same. The 'creation of value' is also 'distinctly more than the satisfaction of desire.'[8]

The scale and extent of our problems, not least the *entanglement* of our global systems and economies, simply means that we cannot act alone. Intervening in only one part of the system will prove insufficient to resolve the problems of society as a whole. We need to act jointly and in a coordinated manner in our efforts to find workable solutions with lasting impact at scale. Government-public-private sector partnerships, working together with civil society, all need to be pulling in the same direction. To 're-boot' the global economy and restore peace in the world, we *all* need to use our best efforts collaboratively.

'Stakeholder capitalism is not about politics . . . . It is capitalism driven by *mutually beneficial relationships* between you and the employees, customers, suppliers, and communities your company relies on to prosper.'[9]

Good business is, in essence, about building good relationships. Trust is the foundational cornerstone, which enables business leaders to evolve their business models, and organisations to become fit for the future. There needs to be consistency and deliberate ethical directionality in its formation. This requires a radical shift in mental models, recognising the *nature* of the ethical *challenges* facing the organisation has changed. The new possibilities afforded by processing large volumes of data at scale must also be supported by an inclusive, equitable, and resilient socio-economic ecosystem, with beneficial outcomes *deliberately* being sought by those designing and deploying *algorithms* embedded within increasingly complex and adaptive Socio-Technical Systems. Understanding that we are all entangled in a complex web of connectivity that is continuously evolving; and that our efforts will be rendered futile, if we try to resist the tidal wave of rapid change.

'In a real sense all life is inter-related. All men are caught in an inescapable network of mutuality, tied in a single garment of destiny. Whatever affects one directly, affects all indirectly . . . . This is the inter-related structure of reality.'[10]

Ethical leadership is business critical. Ethical decisions have a transformative power within the Enterprise. People are more willing to unite around a common cause, motivated by a shared set of values. Clearly defined values are essential for *re*-building trust and confidence, notwithstanding the challenges the Enterprise may face. The moral philosophy of the Enterprise creates social cohesion and provides a powerful sense of direction, identity and belonging. It instils a strong sense of purpose and fosters stability, as leaders grapple with the complexity of the modern world and its unexpected challenges. Ultimately, the *right* actions in response to visibly difficult situations drive superior levels of performance, engender new competitive advantages and attract new talent. Notwithstanding the challenges presented by an all-encompassing use of Socio-Technical Systems, strong ethical principles must be embodied within the fabric of the Enterprise for enduring business success. Ethics is the key to unlocking widely shared prosperity for multiple diverse stakeholders. If we aspire to do the right thing, we are creating a 'virtuous' growth cycle and a more harmonious set of relationships across the globe. If this is the change we are seeking, we simply need to act without fear, anxiety, or anger.

The moral question extends to the quality of work, how we carry out our duties and how we choose to live our lives. As business leaders, we can choose to bring business ethics to the fore, proactively restore trust with real vigour and commitment, and thereby begin re-imagining our digital future. Good business ethics can be practised, for example, by extending the principle of transparency and fairness across the organisation. Not just in terms of decent working conditions, equitable pay structures and appropriate financial incentives, but also gender parity, equal treatment and proportionate representation across all social groups, being mindful and respectful of different cultures and values across the business ecosystem. Ensuring diversity of thought, guaranteeing freedom of expression, whilst proactively mitigating *algorithmic* biases, to ensure all staff members are treated in a fair and equitable fashion. Treating people with dignity and respect necessitates *meaningful* growth, *fulfilling* and *varied* employment opportunities, where individuals may complete 'whole' tasks, as part of *autonomous self-organising* working groups. Bridging the 'capability gap' entails solving the generational divide, forging new synergies across *multiple* disciplines to create well-rounded successful organisations that richly benefit from benchmarking wisdom and continuity, while allowing for innovation, enhanced by the cross-stimulus of different age groups, genders and ethnicities working together. The transition to a new phase in the evolution of the Enterprise should not be viewed through a simplistic *mechanistic* lens, as merely transactional, no matter how pressing cost reduction measures or other pressures may be at any given moment in time. Business is first and foremost *relational*.

Ethical choices substantiate the legitimate purpose of business. In every crisis there is also an opportunity for deeper reflection. Through the process, we may discover valuable insights that help us make the *right* decisions and enact *more beneficial* outcomes. Leaders must make conscious efforts to develop new technologies for the benefit of humanity and the planet. Technology should be valued as a *useful* tool; it should not be used antagonistically or as a *proxy* for government and religion. Individual freedoms and human rights must be guaranteed, including human *autonomy* and the right to *privacy*. The indiscriminate use of technology to gather copious amounts of personal sensitive data, including biometric data, without prior consent and proper scrutiny of how this data is used, shared and stored will cause society to fall apart, provoking distrust and unnecessary hardships. The growing asymmetry of information is tantamount to the asymmetry power and invariably a destabilising force within society. Without civil obedience, there is no social cohesion; and no government can *assure* safety and security for all citizens, *without* peace and stability.

The loss of individual privacy is symptomatic of a new fragility that has crept into the Enterprise. Everything that is part of the network is inherently vulnerable to attack and by definition, insecure. Whether inside corporations, governments or any other institution, excessive structural rigidities reinforce systemic weaknesses that inevitably result in security failures. Data leakages are akin to gross misconduct and may prove catastrophic for market valuations. Large corporations may never recover from the ensuing reputational damage. Without protecting the individual's right to privacy and giving them control over how their data is used, it is difficult to see how collective security may be served.

'There will never be a really free and enlightened State until the State comes to recognise the individual as a higher and independent power, from which all its power and authority are derived and treats him accordingly.'[11]

Individual autonomy is not necessarily incompatible with social cohesion. On the contrary, self-awareness and self-respect are necessary components for any organisation and society to function properly as a whole. Non-coerced self-expression and natural spontaneity constitutes the necessary dynamism in society, fostering human progress. Whether for the State, the Corporation or Civil Society in general, there needs to be a healthy counterbalance to salient issues; in matters of morality, each individual person must be free to exercise their own conscience and evaluate *what is right* and *what is wrong*, both in relation to their own individual needs and those of others. In contemporary society, clear sight of guiding ethical principles is sorely lacking. Owing to omnipresent digital communication technologies, there is a degree of confusion with regards to self-identity and a significant distortion of what it means to be a human being.

In the vortex of change we are currently experiencing, the so-called VUCA[12] environment, business leaders can no longer shirk their responsibilities and accountability in exercising their 'duty of care' towards individuals and society as a whole, through the delivery of long-term value. In essence, they must *carefully* consider the *nature* and the broader implications of the new *dynamics* of change. Resisting the easy options, they *should* instead *explore* new possibilities further along on the horizon, in order to gain a better understanding of the complexities and ethical *challenges* before them. They cannot solely rely on data, but must engage frequently with multiple diverse stakeholders, in order to make better-informed decisions and value judgments. In particular, they must look for critical connections, and identify areas where they can make a difference, tackling the 'big problems' such as climate change, *holistic* health and wellbeing, environmental degradation and other intractable societal challenges, while simultaneously managing *multiple often divergent, stakeholder interests*. They must also steer their own course to create better futures through *useful* and productive innovation that is worthwhile, whether in response to pressures and demands from governments, investors, employees, customers and the wider society. They must also confront the lack of clarity in the available sources of information and take into account there may be restrictions in the freedom of speech.

'The Web as I envisaged it, we have not seen it yet. The future is still so much bigger than the past.'[13]

Notwithstanding unscrupulous actors,[14] the World Wide Web may afford governments and businesses alike the best opportunity to create more equitable digital futures for all members of society. Access to the Internet as a *global public good* is deemed a *human right* in many nations. The Internet may yet foster enhanced collaboration within a global governance structure to ensure a free, safe, secure, productive and collaborative environment. The principles of non-exclusion and non-hostile, non-adversarial relationships may yet engender *true* innovation on a global scale, provided there is access to good education in order to validate *technological inputs* and verify best uses. Owing to the immediacy and the direct impacts of technological disruption, we must seek to improve our capabilities and raise standards of education in schools and in businesses in order to enhance human performance. We must also seek to establish better forms of government, improve critical infrastructure and create more *flexible* organisational structures, while meeting existing and unmet needs of society.

It is ironic that a great deal of 'noise,' *disinformation* and *misinformation*, permeates the 'Age of Information.' As technology evolves, less scrupulous actors shielded with impunity, owing to their monopolistic tendencies, are causing *real* harm in the *real* world. From 'deep fakes,' to 'tokenisation' and the 'metaverse,' new challenges are emerging as human weaknesses are ruthlessly exploited for *exclusive* commercial *ends*. Clearly, the geopolitical, socio-economic and global health challenges we now face are an order of magnitude greater *than previously known*. Coercive 'control power' is no longer confined to armed conflicts. It can be exercised on a mass scale *instantaneously*, globally and it is *unprecedented*. Is there no escape? It is highly doubtful the Internet Communication Technology 'explosion,' steered towards exploitative ends, will enable us to realise its potential and 'real' value. Perhaps the Internet and the Internet of Things as it stands today was *not* the aim for this technology in origin.

'Any organization that designs a system (defined broadly) will produce a design whose structure is a copy of the organization's communication structure.'[15]

The task at hand is to seek clarity and create better forms of communication and quality sources of information. Tim Berners Lee had conceived of the World Wide Web, as a mechanism to facilitate sharing knowledge on a global scale; and it is potentially the most liberating general technology of our time. But, *what if* 'Artificial Intelligence' was enabled to moderate content? As things stand, it would seemingly further obfuscate the reality. Too few players hold the reins of power and the risk of hegemonic control is increasingly likely.

Most Enterprise Management Systems are designed with insufficient flexibility to enable good communication at all times. They may fail to sufficiently account for organisational factors in the original intent; design is generally focused on *technical* constraints, while discounting human needs. However, the *full* potential of the Enterprise cannot be realised without effective organisational design, which necessitates *flexibility*. Systems must continuously evolve to reflect the changes in communication requirements and the organisational structure itself. Understanding how data and information is shared within complex social systems, while securing the transfer of knowledge is business critical. Envisioning how to optimise human interactions within complex adaptive Socio-Technical Systems, powered by 'Artificial Intelligence' necessitates greater care and consideration and above all the involvement of the *participants in the system*. What might the desirable outcomes be? Ambitious results are best achieved by being responsive and adaptive to change in an orderly manner, whilst allowing *sufficient* room for manoeuvre. Understanding the complexity of human relations will afford us the opportunity to find better solutions.

This is a unique *'what if'* moment in our human history. Extensive structural and systemic change across institutions, businesses, supply-chains and *natural ecosystems*, as well as the functioning of governments themselves will invariably send shock waves through the Global System. The forces of change are complex, non-linear, multi-dimensional and multi-directional. There is no clear-cut answer for what is *right* and what is *wrong*. Leaders must *sense* the emerging reality, seize new opportunities and re-configure their organisations as they seek to navigate towards safer shores. Whilst re-defining the meaning of *value* and the very existence of the Enterprise itself. In today's complex and turbulent environment, there is a longing for stability. Supply-chain interruptions are intensifying; there are more stranded assets and sabotage in the flow of information is prevalent. Quite apart from pervasive technological disruption across industrial sectors, the recent outbreak of war in the Ukraine,[16] has added further layers of complexity with long-lasting effects exacerbating geopolitical uncertainty. There is no graver, nor greater threat to humanity than the catastrophic consequences of war, famine, disease and now climate change.

Our quest must be to enrich the lives of people around the world, whilst building an inclusive, equitable and sustainable digital future. The Enterprise ought to be self-sustaining and *fully* integrated within society, seeking to optimise human wellbeing, whilst innovating *with* nature to realise *mutually* beneficial outcomes. There is an urgent need to realise long-term value creation for *all* the stakeholders. True stakeholder value over the long term can only be secured if we focus on individual human needs, while optimising for the long-term public good.

Our universal human 'virtues' beget *more* value, and it's certainly not the other way around. Better to focus on that which unites us rather than that which divides us. Our whole existence depends upon a deep-rooted relationship with nature and with others. Whichever lens you choose, there is one fundamental truth: the laws of nature cannot be ignored, and if we persist, it will be to our own detriment. We can no longer view the environment and Life on Earth as separate. They are intertwined and irrevocably so, just as human survival, health and wellbeing are tied to restoring *natural* ecosystems, safeguarding *all* Life on Earth.

This is a significant paradigm shift. It will require radical change in our way of thinking, the way we evolve organisations, structurally and systemically. The magnitude and increasing complexity of this change will be explored in subsequent chapters. How we manage the transition will be critical: deep-rooted divisions in society, technological disparity, climate change, long-lasting effects of pandemics such as Covid-19 and intensifying geopolitical tensions will impact possible pathways to the future. Societal and environmental implications can no longer be ignored and must be addressed by nation-state governments, international institutions, corporations, businesses of all sizes and citizens globally, as a matter of urgency. There also needs to be an open and vigorous debate so that we can find a new consensus around the manner in which powerful new technologies are deployed.

The urgency has never been greater to harness the true potency of emerging new technologies and to create new pathways towards a sustainable digital future. However, this means working on the definition of *what is* desirable and *what is not*. We need to consciously craft our future as opposed to blindly following the path of least resistance, simply because it is *technically* possible to do so. We can no longer continue being reliant upon technology to solve our problems; instead we should focus on the *quality* of our decisions and actions, the pathways we have chosen and the directionality of change, in order to build a *sustainable* digital future. Emphasis being placed on what is humanly possible and desirable, to avert self-destruction and extinction.

Adaptive Resilience™ is both a physical state and a presence of mind. It is the willingness to explore and make sense of the contextual reality with sight of the horizons. It pertains to *flexibility* designed into the organisational structures and *knowledge* management systems of the Enterprise. This will help foster human progress and steer the Enterprise and society in the *right* direction. In practical terms, the organisation's responsiveness to change, structural *flexibility* and its systemic capacity to *adapt*, together with its *preparedness* for the future will ultimately strengthen its *resilience;* its ability to overcome adversity and withstand *unforeseen* externalities. This is with the understanding that the depth and complexity of the situation requires deeper reflection, broader collaboration, diversity of thought and trans-disciplinary experiences to foster *more* creative solutions for intractable societal problems. We already have the tools at our disposal to discover new pathways for inclusive, equitable and sustainable growth. We *should* deliberately strive to engender multi-stakeholder value. The next phase in our transition may be turbulent or else *it can be smooth.* The *choice* is ours to make.

Chapter 1

Vision
/ˈvɪʒ(ə)n/

HORATIO:

O day and night, but this is wondrous strange.

HAMLET:

And therefore as a stranger give it welcome.
There are more things in heaven and earth, Horatio,
Than are dreamt of in (y)our philosophy.[1]

Vision is about conceptualising new ideas. It has both a philosophical and an *embodied* psychological dimension, since it emanates from a complex visual-sensory system. Our vision enables us to process and make sense of information we 'perceive' in the external physical environment. Our perception and awareness of 'objects' in the environment, form a *dynamic* internal 'symbolic representation' of the reality, whilst our understanding and knowledge is enhanced by accessing knowledge stored deep within our 'memory.' Human perception is therefore a complex set of processes, comprising multisensory integration and intellectual synthesis. It is the primary way we 'see' and make sense of the world, whilst learning and acquiring new knowledge through complex cognitive, emotional and sensory processes. Our understanding of the reality is enhanced through our personal interactions with the environment, social interactions and contextual experiences. Human perception is constantly evolving, shaped by learning, memory, cognition, expectations, sensations, experiences and attention, which is of course selective. We *naturally* choose what we wish to focus on. We are sentient beings, and our unique abilities to perceive and *feel* 'objects' in our surroundings, extends our knowledge and deepens our awareness. As human beings, we are able to discern complex emotional and aesthetic influences, as well as experiencing physical 'phenomena,' in our reality. However, we may not be able to *fully* explain everything through rational or conscious thought.[2]

Hamlet's conjecture is that everything we 'see' and all that we 'know' is not necessarily *complete* knowledge. We may not have sufficient information to understand the *whole* reality before us. Through the metaphor of Hamlet's feigned madness, Shakespeare entertains the duality of rationality and irrationality, which paradoxically may co-exist. Hamlet's disguise is an attempt to 'see' the 'truth' more clearly. He observes we should remain open to alternative explanations of the reality we see before us, hinting there may be limits to our rational thinking. When interpreting the reality before us, there is a natural rivalry between conscious and unconscious thought.[3] There are sensations we may 'perceive' more vividly, within our imagination, *phantasia*, than may appear to be 'true' in the physical 'objects' of our reality, *phantasmata*.[4] As we look through this multi-faceted prism, the light is refracted in a myriad of ways; depending upon which lens we choose, we may see one aspect, one colour, and then another. Hence, we may never be absolutely certain of the reality before us. Preferably, we should entertain the 'wonder' of events as they unfold, in order to make sense of the present and envision future possibilities.

Aristotle observed our attention is paradoxically 'voluntary and involuntary, perceptual and intellectual.'[5] We may choose to interpret the existing reality through a 'rational search' of our human memory, whether recently created or inherited, and at the same time respond reflexively to external stimuli through physical actions and orientation in the reality, as we explore both time and space. Additionally, we may consciously use our intellect and imagination to make sense of our surroundings. We have a subjective notion and sense that we are in control of our actions, such that we may exercise our human agency and 'free will.' In reality, there may be an element of causality, to the extent that subsequent events may be influenced by prior events. Thus, we may experience moments of serendipity, creating an element of 'chaos' in our lives; until we are able to rationalise and make sense of any unexpected events we may experience.

There is a hint in Hamlet's conjecture that the world is *not* an orderly place, whereby one can simply apply logic or reason to ascertain 'universal truths.' Perhaps, they do not exist and we should be willing to question our understanding of the same. The implication here is that there are multiple dimensions and layers of meaning to be discovered upon deeper reflection. We should also be aware that preconceived ideas or biases may distort our perception of the reality; and so we should take the time to further investigate any logical conclusion that may be derived from the 'signals' or cues that may be visible at first sight.[6] It seems 'seeing' is not quite 'believing.' Thus, we may undertake an initially 'chaotic' process to further explore the significance of our human existence, as we try to *make sense of* and ascertain meaning from our perceived reality. The 'symbolic representation' of reality is therefore insufficient to describe its full depth of meaning. There is a non-linear progression in our acquisition of knowledge, which remains open to serendipity, events we were not expecting. In many ways, it is often by accident that we make our biggest discoveries, and further understand the 'notion of truth.' It is as much a philosophical journey, as the consequence of complex visual-sensory processes.

Aristotle referred to 'perceptual awareness' as a proxy definition for human consciousness. The information we receive from physical stimuli in our external environment, *phantasmata* is scrutinised by the intellect *phantasia*, and processed selectively, depending on the intensity of the 'signals.' For Aristotle, our 'perceptual awareness' consists of the relationship between the *conscious* mind and a 'higher order' *unconscious* mental state that may exist *only* in the realm of the imagination. Modern science supports this notion, adding a degree of complexity, since the conscious state comprises two parts, one of which is an *awareness* of the other. Thus, the 'first order' perception of the physical 'object' interacts with the 'higher order' value judgment of the same. Without this integration of sensory perception and intellect, we cannot be certain that the 'object' exists in the reality.[7] Aristotle recognised human consciousness (awareness) could be an 'immaterial perceptual activity.'[8] Human intelligence cannot be explained purely in 'symbolic' terms or formal mathematical logic. Aristotle refers to the intangible quality of human consciousness (understanding), which he believes to be an inherently *dynamic* process.

Whether or not there is a hierarchy in our human consciousness, or whether there is a spiritual dimension and a higher order of intentionality, is still a matter of scholarly debate. For Aristotle, human intuition, *phantasia*, is of a higher order than *phantasmata*, the material substance or 'object' of our thoughts. Thus, the visual, sensory, and physical experience of the external reality we perceive is of a 'lower-order' representational state. A student of Plato, he already knew intuition was a necessary component in order to *fully* 'see' and extend our knowledge and deepen our understanding of the existing reality; while at the same time *sensing* the emerging reality. In the context of reason, Plato asserts intuition draws upon 'pre-existing knowledge,' ultimately enabling us to comprehend the 'true' nature of the reality we perceive.[9] It is the quality of our *tacit* knowledge, things we 'know' implicitly, *without knowing we know* that can be accessed through our subconscious and unconscious state of mind, which constitutes the uniqueness of our human intelligence.

Significantly, if we combine rational *conscious* thought, our innate ability to reason using logic, with our 'higher intellect' intuition, and abandon any preconceptions, there is no limitation to our 'higher order' thinking, the human imagination. We can *sense* much more than we can explain, in relation to the physical 'objects' we actually perceive in the reality and perhaps choose to describe through our use of the human form of natural language.[10] For Plato *tacit* knowledge is the 'soul of eternity.' Through our individual 'perceptual awareness,' we have a unique ability to perceive a multifaceted reality, if we are so inclined to 'see' the possibilities that may not yet be visible.[11] Human consciousness is the critical differentiating factor defining the nature of our humanity; it constitutes the essence of our unique identity and our biological selves.

Perception is therefore a complex phenomenon, while attention is of necessity a selective process. It is energy-intensive and we simply cannot focus our attention everywhere; so we have evolved human intelligence to prioritise the tasks we wish to focus on, subject to our needs. Information is then actively filtered by our own individual mind, based on *how* we choose to respond within a given context. We have the ability to find appropriate responses 'automatically,' often without making use of conscious thought processes and deliberate reasoning. Contemporary scientists have suggested our intuition has evolved to further our capacity to spontaneously understand changes in the environment and more easily relate to others, enabling us to sense and anticipate their responses. This may be referred to as *adaptive intelligence*, which comprises dynamic interactions with the environment. We instantaneously adapt our thinking to the changing reality, necessary for beneficial social interactions and our own survival.

In our quest to find meaning, we continuously learn and evolve our thinking over the course of the human lifespan. It is a dynamic process and forms part of our lifelong human development. Through our complex visual-sensory system, we can acquire and process new information and simultaneously access knowledge that may be stored deep within our subconscious memory. The human brain is the most powerful autonomous control and self-regulatory system we know of, that is both adaptive and resilient. It controls, regulates and coordinates all the physical and mental 'activities,' making 'adjustments' as required. Electrochemical 'signalling' and kinetic 'information' enables us to interpret 'objects' in the environment. Our understanding of the reality is therefore enhanced by our 'direct' and 'indirect' experiences of the same; and the 'information' we perceive through our complex visual-sensory system. As a result of which, the human brain determines our thoughts, actions and behaviours. It *self-organises itself*, selectively identifies and interprets the relevant sensory information perceived through the physical body and combines this with our own awareness of our *inner* mental state. The 'human mind' constitutes a 'unified perceptual landscape,' a unique individual representation of the reality. Human awareness is therefore intentional, both in terms of our own 'inner mental state' and of the 'objects' we 'see' in the external world.[12]

'We think about actions before we perform them. We make representations of them, but why? We expect and act according to the expectancy .... Expectancy is a preparatory action.'[13]

Human consciousness 'acts' both as an anticipatory and regulatory mechanism to shape and influence our behaviours; it enables us to 'play' our intended actions forward in the 'inner space' of the mind, in anticipation of the desired possible outcomes. In a sense, the inner space of our mind affords us the safety of a 'learning zone.' Once the decision is made, our choices are exemplified through physical actions or behaviours. This constitutes an intricate interplay between the human form of communication, namely the expression of our thoughts through the use of language; 'play,' the acquisition of new knowledge through experimentation and 'real' life experiences; and manipulation of the tools we 'choose,' namely *prâxis*, practice and use thereof for a specific purpose. Our unique ability to communicate and 'play,' entertain counterfactuals or possibilities not yet realised, combined with our extensive use of 'artefacts' and creativity constitutes a 'qualitative jump' in the evolution of our human capabilities over time. No other animal, living organism or human-made 'artefact' is able to seamlessly and spontaneously perform this unique combination of skills simultaneously. In a difficult situation, we naturally 'look for' other possibilities and create new 'options' for the actions we may take, by ourselves. Before taking any action in the 'real' world, we carefully evaluate the consequences of the possible responses that are pertinent to the situation at hand. Should we misunderstand the facts as we perceive them, misinterpret the 'objects' in the environment and make an error of judgment, we quickly and autonomously course correct.

How we respond to the external environment depends upon the relative intensity of internal and external stimuli; essentially, our expectations are determined by our perception of the same through our senses.[14] In effect, while forming a single view of the reality, our human brain also differentiates the relative importance of one sense over another in a specific situation, in order to build realistic and plausible hypotheses of possible actions and their likely outcomes. Anticipation of those likely outcomes enables us to cope with any disruptions and uncertainty in the environment, building our innate resilience. Since our choices are subject to change according to our human needs within a given context, human beings are also highly adaptive. Whilst we cannot predict the future, we can prepare for the 'best' possible responses. This helps explain the nature of human memory, an integrative functionality that helps create a bridge across different time horizons. We may also choose to 'save,' whether consciously or subconsciously, seemingly insignificant information in a given context for later use. Owing to the natural *flexibility* in our human *thinking* processes, we can go backwards and forwards, as often as required, to explore all the possibilities in a given situation. If we then choose to reflect upon the past, it may serve to enhance our understanding and knowledge of the present, as we entertain future possibilities through continuous learning. In effect, we use our memory to better understand the present and 'optimise' present behaviours, as we prepare and organise ourselves for future adaptation. The human brain is effectively a 'highly distributed self-organising system;' it comprises rich and highly complex thought processes associated with space and time, that we interpret through a variety of dense 'highly distributed patterns' of neural activities.

Our innate *adaptive resilience* acts both as a control and regulatory mechanism; and since the human brain uses energy efficiently, there is a reason for the activities it engages in. Thus, as sentient beings, we are able to anticipate the likely outcomes of our actions and make the relevant contextual choices as required. Though the exact nature of multisensory and multidirectional connections from the brain to the physical body and vice versa are not yet fully explained, neuroscientists reference the *integrative* nature of human experiences. Our *unique* individual experiences are 'known' to influence our subjective and objective understanding of the reality and *inform* our patterns of behaviour. [15, 16] Perception is defined as a function of physical stimuli being sent to the nervous system, which in turn trigger chemical reactions.[17] In reality, there is no arbitrary or 'binary' separation between the sensations we perceive in the physical body and the 'images' or 'symbolic representations' we experience in our minds. As a result of which our thought processes and behaviours are highly complex. There is nothing *mechanical* about the integrative thinking processes taking place; the seamless 'alchemy' and 'energy' being 'generated' and exchanged at a cellular level is *synergistic*. We can create a comprehensive view of the reality, which we not only 'see,' but also instantly put into context and understand.

'Reasoning draws a conclusion, but does not make the conclusion certain, unless the mind discovers it by the path of experience.'[18]

Human experience is therefore an integral part of our *thinking*. Remarkably our 'inner-vision' or intuition serves to *anticipate* the emergence of new 'events,' plausibly and reliably. It helps us transcend doubt, fear and uncertainty and *informs* our responses to the reality we are experiencing. The 'immaterial perceptual activity' Aristotle referred to is a *unique* human property, belonging to the *dynamic* nature of human intelligence. It is difficult to replicate or simulate these capabilities in algorithmic 'machine learning' systems and computation. Human consciousness has a unique 'subjective' quality and a spiritual dimension, an ethereal beauty that rests within the eye of the beholder. In this sense, 'real' life experiences and our 'diverse' perceptions of the reality are *dynamically* unique to each individual person. Thus, predicting human decisions, actions and behaviours, whatever the circumstances, whether rational or reflexive is an *arduous* task. This is further complicated by the 'intersubjectivity' of human relations, our human need and ability to understand the environment through interactions with others and our own interactions with the *perceived reality* combined. This is perhaps one reason why some leaders shy away from the 'messy middle,' the business of proactively shaping corporate culture. In today's increasingly automated, *artificially connected*, 'big data' driven world, this is a 'big' mistake.

The practice of spontaneous adaptation as the situation requires entails *phrónêsis*. It constitutes the 'practical wisdom' human beings develop over time, through experience. Thus, we develop our understanding of what is required in a given situation and refine our ability to deliberate between *what is right* and *what is wrong*. There are no hard and fast rules. Moral reasoning is a form of *intuitive* reasoning, which stems from an awareness of *epistême*, scientific knowledge, a more precise qualification of 'true' belief; and *sophía*, wisdom, ultimately our *tacit* knowledge and understanding of the reality. Drawing inspiration from *sophía*, the noblest form of the human intellect, we may counter uncertainty and build our innate *adaptive resilience* over time. *Phrónêsis* is then 'a true and reasoned state of [the human mind and] capacity to act with regard to the things that are good or bad.'[19] In effect, it constitutes the unique human ability to apply clear moral reasoning and *ethical* principles to guide our actions, tempered by the contextual reality.

Our aim through *moral reasoning* is to discover and take the *right action* at the *right time* in the *right context*. Phrónêsis is the 'highest intellectual response' a human being can put into practice, encompassing a broader vision and understanding of the reality. This contrasts with *téchnê*, the narrow focus of *technical knowledge* or expertise required to perform a specific task, in a given situation. For Aristotle, *téchnê* is the supporting subordinate or intermediate purpose, serving as a means to achieve a 'good' end. The application of both *epistême*, scientific knowledge and *téchnê*, technical knowledge, has a cybernetic[20] quality. The orientation of the 'object' in the environment is defined through recursive 'feedback loops' and mistakes can be corrected within the 'boundaries' of the system. Our focus in terms of leadership should be directed more towards the practice of *phrónêsis*, 'a state of grasping the truth, involving [moral] reason[ing], concerned with action about what is good or bad for a human being.'[21] Human discernment of whether something is 'good' or 'bad' of necessity encompasses a social and an ecological dimension.

Human *thinking* in its most *tangible* form (*artefact*) is concerned with achieving a certain *télos* (*final cause*), as a reflection of human intentionality and the ability to anticipate the *right* course of action, in alignment with our own moral values. It is a dynamic process reflective of our capacity to continuously learn and improve, since we have a natural affinity for *adaptive resilience*, both as individuals and collectively as voluntary participants in society. In the absence of clarity in our rational thought processes and moral reasoning, we would become weaker. Society is in effect incapacitated, when our *human values* are denied. Consequently, the Enterprise itself is also denied its legitimacy, its *raison d'être*. Values, beliefs and passions are intrinsic motivating factors for all human beings, comprising a myriad of cultural, historical and evolutionary influences shaping human civilisations through the ages. In contrast, 'machine learning' algorithms deployed in modern Socio-Technical Systems are constrained by past events and arbitrary inputs limited in both time and space, as they attempt to simulate complex human thought processes, through mechanistic means.

However, algorithms have *no* awareness (consciousness), no understanding and no knowledge of the reality. They do not have any capacity to 'know' or 'understand' *how* they may cause harm to a *biological* human being; they cannot *autonomously* assign a value to a human life or another 'object' in the reality. They do not have the ability to take 'self-corrective' actions, without human intervention at some stage in the process. A *machine* is a simply an *empty vessel*, prior to any interaction with a human being. Thus, a computational system does not have any cognitive ability or capacity for self-reflection. A computer does *not* 'know' whether a decision being effected through a *mechanical process* is socially acceptable and morally justified.[22] Machines have the ability to produce outputs, subject to human inputs; and they do not have the inherent capacity to effect change or reproduce themselves and their components from within. On the other hand, living organisms have an innate capacity to effect change and self-reproduce their constituent parts autonomously from within, through self-reliant processes, using nothing other than intrinsic parts to make up the whole. It constitutes an *organic* self-generative process known as 'autopóiesis.' Our human faculties, rational, emotional, social and moral reasoning, cultural values and our unique individual 'potentialities' develop over time. As Aristotle suggests, we continually 'grow' our human 'virtues' through practice, which serves to improve our knowledge, awareness and understanding of the reality. The more individuals consistently practise their 'virtues,' the more society acquires wisdom.

Consciousness is derived from the Latin *conscientia*, which means *shared knowledge*. By extension, it constitutes the 'virtuous' application of human knowledge, learning experiences and wisdom being shared with others. It builds *adaptive resilience* in a harmonious, ordered and properly functioning society.

The 'hard problem'[23] of *human consciousness* for philosophers is to understand the connection between conscious rational thought, living and lived experiences, in order to ascertain to what extent *subjectivity* influences our intentions and subsequent decisions or actions. Sensitivity to *qualitative* changes perceived through 'stimulatory movements,' whether 'sensory impressions' of a physical 'object' in the external reality or a *reflection* of the 'soul' and the innermost *beauty* of the mind, gives rise to *unique* individual experiences.[24] The qualitative component of human intelligence pertains to aesthetic values, while the sensory perception of *phenomena* purposefully drives actions towards *effective learning* and adaptation. There is an imperceptible very fine line that almost cannot be drawn between philosophy and psychology, since human *intelligence* cannot be disassociated from the *subjectivity* of human experience. At the time of writing, it is doubtful whether computers, *inanimate* empty 'objects' will ever acquire 'human-like' cognitive abilities, whether described as consciousness or intelligence. It is highly unlikely they will ever acquire the intrinsic capabilities of *biological* human beings, who are 'intellectually alive,' conscious, sentient, cognisant, emotionally and socially intelligent *living beings*. Thus far, there is no agreement of the exact philosophical and scientific definition of human consciousness. Seemingly, no other form of 'known' consciousness in other living organisms comes close.[25]

'Life does not consist mainly or even largely of facts and happenings. It consists mainly of the storm of thoughts that is forever blowing through one's head.'[26]

The richness and complexity of human experience exemplified in the *dynamics* of living life, differentiates human beings from other living organisms. Our thoughts and emotions are subjective, our behaviours complex, non-linear and unpredictable. They are difficult to categorise and do not fit neatly into the linear logic of a mathematical relationship or equation. In modern psychology, 'sensations, perceptions, ideas, attitudes, feelings' have an emergent quality. An individual or a group of people *being* or *becoming* aware of the same, experiences *perceptions* differently at any given moment in time. The axioms and principles of mathematics do not *sufficiently* explain human consciousness and the 'reality' as a *whole*.[27] Human decisions, actions and behaviours have emergent properties that are 'hard' to define. They are governed by how we *feel* and by how we *think* and yet they cannot be 'broken down.' Consequently, scientific knowledge is dependent upon reasonable assumptions to help us understand the reality; and subsequently these *assumptions* inform the construction of 'artificial intelligence.'[28] However, human thinking is *not* static and cannot be 'viewed' in contextual isolation, by an external observer. It is *not* possible to define every aspect of *human intelligence* in terms of formal mathematical logic.

The human brain is the most complex adaptive system known in the universe, though it is *not* yet *fully* understood. It is *not* simply a mechanical or computational structure with 'distinct components operating on purely abstract, formally defined 'symbolic' terms. The human mind is not *simply* a 'hierarchical computational machine.' Thus, it cannot be ascribed definitively to a physical entity, even though it is usually associated with the human brain. The human experience of the reality is of necessity multidimensional and multi-directional, since the brain acquires a *dynamic* model of the physical reality, through its own evolution, development and *adaptive learning*. The brain effectively oscillates between a state of 'chaos' and order, as it continually seeks to maintain 'homeostasis,' paradoxically in a *dynamic* mode of operation.[29] Like a pendulum in a *constant* state of 'perpetual motion,' it performs 'complex tasks' *instantaneously*, across multiple regions that are at once modality specific and at the same time integrated generalised multimodal activities. The human brain operates in an energy efficient manner, dynamically transitioning between mental states. Pure mathematical logic alone cannot capture the *semantic* depth, breadth and *full* richness of the human form of natural language, reflective of the subjectivity of human consciousness and the *uniqueness* of human experiences. This rich nuance and the variety of cultural influences, historical, evolutionary and developmental traits constitute the *multidimensionality* of human intelligence. Common sense reasoning and epistemic knowledge are missing elements in 'machine learning;' although *artificial* 'deep neural networks' represent a kind of *mimicry*, part of the *functionality* of the human brain, based on what we *know* so far, about its structure and can measure using available instrumentation.[30]

The *power* of human *thinking* extends beyond the *limited* functionality that may be simulated by a 'Turing machine.' While the human form of *natural* language is *rich* and *varied*, presenting a high number of variables not readily captured in a 'machine learning' models. It also constitutes the essence of human relations and the *unlimited* expression of human thoughts. The human form of natural language comprises syntax (word order), grammatical structure and *multiple* semantic layers to form meaning. Owing to the complexity of human thought, the articulation and transmission of meaning is an 'art form,' which cannot be reduced easily to a uniform computer programmable language. Different kinds of expression, whether in oral or written form, encompass a *myriad* of nuances and non-verbal cues, to convey rich and complex *meaning*. While algorithms 'work' on randomised pattern recognition by association, based on formal mathematical logic and quantitative analysis of vast volumes of data; mere 'fragments' of the reality, deprived of the *qualitative* aspects and semantic richness of the human form of natural language. It is a somewhat arbitrary task to attempt the reduction of the human form of natural language, within a neat 'set of rules' in a defined closed system. At best, *linguistic* meaning is *approximated* by mechanical means through observation of its word structure or syntax. However, this is not sufficient.

The human form of natural language is a living thing, richly varied and complex through its *idiosyncratic uses*. As a reflection of human thinking, it does not constitute a 'step-by-step' process, no matter how logical or coherent it may appear to be. So much of its rich semantic content is left unsaid, and can be elicited instead from the 'feeling' within a given context comprising cognitive, emotional and social dimensions of richly diverse and varied experiences, including complex interactions with the environment. Consequently, it is difficult to reduce qualitative differences, ambiguity and uncertainty within a defined set of computational parameters. The complexity of the human form of natural language is reflective of the intrinsic complexity of human reasoning. Its eloquence is testimony to the quintessence of the human form of natural intelligence. The ability to communicate effectively, originate one's own ideas, express one's own thoughts *is powerful* and the ability to do so *fluently* in more than one language is invaluable in business.

Mastery of this complex 'art form' enables us to 'discover in any particular circumstance all of the available means of persuasion,' a distinctive human ability.[31] The ability to *freely* construct arguments and elaborate new ideas through the use of the human form of natural language is the hallmark of human intelligence. Aristotle proposed a structure to 'order' our otherwise 'chaotic' thoughts through the use of human reason *lógos*, emotion *pâthos* and moral character *êthos*. In so doing, we are afforded the opportunity to convey a rich and complex meaning, with justification of our unique perceptions of the reality. On the other hand computer programmable 'languages' being used to inform *algorithms* fall short of expressing the *full* richness, variety of cultural values and contextual depth of meaning conveyed through the use of the human form of natural language. At best, algorithms may only analyse the semantic content through probabilistic inferences, by 'guessing' the next 'best' word or phrase.[32] More attention should be given to the *qualitative aspects* of the 'information' being shared through the mediation of computational means.[33]

'Either mathematics is too big for the human mind or the human mind is more than a machine.'[34]

Human consciousness is not so much based on the 'facts' or the 'objects' perceived in the physical reality, but more so on the capacity of the human mind to interpret 'truths' beyond the 'realm of symbolic logic' or probabilistic computation of the same.[35] If the mind were simply a machine, then anything that is not computable through the use of an algorithm would not be understood.[36] However, the human mind has a greater capacity to understand counterfactual realities than 'machine learning' algorithms. It has an ability to perceive 'truths' even if they cannot be proven by mathematical axioms, empirical evidence or by computational means. Human beings have the unique ability to elevate their understanding through the Arts, extend their knowledge by making new discoveries through the Sciences and create useful 'artefacts' to assist and advance human progress. The hierarchy of the 'mind over matter,' stems from our problem-solving abilities and the infinite capacity of the human imagination. Our ability to learn strengthens our innate resilience, with multiple 'recursive' actions taking place even when we sleep, to help us make sense of it all. We can conceive of our own minds and the minds of others; comprehend 'truths' that extend beyond existing human knowledge.

There is a far richer interconnectivity and integrity of 'signals' within the human brain than has thus far been replicated in technology. The speed at which information 'flows' and thoughts propagate in the human mind is 'incredibly fast.'[37] Rapid prioritisation of neurotransmitters according to the intensity of the 'signals' occurs internally and takes precedence over external stimuli. The conscious self creates internal 'feedback loops,' which enable verbal expression and orient our movements and thoughts to help us discover the 'best possible' situational outcomes. We seamlessly navigate different states of mind and respective transitions, reflexive actions and conscious reflection, accessing long-term memory for additional support, as required. The 'inner reality,' constitutes the *uniqueness* of human consciousness, the *intangible* dimension of human intelligence, seamlessly blending perception, cognition and emotion.

The complex 'networks' in the human brain harmoniously coordinate *dynamic* 'feed-forward mechanisms' and 'feedback loops.'[38] These processes are far more complex than simulations thus far achieved in *artificial* 'deep neural networks' or 'symbolic representation.'[39] The richness, depth and breadth of 'information' expressed through the human form of natural language and the 'self-reflective' nature of the *unique* subjective and objective self is not readily captured by 'artificial intelligence.' As human beings, we 'see' through a variety of different lenses, observe our own human experiences and those of others.[40] Our ability to project ourselves into the future, through *dynamic* thought processes, that are separate from any external physical 'object,' fundamentally differentiates us from the 'blind' and 'static' state of computational algorithms, used in 'machine learning.' They cannot 'see' the physical 'object,' understand its 'movements' and any changes *dynamically* occurring in the environment; in effect they have no ability to 'think' or 'reason' about the *reasoning* itself.[41]

Modern scientific theories of human consciousness are based on psychology and neuroscience.[42] They explain human consciousness in

functional terms, 'neural events' occurring within the brain, processing information. Some psychologists believe awareness of one's own
experiences is instantaneous, such that if we were to think something
is true, we might believe it to be true. This is perhaps overly simplistic, since the *fullness of meaning* is revealed over time. Nonetheless,
heuristics[43] impact our daily lives and may be a double-edged sword
in business. Common 'shortcuts' such as 'predictable world bias' or
'confirmation bias' may be supported by randomised 'big data,' which
can be *manipulated* to suit the human-specified 'ends.' The assumption that 'data' has *all* the answers may lead to serious *errors* of judgment. Mathematical accuracy or *computational optimality* does not
necessarily correspond to 'universal truths' in the 'real' world. The
'quality' of the data and subsequent human interactions may introduce 'disturbances' in the computational environment and produce
'anomalies' in *machine-generated* outputs. Thus, the measurement
of 'human variability,' using classical computational methodologies
to determine 'optimality' may not be relevant to the individuals concerned. At best, 'big data' may reveal *generalised* trends, as a result
of probabilistic distributions, but they are not necessarily applicable
to the individual.

Human concerns are varied and cannot be addressed through computational classifications, with a select few variables being assessed
against the 'law of averages.' It is a highly risky and problematic
strategy to pursue since human lives do not fall into one category
or another and cannot be rendered calculable like a sequence of
'binary' randomised moves in a 'chess game.' In highly sensitive
areas, such as healthcare and jurisprudence, the interpretation and
significance of 'big-data' related patterns, requires human intelligence and oversight. In the workplace, 'what if' questions and the
use of inquisitive narratives in decision-making process facilitate
worthwhile explorations and critical analysis of the subject matter at
hand. In this respect, human intelligence is best placed to assist us
in gaining a better understanding of the complexities and emergent
properties of human needs in the contextual reality.[44]

Human consciousness constitutes 'an awareness by the mind of itself
and the world.'[45] It is the means through which we discover our self-
identity, human autonomy and agency. Self-reflection and projection
of 'the self' beyond the immediate physical reality is an *embodied*
experience, *unique* to the individual. Through introspection we continue to learn, grow, develop and refine our 'perceptual awareness,'

throughout the course of our lifetimes. There is a powerful connection between the evolution of the human form of natural language and complex human thought processes, which serve to enhance *natural* human intelligence.[46] The notion of 'free play' in our use of language reveals an inner depth to the various dimensions of perception and outwardly a complexity to the notion of human thinking. As human beings, we have an innate organic 'optionality,' we 'freely' choose how we respond and adapt to novel and unexpected circumstances. The human capacity for agency, our ability to act purposefully, evaluate contextual ethical choices as situations evolve and spontaneously apply moral reasoning to everyday experiences substantively differentiates human intelligence from 'artificial intelligence.' Human autonomy and human agency gives human beings the edge in intelligence; thus, 'artificial intelligence' is in so many ways an inaccurate term.[47]

Human *intuition* is the 'innermost sense,' which guides us to make the right choices, without actually *knowing* precisely why. The non-quantifiable properties of human consciousness prove elusive for 'artificial agents.' They have no ability to discern the 'subjectivity' and 'intersubjectivity' of human experiences.[48] They cannot conceive of human values *autonomously*, nor understand the subtleties of cultural values, 'norms,' beliefs, human 'wants' and concerns, subject to high degrees of variability, and so these elements are excluded from the computational environment.[49] 'Artificial agents' cannot understand the human form of natural language; they are simply programmed to follow a strict 'set of rules' in order to execute a single task, 'the objective function' with mathematical accuracy. They have no capacity to execute any form of *moral reasoning*, other than the programmed numerical analysis subject to inputs and 'stored' data. Anything outside the scope, nature, context and purpose of their *specific* task-led functionality, is unlikely to yield *verifiable* outcomes. Conversely, the human capacity to extract 'truths' from the environment is intrinsic to human nature. Human consciousness entails complex thought processes combined with comprehensive multisensory integration and multimodal activations across several 'regions' of the human brain. These 'activities' form part of a harmonious 'whole' in a continuum. However, the 'true' complexity of human consciousness is not *fully* understood.[50]

'If we use, to achieve our purposes, a mechanical agency with whose operation we cannot interfere effectively . . . we had better be quite sure that the purpose put into the machine is the purpose which we really desire.'[51]

Algorithmically driven 'artificial intelligence' systems have improved significantly in terms of performing single, clearly defined, repetitive tasks. While decision-making efficiency may be celebrated in technical terms, it does not mean the machines are getting better at making better decisions; particularly when they are 'switching' tasks. Outputs cannot be guaranteed; they are not 'fail-safe.' A small 'disturbance' in one part of the system may be amplified throughout the system as whole; owing to the interconnectedness of multiple systems in the 'network,' it may not be possible to detect 'errors' and course correct *before* harms occur. This presents a significant challenge for organisations choosing to deploy these new technologies, as yet not fully mature. They present substantial *material* risks and necessitate significant resources to deliver reasonable, economically viable outcomes. 'Artificial Intelligence' systems are not infallible and without human intervention, it is not possible to guarantee human safety. 'Turing machines' are *not* sentient and lack the *dynamic* capacity of the human mind to *anticipate, regulate* and *control* inputs. Algorithms lack context specificity; they are only concerned with the 'logical sequencing' and 'correctness' of their 'actions' irrespective of the multiplicity of possible interpretations of the reality. Functionality in artificial 'machine learning' models is based on 'binary' decision-making structures, such as decision-trees denoting 'if . . . then' scenarios, and rather simplistic 'cause and effect' solutions.

However, in the 'chaotic' *real* world, 'information' about human beings, is not reducible to a series of 'facts' that can be 'logically deduced' from *calculable* distributions of *generic probabilities,* which do not accurately reflect individual perceptions and interpretations of the reality. Correlations generated by machines may be incorrect since the *relationships* between *inputs* and *outputs* are generally *unclear* in a variety of settings and do not adhere to strict 'computer-generated rules.' There is a fundamental problem with 'artificial intelligence' in so far as its aim is *seemingly* to reduce uncertainty and eliminate ambiguity from the environment. This over-simplification of the pluralistic 'views' and diversities intrinsic to human societies invariably leads to *misleading* and *inappropriate* uses of 'machine learning' technologies, which cause 'visible' harms both to human beings and the environment.

Highly complex social phenomena pertain to a *dynamic* ever changing 'continuous reality,' and transforming the same into a machine programmable 'discrete representation,' that is both *static* and devoid of *meaning*, lessens the *semantic* relevance both to the individual(s) concerned and the situation at hand. Processes concerning human beings cannot be standardised without serious repercussions. Misplaced predictions lead to significant financial losses and 'bad decisions' due to embedded biases in the data and discriminatory parameters used to generate *machine outputs,* cannot be readily reversed in complex adaptive systems. Technical and logical criteria in 'machine learning' are not aligned with human values and 'ethics-based' principles, which underpin society and its institutions. Despite the influx of information, 'big data,' it is *not* possible to 'know' everything. No matter how sophisticated quantitative analyses may be, we still need to consider the *qualitative* aspects pertaining to the 'human dimensions' of the reality and they are *not* suited to 'artificial intelligence' technologies.

Quantification of human societies and their endeavours is categorically *meaningless*. However, in a *mechanical* setting, the use of non-reflexive metrics combined with 'trial and error' methodologies, is highly problematic. Automation, algorithmic decision-making and data analytics conspire to erode *human values* and perpetuate situations of 'unfairness' in pursuit of misguided *technocratic ideologies*, which serve to undermine civil liberties and democracy itself.

Algorithms are not best suited to conditions of complexity, uncertainty and ambiguity. They require accuracy, a clear definition of the problem and indisputable evidence, which is rarely the case in any data-driven context. No matter how large the 'look-up' table, it is almost impossible to list all the possible forms of human interactions, changes in the environment or the *qualitative* aspects of *human* intelligence, values, relations and emotions. 'Artificial Intelligence' is unable to define every possible scenario with precision and determine whether the 'values' contained in the 'infosphere' within the computational environment are pertinent and *applicable* to the situation at hand. While human beings are error prone, we have the intellectual faculties to discern ambiguities in the environment and deal with contingencies, ambiguities, uncertainties and non-linear 'events' in 'real-time,' far better than *algorithms*. The 'logic' of human decision-making and moral reasoning encompasses the ability to make the *right* decisions, even when there is insufficient information and the available data is of *poor* quality, its *value* unclear. Reasoned argumentation pertains to *human intelligence*, rather than 'machine learning' capabilities; thus we should *not* expect *machines* and 'data analytics' to *fill in the gaps*, where knowledge may be incomplete, as if by *magic*.

Automation functions on *mechanistic* principles. It is dependent upon *physical* processes being enacted by the *mechanical* components in the system, like the 'cogs in the wheel,' subject to human and non-human inputs. Thus, it can be considered a 'closed system,' although there may be 'disturbances' in the internal computational environment, as a result of external interferences. Nonetheless, the *decision-making space* is defined by a strict 'set of rules' programmed into the machine. This does not correspond with the variety of cultures, historical influences and evolutionary developments intrinsic to human societies, which are relatively speaking more 'open systems.' Present situations may be related to *historical* events; but there may not be an explicit or direct correlation; and how we 'choose' to respond to complex situations, with no 'clear' answer may require *different thinking* altogether. This is not something that will emerge through automation and data analytics; *algorithms* are designed to 'control' the *status quo*, since they cannot cope with the *uneasiness* of human relations, the *openness* of social systems, non-deterministic outcomes, moral indeterminacy and discontinuity of human societies. Randomised, arbitrary and *inflexible* decisions do not best serve the needs of the individual(s) or society as a whole. We simply *cannot* entrust the *entire* decision-making space to 'artificial intelligence,' when *machine* outputs directly and *instantaneously* impact human lives. In the 'chaotic' *real* world, 'information' cannot be reduced to 'binary categories;' and human intelligence is *not* a 'calculable commodity.'

Human beings are compelled to act as result of their own *unique* autonomous intellect, grounded in *living* and *lived* experiences, human values, beliefs, desires, emotions, passions, rationality and critical thinking; self-reflecting all the while on the *reasoning* itself and the exercising of moral judgment. Thus, the deliberate, ethical and specific use of new technology is preferable to its indiscriminate adoption for any 'general' task, particularly those where the outcomes should be decided upon through democratic processes, based on *pluralistic* 'views' of the reality to avert probable dangers. While human consciousness may not be completely understood, since 'perceptual awareness' is inextricably linked to the 'embodied' experiences and subjectivity of the individual, it is by far the most powerful form of *known* intelligence. Its sensitivity to the *qualitative nature of change*, finely attuned to the environment is unsurpassed. It is doubtful 'artificial intelligence' will ever achieve the same degree of versatility, manual dexterity, simultaneous use of 'tools,' mastery of the human form of natural language, and exceptional intellectual ability to manipulate 'objects' encountered in the environment *instantaneously*. Our intrinsic *human power* lies in controlling the *inputs* rather than the *outputs*; thus we *are* still in a position to determine our individual and collective futures.

The Enterprise remains responsible and accountable to society, and should seek to establish *beneficial* relationships between human beings and 'artificial intelligence.' Human beings do not *function* well, based on classifications, categorisations and the 'law of averages.' They are *unique* individuals and require the Enterprise to be cognisant of their individual needs and aspirations. Human beings are adaptive and resilient, *dynamically* responsive to changes in the environment, destined to create new 'artefacts' and improve their capabilities. While 'artificial intelligence' may prove mechanically efficient in processing large volumes of data, it is not an effective substitute for human *intelligence, moral* and *creative* agency. 'Artificial agents' are not justifiable substitutes for human intelligence, in any circumstance.[52] They do not have the ability to make society fair, just and equitable. They cannot guarantee health and wellbeing, or reverse *wrongful* decisions autonomously. Although the latest forms of generative 'artificial intelligence' models have been rapidly deployed in many sectors, it is worth noting 'artificial agents' are not capable of producing *original* new ideas to create *intrinsic* value for the Enterprise.

Clarity is required in relation to the specific role, use and purpose of 'artificial agents,' to avert *unintended* consequences, as these new technologies are becoming ever more intrusive in our daily lives. Greater scrutiny is required with respect to their intended uses at all levels of society, and potential harms must be mitigated *a priori*, whether in foreseen or unforeseen possible use cases. [53]

'The [AI] problem requires a change in the definition of AI itself; from a field concerned with pure intelligence, independent of the objective, to a field concerned with systems that are provably beneficial for humans.'[54]

If we are to succeed in harnessing the potential benefits of these new technologies, we need to determine the directionality and evolution of the same. It may not be technically and environmentally feasible, still less desirable or beneficial, to ascribe *uncontrolled* 'agency' to artificial machinery, with unbridled access to human lives. The right set of ethical principles must continually evolve and inform *dynamic* governance structures to keep pace with technological change, ensuring appropriate operational safeguards are in place, prior to deployment. Recent advancements in *algorithmically* driven Socio-Technical Systems have wreaked havoc on society. It is incumbent upon leaders to create the right environment, foster collaborative engagement across society and bring new ideas to fruition through continuous learning and improvement. Multiple diverse stakeholder feedback can offer useful perspectives and reliably inform the direction of policy decisions and appropriate actions, while substantiating the legitimacy of the Enterprise.

'The human mind is defined by its wonderful flexibility.'[55] The *unique* human capacity to learn from new experiences across different time horizons makes us *naturally* adaptive to changes in the environment. Human intelligence comprises complex cognitive, emotional and social capabilities; it affords us the faculty of deeper understanding and discernment of *living* and *lived* experiences through our *unique* human consciousness, pertaining to our *whole* being. While internalising visual 'objects' from the *perceived* reality, we conceptualise the same, drawn to contemplate the counterfactual dimensions by our *innate* curiosity. Our responsiveness to change and intrinsic adaptability strengthens our resolve to overcome externalities.

If, as Hamlet suggests, the sum total of human knowledge is incomplete, we should remain open to possible alternative interpretations of the reality. The multifaceted prism of our own unique reality has multiple colours and depending upon which lens we choose, we may 'see' one aspect or another. Wherever we *focus* our *attention is* to some degree, what we actually 'see' and are able to achieve.[56] It helps explain why our own values, judgments and decisions may be momentarily blindsided. Similarly, wherever the Enterprise focuses its attention, its purpose follows and its actions gather momentum. There is no 'guarantee' of neutrality or objectivity in technological processes, subject to *technical* limitations, data selection, human-specified tasks and training parameters. A 'human-friendly' world cannot be compartmentalised; there needs to be room for negotiation and guarantees for the necessary *freedoms* to navigate towards *safer* shores, as storm clouds gather on the horizon. In many ways, we need to 'learn, unlearn and re-learn' what we 'know' and find better ways to live a more *fulfilling* life.

While leaders may be tempted to neglect the *imagination* in the context of the Enterprise, new ideas and inquiries beyond readily available data should be pursued. A healthy dose of scepticism will avert *myopic* vision and the *wrong* focus until the reality emerges with greater clarity. Understanding *how* we learn and communicate is critically important, if we are to build better institutions, business organisations and *beneficial* 'artificial intelligence' systems, incorporating human dimensions and the environment. Most importantly, we need to take into consideration the *experiential nature* of the working environment. The 'true' nature of work *is* learning; and the 'true' nature of learning constitutes the effective application of 'work-in-practice.' This is critically important if we are to successfully *re-imagine* a sustainable digital future.

'The world as we created it is a process of our thinking. It cannot be changed without changing our thinking.'[57]

Vision is a question of leadership and strategic foresight. It should be focused on a set of grounded ethical principles, imbued with clarity of purpose and a *meaningful* sense of direction. If the 'catastrophic' situations we are experiencing are human-made, then we have it in our power to *change* the present trajectory. We can deliberately *choose* to steer the ship in the *right* direction. Against the rising tide of complexity in the modern world, there will always be an emerging reality we should be prepared to 'see' more clearly, using our imagination more so than our conscious rational thought, in order to seize vital opportunities and mitigate existential threats. Long-term thinking should be promoted more so than short-term thinking, to avert imminent dangers by persisting with a *partial* view of the reality. The challenges we face are 'entangled' in complex Socio-Technical Systems that *seemingly* govern our reality. These systems have not been calibrated to meet human needs and they do not reflect human values; and yet automated mechanical decisions 'commanded' by select entities have *undue* influence, affecting almost every aspect of our daily lives. Invariably, there is a disproportionate impact on the more vulnerable members of Society.

The Global System in its current form has instigated an increasingly automated 'zero-sum game,' that is pervasive and self-defeating, in so far as it has interfered with human progress. In the absence of long-term thinking within the *global* political economy and strategic foresight at the Enterprise level, resources are squandered; speculative 'bubbles' invariably lead to 'boom-bust' business and economic cycles. Rising tensions in geographical areas rich with fossil fuels and rare Earth minerals, migration flows triggered by climate change and flight from oppressive regimes, exacerbate intractable societal problems around the world. War, famine and disease; these are not new concerns; they have punctuated human history for millennia. In every crisis there is an opportunity for deeper reflection and change. As business and political leaders contemplate their next moves, the decision must be taken to create new pathways towards inclusive, equitable, sustainable *global* growth if we are to successfully navigate the challenges ahead. Choosing to focus on our *human needs* at an individual and collective level will help unravel the complexities. Through a spirit of renewed collaboration, we can work towards removing the barriers, building healthier societies, while restoring natural habitats and ecosystems that have sustained Life on Earth for millennia. We can no longer afford to pursue a *narrow* financial focus, or continue to take a blinkered 'view' of Ethics. This *notion* needs to become pervasive in business, now more than ever before. In the context of the Enterprise, human values and needs should be factored in from the start, from inception of the organisation, through to the physical infrastructure and modus operandi of these highly complex Socio-Technical Systems.

If we consciously shift our focus towards *human values* and turn towards that which *unites us* rather than divides us, we might productively make a 'big leap' forward. We have the intellectual capacity, scientific knowledge and technological capabilities to forge new synergies at all levels of society and resolve complex societal problems. We can work towards establishing a more harmonious multilateral world order, if we so choose. Ambitious missions always focus receptive minds and help foster broader alliances, through the meaningful engagement of multiple diverse stakeholders. This holds 'true' at the Enterprise level (micro-economy) and the nation-state level (macro-economy) and can be facilitated by more productive (*creative*) policies oriented towards International Trade, much more so than by 'lofty' financial manoeuvres, which do not necessarily correspond with human needs or sufficiently raise productivity levels within the global economy, as a whole. Whilst they may benefit the relatively few, grave structural and *unsustainable* systemic imbalances persist.

Stability requires variety and a continuously *oscillating, self-regulating equilibrium* to secure desirable yet elusive economic performance. It also necessitates the avoidance of the *concentration of power* and *corruption* at any level of society and the *global* political economy.

The Enterprise is the beating heart of society; and now is the moment to leverage its *transformative* power. Without changing the existing thinking and applying sound ethical principles to the Strategy, in support of the Culture, we cannot alter the current trajectory. If the *télos* ('final cause') is human wellbeing and planetary health, then *naturally,* we shall be working towards more *sustainable* societies and human flourishing through more widely shared prosperity. The absurdity of war and senseless killings is plain for all to see. We should move towards *constructive creative ends.* We could be working with nature, not against it. At present, the Earth is the only hospitable planet in the *known* universe.

Since technology is no longer a barrier, we ought to carefully consider, the broader implications of 'artificial intelligence,' both in the public and private sphere; and halt *dangerous* and inappropriate experimentation in the military sphere, with immediate effect. Just because we *can*, doesn't mean we *should.*

Vision is about *re-imagining* a sustainable digital future. It is about evolving our thinking, creating a new philosophy, encompassing what we 'see' and what we cannot yet 'see.' Change is a constant and we need to embrace it. Awareness, Understanding, Knowledge are continually evolving. Leaders may choose to adopt an explorer's mindset, proactively envisioning and bringing to life new possible futures. We have the *unique* ability to *nurture* and cross-pollinate new ideas, while discovering new levels of *meaning.* Knowing we cannot predict the future, we need to focus on making better choices under conditions of increasing uncertainty, and set a new *direction of change.* Without our innate *adaptive resilience*, we would not be able to create new opportunities. Without human autonomy and agency, we would not engage in ethical conduct and strive to reach a higher purpose. Without courage, curiosity, creativity and the unlimited capacity of our imagination, we would *not* 'see' new possibilities; explore new opportunities and develop *flexibility* in our thinking. Without moral grounding, *experience* would *not* be our best teacher. 'Each of us must work for our own improvement, and at the same time, share a general responsibility for all humanity.'[58]

Chapter 2

Strategy
/ˈstræt.ə.dʒi/

'Success is always the result of high intention, sincere effort, and intelligent execution; it represents the wise choice of many alternatives, choice not chance, determines your destiny.'[1]

Strategy comes from the Greek word *strategós*, a directed course of action(s) to achieve an intended set of objectives typically led by a 'general in command.' The rigidity associated with military disciplines and training is often transposed to a civilian context, without taking into account adversarial positioning vis-à-vis the 'enemy' may prove counterproductive. There is a substantive difference between the 'tactical game,' which may be visible to an external observer, and the Strategy itself, which comprises a complex set of adaptive processes, through which the overall success of the Enterprise gathers momentum and evolves over time. The opportunity to secure 'victory' is provided instead by the Enterprise itself, as it clearly identifies its purpose and specifies its intentions, which in turn serve to guide the orientation of the organisation towards a given set of objectives. In the modern Enterprise, the 'general in command' takes on a new form of leadership; while remaining at the helm the role itself is transforming the organisation. It requires multidexterity, the ability to coordinate multidisciplinary actions, while creating learning experiences and new growth opportunities for the Enterprise as a whole. Both to enhance its inherent resilience and its ability to respond efficiently and effectively to challenging externalities. A person or group of people responsible for steering the Enterprise as a whole needs the support of the organisation, while the organisation needs clear leadership, as the structure continually evolves through its interactions with the environment. In essence, it is a reciprocal relationship, based on mutual respect and trust, guiding the requisite set of manoevres with sufficient *flexibility* to realise the *vision* and meet the desired *ends*.

'All men can see the tactics whereby I conquer, but what none can see is the Strategy out of which victory is evolved.'[2]

While *The art of war,* by Sun Tzu, Chinese philosopher of the 5th century BC is often referenced in the corporate context, its teachings are misunderstood. Sun Tzu did not advocate for offensive actions through armed conflict, which drain energy and waste resources; but rather a more subtle 'art form' to defeat the 'enemy' and defend one's own position, through improving one's own self-knowledge, refining one's interpretation and understanding of the reality. 'If you know the enemy and you know yourself, you need not fear the results of a hundred battles.' Just as an individual can improve their self-knowledge and self-understanding, so too the Enterprise can improve itself by embarking on a learning course, removing all the obstacles that may interfere with its acquisition of self-knowledge both individually and collectively at each level of the organisation. The organisation can either be strengthened or weakened by its own structure. As a living organism it is capable of self-regulation and self-organisation and as such it should not be constrained either in identifying its strengths or revealing its weaknesses.

The objective of the Enterprise through 'choice' is to gain further self-knowledge by operating with 'high intention,' 'sincere effort' and 'intelligent execution.' These attributes do not pertain to *mechanical* processes or narrowly focused computational methodologies; rather they pertain to human intelligence. They form part of expansive, explorative, organic, intuitive *critical thinking* processes *envisioning possibilities*, which serve to identify both the risks and opportunities across different time horizons. Human reasoning is highly complex and involves cognitive, emotional and social intelligence, as we develop our understanding and refine our interpretation of the situation at hand, seeking to enhance our human capabilities in response to an ever evolving process of change. Data offers too limited a view of the reality; and much information will be missed if we *only* rely on randomised 'arbitrary' inferences produced by 'machine learning' systems. Wisdom stems from 'embodied' individual and collective consciousness within the organisation, as well as shared knowledge, *living* and *lived* experiences, while it is practised successfully through sincerity, benevolence, discipline and courage. A strategy cannot succeed without intellectual honesty and transparency both in its creation and implementation, failing which the organisation is merely creating an 'enemy' within and will eventually cease to exist.

In the business context, the view that Strategy is a 'war' that needs to be 'fought' is a somewhat outdated description. Defending against externalities, whether unexpected socio-economic crises, geopolitical tensions and energy related shocks, supply-chain interruptions or rival competitors using disruptive technologies requires a wholly new approach. In the digital era, the 'boundaries' between industries have all but disappeared. Thus, an open-minded approach is required, both to ascertain the meaning and vulnerabilities inherent in a given set of opportunities and the threats an organisation may be susceptible to. The organisation itself is capable of determining what is *truly* relevant in a given scenario, whether in a task specific context that requires adaptation or structural changes at an organisational level required to sustain the Enterprise as a whole. On the one hand there is a need for 'homeostasis,' holding a steady position, while on the other the Enterprise must continously undertake a *dynamic* process of change, enabling its constitutents to participate in the sub-processes, which underpin the necessary transitions as the Strategy evolves.

From the vantage point of its constituent parts and the organisation as a whole, as both 'subject' and 'object,' the Enterprise may crystalise a long-term vision and instigate the embodiment of its Strategy at each level of the organisation; thereby enhancing its understanding and interpretation of the reality. The Strategy of the Enterprise may be enacted successfully, by taking an integrative spatio-temporal approach, ensuring there is continuity in its communication systems, by means of multiple 'recursive' feedback loops. This will systematically enable a 'two-way flow of information,' backwards and forwards, taking into account an 'outside-in' and 'inside-out' perspective. It means 'opening-up' a more *dynamic* and *fluid* form of communication within the Enterprise, to strengthen its relationships within the *internal* and *external* marketplace, in order to seize upon nascent opportunities, whilst averting forseeable and *plausible unlikely* risks. Risks cannot be successfully mitigated if they are not accompanied by corresponding actions for adaptation; preferably in an anticipatory capacity to reinforce *organisational resilience*.

The level of preparedness and responsiveness of the Enterprise will be determined by its structure; its capacity to operate both at a 'local to global' level and at a 'global to local' level. In other words, a *decentralised* set of sub-systems contributing to the overall success of the whole. The reversibility of these operational strategies will enhance its ability to provide *pluralistic* perspectives, in order to explain what is happening in the marketplace. Different perspectives from multiple stakeholders inform and shape the evolution of the Organisational Structure, which constitutes the identity of the Enterprise. They also serve to guide developments within the overall System (digital platform) lending support to the configuration of its constituent parts; both the *technical* and *social* sub-systems, vertically and horizontally across different working groups, which make up the *network as a whole*.

Economists adopted the acronym VUCA[3] in 1985, which had originated in US military quarters to describe *volatile*, *complex*, *uncertain* and *ambiguous* challenges faced by leaders; and inevitably there were repercussions in terms of corporate leadership and the organisation of society as a whole. Volatility[4] refers to the nature and intensity of changes taking place in the environment over different time horizons and it is frequently used to describe rapid fluctuations in price, particularly in the financial markets. This translates into a 'negative spiral,' fuelled by fear and anxiety among the market participants. It evinces a certain 'brittleness' in the global financial system, which has been largely automated and only gives the semblance of stability from the outside. The processes inside the system can collapse suddenly, particularly if the system falls under unexpected stress. Recent events have shown it is not resilient and flexible. When the 'load' is too great, the entire system collapses and while 'extreme events' are not always predictable, the consequences are far reaching and impact people's lives for decades. Most economies have not yet fully recovered from the 2007–2008 financial crisis and there are concerns the Global System is on the brink of collapse, yet again. Thus, the Enterprise cannot simply consider local or regional risks; it must entertain a comprehensive, integrated Global Strategic Framework. It should ensure it is *fully* prepared to withstand external shocks, not only aiming to survive without lasting damage to its operations, but preferably striving to 'bounce back' stronger. Having weathered the storm, its Strategic Direction should be informed and reinforced both by individual and organisational resilience of *all* the participants in the System as a whole.

Uncertainty refers to the unpredictability of events occurring in the environment, often beyond the organisation's sphere of influence and control. Unexpected events are often seen as crises, but they may also offer opportunities for the Enterprise, if sufficiently and appropriately prepared to 'seize' the moment. In many cases, insufficient training among employees, results in 'gaps' emerging within the System, as staff members take flight in search of better opportunities elsewhere. Positions left vacant are not easily filled, as skills shortages and competition in the talent marketplace intensifies. The System becomes 'porous;' additional *undue* pressure and excessive burdens are placed on the remaining employees, who in turn suffer 'burnout' and leave their positions. This was demonstrated by the so-called 'Great Resignation' cross-sector in the USA in 2021, following the outbreak of the global pandemic, with similar worker exodus events seen in the UK, China, India and across Europe. While 'gaps' in the labour market and skills shortages persist, *automation* takes a greater hold across industrial sectors. However, this does not solve the inherent fragility of the Enterprise. Despite the 'boom' in 'robotics' and the deployment of 'artificial intelligence' both to fill 'gaps' in the workforce and to cut costs, a variety of new problems are emerging. Companies are not equipped to provide adequate support for employee health and wellbeing, particularly for those who are suffering from anxiety and fear due to increasing uncertainty and the ill-effects of 'long-Covid.' Instability in the workforce further reduces productivity levels and saps confidence levels; performance that is lost is not readily recovered by *machine* subsitutions. Quick fixes may appear tactical, but they do not address the root causes of the labour shortages. More importantly, they do not sufficiently support the long-term strategy of the Enterprise, nor sustain its competitivenes, thereby weakening its overall position.

Complexity refers to multiple factors, which may influence a given situation, including the intricate relationships, interconnections, interdependencies and interactions between human and non-human 'agents' operating 'side-by-side' within the Socio-Technical Systems underpining the Enterprise. The Social and the Technical Systems are 'entangled,' since the constituent parts of the whole system are inextricably linked. The constituent parts of the Enterprise System as a whole, are at once independent and interdependent, such that the 'whole is greater than the sum of its parts.' The sub-systems are 'closed systems' to the extent they can self-organise, whilst at the same time being 'open systems,' since they absorb and exchange 'information' thereby contributing to the whole. Changes in the outputs or the outcomes produced by *interconnected* systems within the network, are not necessarily correlated proportionately to the *changes in inputs* or variations in the contextual paramaters; and any 'disturbances' that may occur, guide interactions both in the *technical* and *social* sytems. Consequently, the behaviour of the whole System cannot be predicted by observing its sub-systems, since the whole 'emerges' or becomes visible only as the sum of its parts. In this sense there is both a structural 'tight coupling' and a 'loose coupling' of the relationships between the whole and its constituent parts at different stages of the learning and development processes within the Enterprise Communication Systems.

Finally, Ambiguity refers to the 'lack of clarity' in the 'real' world surroundings and inconsistencies in the available 'information' within the computational environment. In the absence of a clear 'observable' relationship between cause and effect, multiple components within the System are mediated by randomised 'artificial agents' and no longer reflect *perceived causality* in the 'real' world. Rather 'artificial agents' provide probabilistic inferences and may create further distortions in the qualitative and subjective 'view' of the perceived reality, subject to data inputs and system parameters. Non-linear interactions between the constituent parts give rise to *multiple effects,* which are difficult to predict. Since there is no direct causality evinced by the systems in operation, *mechanical* analyses of the available data may produce heterogenous results and exhibit properties that do not reflect the reality. For example, a voter may change their mind at the last moment; nobody 'knows' what will *actually* happen in the polling booth and this 'eventuality' is not captured in the data, which may only point to the *likelihood* of an event occurring without any degree of certainty. Since accessible data cannot be *fully* explained, or it may be incomplete and inaccurate, ambiguity is an inherent feature of any system, no matter how simple it may be. In living organisations, which are primarily driven by the 'social systems' within the Enterprise, it is *critically* important to understand the psychological and relational informational content that is being 'viewed' through a *mechanistic process*, may *not* correspond with the reality. There are multiple dimensions which need to be examined and understood *prior* to any formulation of the strategy. Data processing 'tools' often detract from the *critical thinking* which needs to take place *prior* to any statistical modelling and preferably *inform* any chosen methodology using quantitative analysis, since the qualitative aspects of the reality and any 'anomalies' found in the data are disregarded for mathematical convenience. 'Machine learning' models currently in use, no matter *how* 'adaptive' they may be, only look at select 'factors' which may influence potential outcomes; they are not exhaustive models of what is actually happening in the reality. At best, they may yield some insight of probable correlations through the observation of randomised patterns found in vast volumes of data; and while causation may be implied, it is not necessarily confirmed by empirical analysis. There will always be a degree of uncertainty since many aspects remain 'unknown unknowns,' and of necessity the Enterprise must learn to navigate the 'nebulosity' that may be present in the environment by cultivating its own *instinct* to make sense of the reality and thereby strengthen its innate resilience.

Exploring the 'messy middle' through *flexible* critical thinking processes will help to take away the fear and anxiety of dealing with uncertainty and unpredictable outcomes. Several semantic layers are missing from 'machine learning' and this is where human beings can fill in the 'gaps' in the analyses and excel. Embracing change as a constant wholeheartedly, while providing the necessary reassurances for colleagues, that if mistakes are made, they can be used as helpful learning experiences, is a good place for Leaders to start. Alternatively, the Enterprise is paralysed by incomprehensible data and hindered by 'risk aversion' to the point of passivity or worse still inertia, where *nothing* happens for fear of reprisals, if mistakes are made. This simply adds to intolerable levels of pressure and toxicity in the working environment and may hasten an earlier demise of the Enterprise, since vital 'cues' or 'signals' are being missed. There will always be tougher challenges ahead and possibly *seeming* contradictions in actions to be taken. And yet the role of Leaders and the organisation as a whole, is not to resolve paradoxes as they emerge, but rather to avert complicatedness in the way that they are being managed.

'Knowing' *anything and everything* can change at any given moment in time is a useful starting point in proactively managing and adapting to unidentified risks as they emerge. 'Artificial Intelligence' cannot solve unanticipated or as yet *'unknown unknown'* risks. However, a well-prepared, healthy, resilient, flexible organisation can respond promptly to any 'hidden risks,' since individual and collective human intelligence can be used to the 'best advantage' of the Enterprise, both to *sense* danger and *adjust* its course with immediate effect. Whether it is the unexpected interruption of 'normal life' due to the Covid-19 pandemic or the sudden collapse of increasingly fragmented supply-chains, the Enterprise needs to become highly responsive and excel even in the face of adversity. It is a condition *sine qua non* for its own survival and a strategic necessity. Hence, the key to a successful strategy is the *willingness to become adaptive*, both in terms of its creation, development and implementation. Strategy needs to become a *living thing*, clearly communicated at each and every level of the Enterprise, informing daily practices through strategic orientation, while becoming an integral part of the *modus operandi* within the Enterprise. In other words, *everyone* needs to be 'singing' *harmoniously* from the same piece of music.

In the modern Enterprise, data is considered crucial to proceedings, and yet 'risk aversion' and 'short-termism' is prevalent. Corporate strategy is usually grounded in theory and treated in isolation, typically remaining at 'arm's length' from the Enterprise participants. In doing so, there is little or no understanding among employees, of the direction being undertaken in any change and digital transformation process. If employees do not understand the strategy, they will offer resistance and are unlikely to follow any 'chosen' pathways for responsible innovation. In the absence of transparency, human beings become nervous and suspicious. Whatever we do not understand may hinder or delay requisite actions, or else it may prove overwhelming and cause 'paralysis by analysis,' thereby lowering *qualitative* performance and productivity levels within the Enterprise as a whole. Whether leaders build trust or evoke distrust, build confidence or instil doubt, these 'social elements' are instantly contagious in equal measure. If 'negative' responses should be elicited through *unclear* decisions, actions or any form of communication, ultimately profitability is eroded. Moreover, a successful strategy cannot be *arbitrarily* distanced from validated, verifiable and the most up-to-date 'sounding boards' within the Enterprise, readily achieved through the daily interactions of employees with 'real' customers in the marketplace.

All too often 'real' direct customer feedback is overlooked, in favour of 'generalised' decision-making practices based on 'artificially' filtered findings, in the form of market 'personas.' Meaningfulness of these 'data-driven' insights is no less ambiguous than any attempted superficial generalisation of 'real' actionable insights generated by human-beings, through *personal lived* and *living* experiences of what is *actually* happening in the marketplace.

The marketplace is, of course, composed of *human beings*, whose behaviours are by their *nature*, unpredictable. Numerical representations of the same, may only allude to *generalised* trends, and ought to trigger *new* strategic thought processes to assess emerging consumer needs. Nonetheless, given the speed at which it is *assumed* new products should be released, data is inevitably and mistakenly viewed as the 'oracle of truth.' This perceived need for undue haste can result in the *unsafe* release of new products that are premature for widescale experimentation. The recent 'furore' and media 'hype' that has irrupted over *artificial* 'large language models,' detracts attention from the deeper 'real' societal and environmental issues. It also denies the Enterprise the opportunity to carefully consider *how* it should build new capabilities and *re-imagine* its digital future, by improving its sensitivity to new consumer demands and its *responsiveness* to newly emerging challenges in the marketplace, thereby strengthening its Strategy.

Shorter-term engagements of the person at the helm, also means that the CEO can become a destabilising influence on the organisation. A reasonable length of tenure is still required to assure the requisite continuity for success, while fulfilling a fiduciary 'duty of care' that can inspire confidence and make reasonable progress with the *enactment* of the Strategy *per se*. Although with the increasing use of automation, the Enterprise is being viewed as a mathematically guided or scientifically 'managed' and 'controlled' system by *engineered digital means*, until such a time as 'artificial intelligence' comes anywhere close to approximating human intelligence, it is *unwise* to substitute human beings for 'artefacts' as yet in their infancy. And yet corporate leaders are beholden or indeed hold themselves accountable to onboarding more automation to 'fix' problems and cut costs notwithstanding 'hidden risks;' since individual performance incentives are inextricably linked to highly volatile, arbitrary market fluctuations. Consequently, short-term thinking dominates the strategic aims of the Enterprise; and longer-term thinking beyond a five to seven year time horizon is remarkably rare. Very few corporate leaders dare to think beyond short-term time horizons, but the few who do are generally more successful. For example, Gucci has reached unparalleled success in the fashion industry, exceeding market expectations and peer performance levels, because it chose to take risks striving towards innovation in uncharted waters, while envisioning a 100-year time horizon.

Market forces also arbitrarily govern government *debt* issued in the form of bonds, with short-term funding subject to a tight three-year cycle. This also impacts business confidence and it is an insufficient time horizon to accomplish meaningful plans of action in the longer term. Consequently, there has been persistent underinvestment in infrastructure at the macroeconomic level, reflected by a lack of investment particularly in workforce education at the microeconomic level. Short-termism does not work as a Strategy; at best it may only provide short-term tactical benefits, upon which the stability of the Enterprise or the nation-state cannot be built successfully. This sense of precariousness generates inertia; the all-consuming nature of the perceived uncertainty and instability created by market forces interferes with substantive efforts to revitalise existing policies and infrastructure, which in turn dissuades businesses from investing in people. The perception that people are a liability while technology is a permissible capital expenditure detracts attention from constructing a resilient Strategy, that can deliver *enduring* value creation opportunities, for the Enterprise, the nation-state and Society as a whole. It feeds into a *negative* self-fulfilling 'prophecy,' while the yearned for stability in the economic environment for long-term investments to become possible, remains an ever *elusive* dream. In the context of increasing market volatility, it seems no government is able to accomplish its intent.

Moreover, the mismatch between rapid automation and the skills required to attain proficiency levels when using 'artificial intelligence' tools, reduces the decision-making space and alienates participants in the system. Discouraged by *algorithmic obscurity* and widespread discrimination *filtered* by mechanical means at speed on a large scale, excludes large numbers of people from entering or remaining in the workforce. At a strategic level, no matter how well-intentioned local and regional government and corporate policies appear to be, it is evident urgent societal needs are *not* being met. In the absence of a coherent industrial Strategy, particularly with regards to the appropriate and responsible use of 'artificial intelligence,' and a clear vision to raise public health standards, education levels and make adequate provisions to safeguard environmental standards, it is inevitable the Global System will continue to *malfunction* as a whole.

Thus, the responsibility for solving intractable societal problems increasingly falls to the Enterprise. However, in most cases the overall Corporate Strategy is not finely attuned to the transformation of society and human wellbeing; and least of all towards taking an 'ecological view' of the economic reality. Without thriving natural ecosystems, human wellbeing is being compromised through the loss of habitats, which in turn influences the *malfunctioning* of the Earth's Systems. Invariably, business is reliant upon natural resources to a greater or lesser extent and people. If we do not proceed urgently with environmental regeneration at a global strategic level, it is difficult to see how we might foster inclusive, equitable, sustainable economic growth at the Enterprise level. Extreme weather events and 'shock' pandemics are not a thing of the past; and while new outbreaks cannot be predicted with certainty, current thinking and business practices have been rendered untenable, irrespective of the time horizon under consideration.

Societal expectations and increasing pressure from investors are becoming powerful forces, requiring a new conceptualisation of the Enterprise and new configurations within the organisation.[5] However, rising geopolitical tensions, misinformation and disinformation,[6] frequently detract attention from necessary long-term planning and corresponding investments. And yet it is against this backdrop of increasing uncertainty that leaders must make their 'choices' and steer their course towards safer shores; astutely disregarding the 'noisy' information increasingly generated by 'artificial' means. Similarly, amidst the 'confusion' genuine opportunities may be missed and the authenticity and integrity of the Enterprise may be compromised. Thus, the Strategy cannot remain 'loftily' removed from stakeholder engagement. It needs to be explained clearly and transparently in an appropriate manner, without compromising the identity of the Enterprise. The Strategy cannot be successfully enacted if customer confidence and trust is eroded; particularly if there is an over-reliance on *mechanistic intermediations*. For example, the semantic content encompassed in any form of messaging filtered by 'artificial intelligence' will be 'lost in translation.' Authenticity is paramount and trust is invariably the most valuable currency in business. Should the Strategy fail to convince investors, employees, shareholders and customers, the Enterprise may fall victim to a sudden loss of public interest or 'attention deficit,' from which it is notoriously difficult to recover.

So how *can* the Enterprise successfully respond to persistent *external* threats and the inevitable *internal* repercussions?

Firstly, we need to understand what Strategy is and what it *isn't*. Strategy is *not* a series of isolated *tactical* manoeuvres to achieve a specific goal. Nor is it a series of moves to guide or manipulate actions in order to attain *narrowly* defined goals.

Strategy is inextricably linked to the broader long-term Vision, Mission, and Purpose of the Enterprise. It underpins the long-term orientation of the Enterprise, in support of its *raison d'être*, sustainable business practices and long-term objectives. A well-defined Strategy has sufficient *flexibility* such that it can evolve *dynamically* in response to emergent changes, while facilitating coordinated actions at each level of the Enterprise. Thus, Strategy is multidimensional and encompasses the rich diversity of stakeholder needs, envisioning a variety of technological options and the development of appropriate capabilities across the time horizons. While the orientation of the Enterprise should be congruent with its core human values, the Strategy becomes *meaningful* when it acts in concert with organisational developments. In a non-linear 'chaotic' world, corporate objectives cannot be realised with *inflexible thinking*. Similarly, competitive advantage cannot be sustained by keeping the strategy 'locked up' in functional 'silos' within the organisational hierarchy. Political 'power plays' and related tensions may emerge, further complicated by vested interests; conversations may be cognitively and emotionally charged, but organisational 'choices' are of necessity 'value-laden' and are rendered *meaningless without due process and ethical reasoning*. Decisions being taken today, particularly with respect to the use of 'artificial intelligence' will shape the present and the future for generations. The strategic direction enacted by the Enterprise, through its policies, systems, processes, daily practices and business activities *profoundly* impacts both Society and the Environment. Thus, a strong sense of duty, responsibility and accountability should not be 'lost' on the strategy-makers.

The purpose of a 'good' Strategy is to enact purposive change for the benefit of the Enterprise, *all* its stakeholders, the wider society and the Environment. The 'Toyota Way' celebrates the Japanese concept of *kaizen,* which embraces this unity of purpose across the generations, focusing on *qualitative* improvements, reduction of waste and the creation of value through *timely* use of materials. At the same time, necessary adjustments are made, while striving for perfection within its organisational structure, processes and daily practices.[7] Ethical principles and core values are systematically implemented and underpin the strategic focus and orientation of the Enterprise. Toyota famously uprooted USA automotive stalwarts in the early 1970s in their home market, by instigating 'lean production' methodologies through meticulous attention to detail. The aim of the Strategy was *not* to pursue *overly narrow* commercial interests, but rather to focus on effectively managing production systems. Specifically inventory levels, precision manufacturing to eliminate waste (defined as anything that used materials unduly, and 'costly errors' on the assembly line, which eroded customer value). In so doing, Toyota achieved commercial success and effected positive change for the *mutual* benefit of society and the environment. Greater profits are the consequence of consistently 'good' actions that satisfy human needs, while being respectful of ecological requirements through the *careful use* of natural resources, in order to avert environmental degradation. Profits do not ensue from the introduction of technology alone; but rather from the combination of human ingenuity and consistent efforts to make *socially acceptable,* 'good' uses of the 'artefacts' we have created.

At this juncture, we need to 'see' a radical paradigm shift. Technology is no longer the barrier; but undervaluing human beings through excessive rapid automation is fast becoming a potential barrier to human progress and wellbeing. We need to address this imbalance as a matter of urgency, at a *global strategic level.* The strategic aim of the Enterprise should be oriented towards human wellbeing and more productive (*creative*) ends. Moving away from the narrow view of *technical* efficiency and the prevailing notion of *value extraction,* towards a more *flexible* and *self-sustaining* business model in pursuit of enduring value creation. This includes human discernment of the situation at hand and *open-mindedness* in seeking to explore and better understand the underlying reasons for 'choices' made in a given situation. 'Wise choices' and 'intelligent execution' in the modern world, constitute the effective management of non-linear externalities, complexities and emergent fragilities *within* the Enterprise.

Flexibility in the organisation supports strategic aims by facilitating *dynamic* interactions and adaptations through continuous learning and continuous improvement. Thus, the Enterprise can ameliorate its *responsiveness* and *preparedness* both in situations of crisis and at the same time opportunity.[8] Empowered individuals can immediately course correct, when adjustments are required in response to changes in the environment. A successful Strategy anticipates the needs of diverse groups of people, participating fully in the evaluation of beneficial ends. The rapid pace of technological change, necessitates new and different ways of thinking, particularly in turbulent market conditions and difficult situations with high degrees of uncertainty. Effective responses require *spontaneous* communication across the Enterprise; sociotechnical systems should facilitate the acquisition and retention of knowledge through multidirectional feedback loops, purposefully orchestrated to lend support to geographically dispersed members of staff. Distributed leadership is a critical strategic concern, as devolved management affords the Enterprise *fluidity* and timely execution of its strategic objectives.

The focus of the modern Enterprise needs to be directed towards effectively co-evolving the human and digital processes embedded within Socio-Technical Systems. They should serve to promote *qualitative* improvements, productivity gains and creativity.[9] Organisational structure is continuously evolving and requires constant attention. From a *technical* perspective, built-in redundancies facilitate quick adjustments, without disturbing the system as a whole. A modular platform-based system lends support to the enactment of *strategic foresight* and contributes to *financial resilience* within the Enterprise, by avoiding 'lock-in' with specific methodologies, suppliers or technologies. This also ensures there are a variety of different options available to support individual autonomy and group-level independence as different teams optimally self-organise, whilst working collaboratively across the Enterprise Value Creation System.

Setting the direction of the Enterprise with a clear sense of purpose will enable change to be effectively and efficiently managed, while smoothing the transitions. A pragmatic approach towards the ideation of strategy and its further development, encouraging employees at all levels of the Enterprise to participate, will prove beneficial in a VUCA[10] environment. Thus, there is an urgent necessity to extend the scope of the Corporate Strategy beyond financial, technological and other constraints to include contributions from *all* functional areas. Efforts to make sense of fast-changing situations will best serve the Enterprise by making *voluntary participation*, a deliberate and consistent practice. 'What if' questions shape powerful narratives, through conversational interactions and help develop critical thinking within the Enterprise as a whole. Efforts to detect relevant 'signals' in fast-changing ambiguous situations help the Enterprise focus its attention on *sensing* future changes; while using effective comprehensive strategic frameworks, bolsters contextual awareness and helps build *adaptive resilience* over time.

Socio-Technical Systems create a 'ripple effect,' impacting communities distant from the operational centre. It is becoming increasingly apparent strategic actions cannot be taken in isolation and intractable societal problems cannot be resolved unilaterally. Strategy at the institutional and corporate level has a disproportionate impact on Society, through the 'digital extension' of the Enterprise. While interconnected Socio-Technical Systems are being deployed around the world, 'intelligent choices' must be made in the allocation of resources together with the pursuit of more 'noble' aims.[11] Public-private partnerships and cooperation at a *supranational* level can accelerate strategic innovation that benefits *all* stakeholders.[12] It should not take a crisis to catalyse *meaningful* change, but the global pandemic triggered extensive competitive realignment of strategic partnerships cross-sector, and brought into being new alliances previously unthinkable. Some industrial groups were forced to make difficult choices, reducing their overall size, others re-focused their attention on core business activities.[13] Any hesitation in *adaptation* posed a serious threat to the economic viability of the entity, irrespective of size and maket position.[14] Over-reliance on economies of scale and other past defences are no longer sufficient.[15]

'Innovations rarely happen within traditional company boundaries any more. The real breakthroughs are achieved by *collaboration* across different sectors.'[16]

Competitive advantage no longer entails defeating industry rivals, rather it involves seeking complementarity through strategic partnerships. Stability and competitive differentiation must be sought *dynamically*, taking into account resources and capabilities may *suddenly* evaporate. Inaction is more of a threat to the Enterprise than reconfiguring potential resources, abandoning bureaucratic processes, which stifle creativity and hinder strategic thinking. Flexibility *must* be embedded in both the production and communcation systems. Newly integrated activities within the Enterprise portfolio, should be proactively managed with the necessary *fluidity*. There should also be a specific focus on the potential 'circularity' of materials being used, whether directly or indirectly by the Enterprise. From a strategic perspective, *specific* attention should be given to the supply-chain, the Enterprise reliance on Nature, and the use of *natural resources* across the entire value chain. Meaningful work is in effect the expression of the Enterprise *purpose* conducted in the service of Society as a whole. The 'choices' made and strategic priorities pursued, ultimately determine the future success of the Enterprise itself.

Strategy in the digital era requires a transdisciplinary approach, creating an *effective* frame of reference, which enables the Enterprise to become more *adaptive* and *resilient*. Boundaries across industries are fast changing, affording the *responsive* Enterprise abundant opportunities to find new pathways for *organic* growth and become *self-sustaining* over time. Technological disruption is occurring everywhere and no business is *truly* safe. Relevance has taken on new meaning, as corporations in the digital era find themselves competing with peers and smaller entities, far more likely to be *adaptive* to the new demands of the marketplace.[17] Moving from a platform-centric strategy to network-centricity requires greater *flexibility*, at the intersection of each node. In practice, this means a greater degree of agency *for self-managing* teams to interact *autonomously* with resource management systems of the Enterprise without being *overly* restricted. Great Strategic Leadership at the helm will help foster and sustain the *momentum* of the Enterprise over time.

The *transition* from a platform-based economy suddenly seems passé, for many *network centricity* is no longer in question. If larger companies wish to take advantage of *nascent* opportunities, they must learn *how* to adapt in *real* time. It is a 'known' fact, innovation happens at the 'edges' of the System. And it is also worthwhile noting the mantra of the Navy Seals, 'slow is smooth, smooth is fast.'[18] 'Break-fast' or 'fail-fast' methodologies are obsoloscent. Deliberately switching positions, changes the perception of the reality, and the way the Enterprise *thinks* about its future, observing *more than one* possibility. It is a completely different *feeling*, if you are thinking about the next 100 years, versus the next three to five years. The Enterprise will *not* be able attract the talent it needs to enact its Strategy, without establishing a 'final cause' that resonates deeply in Society.[19]

Readiness to embrace the *organic nature* of the changes occurring within Socio-Technical Systems[20] enables the Enterprise to successfully develop new capabilities.

Haier is a case in point. An ailing company in the 1980s, the arrival of a new leader at the helm radically altered its trajectory. The new Strategy can be understood as 'respecting human values and market demands,' to become the leading manufacturer of 'white household goods.' Vision, courage, willpower, creativity, tenacity and discipline fuelled inspired leadership teams towards meticulous development and successful enactment of the Enterprise Strategy.[21] There is great *fluidity* in their highly innovative *network-centric* business model, oriented towards extending a broadly diversified portfolio of companies. Participants and new entrants alike must prove their 'value' according to market forces; while the core digital platform provisions goods and services that lend support to their endeavours across multiple market segments. The company *proactively* encourages entrepreneurial activities across its network and promotes upward social mobility to create a *self-sustaining* 'cycle of creativity.' For example, an employee may start at the 'bottom of the ladder,' but gains *meaningful* experience across a *variety* of tasks, such that they can progress quickly up the ladder to become a 'producer,' creating his or her own start-up with the full support of the *surrounding* management team. Whilst the company as a whole operates *globally*, they 'act locally' with the aim of stimulating demand across every node of their network. They continually strive for manufacturing excellence and innovation, build new capabilities, demonstrated by the number of internationally recognised patents and consistent contributions to ISO *quality standards* over the past several decades. The reversibility of the producer-consumer relationship is paramount and constitutes a new paradigm for *continuous innovation* and *continuous improvement*.[22] Having learned from the errors of the past, they aim to be 'environmentally friendly' and have recently embarked on a comprehensive global 'recycling programme,' to ensure resources are not wasted and their 'carbon footprint' is significantly reduced. Governed by a flexible and dynamic strategy, that is both *adaptive* and *resilient* in *relation* to rapid changes in market demands, Haier is remarkably 'nimble.'

Haier has made great strides by prioritising *structural flexibility* and the 'flow' of information across the organisation. At a group level, it affords network participants, both individuals and their respective teams *sufficient* autonomy and agency. With the 'freedom to act' promptly, they can better serve existing and unmet customer needs, without any restriction 'where to play,' whether in adjacent markets or through an extension of core business interests. Their aim is clear and simple: surprise, delight and *anticipate* creating more convenience for digital-service-platform users, whilst working to achieve wider brand recognition in international markets to facilitate future growth *sui generis*. Focusing its Strategy on customer-centric market demands, Haier seeks to 'blend' societal and environmental needs at every level of their network.[23]

Complicated corporate structures *overly* reliant on industry benchmarks accumulate structural 'rigidities' over time. Teams become focused on *formal* data analysis. 'Control' *mechanisms* better suited to *machinery*, than the needs of human beings, are *superimposed* on the complex adaptive 'social systems' in operation. Quite literally depriving the organisation of oxygen, leaving little or no room for manoeuvre. Complicated is not the same as purposefully building complexity into the Strategy for competitive advantage. Network-centricity may create a degree of uncertainty, but structural complexity in the organisation also facilitates the exploration of new opportunities. Paradoxically, it creates more room for manoeuvre, widens the decision-making space and affords the business model new scope for *flexibility*. Opportunities for growth may be 'seized' through timely allocation of resources, anticipation of consumer needs and *adaptation* of existing and new capabilities. On the other hand, complicated structures laden with bureaucracy cause friction, delay responses, constrain learning and drain resources. In the worst-case scenarios, they may lead to 'paralysis by numbers.' Paradoxically, when Strategy embraces complexity and critical reasoning, averting *overly* simplistic assumptions embedded in 'data-driven models,' the organisation is 'free' to breathe. Continuous improvement *naturally* occurs, following the cross-pollination of ideas and osmosis of the same. Every organisation *is* unique and complex Strategies are more difficult to emulate.

'Data is not information, information is not knowledge, knowledge is not understanding, understanding is not wisdom.'[24]

Strategy is born of *evolving* conversations, which in turn shape appropriate responses with respect to the uncertainty and ambiguity present in the environment. Conversations that happen with regularity during the entire *strategy-making* process enable leaders and their constituents to perform a 'reality check' in real time. A shared awareness and understanding of the reality, probing the more difficult questions, bolsters organisational resilience over time. Preferably, the adaptive nature of the Strategy will enable it to flex sufficiently, so that unforeseen changes can be managed with ease. Learning to extract the right 'signals,' sensing the changes as part of the process, becomes a powerful component of the Strategy itself. Relevant context-specific information, whether derived from 'machine learning' and preferably human intelligence can be deliberated upon in formal and informal settings; often the latter are more conducive to new ideas.

'The simple familiar structures are seeds from which people develop a larger sense of what is likely to be occurring.'[25]

Clarity as to the *intentionality* of the Enterprise is business critical. Processes require discipline for success in execution, but they must also afford the Enterprise *harmonious synergies* between the social and technical systems in play. If the Strategy cannot flex, it has failed both the people and the processes. Failure to communicate the strategic intent and priorities of the Enterprise cause the systems to *malfunction*, through the *misalignment* of strategic objectives and corporate values. If the intentionality behind the Strategy is misunderstood, serendipitous moments will be missed and prove *very* costly, should the Enterprise miss the opportunity to *dynamically revive* its competitive position. For example, Cisco faced with strong competition in the software arena, adopted a 'fast agile' strategy to expedite new products and services.[26] Having abandoned *complicated* intellectual property agreements commercial 'deals' with new market entrants could be struck early, thereby capturing more market share and value. While there may be a degree of *uncertainty* at the extremities of the network, the ability of the Enterprise to become self-sustaining will be tested through its *responsiveness* to changes in the environment. The ability to withstand potential risks is business critical; but the Enterprise must also exercise its ability to *seize* new opportunities, *before the moment is lost*.

Through risk mitigation and *adaptation*, the Enterprise continually learns to *self-evolve*, by responding appropriately to changes in the environment. Effective distributed leadership when enacted *informally* requires a high degree of trust, network-centricity and the abandonment of conventional thinking.[27] Strategic foresight proves invaluable when exercised through *flexible* methodologies. Combining quantitative analysis with *qualitative inquiries* enables the Enterprise to explore 'known' and 'unknown' dimensions to acquire a more balanced view. The Strategy itself may *only* evolve successfully, if the data being used is appropriately qualified and *qualitatively* verified. Companies may find adopting a 'risk-averse' stance erodes their competitiveness more quickly; for example, software companies experience diminishing returns in less than a year. Shortcuts aimed at 'boosting' the balance sheet are misleading and ephemeral in nature. They do not confer longevity upon the Enterprise and they are not conducive to *enduring* value creation. While the fast pace of change precludes the realisation of value by conventional means,[28] capital should be directed towards supporting *organic* growth. Economies of scale no longer afford larger firms the protection they once enjoyed; profits evaporate *quickly*.[29]

'In an unpredictable world, sometimes the best investments are those that minimise the importance of predictions.'[30]

There are *no* facts pertaining to the future. Despite the immense volumes of data being collected, 'noise' levels are exceedingly high and may take the Enterprise off course.[31] There is no 'knowable' proof of possible futures, based solely on the computation of *past* events. Raising levels of awareness within the Enterprise is therefore business critical. Everyone needs to *know how* to differentiate 'lagging, current, and leading signals' derived from 'noisy' datasets, in order to make *better* decisions. While *algorithms* cannot provide *definitive* answers, they may prove useful, if the data are of 'good' quality, context-specific and the data sources are either 'known' or *fully* traceable.[32] Leaders cannot legitimately satisfy demands for transparency, if they themselves do not know or cannot verify data provenance; unable to fully track data 'exchange trajectories' across multiple systems. Being 'data-driven' is not as simple as it sounds, since there are many *hidden* risks. Not least 'big data,' an *imperfect* record of *past* events, which may not be relevant to the present or the future.[33] Paradoxically, an over-reliance on data may hinder the Enterprise and obscure new opportunities for Strategic Innovation. Full traceability of data sources and training parameters used in 'machine learning' models is a necessity for the successful integration of 'artificial intelligence' within the Enterprise.

'In an equivocal, postmodern world, infused with the politics of interpretation and conflicting interests and inhabited by people with multiple shifting identities, an obsession with accuracy seems fruitless and not of much practical help, either.'[34]

'Sense-making'[35] as a strategic process enables organisations to leverage human intuition by providing actionable insights, in the context of a comprehensive, *dynamic* and *flexible* strategic framework to evaluate change. All the elements of strategy-making, including societal, political, economic and cultural dimensions, technical, organisational and other operational factors need to be considered *simultaneously*. Technology should be viewed as an 'enabling constraint,'[36] supporting *adaptive* processes and *fluidity* in the exchange of information, as new points of equilibrium are being established. Novel situations can *afford* the Enterprise greater *creative* freedom. Human intelligence, creativity, knowledge and wisdom are essential requirements for an effective Strategy.

Alibaba and Tencent adopt *maximum flexibility* in their strategic approach to growth. Cognisant multiple components within their networks are changing at any one time, they have adopted a 'system of systems' approach, using *multiple* interconnected and interdependent systems to deliver more *functionality* to their users, across the value chain. Complex Adaptive Systems deliver unique capabilities to an increasing number of network users with limited incremental costs. However, they also require the constituent parts, both human beings and 'artificial agents' to operate independently, thereby averting multiple 'single points of failure' occurring simultaneously. Their technology platforms are leveraged with economies of scale to anticipate consumer needs and provide real-time 'greater than expected user convenience.' Their aim is to make the human consumer experience as *frictionless* as possible. Competitive advantage is steeped in a *dynamic* process of continual renewal, enabled by technology, while being driven by evolving their human capabilities. These companies are continuously learning, improving, adapting, experimenting and building resilience; proactively encouraging *unique* consumer-producer interactions, thereby benefiting from the 'network effect.'

Strategy is the means by which we can begin shaping a *more* sustainable digital future. Extreme weather events with increasing frequency and intensity, reveal the devastating effects of climate change, forcing a paradigm shift in the marketplace.[37] Strategy is becoming synonymous with sustainability, encompassing deep-rooted societal problems and environmental regeneration.[38] Companies are recognising human-centricity taken from an ecological perspective is a necessity. Preferential use of renewable energy sources, a reduction in the use of materials, lower carbon emissions, and the avoidance of waste production wherever possible across the value chain, have acquired political and economic significance. However, there is insufficient transdisciplinary research and development, which would have strategic importance to advance those aims.[39]

'The difficulty lies not in the new ideas, but in escaping from the old ones, which ramify, for those brought up as most of us have been, into every corner of our minds.'[40]

Companies unwilling to 'see' and *fully* understand the *power* of the network and its strategic relevance will quickly fade. However, companies should be wary of over-automation.[41] Human intelligence and *consciousness* is *not* a computable commodity. If the aim of corporate strategy is to go beyond cost-control, moving instead towards high levels of productivity, performance and profitability, human connection is essential. Communication should be facilitated not just by *mechanical* means, but rather through knowledge sharing *in person* at a qualitative and experiential level. As Steve Jobs noted during the design of Apple headquarters at Cupertino, the atrium was *purposefully* built like ancient Roman dwellings to facilitate *informal* encounters, in preparation for more formal discourse. Jobs chose to facilitate the serendipity of 'chance' encounters to 'spark' new ideas for innovation. He *knew* intuitively tangible results require *intangible* levels of preparedness. Everyone contributes to the thought process, whether consciously or subconsciously. While conventional wisdom embraces a narrow view of strategy and *technical* efficiency,[42] exercising 'binary' trade-offs, a more *nuanced* approach aimed at new *creative* discoveries is required to create value. Human ingenuity adds to the collective consciousness, which lies at the heart of strategy.

Socio-Technical Systems should *not* be viewed as an opportunity to replace human-to-human connections. Conformity through the standardisation of processes may be required to achieve stability in the *technical* systems, but they should not act as *limiting* constraints for the *social* systems. Strategy fails to be enacted when *technical* systems are *inelastic*. In an effort to solve for the *fragility* of the Enterprise through increased *automation,* we have unwittingly made it *less* resilient. If the workforce is unable to perform its duties without the aid of technology, it begs the question as to *how* the Enterprise can overcome *unforeseen* contingencies. The aim of technology *should* be to facilitate cross-functional collaboration. However, technology may only assist if the information provided is of high quality and it is not voluntarily or involuntarily withheld. Technology cannot solve complex problems by itself;[43] and the future-fit Enterprise should set its strategic priorities in accordance with existing and unmet needs of its stakeholders, rather than be constrained by technology.

Strategy is being reinvented. Whilst the classical playbook focuses on scale and differentiation, there are new dimensions of competition to be considered. Public health, human wellbeing and the establishment of a *trustworthy* relationship between Human beings and 'artificial intelligence,' must now come into focus within an ethics-based frame of reference, as a matter of urgency. In the business context, 'speed to market' has collapsed the 'decision space' without clear benefits for the Enterprise. The aim of Strategy must be to develop beneficial relationships and create well-ordered systems and processes to encourage organisational development, the acquisition of knowledge and *meaningful* information properly structured, stored and accessed in a timely fashion across the Enterprise ecosystem. Adaptive Resilience™, entails a comprehensive strategic framework to foster *flexibility* and responsible innovation within the Enterprise.

'Nothing in life is to be feared, it is only to be understood. Now is the time to understand more, so that we may fear less.'[44]

Strategy is about finding clarity and making the right choices. It is a sequence of events that bestows *significance* on human lives and the environment. How the Enterprise chooses to embrace change is of the essence. And 'choices' *must* be made wisely.

Chapter 3

Culture
/ˈkʌl.tʃər/

'The capacity to learn is a gift, the ability to learn is a skill and the willingness to learn is a choice.'[1]

Culture is by definition a complex network of ethics-based principles, core values and beliefs. It encompasses different patterns of thought, social practices and norms derived from cumulative human experiences, knowledge acquired over time and beliefs *successfully* transmitted from one generation to another. It affords humanity a sense of continuity and heritage, while at the same time being highly dynamic and adaptive to changes in the environment. It is reliant upon sufficient attention and memory being afforded its safekeeping, at an individual and collective level over time, both within the Enterprise and Society as a whole. By its very nature, it is influenced by and simultaneously influences the environment in a highly *dynamic* and *adaptive* fashion.[2] Associated social practices and cultural norms find expression through the richness, complexity, depth and diversity of human thought and the use of the human form of natural language. As a result of which cultural practices, accumulated knowledge and ideas evolve and become reliant for transmission upon a complex web of social interactions, human connections, interdependencies and relationships. The latter transform the meaning of the human values and ethical principles, through the evolution of commonly held beliefs, perceptions, interpretations and understanding of the contextual reality. In the modern Enterprise, the expression of Culture comprises human and 'artificial agents' intertwined in the ubiquitous use of Socio-Technical Systems.

The Enterprise faces a number of different challenges, which in turn may influence and shape its Culture. Some are not new in evolutionary terms such as disease, while other pressures are more closely linked to socio-political, socio-economic and socio-technological changes occurring in the latter part of the 20th century.[3] In particular, the unrelenting speed at which adaptation is now required, creates additional pressures, including financial challenges for the Enterprise. While scientists looked to the 'laws of nature' and genetics as the driving forces of evolutionary change, typically a *very slow* process, the role of Culture is deemed to be a pivotal force in the survival or extinction of our species, Homo sapiens. In many ways, Culture has guided the evolution of our species and shaped our destiny for millennia.[4] Similarly, natural selection plays a part in determining which biological traits and characteristics remain prevalent in human societies, subject to the location of populations globally and the *universal* need for self-preservation. Genetics play a role in guiding our intrinsic motivations and inclination towards collaboration, which in turn fosters a strong sense of belonging and community through social connections and interactions with the environment. At a fundamental level, we seek safety and require security, which translates into the necessity for stability and continuity within the Enterprise.

Culture is shaped and also develops through our own responses, interactions and adaptations to changes in the environment, particularly when we sense *threats* being present. Human beings are *increasingly* at risk of climate change, air, soil and water pollution, loss of biodiversity and natural habitats, disease, famine and further environmental changes. Consequently, socio-economic polarisation and general malaise, whether politically motivated or due to religious beliefs may engender new conflicts and usher in the destruction of war. Human beings are at risk of their own creations, *artefacts* including weaponry, various 'artificial intelligence' tools and technologies, which foster profound changes in society, and in turn *inform* cultural change. Culture is also subject to the transmission of human biases, a variety of historical influences, cultural exchanges through human migrations, evolved nuances in human values, ethical principles and respective changes over time. Thus far, unsustainable approaches in our responses to external environmental change have resulted in deep divisions, inequality, excess levels of waste and consumption being experienced at all levels of Society.

On the other hand . . .

Culture is steeped in richly complex traditions, rituals, Art, scientific discoveries, philosophies, beliefs, creativity and new inventions, which shape the contours of our human existence, influence our worldviews and the acquisition of new Knowledge. Culturally transmitted 'information' from one generation to another, expressed through the human form of natural language, human behaviours and moral conduct, and the use of *artefacts* influences natural selection enacted across the generations.[5] In the interests of *biological efficiency*, the most beneficial traits for our survival are naturally selected and adapted through successive generations. Just as the cellular 'information' is readily assimilated from one generation to the next, cultural adaptations become visible over time, as they are assimilated through tangible forms (*artefacts*) to aid memory and direct *attention* to the necessary learning. It is through a cumulative process of learning over time, that new Knowledge is acquired, reflecting *local optima*, adaptations best suited to the surrounding environment. Culture is *in effect* a sequence of *cumulative adaptations*, which evolve over time, eliciting *dynamic* responses in relation to changes in the environment.[6]

Evolutionary processes have shaped the human capacity to learn and our unique ability to *sense* and respond to change. The acquisition of inherited knowledge, learning experiences and the social transmission of values, beliefs, behaviours, whether by being taught, self-guided and objective observation, constitute the *dynamic* complex array of processes, which instigate cultural development in human societies. Cultural inheritances, distinctive traits and *active* learning processes are visible in all parts of the world. Despite the *intrinsic* subliminal and subjective nature of Culture, it takes on a more tangible form, as intuitive and instinctive *interactions* with the environment are crystallised in new artefacts.[7] Human ingenuity through history has expanded our existing domains of Knowledge, instigated new pathways for growth, prompting new scientific discoveries set to continue for millennia. Exploration of the surrounding environment enhances our perceptions, understanding and interpretations of the complexities in the existing and emerging reality.

Culture creates, shapes and changes a person's inner sense of self and unique identity, learning through *personal* interactions with the environment and the *experiences* of others. It encompasses the wonderful richness and complexity of humanity, which cannot be reduced to a set of numerical values, systematically arranged in simplistic 'categories,' suitable for 'machine learning' and computation. Despite the use of 'multiple artificial agents' embedded in complex Socio-Technical Systems, it is not possible to compute the idiosyncrasies and variety of cultures, of which there are a great many exemplars within the Enterprise. Culture is personal, but it is also embodied collectively within various groups of people. Its evolution and development subject to the *unique* set of *non-linear* social interactions, changing conditions in the surrounding environment and *enactment* of specific values, beliefs and behaviours.

Leaders often underestimate the value and inherent complexities of Culture, its formation, development and evolution. In the context of the Enterprise, there will always be a degree of spontaneity; but equally, the direction of cultural change can be guided through effective leadership and communication. In recent studies, Chief Executive Officers believe corporate Culture accounts for *approximately* 30% of the market valuations, likely a much higher proportion of the company's *intrinsic* value, contributing to growth and innovation. There is also growing consensus the company could do considerably better, if the Culture were nurtured and strengthened. Diversity of thought, enhanced by living and lived experiences, invariably enriches the Culture and bolsters Enterprise *resilience*. Multiple diverse stakeholders create 'virtuous' feedback loops, expand the decision-making space and enhance the process with 'real' insights. Qualitative aspects taken from 'real' world examples often provide high quality 'information' instantaneously; offering valuable actionable insights to inform Strategy and enable senior Leaders to evaluate the development needs of the organisation. And yet few Leaders know how to draw strength from the inclusion of diverse stakeholders in the decision-making processes. However, discounting the rich diversity of thought, historical, socio- cultural, political, economic and ecological influences that contribute to different cultures within their localities is a mistake. A *myopic vision* and *unwillingness* to probe the existing and *emergent* complexities of the reality creates barriers and hinders social progress, denying the Enterprise *vital* new opportunities for *growth* and innovation.

The use of 'machine learning' tools within the Enterprise to 'control' and regulate Culture is a futile exercise, since there is a strong dynamic of autopoiesis[8] at play. The intrinsic values, beliefs and behaviours encompassed within the Enterprise Socio-Technical Systems, self-generate their own renewal and create new complexities. Owing to the proliferation and ubiquitous nature of highly interconnected, interdependent systems both within the Enterprise and beyond, arguably the intermediation of 'artificial agents' influence the direction and evolution of Culture, much more so than we may care to admit. Although extrinsic factors also influence the development of Enterprise Culture, the autopoietic nature of self-governing 'hybrid' socio-technical systems, may to some extent overpower the innate drive for self-identity and the sense of self. This poses a significant new challenge for the Enterprise, in terms of protecting its intrinsic value, authenticity and integrity. It may result in harmful reputational damage, if the appropriate operational safeguards are not envisioned, *prior* to the deployment of these *powerful* 'artificial intelligence' systems.

While human ingenuity and human potential cannot be computed, the probable *'norms'* extracted from 'machine learning' are used as an 'effective frame of reference' during the hiring process. This limits diversity and places the Enterprise at risk of failure, by reducing the *necessary* variety of values and beliefs, which could instead enrich *experiential* Knowledge and strengthen Enterprise *resilience* over time. Awareness of the *internal processes,* which influence both the individual and collective development of Culture and may in some instances proffer resistance to change, requires a more *nuanced* and more 'open-minded' approach. No matter how sophisticated the 'tools' in use, 'machine learning' falls short of the mark in advancing the *awareness* and *understanding* of the Enterprise. Quantitative analysis needs to reach a critical mass before an order of magnitude may reveal 'general' characteristics, through the observation of pattern regularities, subject to select data, which by definition is both flawed and incomplete. Conversely, person-to-person interactions are immediate and *quickly* establish the *qualitative* impact of actions taken in a 'morally charged' situation. A human being can *instantly*, intuitively and instinctively engage in moral reasoning, assess appropriate responses and evaluate the actions required in a given situation. It would seem very few people enjoy interacting with a *machine* to solve their problems.

Culture is a *powerful* force, within Society and the Enterprise itself. It continually develops and evolves *spontaneously*, even though it is increasingly mediated by *artificial mechanical* means. The 'information' contained therein affects every individual and the organisation as a whole. Not all the elements of the 'information' present in the Enterprise environment can be *fully* captured in the information management systems. Tacit knowledge is mainly shared on an interpersonal basis. Inevitably, there are 'gaps' in the Knowledge being stored in the organisation's computer memory; and if people leave the organisation, 'information' is invariably lost. This is highly problematic, since *homeostasis*, the maintenance of a *dynamic* 'stable' state,[9] conducive to 'good' business and business continuity is dependent upon sustaining the Enterprise identity. Paradoxically, this in itself is subject to change over time; as the core values and ethical principles underpinning the *ethos* (character) of the Enterprise *continuously* evolve, adapting to changes in the environment. Fundamentally, it is the people within the organisation who contribute to the formation of Culture, through the exchange of *tacit, practical and experiential* knowledge.[10]

'When distrust is the default emotion in society, we lack the ability to debate or collaborate.'[11]

Culture relies upon the Enterprise's ability to proactively engage in a broad-based dialectic, to foster clear communication and the *dynamic* exchange of information across the organisation as a whole. Trust is effectively the ultimate 'digital currency,' since it determines the *quality* of the 'information' exchanged and stored in the Enterprise's memory. Leaders need to grasp the true nature of the *power dynamics* within and beyond the Enterprise at a local, regional and global level. In other words they need to master the *human dimensions* of change, engaging with the *philosophical* and *psychological* aspects, of necessity intertwined in the human mind. Optimising only the technological side of the System will fail to yield the necessary results.[12] The Enterprise is in essence, a *self-actualising socio-cultural* system; and in this sense Culture sets its own *intrinsic* conditions and strategic priorities at an operational level.

Crucially, the cultural environment within the Enterprise is self-created by the organisation itself; it is *not* the *objective function* of an external 'machine-observable' reality; and it should be *valued* and understood as such. Culture is the expression of the *unique* identity of the Enterprise, both the individuals and the groups of individuals who inhabit the environment and whose social interactions fill the space within. Harnessing its power will propel the organisation forward, creating a *sustainable* competitive advantage, if properly managed. This requires conscious effort and consistent investment in developing *human capabilities* as a matter of strategic priority, through the timely allocation of resources. Failure to do so will deny the organisation the *full* advantages of deploying new 'artificial intelligence' technologies in order to meet Enterprise objectives, whether to mitigate risk, propel *growth* and pursue innovation.

Socio-Technical Systems[13] are generally designed to optimise technical requirements, rather than enhance the 'social systems' and lend support to human interactions. However, a 'self-generating' Cultural System needs to replenish depleting assets in a timely fashion, to ensure its own identity, as a whole, is not 'lost' in the process. The Enterprise is influenced by changes occurring in the internal and external environment, whereby its constituent parts may be renewed, or re-configured to adapt to the changes. Thus, the *human dimensions* should not be forgotten in the structural design of these systems and related processes. The Enterprise as a whole evolves, and the organisation develops through consistent interactions between people, processes, systems and technologies being used to enable the transmission of 'information.' These complex adaptive systems need to be sufficiently *flexible* to accommodate non-linear, *adaptive learning processes*. Human-centricity comprises multiple dimensions, some of which may not be visible at first glance. Hence continuous recursive 'feedback loops' are useful mechanisms to help unravel the complexities of human needs, *enabling* a deeper understanding of how situations evolve, both to improve *systemic* functionalities and foster the acquisition of Knowledge.[14]

Leaders now face the challenge of negotiating an 'infinitely explorable past' through the use of data, and yet owing to 'discontinuities,' the data may offer no further clarity as they face 'a risky uncertain future.'[15]

While there is data in abundance, there is also a risk of being misled by spurious correlations 'invented' by *generative* 'machine learning' systems. These 'confabulations' are built-in *features, artificially engineered* in 'machine learning' models; but *machine counterfactuals* do not have the same resonance and validity as human interpretations of the reality and should not be relied upon without verification. The power of human insights, ingenuity and potential is often undervalued in decision-making process; *de facto* rendered subordinate to the distribution of probabilistic outcomes produced by ever more sophisticated 'artificial intelligence' systems, which may yield fallacious and disproportionate predictions, since they cannot distinguish *human subjects and differentiate human value(s)*. An over-reliance on data is not necessarily the most effective way of reducing uncertainty, and there is a risk 'past events' may cloud judgment. There are no 'facts' available for the future, and the *machines* cannot project themselves and others into future time horizons. The human imagination has its own *predictive* powers and may prove a more *reliable* source of information, if this *energy* is properly harnessed within the Enterprise.

Culture informs the *nature* of interpersonal relationships and human connection. It constitutes our individual and collective responses to internal and external changes in the environment. It is *informed* by our quest for meaning. It constitutes the exchange of Knowledge, which is the foundation of both professional and social relationships. Thus, the structure of the network influences how the Enterprise manages the 'flow of information' and its communication needs, which in turn affects the workflow. The *arrangement* of intersecting nodes within the Enterprise 'network' is therefore business critical. The organisational structure *determines* the capacity of the Enterprise to learn, and thereby its ability to improve its performance, productivity and profitability; subject to the enactment of its core values and purpose.

Culture needs to be in clear alignment with the Enterprise Vision and Strategy. In every game there are clearly written rules. Culture on the other hand hinges on *unwritten rules*, and yet it necessitates leadership and stewardship, constant care and attention in its direction and governance. It requires thoughtful calibration and re-calibration of the forces at play, through a 'virtuous learning cycle' of continuous improvement. Proactive human engagement on a personal level fosters a far greater understanding of human needs, aspirations and expectations, driving the culture forward. Causal effects cannot be 'viewed' in isolation; they are multidirectional and multidimensional. Enterprise Culture is enacted 'top-down,' 'bottom-up,' and across all the nodes of the network.[16] Intentionality drives the orientation of the Enterprise, while sufficient *flexibility* in the System, human autonomy and human agency enables a *dynamic* process of change, organisational learning and knowledge acquisition; above all *fluidity* in the *successful* transmission of 'information.'

The successful transmission of *values, beliefs and behaviours* encompassed in the Culture of the Enterprise entails clear and transparent articulation of core values and beliefs, so that they are in alignment with the strategic direction and purpose of the Enterprise. Contrary to popular belief, 'Culture does *not* eat Strategy for breakfast.'[17] Rather they are two sides of the same coin. One reinforces the other and they are *mutually* beneficial to the realisation of the Enterprise Vision (where its ambitions lie), Mission (what it is setting out to achieve) and Purpose (*raison d'être*). Core values and beliefs need to be continuously reinforced in *good* times and *bad* to ensure they are transmitted successfully to successive generations. Many organisations lose their way once they lose sight of their core values and beliefs. Many more falter when they attempt to sidestep their Culture, and fail to make the *right* choices. Irrespective of crises, the purpose of the Enterprise cannot be fulfilled unless it has successfully extended its shared values, beliefs, ideas, accumulated Knowledge and experiences to new members of staff across successive generations in a *systematic* manner. Culture requires solid foundations and *flexibility*, as it continues to evolve over time, shaping new realities and possibilities through the contributions of successive generations. Culture is a 'Life support System,' a vital force within the Enterprise, underpinning its longevity.

Culture reflects both the importance of continuity (heritage) and the validity of new ambitions, aspirations and expectations in creating present and future value (innovation). As human beings, we take comfort *knowing* from whence we came. It provides an *anchor* for our perception and understanding of the reality, as it continues to be refined over time. Looking forward to the future, we become reliant on learning and new knowledge acquisition, both of fundamental importance for business continuity and sustainability of the Enterprise and Society. The 'predictive' element of the human brain enables us to *complete any missing* 'information,' and by design complements any 'blind spots' in our visual-sensory system. We may 'test' our perceptions, interpretations, understanding and knowledge of the reality, through our own interactions with the environment and with those of others.

Culture is the *relational glue* that holds the Enterprise and Society together. Irrespective of the challenges we may face, it requires conscious *nurture* and cannot be denied *constant* attention.

How the Enterprise *interprets, transmits and shares* 'information' matters. In a very *real* sense, Socio-Technical Systems are 'non-trivial machines.'[18] They present inherent risks and may produce *unintended* outcomes. It is far more difficult for *machines* to emulate the way human beings communicate and *mimic* the human form of natural language, not least because they do *not* understand it. Data does not accurately reflect the subtleties of the cultural values, beliefs and behaviours conveyed through human form of communication. The *qualitative* aspects and nuances of the human form of natural language are 'lost in translation,' particularly following scientific treatments to facilitate 'machine learning' processes. Processes can transform the Culture of the Enterprise (perception, understanding, interpretation, knowledge), as much as *people* can transform processes. For the time being *at least*, Society has the upper hand in terms of Communication. Human interactions with 'chat-bots' are *not always* satisfactory; they may damage the integrity of the Enterprise and alienate customers and employees, if over-engineered to form 'self-recursive loops,' which do *not* correspond with context-specific human needs, aspirations and expectations.

'Despite differences in modes of understanding the world, society nonetheless manages to coordinate itself.'[19]

Cognisance of the *technical* limitations of 'artificial intelligence' is a worthwhile pursuit, when building a harmonious *collaborative* Culture in the workplace. Complementarity is foundational to the Human-AI and AI-Human 'relationships' being established. Human-centricity is paramount; too often *unhealthy* working environments are created because human beings are mistakenly viewed as being *subordinate* to the *technical* limitations of the *machinery*. It ought to be the other way around; how can the machines facilitate human endeavours, rather than 'command' human beings by 'brute force' into futile 'mind-numbing' activities, such as *endless* form filling and *classification* of everyday items. On the other hand, 'routine' tasks, involving human interactions, such as 'customer services' are substituted for *automated decision-making algorithms*, to the detriment of human relations. These *algorithms* contribute to the establishment of *new cultural norms* that are not always *qualitatively* beneficial to the Enterprise.

The *anthropomorphisation*[20] of 'artificial intelligence' has become prevalent in almost every workplace and every aspect of our lives; and yet it can create a degree of confusion. More clarity is needed as to the *intended* role and purpose of 'artificial agents' and their impacts on *biological* human beings should be *carefully* considered. Particularly in light of the failed Eliza experiment in 1964, when a pre-programmed machine was mistakenly attributed human characteristics, equivalent to the dispensation of medical advice from a *real* human being. Similar experiments are being conducted with the latest 'tools,' and Leaders should be mindful of potential *adverse* effects, especially post-Covid-19, as many employees have encountered mental health problems.

System outputs are *not* predictable, and it is worth keeping in mind there may be arbitrary correlations being made by the *algorithms* that are *simply not true*.[21] Thus, we *should* not be making *unfounded* claims that 'artificial intelligence' is set to replace humans. Human intelligence has *not* yet been encoded in the machines. Misinformation abounds and simply creates unnecessary tensions, confusion and apprehension in the workplace, which translates into an overwhelming resistance to change. This defeats any attempt to effect digital transformation processes and detracts from the *fluidity* that is required of creative, efficient working practices and *effective* processes. Preferably, the organisation should be focusing on a 'just' technological transition, including up-skilling or re-skilling individual members of staff, offering a broad *comprehensive* educational programme across the organisation.[22] It is in the best interests of the Enterprise and Society as a whole, in preparation for a sustainable digital future.

Increasingly, there is an expectation that business needs to urgently address the intractable societal problems of our time, including social divisions and unfair practices such as racial or gender discrimination. It is worth pointing out, the machines *cannot* make difficult ethical choices. They can only *follow* rules (as defined by humans) and do *not* have the capacity to interpret *any* exceptions, or identify non-linear career paths that may be beneficial for the Enterprise. Multidisciplinary candidates may be 'seen' as 'outliers,' by the *machines*. It impoverishes the variety of experiences, knowledge domains and diversity among the workforce. It is entirely possible unique and exceptional human beings, who may not 'fit' into pre-arranged simplistic classifications are excluded from the hiring process, and internal opportunities for promotion. Steve Jobs would not be hired or retained by an *algorithm*; his 'background' was *sui generis* and his sources of inspiration eclectic. This is reflected in Society as a whole and those who are denied life opportunities by *mechanistic* means are unable to contribute. This is *simply* holding back human progress.

When the Enterprise adopts human-centricity and consciously works towards establishing an *adaptive* learning culture, it naturally bolsters its own resilience over time, both in terms of attracting and retaining talent. In so doing, it can transform society and make considerable headway in redressing the existing imbalances, both in local communities and society as a whole. While technical skills are reasonably easy to acquire and measure, human potential (hidden talents and the propensity to learn new skills) is less visible and more difficult to quantify. However, that should not deter the organisation from moving towards discovery, identification and recognition of individual talents, interests, aspirations, expectations, role and location preferences, since that will strengthen the competitive advantage of the Enterprise through improved performance. Investment in human beings is a worthwhile endeavour, despite prevailing 'norms' in many large organisations to go in the opposite direction.

For the most part, human potential can be *nurtured* rather than being substituted for technology. Communication should not be limited to intermediation by *mechanical* means since Knowledge will be lost to the organisation, *evaporating* between one node and another across the various sub-systems in the 'network.' Remembering Aristotle's advice, *phrónêsis*, the application of knowledge and wisdom, the higher form of *human intelligence*, needs to be practised regularly, relative to *téchnê*. If the practical application of knowledge is 'too narrow,' lacking in variety of both subjective and objective intrapersonal experiences, then the knowledge gained will not be retained and critical 'information' will be lost. Many companies encounter 'informational entropy,' the dispersal of 'information' between the nodes of the network, such that its significance is lost, diluted or obscured, due to *inflexible* structures and processes. This places the Enterprise at a distinct disadvantage in the Knowledge Economy.

'It is in Apple's DNA that technology alone is not enough - it's technology married with liberal arts, married with the humanities, that yields us the results that make our heart sing.'[23]

By focusing on creativity there will also be less attrition in the workforce as a whole. Holistic health and wellbeing *ought* to be a strategic priority, fostering energy and resilience within the Enterprise for the mutual benefit of Society; and it begins with Culture. Ultimately, business continuity is dependent upon human intelligence; and the sustainability of the Enterprise necessitates *adaptive resilience* reflected by a renewable and *flexible* talent pool. Leaders are gradually recognising technology alone cannot deliver the requisite results across the time horizons. Patagonia is a clear example of combining business objectives with human values. Since its inception it has focused on staff wellbeing and sustainability both in terms of its business model and the environment. Some large corporations are beginning to focus their attentions on *personal development*, leveraging *experiential* training and knowledge acquisition to create *meaningful* work, best suited to the person's *unique* strengths. Systematic identification of *hidden* talents and redeployment of workers displaced by automation is a necessity for sustainable value creation *across* the value chain.

The organisation also has a 'duty of care' to foster social inclusivity and equitable working practices; facilitating *employability* by 'virtue' of the variety of work *being* offered, through daily practices and business activities. Fairness has become a *strategic* necessity, given talent shortages and increasing risks of reputational damage driven by employee and investor 'insurgent activism.'[24] Failure to respond appropriately to pay-gender equality demands, 'missing capabilities,' internal upward *mobility* and other 'gaps' in the Culture System, precludes vital opportunities for growth. Many companies are being driven towards a 'portfolio model' creating *versatile* talent pools within the Enterprise itself. In effect, failure to identify *hidden talents* invariably results in an *underutilised* talent pool, the 'loss of skills' and *intrinsic* value. This will inevitably prove costly across the time horizons, in terms of attracting and retaining the best talent, investors, suppliers and customers.

During the global pandemic, work *suddenly* moved to remote premises and in some instances to emerging 'virtual reality' environments.[25] For example, Accenture experimented with new recruits in the 'metaverse,' though for the most part work transitioned to ubiquitous video calls.[26] While the Enterprise gathered more data, the workforce became more disenchanted. The *asymmetry of information* contributed to growing malaise and in some cases distrust, as private spaces became 'publicly' known through digital channels. As the novelty factor wore off, the conversation quickly turned to new pathologies, including 'burnout' and 'video fatigue,' with adverse effects on long-term health and wellbeing. Invariably, the once healthy boundaries between work and play became blurred. Employers gained unprecedented access to private homes, some making unreasonable demands for employees to 'stay on camera' for the *full* duration of an 'over-extended' working day. Micromanaging at unhealthy levels and exploitative practices took hold in the *mid-tiers* of management, exposing a lack of *preparedness* and leadership training. Fears and anxieties further eroded trust and caused resentment.[27] While statistics showed an increase in productivity, quantitative measurements did not immediately reveal the human cost, which is only progressively revealed and not yet *fully* accounted for.[28] Work continued under intrusive levels of *mass surveillance* or *suddenly* created *mass displacement* and 'financial distress,' whether employment was terminated by choice or forcibly due to uncertainties within the Enterprise.

Covid-19 starkly exposed long-standing *cultural* problems, inadequacies in employment practices, social inequalities and prevailing 'gaps' in policies both within the Enterprise and Society as a whole. Companies responded in different ways. Microsoft chose to re-think its Culture completely, opting to focus on the human side of the equation. Recognising a healthy, adaptive and resilient workforce is a necessity for business continuity and future productivity gains. More attention was given to *qualitative* aspects of employment, moving away from the strict quantitative metrics, which had eroded the core values of the Enterprise. This *sudden* change in direction, championed by the Chief Executive Officer, extolling the 'virtues' of the new company 'mantra,' sought to encourage self-reliance and *resilience* within the workforce, 'being energised and empowered to do meaningful work.'[29] Cultural change *is* difficult but not impossible. It takes time, commitment and consistent effort; it also requires *sufficient* resources. Leaders need to rise to the occasion and exercise their 'duty of care' with renewed authenticity, vigour, and *intentionality*. The reputation of the organisation depends upon it, and it is not simply a 'public relations' marketing exercise.

Change is a constant and while *everyone* has a responsibility to uphold the organisation's cultural identity, Leaders are required to take ownership over the *intrinsic* motivations and necessity for change. Core values, ethical principles, beliefs and *desirable* behaviours need to be supported and *consciously* developed across the organisation. Modelling the same and the provisioning of incentives is important. The Enterprise will not be able to respond, manage or effectively catalyse the necessary changes internally, if there are deficiencies in the levels of *preparedness* and *alertness* across the organisation. Individual human autonomy and agency *actualised* through management systems, processes and structures at each level of the Enterprise is of the essence. While the aim is clear, the transition to a human-centred culture, promoting *holistic* wellbeing needs to be *carefully and properly* managed. If the aim is to thrive, not merely survive, the Enterprise should prioritise *human risks* and seek to achieve 'good' business outcomes through human fulfilment. Optimising successful business outcomes through human *self-actualisation* requires constant attention and investment. Creating the necessary conditions for *effective* learning to occur *dynamically*, entails orchestrating requisite *individualised* support, prospective and existing employees are seeking.

The Cultural turnaround of the Enterprise needs to be rooted more deeply in the fabric of the organisation. Culture should foster trustworthiness, fairness and transparency within the environment, through processes, systems and daily practices. Divergent viewpoints are beneficial for the Enterprise and need not be confrontational, provided there is an atmosphere of mutual respect. They typically help surface *hidden meaning*, new opportunities for growth and foster social cohesion, gravitating towards a common cause. Voluntary participation in frequent discourse is more effective, than imposing a set of rules, pursuing overly rigid organisational structures and over-standardising practices and processes being enacted by the Enterprise. Without sufficient *flexibility* and *fluidity* in the Enterprise Communication Systems, the *human notion* of connection and engagement collapses. Frequent human-to-human interactions are conducive to *harmonious working relationships*, deeper and clearer understanding, fostering *adaptive and resilient behaviours*, as the need arises.

An *effective and efficient* learning system, driven by experimentation and practical experience, will help the Enterprise elevate *general* educational levels, data proficiency and promote an understanding of the Systems in play across the ecosystem. Timely responsiveness to fast-changing situations is always preferable than 'paralysis by analysis.' However, productivity levels will benefit from improved competencies, knowledge of the inherent risks and *technical* limitations associated with 'artificial intelligence,' being more *widely* and *clearly* understood across the Enterprise as a whole. From a structural and systemic perspective, it is important to recognise the Culture of the Enterprise *is* unique. It has its own Code of Ethics, Codes of Practice and professional conduct, educational programmes and 'informational memory,' which are at once independent of the Systems in operation and at the same time interdependent through interactions with the same. While bias and risk cannot be removed completely, effective *mitigation* is derived from a broader knowledge base, as well as *timely access* to the requisite information. Processes should be designed to detect the smallest of changes in the environment, *finely* attuned to the *specific* needs of the organisation, *facilitating adaptation* to endogenous and exogenous changes in *real* time.

Events impacting US employment levels such as the *'great resignation'* and the *'great regret,'* following the Covid-19 lockdowns, seem to have a 'ripple effect' around the world. Many workers abandoned their employment initially due to excessive pressures in the workplace, citing unfair treatment and inadequate levels of pay, across many sectors including healthcare and hospitality. Although many workers have returned, due to the 'cost of living' crisis, rising energy and food prices triggered by the war in Ukraine, the underlying problems have not been resolved. Complex social phenomena, faltering public health and new challenges faced by employers and employees alike are experienced all over the world. Media headlines point to the growing 'talent war' on both sides of the Atlantic, as a *global phenomenon*. Rising geopolitical tensions heighten 'old divisions' and this time it's a veritable 'war' over 'artificial intelligence' technologies and rare Earth minerals, critical for a variety of uses.

As companies endeavour to *automate* their processes, they are unable to hire sufficiently *skilled workers* in the numbers required to advance their objectives. Corporations once dominant in the marketplace, appear to be faltering as the 'next wave' of 'lay-offs' makes *global* headlines. In the context of the Enterprise, research shows pay levels, while a necessary part of attracting and retaining talent, is not the most significant factor in drawing the best available talent. Rather prospective candidates, particularly younger cohorts (millennials and gen-Z) are actively seeking intangible benefits, such as a better work-life balance, happiness, inspiration, personal fulfillment and most importantly *employability*; in other words opportunities for further education supported by their prospective employers. However, employers should not be excluding multi-generational cohorts from their talent pool by *algorithmic* means. The Enterprise can only thrive by successfully integrating multiple skillsets, a richly diverse talent pool drawn from multiple disciplines among its ranks. The successful transfer of Knowledge also requires the fullness of experiences acquired over time and the sharing of wisdom.

A thriving Learning Culture has *suddenly* become the defining factor for Enterprise success in the 21st century.

We need to reconceptualise the *meaning* of work and the 'human dimensions' for present and future generations. Companies are now cognisant with the advent of 'hybrid' business models, where work no longer has a 'fixed' location or dimension that they need to pay more attention to their Culture, talent acquisition and retention requirements, both for business continuity and sustainability. Work needs to *fit in* with a person's life, not the other way around. The *right* solution needs to be part of an experiential learning process, where workers are suitably rewarded, personal data protected and a new employer-employee relationship is established for mutual benefit. There is no playbook, or a 'one-size-fits all' proposition that can foster equitable human outcomes on both sides of the equation. A culture of fairness espouses social justice and has a visible social purpose built-into its DNA. For younger cohorts, opportunities to progress matter more than 'pay and perks;' they are also more likely to be driven by a 'just' cause. In essence, they are seeking *meaningful* work, which resonates with their *own* personal core values, while being *seen*, *heard* and *feeling* valued. They wish to speak *freely*, without judgment being passed on *arbitrary* grounds. Diversity, inclusion and psychological safety are elements that matter in *equal* measure. Cultural *alignment* with *individual values, beliefs and behaviours* is now of the essence.

Culture cannot evolve successfully without nurturing *human* relationships based on *mutual* respect and human dignity. It requires the *continuous application* of Awareness, Knowledge and Understanding of the core values, beliefs and desirable behaviours, at each level of the Enterprise and more broadly across its value chain. Enabling the whole organisation to learn both from its successes and failures is business critical. The 'future of work depends on creating renewable human energy.'[30] Human beings flourish, when new technologies deployed in the workplace are supportive of human endeavour. Leaders need to *personally* invest time and energy in nurturing their talent and 'visibly' exercise their fiduciary 'duty of care' with authenticity, both towards individuals and the Enterprise teams collectively. There needs to be less emphasis on the transactional aspects (*technical efficiencies*) and more focus on creating a Culture that is inspirational, fulfilling and rewarding for people, as they each 'play' to their *unique* individual strengths. The 'best' talent is attracted to business when its purpose is clear; and exceptional Leaders *nurture* the 'best' talent from within.

The Enterprise needs to project its own *unique* cultural identity, endeavouring to rise above *artificially generated* 'noise,' and become a business people *genuinely* want to work for and crucially *believe* in.

Culture is specific to both context and location. As technology continues to evolve and affords society greater levels of convenience, we should *not* neglect 'offline' experiences in the *real* world. Interconnectivity is not a substitute for developing 'good' interpersonal relations, which are conducive to learning and new knowledge acquisition. In essence, we are *social beings* and human connections count. Reductive 'information' may be atomised through 'machine learning,' but it is not a substitute for the acquisition of the broader Knowledge base and wisdom gained through human interactions and experiences, the Enterprise requires. There is no limitation to the human imagination and learning capacity, other than constraints *arbitrarily* imposed within the organisational structure, systems and processes.

New technological advancements and the deployment of 'artificial intelligence' systems call into question what we *know* and *do not know*. For some people, one of the hardest things will be *unlearning what we know*. The only certainty we have is that tomorrow will be *different* from today. If Leaders *choose* to resist the *dynamics* of change, the Enterprise loses its unique identity and ultimately fails, irrespective of external forces, changing markets and competition. The first challenge is to understand the *true* nature of complex adaptive

Socio-Technical Systems. Getting the *balance* right between 'openness' and the 'closed' elements of the system is a *fine art*. It requires meticulous attention to detail, consistent efforts and sufficient *flexibility*, so the system can evolve *dynamically* within the environment. Secondly, how the Enterprise responds to changes, both in the internal and external environment, entails taking into consideration the *impact* of its decisions and actions on Society, as a whole.

Culture has become a *strategic* necessity. Whenever storm clouds gather, uncertainty, fear and anxiety accumulate; and particularly in those challenging moments, Culture must lend support to the Strategy. Investing in people, championing their *unique* talents affords the Enterprise a competitive edge; and enables long-term thinking, bolstering organisational resilience. Resources allocated consistently and efforts made to foster *authentic* collaborations ensure the Enterprise is *fully integrated* in the surroundings and has a *renewable* talent pool. Conversely, a persistently high level of 'toxicity' in the workplace will result in critical failures.[31] The organisational structure and communication systems become more 'brittle' and less likely to withstand external shocks. Internalising externalities is now a requirement and this *specific* capability extends beyond the scope of *machines*. It necessitates mental dexterity, the unique talents and contributions of human beings. Organisations driven by the social purpose of the Enterprise are more likely to focus on broader ecological impacts and equitable stakeholder outcomes.[32] Profits ensue reflective of the measure of success the Enterprise has in reaching beneficial outcomes for people and planet.

'Our aim is to help build a more prosperous society with a business that values respect and fairness and which grows in harmony with the global community. We strive to enhance the quality of people's lives by using our skills and advanced technologies to create great new products and services.'[33]

Increasingly, the Enterprise is operating cross-sector, taking an *holistic* view of its local, regional and global footprints. It needs to act without compromising its leadership position in the marketplace. Trust and resilience go hand-in-hand being built 'top-down' and 'bottom-up.' Enabling teams to self-organise and *grow* creates deeper bonds; and a shared purpose *naturally* propels the organisation forward. Flexibility in the learning and communication systems facilitates change. Conversely, normative scorecards, industry benchmarks and other constraints may interfere with the *organic* nature of the Enterprise Culture as it evolves. Cultural diversity enriches human experiences and enhances Enterprise capabilities, as it is better placed to make the *right choices*. Results are not the priority of Culture; rather the focus is on creating alignment across the value chain with core values, ethical principles, beliefs and behaviours, assuring Quality Excellence in the process.

Collaboration built on trust is the most valuable asset for the Enterprise. Creating synergistic relationships between people, planet and the use of technology is critical. Fostering the Japanese principle of *kaizen*, continuous improvement, the organisation dynamically sustains the evolution of the Enterprise. Toyota is one of the most inspiring examples where trust and human dignity is the bedrock of corporate culture. Their core values are embedded in their code of professional conduct, the 'Toyota Way.'[34] It is infused with the 'spirit' of the company's founder Sakichi Toyoda.[35] His son translated the lessons learned from his father's innovations, automating weaving looms, to pursue his own dream to make automobiles. That 'spirit' is the expression of human values, championing human agency, respecting the needs of diverse stakeholders, combined with the idealistic aim of serving the *global community*. Toyota's culture sets forth a new pathway towards human flourishing and reflects the aesthetic values that are often 'lost' in so many organisations. Toyota celebrates its heritage and the intrinsic value of innovation, working *harmoniously* towards a better future.

'The highest form of knowledge is empathy, for it requires us to suspend our egos and live in another's world.'[36]

At the organisational level, Leaders should consider building a Culture of Excellence, and seek to embed human 'virtues' in the design of Enterprise processes. Human values help sustain competitive advantage and performance levels, as they provide a resource for motivation and inspiration. Feedback loops are less effective without an empathetic approach to human needs. Returns on investments in new technologies cannot be realised without acknowledging the 'human dimensions,' affording the participants *autonomy* and *flexibility*. Self-reliance creates a new healthy *dynamic* in the workplace. From the employee perspective, self-directed learning opportunities are desirable and may be enhanced by 'real' *experiences* across the Enterprise 'network;' thereby helping to raise productivity levels.

Attempts to change behaviours *alone,* is both 'transitory and superficial.'[37] Organisational development requires an integrated approach with a clear sense of direction. As a result of which the *cross-pollination* of new ideas flourishes and bolsters the organisation's *learning capacity;* it confers a *sustainable* competitive edge to the Enterprise.

Culture is a unique environment that both exists and emerges within the Enterprise. It determines the capacity of the Enterprise to adapt to *new* situations. Leaders proactively engaged in espousing the core values, ethical principles and behaviours they seek others to adopt *voluntarily* are more likely to create an *inspiring* learning environment. The learning process hinges upon a variety of views being *'freely'* expressed and 'information' being exchanged, as Knowledge builds *gradually* over time. It requires the *deliberate* abandonment of assumptions and preconceived ideas, a willingness to explore aspirations, expectations and *unmet* needs.

'Owning everything changes the Culture and focus of the business making it more *human.*'[38]

Communication is of the essence. It underpins the core values of the Enterprise and requires clarity in the form of expression. The transmission of shared values across the Enterprise 'network' and by extension Society, also requires meticulous attention to detail, so that the organisation 'stays on track,' averting reputational damage. The influence of the Leader on the Enterprise Culture is undeniable. Culture is inextricably linked with the *personality* of the Leader, strategic orientation and purpose of the Enterprise. Delivering excellence requires a coherent 'single view' of the Enterprise and yet it also needs to convey the 'human dimension' of a harmonious *pluralistic* whole. Culture is the complex mosaic of diverse human experiences, values, beliefs, customs, habits, social 'norms' and historical influences, 'freely' shared and absorbed; consciously and subconsciously, both through formal and *informal* settings and continuous interactions with others and the environment.

Ferrari is one of the best-known brands in the world, synonymous with beauty and engineering excellence. Its response to the outbreak of Covid-19 was exemplary.[39] A small trans-disciplinary taskforce was convened to develop a strategy to resume working and above all to keep everyone safe. In the midst of *chaos,* keeping everyone informed of the changes, whilst adhering to the strictest health and safety standards was no mean feat. It was an extreme 'stress test' of the Culture and core values espoused by the organisation. Through the publication of its 'back on track' strategy, Ferrari extended the knowledge gained through its own experiences to the wider society; the ethos and legacy of its founder Enzo Ferrari, 'never give up,' was still very much alive. The 'ripple effect' provided inspiration, made work meaningful and collaborations cross-sector emerged as companies extended their 'duty of care' beyond normal business activities. Some converted car factories to manufacture respiratory equipment *overnight*, fashion houses turned garments into personal protective equipment and perfume makers attended to the need for hand sanitizers.[40]

Business is relational. Leaders recognise new forms of partnerships and business models are required cross-sector. The levels of investment required to combat *global* problems, such as climate change *adaptations*, necessitate urgent coordinated joint-actions, both to be effective and *achievable* financially. Failure to pursue innovation, mistakenly perceived as the antithesis of business continuity, has frequently resulted in shorter lifespans, as new opportunities for *growth* are missed. In business, if the opportunity is missed, it is often gone forever; or else it has *morphed* into something quite different and may not be worth pursuing. There are well-known examples of corporate giants, failing to *anticipate* changes in the marketplace, responding too late. Errors of judgment are costly and organisations may not recover. Fundamentally, over-confidence and complacency lead to weakened capabilities, and quite often reflect the failure to invest in human ingenuity. It is of course far better to rapidly learn from mistakes than to die from inertia. Leaders should remain open-minded, attuned to the nature and dynamics of change, while learning from *pluralistic*, diverse *living* and *lived* experiences.

Haier[41] is living proof a very large organisation of 75,000 people can flourish through shared values, supported by the *flexibility* of its organisational structure and effective Communication Systems. Dynamic 'micro-enterprises,' teams of 15 people, seamlessly perform their duties by completing *whole* tasks, and effectively communicate in real-time with the entire ecosystem, sharing Knowledge, 'information' and skills. They are resilient self-sustaining 'organisms,' working towards a common cause. While they benefit from accessing shared platform resources and modern technologies, including 'artificial intelligence' they are especially attentive to the 'human dimensions;'

the delivery of great customer care and *mutual* support within the organisation itself. Self-managing teams *adapt more quickly*, defuse tensions and create 'virtuous feedback loops' that are of *mutual* benefit. Extraordinary results ensue from the full richness of creativity and *timely responsiveness* to change. Team cohesiveness is formidable, morale is high and there is a *real* sense of purpose. It is akin to the high performance levels you might see in a Formula One team, which *acts as one. People, processes, systems and technology* operate in perfect *synchronicity* as a *harmonious whole*.[42] Every person has a clear understanding of their own role and each other's role. Every person in the team takes part in the 'pre-race' and 'post-race' briefings. Win or lose, the team *as a whole* continually learns together and most importantly *moves* forward.

'We have intangible value for brands, but not for people's potential.'[43]

The Enterprise needs to continually invest in developing human capabilities, critical thinking, emotional intelligence, human relations, data and more broadly ethics proficiency, if it wishes to harness the full potential of emerging 'artificial intelligence' technologies. Failure to do so means there is a risk its Culture will become impoverished, particularly if insufficient attention is given to the human experiences in the workplace. Accounting practices serve as the measurement of quantifiable items at a specific moment in time; but they do not reflect the intrinsic value of human potential and the dynamic evolution of the organisation. Therein lies the paradox: intangible value is ascribed to brands, intellectual property and *generative* 'artificial intelligence.' And yet the potential value of human beings is unexplained.

'That which is not good for the swarm, neither is it good for the bee.'[44]

Culture needs to be visibly espoused by the Leadership teams across the Enterprise and continually reinforced. If the individual flourishes and succeeds, so too does the team. In large corporations,[45] the emphasis has been on the rigour of the scientific approach to management. However, as technology becomes more pervasive, more attention needs to be given to the 'human dimensions.' Human beings aspire to *live and breathe* in the *creative* dimension, and desire to espouse their own aesthetic values and beliefs. While economists identify 'self-interest' as the motivating factor, we are first and foremost *social beings*. Paradoxically, 'chaos' is a vital component of 'social systems,' and cannot be constrained by a linear order; without sufficient *variety* in the 'social systems,'[46] the Enterprise becomes less stable and more fragile. Variety in the work we do fuels creativity, which is conducive to 'good' health and wellbeing.

There is no longer a single source of human knowledge. Boundaries are fast becoming blurred between the value of human intelligence and 'artificial intelligence,' which is simply *not intelligent* in the *human sense*.[47] It remains a sophisticated computational tool, which can assist the processing of vast amounts of data. Knowledge that is represented or encoded in a form suitable for machine processing will increasingly play a part in our construct of the reality. Experiential learning may shift to the 'metaverse'[48] and other forms of 'mixed reality' both at work and at play. Hence ubiquitous connectivity will transform human-to-human relationships into virtual '3D' *'artificial persona'* relationships, which call into question ethical principles, such as fairness, social equity and social justice. Organisations must give serious consideration to online safety, privacy and accessibility to life opportunities and above all governance structures, owing to the non-deterministic nature of these new technologies.

'I think the fundamental role of a leader is to look for ways to shape the decades ahead, not just react to the present, and to help others accept the discomfort of disruptions to the status quo.'[49]

As 'artificial intelligence' systems proliferate across all sectors, the role of the Leader will become increasingly important, both in setting the tone for the Enterprise Culture and its strategic direction. Culture is 'the glue' that holds people together, and with increasing intermediation of 'artificial agents,' Leaders will need to find new ways of fostering 'good' human relations among their stakeholders. Investment in the *broader* educational programmes will prove critical for business success. Developing *human capabilities* such as *critical thinking, emotional and social intelligence,* as well as advancing the requisite *technical* skills, such as data proficiency and an understanding of the limitations of 'artificial intelligence,' will contribute to the longevity of the Enterprise. Failure to do so means there is a risk the Enterprise Culture will become impoverished, particularly if human-to-human *connections* are not supported, and insufficient attention is given to the *human experiences* in the work place. The 'human factor' in the business equation is of strategic importance for the Enterprise, in light of new challenges emerging from *'hybrid' business models*.[50]

An *adaptive* and *resilient* Culture is a *sustainable* Culture. Forming a protective shield around the Enterprise, it enables the Enterprise to thrive and potentially extend its lifespan, provided the appropriate governance structures and operational safeguards are in place, to safely manage and mitigate emergent risks, owing to the *non-deterministic nature* of Socio-Technical Systems. These systems comprise a series of complex adaptive processes, supporting *dynamic* interdependencies and *intricate* interactions between 'multi-agent systems,' involving people and machines, courtesy of Information Communication Technology. We are on the cusp of redefining relationships, roles, duties, responsibilities and obligations. Inevitably, there are frictions internally, which need to be disentangled, but conflicts may also arise externally, not least because there is no such thing as perfect equilibrium and underlying assumptions of the economic model are fuelled by *imperfect information*.

The dexterity of the Enterprise in navigating complexity *is* mission critical. As complexity increases so too does the need for *flexibility*. A complex adaptive system maintains its identity by preserving the majority of its structural 'couplings,' while *dynamically* adapting to internal and external changes. This may then lead to changes in the 'couplings' over time, but without sufficient flexibility it cannot preserve its identity at each stage of its evolution. Processes should be disciplined, oriented towards *desirable* ends, but they should not be overly prescriptive where human beings are concerned. The strict rules required by 'artificial agents' do *not* apply.

Culture underpins the sustainability of the Enterprise. And yet it is often denied the attention it deserves. It seems ironic in the Age of Knowledge. Philosophers have long debated the source of 'truth' for millennia. Our quest for *meaning* is effectively in 'perpetual motion.' Whether through the Arts, Humanities and the Sciences, our destiny is to continue seeking new horizons. At an individual and collective level, human consciousness constitutes the basis of existing domains of Knowledge, transposed into our Culture. We may choose to make further inquiries, seek to learn from our predecessors and look forward to what *might* be. Therein lies the paradox, since neither Knowledge, nor data or 'information,' is ever 'complete.' Culture continues evolving, and necessitates *room for manoeuvre*. It takes shape through the continued exploration of *new ideas*, without ever abandoning our *quest* for the 'truth.' It is the embodiment of change, Knowledge acquired through a cumulative process of *renewal*, new discoveries and exploration of new possibilities. Envisioning counterfactual realities creates the conditions for enduring 'real' value creation and orients the Enterprise towards *continuous innovation*. Culture is encoded in operational and reputational resilience. It has *organic* intangible properties, which cannot be fully quantified and yet it has a *real* impact on the Enterprise and Society. Culture constitutes the identity of the Enterprise. It *should* be intentional, transparent, self-directed through evolving core values, embedded within the *belief system* of the Enterprise. Culture is *always* work in progress.

Chapter 4

Growth
/grəʊθ/

'Without continual growth and progress, such words as improvement, achievement and success have no meaning.'[1]

Growth denotes 'the process of growing' and the means to increase prosperity.[2] It should be the means by which long-term *real* economic value is ethically created, fairly distributed and beneficially delivered to the wider society. This should be achieved while safeguarding the health of global populations and the precious natural resources of our planet. Hence, both the *direction* and the *qualitative* aspects of growth deserve greater attention than they typically receive. The Enterprise is preferably the protagonist, supported by multilateral governance frameworks to facilitate economic growth. Fully integrated in its environment, it is best placed to fulfil the needs of Society, at a granular level. Its purpose and *raison d'être*[3] is interlinked with human destiny, the Environment and Society, as a whole. Anchored to our fundamental human values, respectful of different cultures, Nature and the demands of the Earth's Systems, sustainable growth assures *continual progress* and *improvement*. It is clear *meaningless* production and expenditures no longer serve us. The *dynamics* of global demand ought to meet supply and vice versa, *freely* oscillating towards desirable forms of equilibria; but first we must learn where 'real' needs exist, understand their true nature, as change continually occurs. We may better respond, exploring new areas of comparative advantage within our respective economies to foster trade, attract new investments and support more efficient industries. We can evolve our capacity to build new 'bridges to the future,' forging trustworthy partnerships of *mutual* benefit *at all levels of Society*, and thereby gain a better contextual understanding of local, regional and global needs. Exploitation of the environment without due consideration for our intrinsic human needs and values,[4] may at best yield limited returns and at worst have 'catastrophic' consequences for our continued survival.

The interconnectedness of the Global Economy and of the Earth's Systems should be considered in the context of current and future growth, if corporations are going to properly embed 'ESG principles'[5] into their Vision, Strategy and Culture and become fit for the Future. The extraction of monetary value is not a *sufficient* determinant of future value, without the legitimacy afforded to it by Society. Nor can we find a 'quick fix' using technology alone, while seeking immediate answers from the data. The changing geopolitical and 'geo-economic' world order requires a broader understanding of the inherent complexities and challenges. We need to *re-imagine* growth in the context of achieving a *sustainable* digital future. This entails working collaboratively towards inclusive, equitable, differentiated growth. The Enterprise needs to effectively and efficiently respond to existing and unmet needs, understanding the ambitions, expectations, aspirations and desires of human populations at local, regional and global levels. While the appropriate 'policy mix' may vary according to the socio-economic needs of each country, emphasis should be placed on renewing infrastructure and institutional reform. The aim is to create favourable conditions for growth in support of human health and wellbeing within planetary boundaries.

It is now clear the Enterprise must give due consideration to the impacts of its business activities, taking into account human health, whilst working towards *regenerating* the Earth's *natural* ecological balance. In many cases, acting in support of localised conservation activities to restore natural habitats and biodiversity can stimulate growth opportunities, benefitting local communities while reducing its carbon footprint and environmental impacts. Additionally, the Enterprise can use its best efforts to implement adaptations to counter the worst effects of climate change and sustain business continuity. Consistent public and private sector investments directed towards the decarbonisation of the global economy will create new opportunities for economic growth, and if properly managed, foster enduring value creation, both intra-generationally and inter-generationally. Notwithstanding the challenges we face, beneficial outcomes can be achieved through improved multilateral collaborations and sustainable economic growth. The impacts of policy decisions and actions in one country are of necessity intertwined with those of another. Efforts to stimulate growth, combat climate change and implement adaptations need to be *coordinated* at a local, regional and global level for the *mutual* benefit of *all* economies and societies.

Governance structures at an international level are of equal importance, provided they allow for sufficient *flexibility* to foster economic complementarity and create the necessary conditions for growth at all levels of Society. Efforts to renew existing trade agreements[6] can facilitate *coordinated* actions at local, regional and global levels, and foster operational safeguards to restore public confidence and trust in the advancement of new technologies, particularly 'artificial intelligence.' The removal of trade barriers, timely macroeconomic interventions, harmonised regulatory and legal frameworks, global *qualitative* reporting standards can engender new possibilities for economic growth. Governments should focus on creating broader alliances, to improve public health and the overall quality of public services and infrastructure, while making adequate provision for reasonable 'social safety nets,' in support of life opportunities. Raising education levels in Society as a whole can also foster new employment opportunities, economic competitiveness and future growth possibilities, smoothing the necessary transitions.

Through a variety of public-private partnerships and a wide range of strategic initiatives, it is possible to achieve effective and efficient collaborations to enact *meaningful* change. Adopting the principle of economic complementarity is key in the 'knowledge economy,' where trade is focused on services in some economies and efficient means of production in others. Where countries are more reliant on the use of natural resources, the aim for current and future growth should be to reduce pollution levels. Adhering to the principle of 'economic circularity,' the endeavour is to limit new waste production, supported by useful technology-knowledge transfers. Appropriate qualitative improvements in systems design, development and deployment can be facilitated by the use of 'artificial intelligence.' Without continuous improvement, growth and human progress, there can be no lasting *meaningful improvement, achievement or success* for the Enterprise, the Economy and Society as a whole. Orchestrating a successful and peaceful transition towards a more sustainable digital future is now a matter of urgency.

For the last thirty years, economies have become more integrated and interconnected within the Global System, owing to globalisation and significant advances in more affordable technologies. The global economy tripled in size between 1980 and 2010 and 1.3 billion people were lifted out of extreme poverty.[7] Incremental improvements in computer hardware and software, telecommunications and related infrastructure enabled Information Communication Technology, such as 'artificial intelligence' to take a leap forward. Rapid digitalisation[8] across multiple sectors, increased connectivity in both scale and speed, lends support to the *instantaneous* collection of data from the Internet and transmission of 'information' worldwide. Overall economic growth fostered by *liberalised* trade removed barriers to human progress, owing to reduced cross-border frictions, enabling less restricted 'flows' of capital, goods and services. Trade and capital flows transformed the lives of billions of people around the world, improved living standards and crucially elevated literacy levels on a global scale. Relatively fewer and less complicated tariffs coupled with relatively unconstrained digital cross-border payments, created new markets and plausible business opportunities for companies to expand overseas with relative ease.

Significantly, international trade accounted for 40% of global gross domestic product (GDP) in 1990 and increased to 57% of global GDP in 2015. At the same time, foreign direct investment increased from 10% to 34% of global GDP. While the benefits of global trade were by no means evenly distributed, emerging regional economies mostly in South East Asia contributed 70% of total global output in 2017, doubling their contribution relative to the start of the 21st century. Increasing local, regional and global competition not only sparked technological innovations in advanced economies, bolstering R&D through the global exchange of knowledge and ideas, it also greatly helped developing and newly emerging economies, which would not have otherwise benefitted from global trade.[9]

Global economic growth between 1980 and 2010 was largely driven by the increase in trade and financial deregulation assisting the flow of capital cross-border. Economists note for the first time trade became truly global, as opposed to being simply international, supported by technology-knowledge transfers, lower tariffs and overall lower transportation costs. Many countries experienced significant levels of economic growth, notably China and India. South East Asia became the global manufacturing hub, as many industries from the Global North *migrated* towards the Global South.[10] Supply chains became increasingly fragmented, while global populations participated for the first time in global economic expansion. Multinational firms grew rapidly, benefiting from lower borrowing costs, buoyant markets, high levels of business confidence; all of which resulted in the acceleration of M&A, as companies sought to diversify and expand their existing portfolios beyond prudent core and adjacent markets.[11]

Nokia ventured into mobile phones, expanding the scope of its core business activities. It began making all the components 'in-house,' and by 2006 at its peak imported more than 100 billion components to support local and regional factories.[12] In 2007, Steve Jobs launched the iPhone; Apple sold 6.1m in its first year and the rest is history. Apple dominates the market today occupying 25% market share, Nokia at the peak of its success held 51% of the market. Owing to the fast pace of change and stronger competition, Nokia and others had to cut their losses; Nokia chose to refocus its attention on core B2B activities. Despite valiant efforts to compete in the B2C marketplace prior to the sale of its handsets business to Microsoft in 2013, Nokia had accumulated 57 incompatible operating systems due to absent interdepartmental communication and other organisational problems. Returning to highly specialist areas in telecommunications, Nokia recovered quickly, strengthened by its acquisition of Alcatel-Lucent in 2016. As technological advancements gather momentum, firms will need to cultivate a strong *adaptive capacity*, focusing on human capabilities and *organisational resilience*, taking care not to exceed their natural *'stretching point.'* Additionally, firms need to direct their efforts towards an orderly 'green transition,' targeting highly skilled ecologically-minded business activities, leveraging the 'knowledge economy.'

While the return of heavy industry and manufacturing to advanced economies in the Global North was previously questioned, it is possible new technologically advanced industries will emerge to replace 'lost' productive capacity, due to rising geopolitical tensions and the 'green transition.' Almost every country is revising existing industrial policies, long-term energy requirements and plans for long-term infrastructure investments. However without renewed 'openness' towards global trade, it will be difficult to tackle the 'bigger problems' such as climate change, societal disequilibria and income inequalities. Countries will be less able to attract substantial capital inflows, direct foreign investments to assist the global transition towards 'clean energy,' and undertake coordinated actions for successful local, regional and global adaptations. R&D directed towards *decarbonising* the global economy will sustain long-term growth and foster 'true' innovation, preferably using readily available nature-based solutions to limit further environmental degradation, catalyse urgent actions and save on costs. Context-specific targeted efforts will be required to effect structural improvements and institutional reforms, oriented towards more inclusive and equitable conditions for *all* countries to access financial resources and new trade opportunities.

Companies need to raise their game, *dynamically* adapt their existing capabilities, while improving leadership and management skill sets across the ecosystem. Simultaneously strengthen their technological capacity and responsiveness to rapidly changing situations, as they enter new markets, defend leadership positions and market share. Increased trade draws economies closer to their respective comparative advantage fostering export-led growth, which serves to enhance 'real' income. Competitive pressures on domestic firms force more effective and efficient use of limited resources, fostering high levels of performance, profitability and productivity, one of the leading indicators of potential future growth. Wages are higher when skill sets and educational levels improve, benefiting aggregate demand and savings. Increased trade in terms of imports allows consumers to benefit from a greater variety, quantity and quality of goods and services at more competitive prices. Overall, globalisation has fostered one of the strongest periods of economic growth in recent history. It correlates with improved living standards, higher education levels and life expectancy.

Notwithstanding the socio-economic necessity for a resilient mixed economy, 'open' to global trade, not all policy makers favour the long-term view of economic development. Some choose to support inefficient industries rendered obsolete by increased competition and turn to protectionist measures, rather than accelerating investments towards large-scale infrastructure adaptations to combat climate change. The notion jobs will be protected is misguided and extremely costly for all members of Society.[13] Tariff barriers damage export-led growth and attract retaliatory responses. Domestic firms become less competitive, no longer economically viable when market conditions change. While tariffs may boost growth temporarily, they introduce hidden costs and market distortions, limiting future economic output and aggregate demand. Import substitution policies prevalent in South East Asian countries inhibited economic growth, prior to countries like India, 'opening' their economies to international trade and financial deregulation, previously unable to benefit from technology-knowledge exchanges and capital inflows.[14] Integrated global trade frameworks lend support to current and future economic growth, enabling business expansion, while improving living standards for local populations.

Where jobs may be lost through *technological competition*, automation of processes and simple repetitive tasks, it is the responsibility of corporations and governments to create appropriate *transition mechanisms* to help jobseekers find new employment opportunities.[15] Inclusive growth renders voluntary participation in the economy possible, while more equitable employment underpins sustainability, as the economy becomes more *adaptive and resilient over time*. Employability is the new competitive advantage. It will help counter *discontinuities* in economic growth, since the current and future value of the workforce and related productivity improvements will not be 'lost.' If appropriate support mechanisms and policies are designed to be context-specific at a local level, they can spur the emergence of micro-enterprises supporting reskilling and up-skilling of displaced workers within local communities. Recent studies have shown investment in technology without corresponding investment in human capabilities leaves firms at a disadvantage, as they cannot capitalise on new technologies in the absence of highly skilled talent pools. Decentralised local interventions are more flexible, timely; and with detailed knowledge, awareness and understanding of local requirements, they are less costly to implement and can be *adjusted* as required. Since central governments do not have unlimited funds to provision 'social safety nets,' investments directed towards helping firms and displaced workers at a local level are essential to reinvigorate the economy as a whole. Failure to do so results in the disintegration of local communities and socio-economic malaise lasting for generations, until appropriate policy interventions are provisioned.

'Investment in education is the most direct way to improve skills and human capital.'[16]

Since the global economy is set on course to grow primarily through the advancement of newly available technologies, companies require financial incentives to support skill conversions and foster employ-ability within their own ecosystems. While individual workers need equal access to opportunities supporting their personal growth and development plans, and independent skill set transitions likely to occur several times within their careers. Education does not end with school or university; life experiences go hand-in-hand with work experiences and need to be supported both at an individual level and collectively for optimal results. Voluntary adherence towards co-evolving new capabilities within the Enterprise is where new sources of value may be discovered. Legacy systems, processes and aging architectures hinder growth opportunities, but the failure to discover hidden talents curtails the ability of the Enterprise to realise its full potential and ambitiously pursue new growth opportunities *organically*.

Efforts should be directed towards creating favourable conditions for growth, proactively exploring new ideas. The Enterprise should focus on developing new business models, supporting entrepreneur-ial capabilities across its own 'network' and extended supply chains. Many organisations focus on *narrowly* defined financial metrics and vital new growth opportunities are lost. Investment decisions are either delayed or distracted by local contingencies without 'seeing' the 'bigger picture,' often discounting the *value* of beneficial societal outcomes. Conversely, enabling each individual to gravitate towards their strengths boosts productivity within the Enterprise at a micro-economic level, which is then reflected at a macroeconomic level to the benefit of Society and the Global System as a whole. Simplifying taxation regimes, regulation and applicable legal frameworks will not only assure compliance and greater transparency, but also reduce the *bureaucratic* burden placed upon the Enterprise, enabling finan-cial capital to 'flow' towards more productive (creative) ends.

A productive (creative) shift towards a new growth paradigm requires a radical *new way of thinking* and an abandonment of 'beggar-thy-neighbour' policies that have taken countries to the brink of war, if not fully fledged armed conflicts over trade and territories for centu-ries. And yet they may pose an existential threat, owing to the latest technology-driven 'arms race.' We could *choose* instead to engage multilaterally, demonstrate a renewed willingness to end nuclear proliferation and autonomous weaponry systems involving 'artificial intelligence,' which do not lend support to *sustainability* in the global economy, whether in the present or the future tense. Technology advancements could be decoupled from the military sphere to foster new scientific discoveries and promote beneficial human outcomes, extend our current knowledge, while safeguarding the environment. We could work towards *mutually* beneficial cooperation on a global scale. Should we choose to look through multiple lenses, we could gain a more comprehensive understanding, awareness and knowledge of the challenges we *commonly* face. The complexities of economic growth unfold progressively over time, and require a renewed appreciation for collaboration, effectively grasping the significance of what is *actually* at stake.

While technology advancements and globalisation contributed to economic progress in many countries, these phenomena also created structural and systemic imbalances. Global economic expansion is correlated with rising debt levels, greater uncertainty, financial instability and heightened geopolitical tensions, as major economies jockey for power and influence. Despite improvements in the relative competitiveness and higher rates of employment in high-skilled sectors, others faltered in advanced economies. Manufacturing decline in the USA and the UK relative to others, such as Germany and France, saw sharp falls in productivity, particularly in the aftermath of the global financial crisis 2007–2008. Income distribution levels were extremely uneven, declining 'real' wages and disposable income exacerbated polarisation in society, leading to increased incidences of 'gun violence,' 'knife crimes' and civil unrest.[17] From a societal perspective, this is further complicated by insufficient investment in the 'public good,' vital public services, healthcare, education, shelter and other social infrastructure.

'Productivity isn't everything, but in the long run it is almost everything. A country's ability to improve its standard of living over time depends almost entirely on its ability to raise its output per worker.'[18]

Institutional deficiencies lead to increased economic costs and inhibit growth. While inconsistent levels of investment in R&D dampen business optimism, they lower *expectations* for current and future growth, offering little incentive for firms to initiate change within their respective business and economic cycles. Whilst economic growth is expected to mirror technological progress, the widening 'capabilities gap' and ensuing 'productivity gap' is not an insignificant challenge for policy makers and firms to overcome. A sharp decline in worker productivity undermines economic competitiveness, which is difficult to overcome should policy misalignment with the pace of techno-logical change *persist*. Interventions overly focused on one side of the equation and not the other do not bolster *economic resilience* and may cause further structural damage due to delayed recovery from unforeseen events.[19]

Some research suggests the USA and the UK have become 'too financialised,' since their 'productive capacity' was gradually eroded, following financial deregulation in the early 1980s.[20] However, *all* economies are entangled within the Global System and it is para-mount to manage each phase of the technological transition care-fully. In so doing, the timing of policy decisions is critical. Austerity policies designed to reduce debt-to-GDP ratios in the UK post 2007–2008 financial crisis, while economies had *not* fully recovered from the cyclical downturn, adversely affected employment levels and life opportunities for individuals, households and businesses alike.[21] Austerity measures undermine business confidence, delay domestic investments, weaken public trust in the institutions and reduce inves-tor confidence in the economy. Conversely, increased government spending aiming to bridge the growing 'productivity gap' and 'capa-bilities gap' increases debt levels, leaving the economy vulnerable to increased market volatility, and at risk of insufficient *capital inflows* to support the deficit should there be a *sudden* loss of confidence.

Finding new ways to improve productivity levels is one of the key challenges for financial services oriented economies, such as the USA and the UK. It drives their relative positions of influence on the global stage, but also creates structural and systemic imbalances. The US has striven for consumer-led demand, supported by a for-midable defence industry; the UK punches above its weight in terms of technological innovation and acts as a global financial hub, part of its historical DNA since the Industrial Revolution. It is ironic both economies have 'lost' their manufacturing capacity, which is not easy to rebuild in a short amount of time. Long-term planning and *flexible* industrial policies across a variety of sectors foster a 'mixed economy,' enabling current and future economic growth, employment opportu-nities more broadly encompassing a variety of talents and skill sets in the population. Relative positions in terms of *global competitiveness* cannot be sustained on *overly narrow* industrial footprints and expenditures. Aggregate demand can fall dramatically overnight as we saw during Covid-19 lockdowns.

While the labour market is said to be more flexible in advanced economies, following the emergence of the 'gig economy,' productivity levels have not significantly improved. The reasons are complex and the 'labour problem' is difficult to solve in the short-term at a macroeconomic level. In some cases regulatory changes have introduced further distortions in the labour markets.[22] In the context of slowing growth, policy makers have sought to restrict migration 'flows' to ease the pressure on local services. However, this serves to compound the problem and vacancies remain unfilled due to shortages in many sectors, including healthcare, hospitality and agriculture in the case of the UK. The *global misalignment problem* in human capabilities and resources affects *all* economies, while the continued exchange of skills and labour to support economic growth is paramount. The difficulty lies in managing orderly transitions, as change is happening so fast. Often institutions lack the capacity to fulfil processing requirements due to inherent cross-border complexities, increasing volume of migration 'flows' and crucially the embroilment of criminal gangs.

Productivity data does not provide a complete view of the reality, since the statistics reflect GDP per hour worked. They do not indicate underutilised capacity or reveal the *true* nature of context-specific 'capabilities gaps,' beyond the general trends and predicted outcomes. It would be more helpful to include *qualitative* elements, such as the variations in education, skill sets and experience levels within the workforce. This would help *qualify* not just quantify current economic performance and guide future competitiveness, revealing the *policy gaps* and investments needed to further 'real' economic progress. Often the 'capabilities gap' is narrowly defined in terms of *technical skill set shortages* currently sought by employers. However, the Enterprise requires a broader knowledge base and a variety of versatile skill sets within its workforce, to satisfy current *and* future needs. This includes the ability to develop an entrepreneurial aptitude, strengthen human leadership and management skill sets, creativity, curiosity and empathy across the Enterprise 'network.'

In the context of the Enterprise, *social progress* correlates with productivity. It entails working effectively in teams, encouraging a collaborative approach towards the completion of 'whole' tasks, ensuring there is sufficient diversity in the organisation as a whole. New technologies that are successfully deployed require diverse skill sets drawn from multidisciplinary talent pools, with the emphasis being placed on flexibility, diversity of thought and the variety of *lived* and *living* experiences. Hybrid business models enable companies to harness external expertise as often as required, including the ability to access diverse talent from multiple geographical locations through remote working. This can benefit organisational development not only through sustainable costs, but also through cultural enrichment if there is sufficient open-mindedness and in-built flexibility within the organisational structure, systems and processes to optimise local, regional and global contributions to economic growth and value creation. The focus *ought* be on the *quality* and *direction* of current and future growth. If a person grows within the organisation and is fully supported, higher performance and productivity levels *naturally* evolve among teams, and greater profitability ensues.

The 'social contract [is] the implicit agreement between government, business, institutions and civil society.' It transpires 'social inequality is set to increase further as the costs associated with the 'green transition' disproportionately fall to the user, taxpayer, consumer and worker.' [23] For example, income disparity in the USA, the world's largest economy, peaked at the end of 2021. The top 1% of the population held 32% total income compared to only 8% total income in 1976.[24] This is highly significant in a consumer-led economy, particularly when it is the largest. As disposable income is eroded in the wider population, domestic consumer demand and savings fall, while the 'spillover effects' impact *all* economies due to complex interdependencies within the Global System.

Social inequality is highly complex. It reflects political and societal disparities, misallocation of resources, policy inadequacies and resulting income misdistribution. It negatively impacts economic growth, since *income and wealth distribution* determines whether there is *sufficient* elasticity in the demand-supply curve and socioeconomic mobility within a population.[25] Insufficient elasticity in the demand-supply curve adversely affects current and future economic growth. A thriving economy necessitates buoyant *expectations* of present and future growth, business confidence, employment opportunities, and demand and supply-side elasticity supported by socioeconomic mobility within and between generations; above all, citizen trust and confidence in both the economy and the policy makers. Multiple barriers may inhibit socio-economic mobility, such as gender and racial discrimination, social stereotyping and other forms of legal and civic disparities, creating deep-rooted social divisions in the fabric of Society.

Increasingly, social inequities, biases and various forms of discrimination and other inaccuracies are embedded in the *algorithms* driving *automated* decision-making tools, deployed within *proliferating* Socio-Technical Systems. Persistent difficulties in finding new jobs or obtaining loans and stagnating 'real' wages for those in work, create strong disincentives for displaced workers to find new work.[26] Processes designed to satisfy the 'needs' of machines render human needs subordinate to arbitrary and erroneous *digital profiling*, which precludes life opportunities for individuals and subsequently negatively affects growth prospects for the economy as a whole. Structural imbalances become entrenched within the economy, if appropriate policy responses do not occur in a timely manner. Without adequate and proactive measures to ensure a 'just transition' as the structure of the economy changes, social unrest is entangled with the ensuing *mismatch* in the levels of education and skill sets required to foster economic progress in the 'knowledge economy.'

Economic policy needs to be *adjusted continually* to keep up with the pace of change, taking into account the human dimension, as the economy undergoes structural, systemic and technological change. If there is insufficient *flexibility* in fiscal policy, as monetary policy tightens to move inflation towards the *agreed target rate*, the burden of taxation and shortfall in public expenditure typically falls on low-to-middle income households. The 'stop-start' *policy dynamics* and further imbalances subsequent to the Global Financial Crisis of 2007–2008, led to a lacklustre rise in 'real' growth and a decline in 'real' wages.[27] Despite 'controlled' low price inflation for discretionary goods and services, households faced increased living costs for essentials, housing, education and healthcare; and more recently spiralling energy and food costs.[28] Unsurprisingly, US households did not invest in income protection, pensions and healthcare due to the 'squeeze' in disposable income. Thus far, 'higher wages' promised by technological improvements are not evenly distributed. Many workers are exploited in extremely poor working conditions and low levels of pay to advance 'labelling' and other related 'micro-tasks' that require human intelligence, in order to advance 'machine learning.'

The net effect is a reduction in pro-capita wealth and a significant fall in living standards for low-to-middle income groups.

The 'missing middle,' arguably the most productive segment of the economy, labour force, education and main contributor to aggregate demand, reduces tax revenues for governments. This creates a 'vicious cycle' and reinforces income disparities, while reducing the productive capacity and resilience of the economy as a whole in adverse market conditions. While an 'open market economy' may in theory foster equal opportunities and promote a fair distribution of income, there are *inherent distortions* in the Global System. We have not yet experienced a properly functioning 'free market system,' where supply *continually adjusts* to demand and vice versa, oscillating towards *natural multiple equilibria*. Consequently, inequality persists in modern societies, since we have not yet corrected deep-rooted structural and systemic malfunctions.

As China transitioned from a largely rural economy towards an urbanised industrial economy, the World Bank described China's progress as 'the fastest sustained expansion by a major economy in history.' China enjoyed uninterrupted double-digit growth for thirty years until 2018.[29] Following market reforms in 1980, China sought to adopt new technologies, building state-of-the-art infrastructure and a manufacturing capacity to meet global demand. It also focused on developing human capabilities alongside its technology and manufacturing capabilities to facilitate current and future economic growth. It sought to improve manufacturing quality standards, advance technology and enhance education levels through cultural exchange, attracting outside talent to realise its strategic intent. It is now the second largest single economy in the world, a centre of excellence for manufacturing and a significant contributor to US capital inflows, lending support to the US federal deficit.[30]

As the world order is changing and the domestic economy moves towards maturity, China is adapting its strategy. Its policy efforts are focused on averting the so-called 'middle-income trap,' the sharp decline that usually follows a peak in economic expansion. In seeking new sources of value and *continual growth*, China is pursuing a global 'infrastructure-first' approach to economic growth, with the aim of boosting domestic aggregate demand.[31] Unencumbered by legacy systems or aging infrastructure, it is relatively 'free' to continue investing in technological innovation, with a sharp focus on developing services in the private sector. Once participants in a 'closed economy,' Chinese businesses and households are now more entrepreneurial in outlook, oriented towards widely shared prosperity. In China's worldview sustained economic development can be achieved by enabling *all* citizens to become producers and consumers. As with any major shift in the global economic land-scape, the right 'policy mix' differs from country to country. There is no 'one size that fits all,' or *magic solution* to fix social and societal problems; and technology cannot provide all the answers. Learning valuable lessons from history is a worthwhile pursuit. Sensing *how* to find appropriate responses in rapidly changing circumstances requires *dynamic* adaptation both for the Enterprise and the global economy as a whole.

Covid-19 created a dual shock initially on the demand-side, quickly turning into supply-side shortages of various goods. A difficult situation was soon exacerbated by the outbreak of war in Ukraine and the imposition of NATO-led sanctions on Russia with the ensuing retaliation. Heightened geopolitical tensions following Russia's invasion of Ukraine caused further *uncertainty* and turbulence in financial markets. Transportation routes suspended due to Covid-19 restrictions intensified supply-side problems and rising freight costs, further complicated by Russia's blockade of the Black Sea ports and violation of international maritime law, temporarily suspending the safe passage of merchant ships. Initial food and energy shortages led to spiralling consumer prices and further compromised global health, food and energy security. Semiconductor shortages due to extended lockdowns and interruptions in manufacturing compounded 'geo-economic' tensions. In terms of global economic growth centred on technology improvements, semi-conductors are critical components cross-sector.[32] Overall global supply chain disruptions due to Covid-19 lockdowns and the war in Ukraine compromised global economic recovery and human health. While the outcome of the war in Ukraine is not yet known at the time of writing, adverse effects on human health, global supply chains, current and future economic growth affects *everyone*.

Firms faced with the ill effects of Covid-19 and a depleted workforce will continue to suffer severe supply-chain disruptions and financial pressures due to rising prices in commodities, energy and borrowing costs. Some corporations suffered further losses as they systematically withdrew operations from Russia.[33] Under these circumstances, globalisation in terms of renewable trade agreements appears to be under threat. Many firms have considered 'near-shoring' or 're-shoring' supply chains and productive capacity, proactively seeking to 'de-risk' over-reliance on any given country. While prompted by the adverse effects of Covid-19 and the war in Ukraine, the impending structural shift in the global economy cannot happen overnight. In some cases, the costs far outweigh potential benefits and 'the switch' may not prove economically viable. At a time of *extreme uncertainty*, it may be wise to postpone *hasty* decisions. Global trade produces greater economic benefits across the time horizons and if properly managed, it can foster *improvements* in global cooperation. Through shared *mutual* interests, strong commitment and strategic foresight, it creates new opportunities for cultural and reciprocal technology-knowledge exchanges to foster inclusive, equitable and sustainable growth. Without international cooperation on a global scale, trade is severely restricted limiting growth opportunities in *all* economies.

During the initial phases of the global pandemic, consumer spending for *discretionary* goods and services came to a grinding halt. The expected 'bounce-back' following 'pent-up demand' created by regional lockdowns did not materialise everywhere in equal measure. Varying levels of fiscal stimulus, severe supply chain disruptions and the ensuing shortage of goods and services,[34] lowered global aggregate demand. At the peak of the health crisis, despite 'furlough schemes' being extended in many countries, many jobs were lost. Retail, hospitality, healthcare and creative industries were the worst affected. Conversely, e-commerce saw 'explosive growth,' as companies found new ways to engage consumers on digital platforms. 'Curb-side' and 'drive-through' deliveries to limit 'social contact' became the 'norm' to limit transmission. Consumer demand 'bounced back' more quickly in the US and by the third quarter of 2020, there were 'signals' the US economy was recovering strongly relative to others.[35] American citizens experienced strong fiscal stimulus, as the US Presidential election drew near. In December 2020, USD 900 billion was injected into the US economy under the Trump administration, and a further USD 1.9 trillion under the Biden administration in March 2021. While economists disagreed on these measures, inflationary pressures began building in the final quarter of 2020 and the spring of 2021, as buoyant domestic demand far exceeded the available supply of goods and services. This set the largest global economy on course to 'overheat.'[36]

The Federal Reserve did not immediately activate its macro-prudential policies due to concerns consumer demand might falter, triggering a deep recession. Perhaps the Federal Reserve hesitated due to the pending re-election of its chairman. In any case, it did not raise interest rates until early 2022.[37] Similarly, both the Trump and Biden administrations had not anticipated supply-side inflationary pressures, when considering their respective policy responses to the Covid-19 crisis. Some economists believed the US fiscal stimulus was 'too generous' relative to foreseeable domestic demand.[38] In reality, global supply chains did not recover *quickly* enough to meet US domestic demand. Reduced output particularly in China exacerbated supply-side shortages, further complicated by interruptions in critical transportation routes, especially sea freight. Firms and consumers faced challenging circumstances; lower forward investments and output projections fuelled uncertainty and made the Federal Reserve unduly cautious in the immediate aftermath of the crisis.

The fiscal stimulus in the Eurozone was significantly lower, based on the relative financial positions and population size of its members. And yet they were not immune to inflationary pressures fuelled by the food and energy crisis.[39] European countries heavily reliant on Russian oil and gas could not easily switch to alternative energy sources. Consequently, the *sudden* reduction in Russian oil and gas, led to 'energy rationing' across the Eurozone (notably Germany), not seen since the 1970s. As the global economic situation worsened, rising energy prices (arbitrarily impacted by a further reduction in production by the OPEC countries)[40] coincided with severe food shortages. Multiple factors led to a significant slowdown in economic output;[41] not least the lockdown restrictions halting manufacturing to avoid transmission of the virus coupled with spiralling food and energy prices that provoked a severe 'cost of living' crisis *everywhere*. When advanced economies falter, the 'knock-on' effect is disproportionately felt in low-to-middle income countries more susceptible to *debt distress* and *limited access* to credit due to *perceived* financial risk. While the impacts of economic sanctions are not symmetrical, they rarely achieve the desired effects. On this occasion, developing economies on the verge of bankruptcy and those already compromised by debt distress, suffered extreme hardships.[42]

Businesses focused investments on new technologies, both to manage fluctuations in demand and control costs. And yet the pursuit of *technical* efficiencies deemed a necessity, was *suddenly insufficient*.

Sought-after short-term gains in the marketplace were no longer without risks. Multiple 'cascading risk' factors ranging from financial instability, economic uncertainty to extreme weather events no longer confined to specific geographies, intensified inherent business risks and vulnerabilities. Rising geopolitical tensions have either slowed or precluded broader multilateral trade agreements. No matter the size of the Enterprise, global supply chains *continually* disrupted are not easily disentangled from the Global System. Raw materials, manufactured, semi-manufactured goods and services form part of complex and highly fragmented supply chains. If people are incapacitated by ill health, due to 'long Covid,' now a *global* health phenomenon, they cannot produce and consume. As one side of the demand-supply equation is heavily impacted the other cannot properly function. Hence the 'S' – Society and social factor framed by the 'E' (environmental factor) and the 'G' (governance factor) on either side of the '*messy middle*' cannot be ignored in the context of *sustainable* growth. The *direction*, *qualitative* and *ethical* aspects of *growth* must now come to the fore of the debate.

Large corporations oriented towards short-term 'trade-offs,' often fall short in the exercise of their fiduciary 'duty of care,' social responsibility and environmental accountability. When taking an overly narrow financial view, simplistic cost-benefit analyses do not encompass complex Human, Ethical and Nature Risks intrinsic to the financial risks of the Enterprise. Risk-averse behaviours frequently conceal the innate reluctance to reconcile multiple diverse stakeholder interests. Boards, CEOs and Senior Executives are misguidedly curtailing present and future growth opportunities, while placing business continuity at risk. Although sentiment is changing, many US companies interpret their fiduciary duties as being primarily concerned with shareholder value. And yet firms are discovering the real limitation to growth is not the lack of ambition and access to new markets, but the scarcity of highly skilled workers to make the best use of increasingly affordable technologies, such as 'artificial intelligence.' There is no 'one-off' cost where technology is concerned. At present, 'artificial intelligence' requires intensive use of resources and the deployment of human intelligence to function properly. Disappointment invariably ensues when the predicted returns on investment fail to meet expectations and do not quickly materialise on the balance sheet.

Decades of inconsistent investments in human capabilities, an over-reliance on automation and the lowering of quality standards in pursuit of technical efficiencies and cost savings have introduced new *fragilities* in the Enterprise ecosystem. The inherent structure of the organisation has been weakened, and so too its ability to withstand externalities. Exogenous and endogenous shocks are quickly assimilated, due to the permeability and porous nature of Enterprise systems and processes, frequently guided by unsupervised 'artificial intelligence.' Financial capital has not always been directed towards productive (creative) ends, especially where human capabilities are concerned and the intrinsic competiveness of the firm rendered lacklustre. This has created a sizeable 'growth deficit' that is challenging both for the Enterprise and global institutions; and it cannot be quickly remedied, especially under difficult economic circumstances. Therein lies the growth paradox: long-term investments in both people and technology are required for consistent growth and innovation. And yet long-term investments cannot be successfully enacted and sustained in a persistent turbulent economic environment. On the other hand, the timely allocation of resources coupled with an *adaptive resilient* mindset is a prerequisite to extend the growth of the Enterprise beyond its present needs and secure its longevity.

While a strong financial position is essential, it should not be the end in itself. Consistent efforts to build unique human capabilities will enable the Enterprise to sense emergent changes and seize new opportunities for continual growth, while dynamically reconfiguring the organisation in preparation for the next innovation frontier. Irrespective of size, growth in any business is reliant upon the *adaptive resilience* of the Enterprise and its ability to adopt different business models and organisational configurations in fast changing market conditions. Breaking down the internal barriers to growth is essential. Growth is enabled by consistent investments in people and technology, financial flexibility and *organisational resilience*. Shareholder value is created and best protected by creating and protecting *stakeholder* value.

While Knowledge underpins the success of the Enterprise, the *growth process* necessitates careful orchestration. The scientific methodologies of the previous industrial era coupled with overly narrow economic assumptions, though prevalent in the mindset of many, have been rendered obsolete. Beliefs, desires and intentions cannot be automated; and yet they are the prerequisites of growth and innovation. Paradoxically, the increasing automation of various decision-making tasks by means of 'artificial agents' has not reduced the inherent financial and non-financial risks of the Enterprise.

Human creativity, strategic foresight and regular 'stress testing' prove far more effective in terms of efficient risk-management processes, both to mitigate and enact the requisite adaptations. While 'artificial intelligence' may help identify pattern regularities with respect to past events, human intelligence can more accurately detect unlikely but plausible scenarios, thereby increasing the level of preparedness and alertness within the Enterprise as a whole. At a fundamental level, 'artificial intelligence' raises critical questions concerning the nature of work and the future of the Enterprise. Just as organisational structures, systems and processes are being called into question, so too is the nature of meaningful growth and innovation.

While there is a concern 'real' economic growth may be at risk due to the over-financialisation of the Global System, the *growth problem* can be defined more broadly, as the risk of *over-automation* in the absence of due process and the presence of immature technologies. The inherent structural and systemic risks have been accumulating from the start of the century, and have intensified since the outbreak of Covid-19. Socio-Technical Systems driven by 'artificial intelligence' technologies have been deployed in all sectors, irrespective of the technical shortcomings, social inadequacies and lack of appropriateness for the task-in-hand. Insufficient attention has been given to the 'fitness- for-purpose' of 'artificial agents' operating without human supervision, and in most cases, without the necessary operational safeguards. And yet the legitimacy of the Enterprise and government institutions alike is determined by Society. The value of economic growth and innovation must be meaningful to Society, and its contribution and distribution among citizens, inclusive and equitable. As financial and other automated digital services in critical sectors such as healthcare and education gain prominence relative to other productive segments of the economy, greater public scrutiny is required. It is *growth critical* to ensure financial and other digitalised services remain accessible to the wider populations. Fairness and economic resilience are prerequisites for governments and businesses alike to effectively maintain their 'social licence.' Acquiescence and arbitrarily imposed subordination to 'machine intelligence' or 'artificial agents' is detrimental to human health and wellbeing. It negates human values, human autonomy, human agency, human dignity and human integrity; and introduces 'extreme risks' both for the Enterprise and public bodies, due to the unintended consequences, adverse social and societal outcomes and further environmental degradation.

The challenge is to *envision* creating the necessary conditions for 'real' economic growth, using new technologies *wisely*, such that actions in one part of the world do not harm another. Owing to the interconnectedness and interdependencies of national economies in the Global System, new forms of equilibria pertaining to demand and supply in the 'real' economy need to be established through reciprocal and coordinated actions typically enacted through trade agreements; with environmental, nature, ethical and human risks being factored in at all levels of socio-economic and socio-political activity. If we fail to take into account the 'S' factor at a granular level, we will continue making the same mistakes, and remain under the illusion overly narrow economic assumptions and a partial view of the reality through the use of incomplete data will lead us to the *right* decisions. Since the 1950s, economists have traced a 'pattern of [wealth] accumulation in which profit making occurs increasingly through financial channels rather than through trade and commodities.'[43] Financial-sector driven profits are not necessarily the issue. The issue is more about *how* financial capital is used and where it is deployed. The focus on growth needs to be much broader than previously imagined. It is not simply about revenue, income and output growth. Preferably, growth should be oriented towards economic prosperity, encompassing human health and wellbeing, which has a transformative power in Society and overall economic benefits for the Enterprise and institutions alike.

The rules of the game are changing and it is no longer sufficient to shore up the financial position of the company, believing it will suffice to sustain the Enterprise for the duration of its lifespan. Business leaders are no longer able to sidestep the demands of their constituents, no matter their ambitions for short-term financial gains. Therein lies the growth conundrum for the Enterprise. Existing socio-economic structural and systemic imbalances pose a significant problem in terms of the workforce and the challenge is specifically *how* to accelerate growth without causing further environmental damage, whilst navigating destabilising forces within the geopolitical sphere and extreme weather events intensified by persistent imbalances in natural ecosystems. Further pressure is being applied by institutional investors, consumers and employees for something to be done about these fundamental problems. Ultimately, the *continued success* of the Enterprise is reliant upon its integrity and the trust it earns among its constituents over time.

Since the 1990s, the Internet has enabled new forms of economic activity such as e-commerce, which are known to represent an increasing proportion of GDP, although quantitative and *qualitative* changes resulting from the Internet-based activities are not easily measured.[44] The problem for economists is not only how to measure 'free' goods and services, but also the *economic benefit* and intangible value, such as health, wellbeing and education derived from engagement with digital services in civil society. For the most part 'consumer surplus' is imperfectly measured and can provide a misleading picture of the economy and the impact of technology itself in terms of economic value, measured where possible in terms of price and output volume. More importantly, GDP fails to capture externalities including pollution, congestion and 'non-market' activities, such as caring and household duties for which there is no market value (price) attributable to those carrying out those duties. Work in these instances has no value; and yet it is vital to support social, societal and economic wellbeing. The 'human dimension' of growth is therefore not well understood; and policy makers have an imperfect purview of the reality.

The advent of 'generative artificial intelligence' further complicates existing structural and systemic imbalances and gives rise to new 'extreme risks,' affecting the digital economy as a whole.

While there is arguably less friction in the modern financial system, due to the velocity of automated digital transactions, algorithmically driven 'artificial intelligence' systems are *not immune to failure*. Inherent fragilities and 'brittleness' of the systems 'in play' are an order of magnitude greater due to the interactions of autonomous 'artificial agents' presenting new capabilities, including 'confabulations' and 'impersonations.' As more data is collected and individual citizens are required to prove their identities to 'machine intelligence,' so too structural and systemic risks in the economy have grown exponentially. Citizens do *not* have control over their personal and sensitive data; while systemic 'errors' including embedded biases and discriminatory practices preclude *life opportunities*, such as becoming successful bank loan and job applicants. If the algorithm detects an *anomaly* based on gender, race, health conditions, postcodes or any other variety of singular and combined data-points, 'evaluated' against statistical averages and probabilistic outcomes, there is often no means for *individual citizen* recourse in the event of unfair treatment, due to the lack of *transparency*.

At the macroeconomic level the Global System is susceptible to multiple 'errors' escaping detection due to the interconnectedness of Socio-Technical Systems difficult to 'control' cross-border. Cyber attacks involving dangerous 'artificial intelligence' capabilities, amplify potential 'cascading risks,' due to automated *non-human* errors. As demonstrated during the Ukraine war, critical infrastructure anywhere and the global financial system are increasingly susceptible to 'catastrophic' systemic failures. In the context of global economic uncertainty, rising inflation and high debt levels, the stability of the financial system is in question. At present, there are no 'real' anchors for the value of money; the electronic debt exchange mechanism is governed by a handful of 'fiat' currencies.[45] In effect, any distortion introduced into the system affecting US dollar denominated transactions in particular is transmitted globally.[46] The 'domino effect' when the system malfunctions triggered by a sudden loss of confidence is catastrophic. The US subprime mortgage crisis in 2007–2008 is a case in point; and the 'spillover' effects persist worldwide.[47]

The speculative 'housing bubble' in the US set in motion a global liquidity crisis and global economic slowdown not seen since the 1930s.[48] Fuelled by high borrowing levels and unsecured lending, the crisis was compounded by the reckless actions of a few 'big players.' House prices fell sharply and failed to recover quickly; wide-scale de-leveraging accelerated foreclosures. Overlapping events in the UK and the EU Sovereign Debt Crisis in 2009 forced governments to 'bail out' the banks at their citizens' expense. The 'credit crunch' and ensuing austerity inhibited economic growth for more than a decade. The US Financial Inquiry Commission summed up the *global financial crisis*:

'The crisis was avoidable and was caused by [. . .] widespread systemic breaches in accountability and ethics at all levels.'[49]

The *moral hazard* reverberated across the globe. It evidenced the need for shared accountability, highlighting the *inescapable* 'truth,' integrity cannot be bought or legislated. Institutional oversight failures coupled with the unbridled power of *influential* elites interfered with 'free market' *dynamics*. Speculative 'financial bubbles' favoured monopolistic 'zero-sum' games in the misguided belief large financial institutions were 'too big to fail.' Missed opportunities to serve broader societal interests undermined *public confidence* in the *regulators*, not entirely without justification, as widespread corruption was revealed.

The inability to establish a stable multilateral world order has undermined efforts to create sustainable growth since the end of WWII. Reconstruction efforts in Europe under the US Marshall Plan and Bretton Woods System fostered the 'economic miracle' in the 1950s and 1960s, but success was short-lived as the Bretton Woods System,[50] collapsed in 1971 on the eve of the first 'oil shock.' Financial instability underpins *economic uncertainty* still today. US domestic debt levels skyrocketed for the first time, partly to fund military interventions in Vietnam and have continued rising. Compounded by US dollar denominated debt under IMF and World Bank rules, developing and emerging economies are inhibited in their growth aspirations, all of which is inextricably linked with the profound structural imbalances and systemic risks as yet unresolved. Gold reserves stored in the vaults of the Bank of England support the London Stock Exchange, which remains a global trading centre for commodities and partly explains the 'special relationship.' However, the US dollar is vulnerable due to unresolved historical geopolitical tensions and intensifying competition among 'fiat' and emerging digital currencies, not least 'geo-economic' technology-energy rivalries among the USA, Russia and China.[51]

Economic growth is often viewed as a *straightforward* change in GDP. And yet historical complexities, structural and systemic imbalances are *global challenges* of a scale and magnitude that extend beyond national borders. Simon Kuznets, the economist who invented the current method of accounting in the 1930s, readily admitted it did not accurately reflect the distinction between the 'quantity and quality of growth, between its costs and returns and between the short and the long term.'[52] Irrespective of the frequency of measurement (quarterly), GDP statistics arbitrarily reflect *price* and *quantity*, but provide no insight into the state of the economy, value and benefits awarded or denied its citizens at an *individual* and collective level. The *market value* of select goods and services are aggregated, whilst economic activities that cannot be *fairly* estimated in *numerical* terms are excluded. Kuznets recognised these limitations and recommended going beyond such a *narrow* definition.

'Goals for more growth should specify more growth of what and for what.'[53]

The direction, quality and intrinsic properties of growth matter. We can no longer account for growth in quantifiable atomised form and monetary terms alone. Kuznets's earlier intentions may have been to introduce a measure for economic welfare, but in the event GDP became an *efficient* way to calculate *how* people and other forms of capital could be diverted to wartime production efforts.[54] Though GDP measurement has been revised several times, technical efficiency has since dominated economic thinking,[55] and influenced policy makers. Computational parameters have become more sophisticated with the advent of 'artificial intelligence,' but we need a *broader definition* of growth. Key factors of *economic value* such as work-life balance, the quality of life, independent life choices, freedom of speech and happiness are not usually measured in accounting statistics; and yet they are critical indicators for current and future economic growth.

If the Global System is broken, it begs the question as to what comes next. Stakeholder capitalism is a term often used, but perhaps not *fully* understood. Crucially, it requires a renewed focus on the 'S' factor, *societal* element and the 'E' *ecological* factor that have been neglected. The 'human dimension'[56] entails focusing on individual and collective human needs, rather than pursuing conformity to an arbitrary median value, which typically lowers *qualitative* and ethical standards. At the same time, aggregate values may lead to the misallocation of resources, owing to a superficial assessment of human needs. Human health, fair and equitable distribution of income, equal access to life opportunities seem elusive, but the complicatedness of the systems in play obfuscate possibilities that could be explored, taking a more *flexible* and *open-minded* approach towards emergent challenges. While technology is intended to spur economic growth and make our lives easier, it would appear 'artificial intelligence,' in its present form, is set to create new societal harms and worsen environmental degradation.

Adaptive Resilience™ underpins a process of continual change, focusing on the quality and direction of growth and innovation to foster enduring value creation. *Extreme risks* have suddenly become the 'norm' and necessitate urgent adaptations. Ranging from 'generative artificial intelligence' systems, designed, developed and deployed without appropriate operational safeguards to extreme weather events, future pandemics, geo-political and geo-economic risks, they are *powerful* forces inhibiting or delaying requisite investments in human capabilities and technological advancements. Resilience constitutes the ability to 'bounce back' from adversity and envision plausible 'exit-strategies' from the next series of 'shocks,' while creating innovation pathways across *all* functions of the Enterprise ecosystem.[57] Business leaders choosing to accelerate a 'virtuous growth cycle,' *qualitatively driven growth* based on human values, achieve greater rewards through their ambitions to deliver beneficial outcomes. Re-imagining the purpose of the Enterprise, they are able to activate the inherent *dynamism* of the organisation, working towards improving aspects of the world that *must* change. The *successful* advancement of economic interests at all levels of Society necessitates shared responsibility and accountability on a global scale.

Growth in the 21st century should be evaluated through multiple different lenses, taking a *holistic view* and an ethics-based approach, while *proactively* working towards solving the most intractable problems of our time. The technology-knowledge driven exchange mechanism is a *powerful enabler* of growth and innovation, paving the way for global trade and new forms of *economic complementarity*. Developed nations acting in support of developing and emerging economies to bypass the polluting phase of industrialisation reap *greater* rewards and benefit *all* economies. A renewed focus on nature-based solutions to combat climate change, accelerating the *global transition* towards renewable sources of energy, lessens the reliance on fossil fuels and hugely benefits *human health* and *planetary wellbeing*, globally. New strategic partnerships afford the world 'safe passage,' through the deliberate *avoidance* of armed conflicts and '*weaponisation*' of food, energy and technology supplies.

Growth is a *cultural* phenomenon. Socio-economic progress requires a *fresh look* at the things we value, rejecting those that present an existential threat and we should *not* entertain. Careful consideration must be given to the direction of present and future technological advancements. Human-centricity necessitates a broader *ecological* view of the reality, shaping growth and innovation for the benefit of Society and the Earth itself, arguably one of the biggest challenges in the 21st century. *Meaningful* growth and innovation is of necessity inclusive, equitable and sustainable.

Chapter 5

Innovation
/ˌɪn.əˈveɪ.ʃən/

'I'm enough of an artist to draw freely on my imagination. And imagination is more important than knowledge. Knowledge is limited. Imagination encircles the world.'[1]

Innovation is the art of transforming *valuable* new ideas into reality. It is a *dynamic* process fuelled by curiosity, creativity and courage, enabling us to envision new ways of doing things. The aim is to build *adaptive resilience* within the Enterprise to foster sustainable growth and enhance the *quality* of our lives. Harnessing the power of the human imagination is paramount, as we are able to transcend inherent barriers towards sustainable growth and overcome global political, economic, societal and environmental challenges. Human ingenuity knows no boundaries. Unconstrained by the limits of current knowledge our imagination runs *freely*, conceiving of new ideas, recombining those that already exist to evolve new forms of expression. While drawing inspiration from Nature we enact new scientific and artistic discoveries that enrich our daily lives. True innovation is transformative. When breaking new ground, we actively embrace uncertainty, seeking to address the challenges before us. The Enterprise proactively pursues innovation, adopting new ways of thinking, taking different approaches to *known* challenges and those as yet *unknown*. Consciously raising its level of preparedness and alertness to bolster its adaptive capacity and enhance its resilience in light of contextual contingencies at a local, regional and global level. In so doing, the Enterprise is able to create new sources of value that will stand the test of time for the benefit of humanity and the planet.

Imagination affords humanity the freedom to explore, experiment and discover new conceptualisations of the realities before us. Through our own individual and collective experiences, we may choose to create new 'artefacts,' enacting appropriate strategies to create a better world. Our innate human desire to seek new beginnings and the excitement it creates propels Society forward. Technological progress has recently accelerated change, at a slightly faster pace than we are able to *collectively* absorb, comprehend and comfortably adjust to. Notwithstanding the 'chaotic' transitions, new technologies such as 'artificial intelligence' have significantly shortened the timeframes for new scientific discoveries, creating both new opportunities and *risks previously unknown*. While the development of the Covid-19 vaccine was extraordinarily fast, assisted by computational power and synthetic data, accelerated human trials and virtual collaborations among scientists on a global scale; it also begs the question of fairness and social exclusion, applicability and acceptability in the wider society. The ethical questions pertaining to global human health and bioengineering are highly complex and thus far remain unanswered. Time will tell to what extent we may have compromised our natural defences and further debilitated the human immune system. As a Society, we shall need to decide to what extent we might pursue bioengineering without causing *undue harms* to human beings and the planet. In many ways, sustaining human health and wellbeing requires a new way of thinking and necessitates addressing the root causes of human diseases, not least environmental degradation. The inexorable pace of change requires a renewed focus on what *really* matters.

Innovation within the Enterprise is driven by an authentic Vision and a clear Strategy, underpinned by a strong sense of purpose and a propensity towards achieving 'real' growth. It requires Global Strategic Leadership, strategic foresight, discipline, emotional and social intelligence, organisational flexibility coupled with dynamic processes, oriented towards building a sustainable digital future. There are many different phases when undertaking a deliberate process of *continuous innovation*. They require careful orchestration both to sustain the momentum of positive change and satisfy concurrent, often divergent needs, while ensuring disruptive elements can be brought to fruition. Internal and external influences may interfere with progress, underscoring the importance of conducting fundamental research. Anticipation of potential changes in the environment will facilitate effective transitions along new innovation pathways. In the event of rapid technological change, the Enterprise can no longer rely upon incremental improvements or count upon isolated initiatives to sustain its market position, employee engagement and customer loyalty. Faced with accelerating changes in the environment, radical re-invention of the Enterprise itself is required at a structural and systemic level.

The continued evolution of Society and our surrounding Environment requires more careful scrutiny. Taking a holistic view of the situation at hand, we are better able to assess the impacts of our individual and collective actions. Finding inspiration from new connections and ideas drawn from multiple disciplines, we have the ability to continue searching for the *right* answers to solve complex problems. In the context of the Enterprise, radical innovation entails the removal of barriers to communication and the sharing of 'information' in a timely manner. Entertaining *new forms* of collaboration across the ecosystem while eradicating organisational silos, which deny the Enterprise new opportunities to create enduring value. Owing to geopolitical and 'geo-economic' uncertainty, highly volatile market conditions and frequent changes in consumer preferences, the enactment of *human values* strengthens *organisational resilience* and provides a suitable anchor for innovation. The acquisition of Knowledge through practical experiences surpasses technology, which cannot of its own accord enact meaningful change. Digital transformation strategies enacted within the Enterprise are of necessity oriented towards the decarbonisation of the global Economy. No single actor can tackle climate change without engaging in peer-to-peer collaborations cross-sector while enlisting the support of Civil Society. In the digital era *human needs* must of necessity shape technological innovations, contextualised within the safety of planetary boundaries to prevent undue harms. Redefining human interactions with technology and the environment is a prerequisite of responsible innovation.

The *effective and efficient* use of natural resources necessitates a new approach to the creation of value within the Enterprise.

Advancements in scientific discoveries made possible by recent technological developments can foster the invention of new materials and alternative sources of energy that are respectful both of Nature and the *dynamics* at play within the Earth's Systems. The Enterprise needs to focus on sustainability both to preserve its economic viability and effectively respond to increasing demands from customers, employees, suppliers and investors for increased *transparency*. Operational opacity is no longer a viable option with respect to carbon dioxide emissions, Nature *regeneration* and *conservation* initiatives and raw material procurement across the supply chain. Consumers are interested in *knowing* the sources of materials, processes, practices and behaviours of the Enterprise in relation to its *ecological* footprint. Consequently, sustainability must become the cornerstone for *any* innovation pathway being pursued within the Enterprise. In order to successfully identify new sources of value, innovation strategies require frequent adjustments, peer-to-peer collaborations even among rivals cross-sector, enlisting *proactive feedback* from *all* the stakeholders whether directly or indirectly impacted by the activities of the Enterprise.

Rapid advancement in digital technologies and in particular 'artificial intelligence' greatly extends the scope, nature, purpose, context and reach of Enterprise innovation. Engaging the entire organisation to develop and enact the best ideas is not only a wise decision, but also an *economic* necessity. The Enterprise cannot compete successfully without drawing upon diverse *lived* and *living* experiences of its workforce. Human ingenuity, creativity and technical proficiencies shared cross-functionally, lend support to constantly evolving, *coherent* innovation strategies. Dynamic *adaptive processes* reduce inherent risks and uncertainties, whilst proactively strengthening the willingness to explore new ideas, effectively and efficiently nurturing the *collaborative spirit* across the entire value chain. The Enterprise as a whole benefits from instilling a strong culture of innovation, reinforcing integrative efforts to orchestrate requisite organisational changes. Processes to facilitate innovation are best arranged through the active participation of those directly affected by them, ensuring communication systems are 'open' and sufficiently *flexible* to deliver desirable outcomes.

Growth is accelerated by 'scouting' the right innovation opportunities in the 'real' world, deftly using 'artificial intelligence' to provide reliable 'information' to help evaluate market conditions and latent demands. Data collection should be performed with extreme care, identifying specific contextual uses, necessity and proportionality, while taking into consideration 'real' human needs and potential unintended consequences when 'errors' occur. Implementing privacy protections for users and contributors, ensuring informed consent is business critical. Whether enacted by human or 'artificial agents,' users and contributors should be made fully aware how and where their data is being used and how long it will be retained. Clearly defined data acquisition, retention, use and management practices are paramount. Privacy safeguards bolster *security resilience*, reducing exposure to cybersecurity threats, while enabling the Enterprise to *proactively* sustain its integrity and trustworthiness among *all* the stakeholders for the duration of its lifespan. Never has the need been greater to integrate R&D, strategic intent and analysis into daily practices. Conceptually, innovation should become embedded in the business model, the fabric of the Enterprise and its *modus operandi* with 'flexible controls' to facilitate *smooth* internal transitions. New ideas fuel creativity, driving the *forward momentum* of the Enterprise.

Socio-Technical Systems *should* enable the continuous development of organisational capabilities, supporting creative breakthroughs. Cross-functional collaborations enhance valuable learning opportunities across the innovation ecosystem, while reinforcing the intrinsic value of the Enterprise, its core competencies and *raison d'être*. In essence, a strong innovation culture demands sustainable energy, creativity and new ideas being formulated with ease. Innovation may begin with small incremental improvements but technological advancements will of necessity increase the forward momentum. Enterprise leaders need to be prepared to embrace the flow of energy, and seek to reinforce the adaptive capacity and innate resilience of the organisation. Flexible 'controls' coupled with the right incentives will provide renewed impetus for successive waves of innovation. Enlisting the full commitment of every participant is key for innovation success, while leaders ensure process *fluidity* and 'two-way communication,' adjusting risk tolerance thresholds and organisational practices, as required. The ability to transcend hidden barriers towards the realisation of *qualitatively* enhanced value assures beneficial outcomes for all the stakeholders. While anticipating trends in disruptive technologies and industries is an economic necessity, understanding emergent complexities and the potential impact of changes in the geopolitical and geo-economic landscape, demographic variations, migration flows and other climate related factors *is* transformative. Addressing human and planetary needs *simultaneously* is a necessity, orienting the Enterprise towards sustainable competitive differentiation in the marketplace. Both the possibilities and challenges are revealed when taking a self-referencing and synergistic approach towards change. Leveraging global Knowledge, local and regional insights *beyond* the Enterprise's direct sphere of influence enables the Enterprise to identify new opportunities.

Innovation affords the Enterprise a *meaningful* existence, reinvigorating organisational resilience, through a process of continuous learning and improvement. It propels the Enterprise forward, readily adapting to changing circumstances, not least disruptive technological changes. While innovation sustains competitiveness and economic viability over time, it also influences the strategic direction of the Enterprise. The business model is continually shaped through *adaptive processes*, prompting refreshingly new responses to a fast changing environment. Scientific breakthroughs are happening at a faster rate than ever before, and the Enterprise should pay specific attention to new possibilities previously unimagined. Enhanced connectivity, quantum computing and newly emerging capabilities particularly in widely available 'foundation models' will transform the nature of human-AI and AI-human interactions, influencing decision-making processes within the Enterprise. Alongside ease of access to new digital services, *disinformation* and *misinformation* will become heightened security risks, if not properly managed. Decentralisation, remote working, new forms of digital payment, cryptocurrencies and digital authentication necessitate *re-imagining* Enterprise management systems and related processes, coupled with *regular training exercises* to continually 'test' the systems in play. The Enterprise innovation strategy should include a broader education programme encompassing new capabilities and heightened awareness of the potential systemic risks across the entire workforce.

Innovation is of necessity a process of continuous change. Frequently, it constitutes the response to perceived changes in the environment, industry and marketplace dynamics, consumer preferences and various externalities.[2] The Enterprise should also proactively pursue innovation in anticipation of unmet customer needs, thinking beyond conventional practices to extract 'exchange value' in monetary terms and narrowly defined performance metrics. Considering instead the *relational dimensions*, encompassed within system dynamics and user interactions, to identify changes in 'signals' and observable 'norms' to get a sense of evolving societal values and newly emerging demands. Taking care not to over-automate internal processes and become *overly* reliant on data that may obscure the reality. Consistent investments in R&D, human capabilities and the avoidance of short-cuts will avert potential shortcomings, ensuring valuable opportunities are not missed and future staffing requirements are adequately resourced. Proximity and consistent engagement with customers, employees and suppliers best informs innovation strategies and effective innovation processes, thereby creating 'real' opportunities for the Enterprise to enhance its present and *future value*.

As more elements of the 'real-world' are encapsulated in a deluge of *terrestrial* and *extra-terrestrial* data gathered from outer space, high-level political and economic decisions will undoubtedly change course. The Enterprise needs to remain vigilant and identify the relevance and potential impact on its own operations. There may be new hidden risks and new opportunities, taking into account large text and image 'foundation models' are being managed by the relatively few. Digital 'core identities' and 'digital twins' provide insights in real time, but they are also susceptible to hacking and other criminal activities. Modular open-sourced digital platforms and related services facilitate access to new technologies and reduce development costs for many customisable solutions and applications, but they also introduce new vulnerabilities in the Enterprise systems. It begs the question as to whether the Enterprise should build its own 'foundation model' though costs may be prohibitive. The *value* of data in the digital era also needs to be carefully considered and continually re-evaluated in the context of *human needs*, emergent risks and environmental damage.

Notwithstanding vast volumes of data being collected from the Internet, including data generated by 'artificial agents' and other sources, we have not yet discovered the source of 'perfect information.' Engineering breakthroughs and an increasingly large number of parameters in both text and image 'foundation models' facilitate ever faster incremental improvements, but 'artificial intelligence' models still present significant technical limitations. Not least the inability of multimodal models to process an infinite variety of data types, as would occur instantaneously in the 'real' world occasioned by the human mind and our interactions with the environment. Generalising the use of text and image 'artificial intelligence' *foundation models* across a variety of tasks is not the same as 'artificial general intelligence,' which would *generally simulate* some aspects of human intelligence, such as the ability to perform multiple tasks simultaneously and perhaps make use of 'common sense' Knowledge. Time will tell if *machines* will *ever* reach this threshold and whether broad commercial use cases can be safely managed. At present, the *ability* to discern nuances in advance of current and future market demands of significance to the Enterprise requires *human intelligence.* Embedding human supervision in various data processes will help prevent 'catastrophic' failures. In addition, a significant amount of energy is needed to cool large-scale data centres and computational equipment causing further environmental damage due to the persistent use of fossil fuels. Lifetime harms due to the unintended consequences of non-deterministic technologies range from an existential threat to humanity at one end of the scale to the potential *weaponisation* of 'artificial intelligence' in Civil Society at the other. The inevitable loss of employment opportunities coupled with far reaching societal harms due to *hidden biases* in the data sets is fast becoming the reality.

Disruptive technologies influence human behaviours, challenge cultural 'norms' and have profound societal consequences. New tools provided useful *learning* opportunities for millennia, furthering socio-economic progress on a wider scale following the Agricultural and Industrial Revolution.[3] However 'artificial intelligence' conceived without the requisite operational safeguards to *guarantee human safety* could pose an existential threat if misused. Foundation models in their current form offer no guarantee for citizen safety and the lack of transparency gives rise to legitimate concerns. The Enterprise needs to carefully consider its choices and risk profile, whether it wishes to engage in certain types of experimentation and any potential implications due to *unidentified* use cases hidden in the value chain. Extreme caution is required with respect to impending military uses and carbon-capture technologies. The Earth's Systems comprise innumerable non-linear dynamic interdependencies, which are *not* fully understood. Interference with the Earth's climate taking an over-simplified *mechanistic and reductionist* view is highly dangerous. Technology may assist new scientific discoveries, but it *cannot* solve everything, least of all the problems created by a fossil-fuel–driven economy. The solution is to re-integrate Nature as the protagonist in the Global System and for the Enterprise to move away from fossil fuel extraction and derived products with immediate effect. The issue of stranded assets and the vested interests of the few who engage in potentially harmful experimentations *do not warrant interference* with Life itself, whose intricate complexities we barely understand. Geo-engineering and bioengineering raise serious ethical questions, which cannot be decided upon by unelected or elected leaders without consultation with Civil Society. It demonstrates a profound error in judgment and a thoroughly misguided attempt to reduce the inherent complexities of the Earth's systems and Life itself to a *machine*.

In the context of the Enterprise, the ubiquitous presence of 'artificial intelligence' and sensors embedded in various systems may prove useful in specific contexts. However, recent technological advancements may also prove highly problematic since they affect human thinking and our innate ability to 'get the job done.' There is a genuine concern human intelligence is being reduced as 'artificial agents' are disproportionately used in a variety of settings. The global pandemic forced remote working cross-sector, driving increased use of sensors and interoperable systems in different sectors, ranging from finance to healthcare, education, 'smart' workplaces and 'smart' cities. The latest surge in the adoption of 'artificial intelligence' and blockchain is fast transforming the Internet of Things (IoT)[4] and very soon it will become the Internet of Everything (IoE),[5] moving beyond technology-intensive industries into the mainstream. The IoE will make technology more pervasive in our daily lives; people, data and processes becoming intertwined through connected physical devices, as part of a unitary whole. Public and private entities are seeking to overcome considerable technical challenges, as they transition from complicated legacy systems. However, this next phase entails immense mass accumulation of personal and sensitive data, including biometric data, which undermines civil liberties, human rights, privacy, public safety and security. There are unresolved tensions in public discourse over these issues, heterogeneous and divergent views on *how* best to proceed. But, these inevitable frictions are necessary since 'artificial intelligence' is set to become the most *transformative* technology in human existence.

Innovation in many cases has become synonymous with digitalised automation, technological change and 'big data,'[6] used to derive probable outcomes through statistical analysis. Data is believed to hold the key to maintaining the present value of the Enterprise, while unlocking its future value and longevity. However, it is not that simple. The reality is far more complex than any 'information' that may be inferred from the data being processed through Socio-Technical Systems. The dynamics of change are complex: multidirectional and multidimensional. The intricacies and unpredictability of human interactions, interdependencies and interrelationships are not fully captured in machine learning models. While machine learning is considered a necessary element to reduce uncertainty, given the volume of data and recent acceleration in the pace of change, it is not sufficient. Paradoxically, it may add layers of complicatedness and interfere with human *moral* judgment. Data may be relevant to a specific context, but it does not provide *all* the elements for a deeper analysis and a more *nuanced* understanding of the changes. It does not encapsulate the non-linear nature of emergent changes in the surrounding environment, nor the dynamics of human behaviours and peer-to-peer interactions increasingly intertwined with those of 'artificial agents' operating in Socio-Technical Systems. The *meaning* of these changes manifests *gradually* over time and may not become *fully* apparent in *atomised form* at a given moment in time, owing to the continuum of change.

The 'events' in a given data sample represent a historical record of what happened at a given moment in time. Data may help explain how we reached a certain point, but it rarely provides 'complete information' about the present or the future with *any* degree of certainty. On the other hand, dynamic inquiries, observations, dialogue and experimentation spur innovation. We can make *sense* of the emerging reality, using our unique human faculties of interpretation and our imagination.[7] Data processing and statistical analysis should only be the starting point of *an evolving* conversation. Statistical significance is subject to the clarity of the *objective function*, the *quality* of the input data and its provenance. It may serve as the germ of an idea, a hypothetical situation that is seemingly true but warrants investigation. In other words, what the data suggests may not be true. When various technologies are combined in complex adaptive systems, further demands are made on the core competencies of the Enterprise.

Should the Enterprise opt for complete automation and standardisation of repetitive tasks to reduce costs, it will be at risk of losing its capacity and ability to learn on a continuous basis. It may suffer 'informational entropy,'[8] where the information is readily dispersed within disparate systems and the Knowledge is not easily retrieved. In the absence of 'real world' encounters, remote working and the emergence of 'virtual workplaces' may make it more difficult for the Enterprise to innovate meaningful Intellectual Property. While there may be technical constraints and security concerns, information needs to be shared as 'freely' as possible. Securing communication pathways is of the essence, but so too is enabling *fluidity* in the exchange of 'information' and shared experiences in a variety of ways. As every entrepreneur knows, timing is everything. A missed opportunity may be lost or become less attractive due to delay. Technology providers are moving towards standardisation driven by cost efficiencies and interoperability between systems; and yet the creative enterprise necessitates more flexibility to promote spontaneity and spark novel ideas for innovation. Often there is a difficult trade-off between security, privacy and flexibility, subject to the levels of risk tolerated by the Enterprise.[9] Given the rapid pace of change, a more 'elastic' approach is needed to promote new innovation pathways.

At maturity the Enterprise is more likely to pursue 'innovation' in response to changes in existing customer needs and industry regulation. Rarely is the 'bigger picture' taken into consideration, to spur more creative efforts. For those operating within a classical business model, shareholder value is paramount, typically associated with narrowly defined financial metrics. However, it is difficult to see how the Enterprise may fulfil its potential and experience the *full* benefits of innovation for its own sake, by creating new sources of value. Innovation ought to be the *freely* chosen, preferred pathway for the Enterprise. And yet the *entrepreneurial spirit* is often submerged by multiple constraints not least overly burdensome bureaucratic procedures. Innovation requires consistent efforts over time to avert losing the spark of new ideas amidst mounting administrative requirements. The right balance needs to be struck between compliance, responsiveness to regulatory changes, financial pressures and technological constraints, while averting self-imposed restrictions in thinking, particularly when limiting opportunities for the exploration of new ideas. Resource scarcity, regulatory and technical constraints are often cited as limitations to innovation, but rarely is the focus of the Enterprise re-directed towards developing its *human capabilities*, an indispensable component of Enterprise resilience.

Innovation becomes *meaningful* when seizing emergent opportunities on the horizon. The Enterprise has a critical role to play in creating sustainable value for Society, through the enactment of new business models to foster innovation, nature-based solutions and customer-focused services. Since the Enterprise owes its existence to a healthy environment and a revitalised thriving society, it makes perfect business sense to align its objectives with multiple stakeholder requirements, while raising the bar for *qualitative* improvements in its products and services. In a world where there are 'n-sided' markets afforded by social networks and the Internet, focusing on the specific needs of *known* stakeholders is essential, but it may not be sufficient. Seeding newly emerging markets quickly may require frequent adjustments in the business model and in some instances radical change. Knowing *how* to transition smoothly from the old to the new is critical for successful innovation. Understanding disruptive business models, particularly circular business models and peer-to-peer customer-producer 'experience platforms,'[10] fosters new innovation pathways, leveraging strategic partnerships.

While new inventions are desirable, they may not always be necessary. In highly competitive markets, it may simply be a case of identifying the right 'mix of ideas' to enhance present and future innovations. Expanding available resources within the Enterprise network is no longer prohibitive in terms of costs. Uber and Airbnb do *not* own their assets. They both *crowdsourced* underutilised resources whether private cars or private rooms for hire, serving the more competitive tiers in the marketplace initially, and progressively disrupting the entire transportation and hospitality sectors, respectively. Crowdsourcing increases diversity of thought and lived experiences, providing rich sources of Knowledge, creating more opportunities for innovation. Peer-to-peer 'smart contracts,' new digital lending platforms and crypto-currencies are disrupting how individuals access funding through micro-finance.[11] ICT also enables real-time virtual interactions across the globe, reducing the costs of creating and developing new materials, products and services. Open-source access to new technologies encourages new 'virtual' strategic partnerships, accelerating speed to market and the realisation of new sources of value. 3D printing technologies are being experimented with in a number of different settings, including a newly built steel bridge in Amsterdam. While embedded sensors enable real-time maintenance and reduced costs ongoing, the 'digital twin' also enhances learning opportunities and potential new applications. With industry lines blurring, new public-private partnerships are emerging cross-industry, enlisting the help of multiple academic disciplines to tackle one of the biggest problems, climate change. Through joint efforts in R&D and shared experiences, costs are effectively being reduced in the search for suitable climate adaptations. While technological advancements may be necessary, they will also radically alter the quality of our lives. Just because we can doesn't *always* mean we should.

As the Enterprise seeks to differentiate its competitive position, it is becoming increasingly apparent it must do so through an open platform for innovation, facilitating joint-project work even among rivals.[12] The 'window of opportunity' has significantly narrowed and speed to market is of the essence. Focusing on the *right* forms of collaboration the Enterprise instigates a self-fulfilling promise of *continuous innovation*. The best performing companies have embraced this *paradigm shift* and continually make adjustments to meet their customer needs. Working towards *lifetime customer value*, they strive to build bridges from one generation to the next, continuously developing their value proposition. Sales Force is a case in point, making a bold statement as a young start-up that it would disrupt CRM Systems; and it has done so. Through continuous improvements to its business model, it has developed *dynamic adaptive capabilities*, while expanding its network of external practitioners to further extend its reach. Sustaining innovation requires astute management of resources across the value chain. Practice makes perfect and the Enterprise is able to take significant strides towards operational excellence, through operational efficiencies, and fast 'pivots' as conditions change. How far the Enterprise is able to progress depends upon its willingness to embrace uncertainty, its ability to take entrepreneurial risks and explore new sources of value creation.

Effortless continuous innovation fosters successive 'virtuous growth cycles,' creates value and reciprocal benefits for the Enterprise and its stakeholders. Human potential is the most valuable asset within the Enterprise, whose *intrinsic value* is rarely discovered. Whether it is a failure of leadership, structural or systemic deficiencies, the *nonsubstitutable value* of the individual across the ecosystem is hardly ever realised.[13] Underestimating the value of *dynamic* human interactions in real time curtails overall performance. Some managers take an overly narrow view of the reality, whether due to risk aversion or skewed incentives; they do not fully commit to innovation nor support *nascent* talent pools. And yet the *idiosyncrasies* of individual talent and collectively the talents within teams confer an unassailable competitive edge to the Enterprise since *unique* individual and team core competencies are more difficult to imitate than data and machinery.

'Discovery is simply seeing what everyone one else has seen – but thinking what no one else has thought.'[14]

Disruptive Innovation requires sufficient time, space and effort.[15] It necessitates a compelling vision of the future and successful cross-disciplinary partnerships, realised through human ingenuity, enabled by technology. It begins with the successful design of a vibrant innovation ecosystem, which enables the Enterprise to identify, understand, clearly define and refine *new ideas*. Exploration extends across core business activities, new addressable markets and emerging *breakthrough technologies* that contribute to the intrinsic dynamism of the Enterprise. New discoveries are often 'at variance with existing knowledge,' and effective progress is made over time. Tensions and frictions may arise; but surfacing conflict in a respectful manner enables the learning process to evolve. The effective pursuit of innovation necessitates the ability to comfortably and systematically question the *status quo*.

Competition effectively stimulates the vitality of the Enterprise, whether it exerts its force from inside or outside the organisation. Innovation is set on pushing the boundaries to explore new realities. Expansion of existing Knowledge enables the Enterprise to shape its future and remains within its sphere of influence no matter the challenges presented by externalities that lie beyond its control. President John Kennedy announced in 1961 American astronauts were going to the moon by the end of the decade not because it was easy, but because it was hard. In reality, the USA was competing with the USSR and wanted to get there first.[16] While few entrepreneurs *fearlessly* undertake the journey, they *know* without entertaining possible 'moon shots,'[17] chances the Enterprise will run its course are reduced. Increasing industry convergence and overlapping ecosystems require a variety of responses. They may on occasion need to be reactive; but preferably they should be proactive. Breakthrough scientific discoveries arise through competitive tensions and the same is true of the Enterprise.

'Innovative entrepreneurship is not a genetic predisposition, it is an active endeavour.'[18]

While innovation impacts the organisation as a whole, effective cross-pollination of ideas requires strong entrepreneurial leadership and the astute orchestration of limited resources. The CEO plays a pivotal role, galvanising actions and decisions at the *right* time, even if there is insufficient 'information.' Multidexterity becomes the mental model of the Enterprise. Understanding the multidimensionality of change in the digital era entails learning to navigate multiple ambiguities and uncertainties in the environment. Embracing different perspectives uncovers *unexpected connections*, particularly if there is *fluidity* in conversations taking place. Existing roles, relationships, practices, risk thresholds and controls are disrupted in the process of radical change. Strategic partnerships become a *natural* extension of the Enterprise and form an *integral part* of the innovation process. The Enterprise is rewarded with the transfer of valuable tacit knowledge through its practical application. Trust is earned through reciprocal efforts towards continuous improvement across the innovation ecosystem. In essence, the organisation is optimised towards the *systematic genesis* of new ideas, novel products and services that add value and *usefulness* for customers, whether in tangible or intangible form, through the careful selection of new technologies and new ways of operating. Innovative processes and organisational structures crystallise new sources of value. Contrary to accepted norms, the fastest route to market is *not* necessarily the most successful.

Evolving the adaptive capacity of the Enterprise is a strategic necessity, improving its responsiveness to fast changing circumstances. Innovation is no longer a question of 'value capture' since customers, employees, suppliers and investors expect so much more. They are demanding significant *qualitative changes* to the Enterprise value proposition. Earning and retaining their trust necessitates a demonstrable commitment towards *sustainability* across the value chain. Taking a short-term view of disruptive opportunities in the marketplace, even with the means to combine and recombine different technologies will prove *meaningless*, if innovations fostered by the Enterprise fail to enhance the quality of people's lives. The intrinsic aesthetic value of products and services that surprise, delight and reward customers is paramount. Meaningful unicorns are very few while incumbents resisting change are far more numerous;[19] and yet *purposeless* innovations likely result in costly failures more so than resounding successes.

The ability to find new innovation pathways is both an Art and a Science. It requires a unique combination of Knowledge and intuition coupled with a detailed analysis of the surrounding environment to gain a proper *sense* of the emerging reality. Tacit knowledge[20] is personal, gained through lifetime experiences and provides context for intuitive ideas to be developed and refined by *testing various hypotheses*. This is crucial to counter the loss of momentum and potential inertia that creeps into business practices. Whilst an 'orderly' process is beneficial for established business activities, disruptive innovation comprises seemingly random encounters, necessitates *time and space for creativity*, a fair amount of risk and 'errors' deemed valuable learning experiences. The aim should be to afford the Enterprise a 'cumulative synthesis' of discoveries to continually guide the innovation process. 'Light bulb moments' are spontaneous and occur in a non-linear heterogeneous fashion. Innovation in the digital era is of necessity a multidisciplinary, cross-functional and *purposeful* business activity, guided by a clear vision from which it derives its *meaning*.

'The greatest danger for all of us is not that our aim is too high and we miss it, but that it is too low and we reach it.'[21]

The aim of the Enterprise should be set high since it constitutes the vital *life force* of the organisation. Tackling the difficult questions is a growing expectation among key stakeholders. Knowing, understanding and being aware of individual perspectives, aspirations and expectations, taking a genuine interest in personal histories and specific pain points within the organisation constitutes transformative leadership. Akio Toyoda espoused 'genchi genbutsu,' *going to the spot and seeing for yourself*, instigating an evolving conversation to get a better grasp of the organisation's challenges.[22] If the diagnosis is flawed the CEO cannot effectively evolve the values, beliefs and behaviours of the organisation. By virtue of entering into the *dynamics of continuous innovation*, creativity emanates from the Enterprise Culture, embedded in the systems, processes and daily practices, so that *everything* is conducive to finding innovative solutions. The spark of *valuable* new ideas can originate anywhere and should not be dismissed out of hand.

The *Ren-dan-heyi* business model adopted by HAIER comprises *self-organising* micro-enterprises within a multi-tiered network that can accommodate different velocities and stages of development within the Enterprise ecosystem. While participants benefit from centralised platform services, access to finance, IT and HR services, they retain full autonomy and 'switch' business partners and services as they see fit. Adopting *fluidity* in the thought processes and *integrative* thinking across the Enterprise fosters 'autopoiesis,' self-creation and self-development. Every actor contributes to the process and *co-evolves* products and services through *competitive collaboration*. The ethos is that 'users, stakeholders and enterprises can co-create and win together.' The connectivity provisioned by the central platform enables the transfer of *real-time* 'information' in a process of *continual renewal*. BrandZ is Haier's pathway for continuous innovation. It became the most valuable *global* IoT ecosystem, worth USD16.3 billion in 2019. The 'Smart Home' service ranked 448 on Fortune Global 500 list with revenues of USD 27.7 billion. The Haier group became the leading global 'white goods' manufacturer in 2020, and the first Chinese company to be awarded ISO900 certification for upholding quality standards.[23]

'It is in Apple's DNA that technology alone is not enough – it's technology married with liberal arts, married with the humanities that yields us the results that make our heart sing.'

Steve Jobs understood the essence of disruptive innovation.[24] He contemplated the 'jobs to be done' from the customer's perspective, knowing intuitively innovation stems from *unknown* intrinsic desires. Customers adore surprises and readily embrace novelty, provided new products and services enrich the *quality* of their lives. Unafraid to explore human emotions and connect with target audiences, he sought to create 'unforgettable experiences' drawing customers to the entire suite of Apple products. Corporate launch events were infused with the same suspense and excitement of fashion shows, a far cry from the 'dry' technical presentations 'tech savvy' audiences were used to. At every launch of the new Mac, iPod, iPad and iPhone, the air was filled with wild enthusiasm as Apple's *loyal fans* wrapped around Apple stores situated in the *best known* shopping arteries worldwide. People were *energised* as they joined endless queues and slept on pavements to 'win' the privilege of being the 'first in line' to purchase Apple's latest offerings. If Apple product launches were atypical, so too were the lifetime experiences of its entrepreneurial co-founder. Steve Jobs dropped out of college, studied Eastern philosophies and the Art of Calligraphy. If he had not discovered its intrinsic beauty and subtleties, we might still be staring at the robotic blinking light of a cursor jumping around the computer screen.[25] He honed his leadership skills at Pixar, having been dismissed by the Board of his own company in the early 1980s. Momentary defeat did not deter him from *being creative*; he personally invested and revived the ailing fortunes of Pixar, realising sooner than others the *potential consumer value* of 'complex 'complex graphic visualisations;' lessons he then brought to Apple a decade later.

Apple is one of the very few trillion dollar companies that exist in the world today. And yet the company did *not* subscribe to the 'build and fail fast' school of thought. There were no 'sprints' or lean production methodologies at the outset; time, space and effort afforded Apple multiple 'trial and error' experiments and a steep learning curve ensued both for the Macintosh and its companion products. This is sometimes forgotten in the modern setting, where 'quick wins' seem to be the *only* priority. Steve Jobs *knew* intuitively which technologies had potential and was prepared to *take the risk*. He chose to facilitate 'brainstorming' activities at the Cupertino HQ, and *consciously* developed *creativity* across the Enterprise. The most striking product innovations, all closely guarded 'secrets,' appeared in the late 1990s, starting with the iMac in 1997, the iPod in 2001[26] and the iPhone in 2007. However the products are only part of the story. Steve Jobs also disrupted the music industry with the launch of the 'App Store.' While Apple held on to its IoS until 2010, it has since opened up the 'App Store' to multiple developers benefitting from 'open innovation' and further strengthening its ecosystem. It was the first technology company to reach the milestone of 'one trillion dollars' in 2018, 42 years after its inception, doubled its market value in 2020, rising to 'three trillion dollars' in January 2022.[27] Few companies have the ability to sustain market value through incredible customer loyalty. Apple is currently holding steady, focusing on *incremental improvement*. However, disruptive innovation is part of its DNA. It remains to be seen which market forces may yet influence its future.

The Apple story is extraordinary. Steve Jobs' vision was to create 'an enduring company where people were motivated to make great products.'[28] Whether at Pixar or Apple, Steve Jobs knew engineers and computer scientists, artists and designers all needed to work side-by-side, recognising the best ideas emerge from the intersection of science, technology and the humanities.[29] Inspired by emerging technologies in Silicon Valley, Italy and Japan he sought to combine utility, functionality and beauty in the 'look and feel' of the product. Jony Ive and Steve Jobs paid meticulous attention to detail; beauty was paramount in every design aspect and technical element to improve performance. Above all the customer experience needed to be memorable. Multidisciplinary teams were primed to work together, whilst also competing with one another to overcome technical limitations. Product excellence was oriented towards improving customer outcomes, with the aim of surpassing expectations. Apple was *not* concerned about 'cannibalising' its own products and set the highest standards in every aspect of design, product engineering and manufacturing without neglecting the finer details, including the packaging designed to elicit delight in the end consumer. Steve Jobs was not thinking about profits, but rather of 'producing something that would bring happiness to *many people all of the time.*' This has drawn generations of customers and attracted new talent to one of the most iconic and enduring brands born in the 20th century. The 'subtle difference' of switching the priorities from making profits to making great products, 'ends up meaning everything.'[30] While the transformation of the industry was *radical*, so too were the *expectations* of Society.[31]

'Technology inspires art and art challenges the technology.'[32]

Steve Jobs paid meticulous attention to every detail of the Enterprise. Unwilling to compromise on *quality* and *customer value*, the mission was to make computers 'friendly' and aesthetically pleasing to the eye and draw the attention of a *non-technical* audience. The purity of design and seamless finishes to the materials used was a remarkable feat of engineering and Art combined; it set a new benchmark for industry rivals and enabled the company to command premium prices. Jobs solved the 'Innovator's Dilemma'[33] by *continually* enhancing *creativity* in pursuit of excellence without ever reaching a specific destination.[34] Strong visionary leadership enabled the company to thrive under conditions of extreme uncertainty.[35] He also *knew* few are willing to explore uncharted markets, which ultimately shape both present and future opportunities. Jeff Bezos also underscored the value of experiential knowledge. He encouraged co-workers to entertain the 'wandering mind' and actively pursue 'blind alleyways.' In so doing he systematically embedded the *explorer's mindset* into systems, processes and organisational structures. The quest was simple: 'if we can get processes decentralised, so that we can do a lot of experiments without it being very costly, we'll get a lot more innovation.'[36] The creative process is an effective and *necessary counterbalance* to technical efficiency. 'Every day is day one' at Amazon and this *ethos* has helped the company foil corporate inertia. It is a powerful tool that *unlocks* the *hidden potential* within the organisation.[37]

Understanding the *innovation process* within the Enterprise ecosystem is business critical. Through the explorer's gaze, *visionary leaders* 'see' the reality from multiple different angles. They are prepared to take a 'leap of faith' as they 'look out' onto the horizon. Elements of significance emerge at different times; some ideas may not have immediate relevance or else their meaning may be altered and so they are discarded. Patience and discipline yield far better results, as the journey unfolds, safe in the knowledge significant performance, productivity and profitability improvements will take time. Through continuous improvement, the Enterprise reaches a higher level of preparedness and learns to mitigate security risks across the value chain;[38] given the complexity of Socio-Technical Systems in operation, 'there should be no single point of failure.'[39] Since information flows through complex networks in multiple directions, the attempt to bring everything under a unitary control centre is technically challenging and potentially counterproductive, especially as the Enterprise extends its reach across the 'real' physical world, virtual and mixed realities.

'Creativity is connecting things in novel ways.'[40]

The notion of combining the Arts and the Sciences is best exemplified by the 'Medici effect,'[41] which prompted a 'creative explosion' during the Italian Renaissance in Florence. The leading thinkers, artists and scientists came together at the behest of the Medici family. 'As these individuals connected, new ideas blossomed at the intersections of their respective fields, thereby spawning the Renaissance, one of the most inventive eras in history.'[42] More recently, correlations have been found between creativity and economic growth. And yet, in many companies hardly any space, time or effort is afforded true creativity. This is a mistake. The human imagination is the most powerful tool we have to counter uncertainty. Harnessing the power of human ingenuity amplifies Enterprise resilience and its ability to withstand future shocks, which may adversely affect overall performance and threaten its existence. The more diverse our experiences and the richer our domains of knowledge, the more versatile our thinking becomes and our innate curiosity can be fulfilled. Spontaneous and relatively unconstrained thought processes are beneficial in highly complex situations. They enable human beings to disentangle what is happening and determine the best course of action. Whether or not it is explicitly acknowledged within the Enterprise, it is the ability to pinpoint unseen connections, through seemingly unrelated associations, which often leads to the most successful innovation outcomes.[43]

Where there is low cognitive control, non-conscious forms of 'information' yield effective evaluations of complex situations. 'Perceptual awareness' is intuitive and should not be *artificially constrained*. Human rationality is a secondary phenomenon, which follows what *we already know* from our own intuition. Since empirical evidence may have a *plurality* of meanings, we need to *trust* our own instinct in relation to contextual significance, before taking hasty decisions derived from flawed or incomplete data. First principles such as time, space, cause and effect are necessary, but taken in isolation they are not sufficient to *make sense* of the inherent complexities in the reality before us, particularly in *fast changing* situations. They do not provide *instantaneous explanations* nor 'complete' Knowledge of the *emerging* reality, initially experienced intuitively and therefore subjectively. After which we may apply 'objective assessments' within spatio-temporal frameworks, constructed for shared analysis. Innovation is inherently an *organic process*, usually led by the CEO to inspire the organisation, set the rhythm and regulate the pulse of the Enterprise to sustain momentum. Informal interactions across multidisciplinary teams create new possibilities and a variety of innovation pathways, to enrich available options for the Enterprise in pursuit of its strategic intent. Working towards a comprehensive view of the reality and a deeper understanding of the multifaceted interactions, interdependencies and interrelationships within the Socio-Technical Systems.

True innovation *ought* to be the triumph of novel ideas, curiosity, courage and creativity. It requires a paradigm shift and renewed focus on the 'uniqueness of individual creativity,' rediscovering what matters most, expressed in terms of human values. The Enterprise becomes adaptive and resilient through effortless practice,[44] when undertaking a deliberate process of continuous innovation. The emphasis is on creating sustainable value – *how* the enterprise is making a product or service, limiting waste, pollution and environmental damage – and *how* far its core values correspond with human needs, expectations, values and beliefs held individually among its constituents and collectively in the wider Society. Notwithstanding challenging geopolitical and geo-economic contingencies, the motivation of the Enterprise is driven by 'going the extra mile,' without ever compromising on the intrinsic aesthetic values of products, services and its integrity. Innovation is therefore the Art of harnessing the human imagination and the ability to transcend perceived barriers to growth. Success is the ability to *dynamically* re-imagine a sustainable digital future. The ambition to do so is the quintessence of innovation.

'While some may see them as the crazy ones, we see genius because the ones who are crazy enough to think that they can change the world, are the ones who do.'[45]

Chapter 6

Transformation
/ˌtræns.fəˈmeɪ.ʃən/

'Whereas moral courage is the righting of wrongs, creative courage, in contrast, is the discovering of new forms, new symbols, new patterns on which a new society can be built.'[1]

Transformation constitutes the transcendence of barriers to human progress through a process of continual renewal. It entails the deployment of 'creative courage' to discover new forms of existing within Society, while being respectful of our planetary boundaries. Embracing the dynamics of change, the Enterprise intelligently executes wise choices of the many alternatives afforded by new scientific discoveries and technological advancements. With high intention and sincere effort the Enterprise seeks to address complex challenges with the 'end goal in view,' oriented towards a sustainable digital future. Amidst an all-pervasive digitalised reality, a sizeable gap has emerged between technological advancements and human attainment. Through a process of continuous learning and improvement, the Enterprise is consciously engaged in developing dynamic human capabilities. Pivoting quickly to unlock hidden market opportunities, the Enterprise embarks upon a 'virtuous cycle' of growth and a process of continuous innovation, successfully transforming new ideas into reality. The unprecedented impact of the global pandemic has accelerated the adoption of new technologies beyond our expectations. Harnessing the power of the human imagination, the Enterprise proactively pursues the discovery of 'new forms' of existence and existing, creates new 'symbols' or artefacts and evolves new 'patterns,' values, beliefs and behaviours on which a new society and its own future can be built successfully and *meaningfully*.

The Enterprise *cannot* exist in a vacuum. It forms an integral part of a highly complex network of natural and human-made systems. As much as it may exert its own influence on the reality, it is simultaneously influenced by its interactions with the systems in play and the Global System as a whole. Understanding its dependencies and interdependencies within the physical reality and increasingly the interconnectedness with digital 'networks' is business critical, owing to the inexorable process of change both within and between industries. The pursuit of sustainable growth and innovation in an increasingly challenging business environment necessitates *radical transformation*. Whether at an individual or at a collective level on a local, regional and global scale, 'moral courage' is urgently required to redress the 'wrongs' that preclude human progress. There is an opportunity to exercise our individual and collective wisdom to steer the Enterprise in the *right* direction. Its present and future longevity is inextricably linked with the integral regeneration of Society, the Environment and ultimately the Enterprise itself carefully *choreographing* the necessary momentum to transform its own existence. Attentive to changing human needs and those of the surrounding environment, the Enterprise is best positioned to navigate the most effective and efficient innovation pathways. Surpassing inherent limitations the Enterprise transforms both itself and Society.

The Global System in its current form is *not* sustainable. It requires concerted efforts to address both the effects and the root causes of structural and systemic disequilibria that have persisted for many decades. How we *transition* from the current state towards a more desirable future state is the crux of intense debate and increasing public scrutiny, specifically concerning energy sources and recent technological advancements in the field of 'artificial intelligence.' Automation in the form of 'generative artificial agents' embedded within Socio-Technical Systems seemingly exerts a negative influence on productivity both within the Enterprise and the wider Society.

Some jobs will be lost and it is possible relatively fewer new jobs will be created, subject to requirements and the *ethical choices* being made by individual companies and respective governments. Undeniably, the effects of 'artificial intelligence' are all-encompassing and invariably have a profound impact on Society and the Environment, given high levels of fossil fuel energy requirements. In the context of the most transformative technological change in our lifetimes, it is worth keeping in mind the higher purpose of the Enterprise, its pivotal role in Society and its responsibility towards protecting our most precious resource, Nature itself.

Digital business transformation fosters a self-fulfilling 'virtuous growth cycle' since it entails finding new forms of collaboration, communication, connection and coordination of efforts among people, processes and technology. It requires a clear vision of the future built on a deeper understanding, awareness and knowledge of the past and a coherent strategy to facilitate seamless transitions across the Enterprise ecosystem. Digital business transformation is not about fighting the existing reality, but it is about *consciously* pursuing a new direction. In a fast-changing turbulent world, the Enterprise experiences unexpected challenges and sudden changes in the business environment. Understanding the complexities of the external and internal forces in play, Enterprise Leaders recognise relationships, institutions, boundaries within industries and the regulatory environment are subject to change and include factors outside their control. Legal and ethical thresholds are being exceeded due to disruptive and rapidly evolving technologies, which *continually* exert a 'force multiplier effect' both on the Enterprise and the wider Society. The ability to discern the ramifications of actions and decisions to be taken, both the effects and underlying causes strengthens Enterprise resilience, its strategic intent and the directionality of change.

Through the creation of new 'artefacts,' the Enterprise effectively continues to evolve its *raison d'être* and thereby enhances its intrinsic value, seeking an unbreakable bond with its customers and primary stakeholders. Leveraging specific contextual human experiences, Enterprise Leaders focus their attention on delivering success through the active engagement and participation of the stakeholders, taking into consideration inflection points on the horizon at the intersection of human and environmental needs as well as the changes introduced by emerging technologies. Efforts are directed towards timely adjustments and the effective allocation of resources, in response to and in anticipation of changing aspects of the reality, within the Enterprise's control and its own sphere of influence. Fast-changing customer demands, cross-sector competition and disruptive technologies call into question the legitimacy and economic viability of the Enterprise and this necessitates a *paradigm shift*. A veritable mindset change at the higher echelons averting wasteful and unproductive uses of natural resources. Moving away from meaningless extraction of monetary value and senseless exploitation of available resources towards beneficial societal and environmental outcomes. Human health and wellbeing catalyses growth and the self-fulfilling promise of enduring value creation for present and future generations.

Enterprise resilience stems from instilling a vibrant culture of continuous growth and innovation within the Enterprise, centred on individual and collective human values, beliefs and intrinsic motivations. The social and relational dimensions of business provide an inexhaustible flow of energy and a source of inspiration. If properly arranged, people and processes propel the Enterprise forward, rather than the technical means, which might otherwise serve to enable human endeavour, creativity and ingenuity. Enterprise leaders focus their efforts on effecting necessary structural and systemic changes enabling new forms of collaboration to emerge. The Enterprise sets in motion a process of continuous learning and improvement, coordinating its efforts across the entire value chain to achieve meaningful change and stay ahead of the competition. Purposefully re-configuring the organisation, constructing an *open system* of communication to enhance the ability of the Enterprise to make new connections in the 'informational' environment. Notwithstanding the level of uncertainty and ambiguity in the environment, the actions and decisions taken by the Enterprise are intentional and continually aligned and re-aligned with its core purpose and values. Digital business transformation is an evolutionary process comprising meaningful changes at all levels of the Enterprise. It entails changing processes and other elements within the Enterprise's control and sphere of influence to enable new forms of collaboration to emerge.

Transformative leadership fosters 'real' growth and true innovation by fully respecting individuality, human autonomy and human agency, while leveraging the rich spectrum of human consciousness and talents within the Enterprise. Leaders seek to create synergistic relationships among teams, enhancing their understanding and awareness of the strategic objectives and direction of the Enterprise, and their ability to contribute towards achieving a harmonious whole. Conscientious teams are more capable of acting with integrity, focusing on improving performance in a more impactful and ethical manner, finding new and better ways to surprise and delight their customers. Individuals become fully engaged when they are seen, heard and their feelings are taken into account as part of the *transformation processes*. Their enthusiasm reverberates outside the Enterprise creating a 'virtuous cycle,' obtaining valuable 'real-time' feedback from their customers as part of a 'two-way conversation.' Seamless transitions can only be achieved through the continued successful *cultural transformation* of the Enterprise, which is influenced from the 'outside-in' and the 'inside-out.' It is never a destination, but rather a proactive human endeavour underpinning a process of continual renewal. In essence, the cultural transformation of the Enterprise comprises rich patterns of thought, values, beliefs and behaviours for which everyone is responsible and accountable. Knowledge and technology can only be successfully integrated within the structure, processes and systems of the Enterprise, through embodied values such as empathy and compassion, strong leadership and sensitivity to individual human needs and those of others both within and among diverse cross-functional teams participating in the Enterprise ecosystem.

The Leaders' endeavour is to choreograph a delicate and intricate dance, creating a system of responsibility and accountability both at the individual and collective levels, ensuring collaborative outcomes and contributions to the whole task are articulated and celebrated. Clearly identified roles and interrelationships lend support to shared agency across the Enterprise ecosystem, and afford the organisation seamless interactions with new technologies. Successive waves of active learning accrue to enhance Enterprise Knowledge, Understanding and Awareness. Together these elements form an integral part of Enterprise Wisdom, embodied by its participants and expressed through the practical application of sound moral principles, human values and Knowledge encompassed within the social and value systems that are continually evolving. However, this is not a destination per se. Rather, it is a circular motion, which leads to the consideration of an infinite variety of possibilities as the Enterprise 'grows' over time. Continually refining its ethos, the Enterprise proactively focuses on creating new products and services. They serve as exemplary 'symbols' of an unbreakable bond with its customers, who ensure in turn the relevance and usefulness of the Enterprise resonates within Society.

The successful adoption of new ways of working and new technologies requires clear and effective communication of both the Vision and the Strategy as a constant. Resistance to change frequently occurs when the current culture, levels of Knowledge, daily practices and 'comfort zones' of individuals and collectively among teams are underestimated during the process. Inherent biases, obsolescent processes and existing paradigms create formidable barriers, if they are not addressed *a priori*, with due concern and sensitivity. Actions follow intentions and in this respect data is not a reliable source of 'information.' Leaders will only ever gain an *approximate* understanding of the pulse of the Enterprise, if they eschew direct engagement with their stakeholders. The *pattern matching* functionality of 'artificial intelligence' is not *fully* reflective of the deeper 'values' and 'beliefs' at play in the Enterprise, which influence interactions with Socio-Technical Systems and daily practices. If the purpose of key processes and underlying paradigms are not clearly understood, any changes made, new processes and technologies are likely to fall short of the mark. Separating the users impacted by the change from the relevant processes undermines their effectiveness and may prove an insurmountable obstacle once they are deployed. If the aim of the Enterprise is to achieve 'actionable' insights derived from data, a good starting point is to undertake thorough consultations with individuals and teams *involved* to ascertain human needs. In the early stages of digital business transformation, it is an arduous task to distil 'information' from historical, current and disparate sources of data, which may be riddled with inaccuracies and duplications without full participation of those directly affected and due consideration of the impact on others.

As digital transformation reaches maturity, the mistake is often made to *fully* automate existing processes, so-called 'routine tasks' without undergoing a thorough process of renewal. Novartis met with obstacles during the early phases of its digital transformation because the *technical* development teams had been acting independently of the *business* teams. Consequently, new processes did not reflect their needs. However, remote working during the global pandemic interrupted 'business as usual' and teams across all functions within the Enterprise began *working together* to modernise systems and processes. Invariably, development and business teams working together were able to deliver far better outcomes, updating and changing internal processes to better suit their needs and their ability to respond fast to changing customer demands. Less haste constitutes more speed through a process of consultation and continued dialogue to enhance the effectiveness of investments in people, processes and technology. Thereby averting costly 'errors' through a lack of engagement due to the Enterprise's failure to meet the *human needs* ahead of the *technical constraints*.

As the Enterprise transforms through the adoption of newly emerging technologies, so too Society is affected by the changes. The transformation of Society hinges on broader socio-cultural, political and economic changes in the environment and this needs to be taken into consideration by the Enterprise since the wider Society is *partly encompassed* within 'artificial intelligence' models that may be deployed within the Enterprise. At present, human relations both within the Enterprise and Society are increasingly mediated by *technical* means. The misguided use of 'big data' may on occasion supplant ground truths in the interests of speed. However, it is a mistake to make assumptions based on assumptions previously made by *unknown* parties and *undisclosed* methodologies. Contrary to popular belief in some arenas, 'big data' does not necessarily provide 'a higher form of intelligence and knowledge,' which is strictly speaking a human endeavour. 'Big data' comprises large volumes of text and image data collected from heterogeneous sources that have not been independently verified. However quantity does not substitute for quality; even though modern algorithms work best on large amounts of data, it does not detract from the inherent flaws in the data, inconsistencies and inaccuracies; the lack of validation and 'informed consent' from the individuals concerned as a result of current *data practices*.

The 'modern massive data sets' used to train 'machine learning' models, are subsequently embedded in *algorithmically* driven 'Socio-Technical Systems.' At present, the outputs cannot be *fully* explained. Scientists and engineers are unable to unravel the steps taken by an autonomous 'artificial agent' to reach a given output, and users are left none the wiser even though they have access to a natural language interface. Despite sophisticated data processing methodologies, the data are *not* free of implicit biases,[2] and often lead to discriminatory practices. It is difficult to use pure mathematics to provide a properly 'objective view,' a logical and linear assessment of an individual or group of individuals, simply because the data are mere fragments of the available 'information' in the environment. Human experiences, patterns of thought, idiosyncratic uses of language, knowledge and behaviours are by definition the exact opposite, *non-linear*. At best, they may only be *approximated* by 'applied statistics' used in modern computational algorithms involving 'artificial intelligence.' Owing to the vast volumes of data being collected, the transformation of 'information' by *mechanical* means is subject to *automated filtering*. 'Multiple comparisons' may result in spurious correlations, often non-causal coincidences that could eventually harm Society.[3] It is difficult to avert discriminatory practices without human interventions, continuous monitoring and human supervision of the models in play, including independent assessments to verify the validity of the data and data practices being used to collect, manage and store the same. Once biases are embedded in the datasets or they are introduced through subsequent inputs in the data processes, they become more difficult to isolate and may prove too 'costly' to remove. However, the Enterprise will also need to evaluate the cost of *not* doing so.

Data has no intrinsic value without specific social, economic, cultural, demographic and political context. Current methodologies used in 'machine learning' do not require causality to deliver predictions and do not take into account *human values*. Where quantity is privileged over quality, the complexities of human relations may be 'lost' in translation, particularly where *parallel* data processing mechanisms are embedded in multi-agent systems. Large data sets effectively comprise billions of tiny numerical fragments dispersed in cyberspace, recomposed by *mechanical* means, but not reconstituted and restored to their original state. Working with the data which is by definition incomplete, inexact and difficult to verify is nonetheless a subjective experience. Individuals may perceive *meaning* differently; thus data is no closer to the 'objective' source of truth than the interpretation of a human being and the transfer of Knowledge remains a distinctly human endeavour. Fundamentally, 'information' stored in the memory of a digital platform and related computational systems represent multiple heterogeneous datasets, which attempt to *simulate* the reality, but only partially succeed. They can be interrogated and manipulated so that they become useful, but questions should be asked as to the relevance of the relationships they *seemingly* reveal. There should also be full transparency as to 'who' or 'what' has intervened in the composition of the requisite datasets.

The emergence of 'generative artificial agents' could 'cloud' judgments on the 'patterns of behaviour' being analysed simply because they are not equipped to discern 'objects' of value in the computational environment or evaluate their relative significance. In other words, 'artificial agents' have no *universally applicable moral* code or professional code of conduct to which they are bound; any inbuilt 'guardrails' in large language models pertain to the 'task' they are required to execute with *mathematical accuracy* and have thus far proven inadequate. Computational *algorithms* are simply programmed to execute a particular 'task' and are in effect 'blind' to the outcomes. They utilise sequential linear logic and cannot successfully make connections between non-linear events. The stored data used to train 'machine learning' models entails static historical components, and the models cannot be easily updated. Conversely, *dynamic* forms of current *real-time* data, including various other types of interconnected data beyond the limitations of text and image, enable human beings to make informed, intelligent decisions instantaneously, subject to the requirements of the situation at hand. The actions of 'artificial agents' are not intelligent, adaptable or intentional like those of human beings, rather their *performance* of a given 'task' is limited to a specific 'element' of the task in hand. Although data is the basis of 'artificial intelligence' the 'information' that is generated becomes Knowledge *only* when *meaning* is added, and it is connected with other forms of data, beyond the limitations of 'text and image,' which are the only *types* of data that can be processed and/or generated by 'artificial intelligence' systems at present.

Knowledge stems from human experiences and encompasses human intelligence, adding *meaning* to the 'information' we perceive in the reality. It is far more complex than the 'decisions' taken by computational algorithms based on the *limited availability* of the data they have access to. Particularly, if we consider human actions and decisions are the result of 'common sense,' uniquely subjective and dynamic real-time perceptions and interpretations of the reality. They are also context-specific, which relates to the practical application of implicit and explicit Knowledge used *intentionally*. This cannot be *broken down* so easily and therefore the faculty of *understanding,* 'perceptual awareness,' human intelligence, the idiosyncratic use of the human form of natural language and consciousness are *exclusively* human capabilities. They cannot be accomplished by computational systems, even with state-of-the-art 'artificial intelligence' and the most advanced 'machine learning' models. In the context of the Enterprise, 'good' practice entails educating the entire workforce, so it is better able to use these sophisticated and increasingly *powerful* computational tools. Notwithstanding the technical limitations, incremental improvements in 'artificial intelligence' models are moving very fast and new capabilities are emerging daily, through *continuous human interactions,* particularly with large language models. Thus, data proficiency among *all* the constituents of the Enterprise and a thorough assessment of 'fitness-for-purpose' prior to deployment of the 'machine learning' models is a prerequisite for successful digital business transformations.

Insufficient levels of education and the absence of broader Knowledge domains in existing curricula constitute a limitation to the advancement of Society and the capacity of the Enterprise to derive *true* value from its investments in technology.[4] A well-rounded education necessitates liberal Arts as much as the Sciences, data proficiency and consistent training in ethics-based principles in readiness for practical applications, across *all* organisations creating, developing and deploying 'artificial intelligence' both in the public and private domains. Wrongful conclusions may be hastily drawn from the outputs provided by 'machine learning' systems, owing to the immediacy of responses and a lack of understanding *how* the machines *actually* work. There is also a 'real' risk the speed, volume, scale and manner in which data is collected, stored, processed and standardised to deliver 'actionable insights' or 'actionable knowledge' as many have claimed can lead to an impoverishment of human intelligence and an erosion of human agency due to automation. At present there is insufficient discussion of the *semantic weaknesses* of 'artificial intelligence' and its inability to *understand* the human form of natural language, let alone discern the complex relationships among human beings, both their interactions with each other and the environment. The philosophical and ethical dimensions underpinning the process of digital business transformation are hardly ever discussed, and yet they are a prerequisite for delivering *meaningful and beneficial* human and planetary outcomes. Knowledge cannot be substituted by a 'superficial' peripheral view of the reality, limited by observable elements and quantifiable aspects of human experiences should they be so perceived. Computational analytics are essentially based on mathematics and linguistics, which are important for the *mechanics* of 'artificial intelligence' systems. The formulation, classification, labelling and contextualisation of data require human interventions throughout the process, but necessarily take a reductionist approach to render the data in a suitable form for 'machine learning.'

It is worth noting public and private sector entities as well as government institutions may be data rich, either because they have collected or have access to large volumes of data, but they may still be *insight* poor should they become *overly reliant* on data alone. It is worth noting there is a significant 'capabilities gap' between the velocity at which the technology is being developed (including hardware and software, computational power and storage capacity) and the capacity of the Enterprise and Society to absorb the *significance* of the changes taking place and successfully utilise the tools for *beneficial ends*. At one end of the scale there are instances of 'perfect synchronicity' and at the other, bewilderment and confusion. A Formula One driver prepares for the race ahead, and in many respects trains more successfully when using the simulator due to the immediate feedback loops from the *telemetry* that becomes available for the *whole* team to examine and make *instantaneous* improvements to the car *prior, during and post*-race performances. It constitutes a process of continuous learning and improvement with harmonious and synergistic relationships being developed with the technology and the *whole* team ongoing. The relationships are built on *transparency and trust*. Thus, the data is only one component of the distinctive *human endeavour* to strive towards operational excellence, team cohesion and outstanding levels of overall performance. This is not quite the case in corporations. Often there is a misguided perception digital transformation and specifically more automation *is* the answer to all the underlying problems, whereby the ultimate destination is usually conflated with short-term gains. However, the interpretation of data is more an Art than a Science; it necessitates practical 'know-how' and the consistent application of *human wisdom*, connecting the dots to find new innovation pathways beyond the telemetry engineers receive in the case of a Formula One team. Intentionally building dynamic human capabilities and knowledge through *in-depth testing* of frontier technologies prior to implementation will help surface implicit and explicit biases, which may not be immediately apparent.

In the context of the Enterprise, 'good' practice includes multi-stakeholder engagement and the application of ethics-based principles at all levels of the organisation, from the design of new 'work flows' and processes through to the safe and reliable use of 'artificial intelligence.' Regulating multidirectional influences on the Socio-Technical Systems in operation within the Enterprise is no mean feat; it extends beyond the realm of engineering and the organisation's control. Cyber security risks abound, and it is becoming increasingly apparent 'bad actors' are using relatively 'simple' techniques to create a 'back door' entry point to exploit weaknesses in the value chain. Sample data sets used to train the 'machine learning' models are *not* free of implicit biases and although there are human interventions and 'data cleaning' processes in play, biases are very difficult to remove or 'balance' during production. This may lead to reputational damage in the event unintended consequences, directly and instantaneously impact human users, consumers and recipients of automated digital services. Preparation for such eventualities necessitates the dynamic implementation of due processes and a healthy dose of skepticism and vigilance among internal and external stakeholders to question highly improbable outcomes in a timely manner. This includes business, scientific and technical teams working collaboratively, while engaging in frequent 'two-way communications' with internal and external stakeholders to ascertain effective processes and technical 'action systems' are proactively maintained and continually adjusted to meet specified human safety and international security standards.

Notwithstanding strong headwinds, human creativity and ingenuity have thus far prevailed. The human form of natural language is the most wonderful expression of human agency, steeped in cultural richness and *meaningful* expression of new discoveries and interpretations of the reality. The human mind is the most powerful capability we know, capable of creating infinite new ideas and possibilities, instigating new courses of action in conjunction with others. Human creativity and ingenuity cannot be replaced by existing technologies. Large language models cannot enact thoughts, values, beliefs, feelings or initiate actions and form current or future goals for the time being. They do not have human-level intelligence and they do not have sentience. They lack a 'real' conception of the physical world and can only estimate the 'value' of an 'object' in the reality by so-called 'weights' being adjusted in the training parameters used to run the computer program. Iterative 'trial and error' adjustments in statistical 'weights' to determine probabilistic outcomes are not the same as human experiences, implicit adjustments, dynamic 'real-time' learning and knowledge acquisition. Although the extensive parameters included in large language models form a sophisticated 'probabilistic map' of the reality, 'machine learning' capabilities at present *cannot* compete with human-level intelligence.[5]

Large language models may be described as the *digitalised mimicry* of human thought patterns and as a result they have created a degree of confusion in Civil Society. Despite the recent euphoria, they still lack the ability to create any *meaningful* interactions with human beings, since they have no sense of purpose, intention, human values and much less the propensity to lean towards the 'truth.' While human beings may 'playfully' deceive depending on the context and the manner in which the game is played, they do not in general pose a threat. However, large language models such as 'ChatGPT,' (OpenAI) Bard (Google), Bing (Microsoft) or LLaMA (Meta) may potentially pose serious risks if *misused* and deployed in highly dangerous settings. These *tools* are causing consternation since they have been trained *indiscriminately* on *unverified* Internet data and are now masquerading as 'weapons of mass disinformation,' generating 'hallucinations' or false 'information,' deep fake videos, fake voice recordings, impersonations of persons no longer alive and living high profile industry leaders and politicians; or else they *generate completely re-invented fictitious personas* that have never existed and yet *seem very real.* False 'information' or 'confabulations' as they are sometimes called, could potentially lead to *serious harm* in a highly volatile geo-political and geo-economic environment.

While the ability to produce 'confabulations' is an 'in-built feature' of large language models and undoubtedly a remarkable feat of mathematics and engineering, the threat becomes 'real' if human beings are no longer able to discern the difference between 'fake news' and 'fake personas,' and other types of data populating the Internet. The 'real' issue is the increasing risk of potential *systemic failure* and the complete breakdown of human relations owing to a *profound distrust* of mainstream media, once authoritative sources of 'information.' In the absence of adequate operational safeguards and specific governance structures, more recently concern is growing over *artificially* generated data now emerging in cyberspace. However, the disharmony being caused in Society has more complex profound causes that cannot be solely attributed to the technology.

Amidst this maelstrom of confusion, the Enterprise must carefully navigate its chosen growth and innovation pathways, leveraging dynamic human capabilities to overcome new challenges in the business environment. While successfully staking its claim to the future by transmitting its shared values and beliefs with authenticity, across the ecosystem and broadcasting with sincerity its 'good intentions' externally to the wider public. Rising above intensifying 'noise' levels that produce undue distortions and distractions is no mean feat. However, the Enterprise has a leadership role to play in shaping the future of humanity and the future of our planet. The righting of 'wrongs' cannot be achieved overnight, but the moral and creative courage inherent in the Enterprise can become a beacon of light. Enterprise leaders can engage with multiple stakeholders and facilitate negotiations with a view to neutralising structural and systemic imbalances, inequalities and inequities within their immediate sphere of influence. In so doing, they create a 'ripple effect,' which can reverberate and inspire similar actions across the world in 'real-time,' thereby using modern communication technologies for the 'good.' There have been attempts to establish *grading systems* for 'artificial intelligence,' but they provide insufficient guidance due to rapidly evolving developments in the technology. In part this is due to 'open source' access to emerging technologies, which thus far has not been subjected to independent verification and public scrutiny with respect to applicable safety standards.

The Enterprise has a moral obligation to fulfill its fiduciary duties. In decades gone by the fiduciary 'duty of care' towards social responsibilities and the protection of the environment were neglected in favour of short-term gains and further efforts to stem market volatility. However this financial posture is no longer sustainable; cash flows and revenue streams may *suddenly* falter, while assets are threatened and liabilities appear to be increasing. Working with greater *flexibility* across the time horizons, taking a more holistic and integrated approach towards short-, medium- and long-term goals, while making timely adjustments is a matter of urgent necessity. While further automation of business processes and cost containment may be deemed priorities, they are no longer sufficient. Digital business transformation can no longer be so narrowly defined. Since the outbreak of the global pandemic in 2019, there is a new level of awareness within Society about what needs to be done and a growing distrust of the *means* being used to address existing problems. The new paradigm shift towards *sustainability* is paramount. It entails the attainment of social purpose, social justice and social equity encompassing human health and wellbeing and that of the planet.

Primary stakeholders including investors, customers and employees are making stronger demands, exerting pressure on the Enterprise. Representatives from local communities and 'protest groups' in the wider Society are placing additional pressures on the Enterprise to deliver *meaningful* change. Overall they are demanding demonstrable proof the Enterprise is being respectful of diversity and inclusion, human health and wellbeing, while moving away from fossil fuels, plastics and other waste products in order to safeguard the environment. Impending changes in legislation and regulation will instigate further changes in the strategic direction of the Enterprise, with renewed emphasis on its social responsibility and accountability for environmental protection. The new requirements for compliance will necessitate reconfiguring the organisational structure, systems and processes to limit further environmental damage and prevent social harms, including the reallocation of resources towards 'just causes.' Heightened awareness of social inequalities combined with the 'cost of living crisis' renders the attainment of social justice and social equity a strategic priority, but also a necessity for growth.

The recent surge in legal and regulatory activity in many jurisdictions surrounding the use of 'artificial intelligence' bears witness to growing concerns of the potential societal harms that may be caused by *unsafe* releases of new technologies *untested* in the public domain. Many 'red lines' have been crossed such as increased public and private surveillance, including the controversial use of facial recognition without clear benefits for Society.[6] Similarly, 'true' scientific discoveries with societal benefits in mind have slowed as funds are diverted to other uses. The most dangerous uses lie in the military sphere, causing serious global safety, security and ethical concerns, as yet unanswered. In the context of the Enterprise, it will be necessary to create *dynamic* governance structures specifically for the use of 'artificial intelligence.' Since it is embedded in the Socio-Technical Systems in play, the Enterprise will need to provide *full* transparency and assurances for its stakeholders; proposed uses are both necessary and substantiated by trustworthy actions. 'Artificial intelligence' will invariably change the structure of the organisation, modify its modus operandi and *transform* the nature of the Enterprise itself. Non-deterministic technologies such as algorithmically driven 'machine learning' models may introduce *unknown* risks and unsettle the workforce. Efforts to introduce new technology-based efficiencies may become counterproductive should the Enterprise fail to properly assess potential *downside risks* that may be 'hidden' in specified uses prior to deployment. At the same time, the impacts on the workforce should become the priority, taking into consideration *plausible unlikely risks* and the likely unintended societal and environmental consequences prior to implementation.

A risks-based approach to digital business transformation is the minimum requirement since *hidden risks* may be introduced unwittingly into the Enterprise ecosystem through third- and fourth-party service providers, developers, productivity applications and so on. Unless the Enterprise has the means to curate its own proprietary models and its own data sets without recourse to third-party external providers, integrations and data sources, it will be difficult to *fully* manage and mitigate the inherent and emerging risks. Securing contractual cooperation and *transparency* from third-party providers is paramount, including verification of data sources and training methodologies, prior to deployment of any third-party solutions, no matter how 'trivial' they may appear to be at first sight. However, in the context of 'artificial intelligence' *nothing is trivial*. Although significant advances have been made and incremental improvements in 'artificial intelligence' are progressing very fast, there are many *technical limitations* and immature aspects of the technology, which increase the risks for the Enterprise both during further development, customisation of *generic models* and subsequent deployment. It is advisable to create multidisciplinary cross-functional teams to address the ethical and moral concerns as they arise, as well as ensuring *continuous monitoring* and *human supervision* throughout the model lifecycle, particularly after decommissioning and/or changing designated uses.

The quest for the Enterprise is no longer to simply produce products and services at more competitive prices, but rather to consider how it can add meaningful value to the quality of people's lives, both within its own sphere of influence and beyond. Stakeholders are seeking further guarantees that the interests of the Enterprise are morally grounded and its use of technology does not veer into unacceptable uses. In the absence of adequate operational safeguards embedded in 'artificial intelligence' systems by the technology creators, the Enterprise is being called upon to demonstrate exemplary Leadership (Vision), Stewardship (Governance) and Direction (Strategic Objectives), enacted through carefully chosen Growth and Innovation pathways. In response, ethical choices being made by the Enterprise need to be clearly articulated and communicated transparently, both to establish a stronger connection and the sense of belonging, its stakeholders are seeking; demonstrating a higher sense of purpose to justify its own existence. The new competitive advantage will be evaluated against the new digital currency: trust. Differentiating through trustworthiness is a distinctly human endeavour; while Enterprise systems and processes may be enabled by technology, the *effective* creation, distribution and delivery of value to customers, stakeholders and the wider society will always be enabled by people.

While technology and organisational structures are subject to *continuous* change, Enterprise leaders should strive to sustain strong *morale* within the workforce. There is an urgent necessity to *re-humanise* the *use* of technology, and it stems from the fact that human beings learn best through *responsible autonomy* and *practical experience*. Employees in particular need to *feel* their values and beliefs are being respected, and their efforts are not *invalidated* by *meaningless* tasks they are directed to perform by 'dumb' and 'blind' algorithms. Uber is a case in point. It often uses *gamification techniques* to lure its drivers into working longer hours in pursuit of the company's interests, but at great cost to the drivers who incur lower fees due to the laws of supply and demand.[7] Information flows should be more *transparent*, enabling those *directly* affected to *self-organise* and 'freely' decide how best to execute their tasks and subsequently share *their* Knowledge. Disempowering the workforce, whether contractual employees or 'freelancers,' through external supervision across the enterprise networks, performed by unknown centralised 'agents' with no direct relevance or personal connection to the individuals and the groups concerned is counterproductive. Employees appreciate clarity in the organisational structures and procedures they *choose* to follow, but they thrive when they *know* there is an opportunity for *personal growth* and *self-improvement*. Moreover, commercial success is dependent upon fully committed employees who *voluntarily* rally around the employer's interests, provided there is an underlying *'just cause'* to *inspire* and *motivate* them. Purpose and meaning may be derived from many different contexts, but customers and employees must be given a high priority. The Enterprise cannot function properly on machinery alone; the socio-cultural and power dynamics in play, human relations and value systems ultimately sustain its success over time.

The use of disruptive technologies must be viewed from multiple perspectives, taking into account *longer-term consequences* and not just the potential short-term gains.[8] A highly motivated, engaged and fully committed workforce is of the essence. If the goal is to avert *unintended* security breaches and defend against internal and external threats, including probable *interference* from 'generative artificial agents,' a new 'balance' needs to be struck. Emerging 'artificial agents' are capable of 'hallucinations' and 'impersonations,' which could easily 'fool' people; and yet, *some* internal controls need to be loosened to enable spontaneity in the 'flow of information' and *'good'* levels of communication between all the *participating* members of the Socio-Technical Systems in play. At the same time, some 'controls' need to be reinforced to defend against potential 'new threats' on the horizon, which cannot be *fully* controlled within the Enterprise. Flexibility and timely *dynamic adjustments* underpin the overall performance at a structural and systemic level. In the context of 'generative artificial agents' the *human dimension* cannot be discounted. There is an increasing need for *specific training* and frequent 'stress-tests' being embedded in daily practices performed across the *entire* organisation.

The impact of automated algorithmic decision-making on the human consumer is instantaneous and there is often no effective recourse for individuals to seek remedial action. Employees are left *powerless* to take corrective actions, due to automated *mechanical processes*. And yet they could solve the customer's problem swiftly and easily with *less cost* to the Enterprise and crucially *less damage* to the quality of human relations. Disempowerment of front-line employees, who are vital to the success of the Enterprise is often one the critical points of failure in digital business transformations. This typically occurs where automated digital services are introduced without *prior* consultations and *processes* are viewed purely from an engineering perspective, 'optimised' for *technical* efficiency. Full automation without human supervision may mask 'glitches' in the systems and cause unintended harms to the recipients. Adverse effects impacting Society can result in significant fines and lasting *reputational damage*. Quite apart from quantifiable financial losses, commercial value is eroded and customer loyalty is invariably lost. It may be necessary to make additional financial provisions to mitigate 'high risks' resulting form the operation of Socio-Technical Systems, but it is not sufficient or efficient.

The implications of moving towards 'hyper-automation' in the global economy are profound. Thus far 'highly personalised' services have eroded individual right to privacy and fundamental civil liberties, since data is often collected without 'informed consent.' In many ways, automated digital services are far from being *personal*, owing to the underlying methodologies employed by digital service providers. The ubiquitous *profiling*[9] of individuals provides substantial revenues for the creators of the technology, despite *unscientific* claims the software can perform a 'complete' psychological assessment of an individual person. From a linguistic perspective, it is highly improbable since 'artificial agents' do *not* understand the human form of natural language. In practice, the identification of 'regularities' in statistical patterns recorded as a result of 'past behaviours' can be *misleading* since implicit biases cannot be entirely removed from sample data sets selected to train the models. Predictions of human abilities formed using a *rigid* outline, viewed by an 'artificial agent' that is both 'dumb and blind,' producing probabilistic inferences outside context-specific dynamics, are not *truly* reflective of the *specific* individual and their *unique* characteristics. Personality traits are highly complex and human intelligence is multidimensional. It is difficult to see how a computer *algorithm* guided by a linear programme and a standardised set of rules can encapsulate all the elements, which make up the wonderful complexity of the human mind, the hidden talents and abilities of a highly unique individual *human being*. If the bar is set so low, using immature technologies to evaluate talent, the Enterprise will ultimately become impoverished both in terms of Knowledge and Wisdom.

The analysis of patterns in human behaviour is an overly narrow lens to infer the *unique human potential* of individuals. Despite *generalised* inferences that may be derived from any given data set, statistical significance based on the law of averages may not be relevant to the specific individual.[10] Inferences reached by *mechanical means* are by definition probabilistic and mathematically accurate, but they merely suggest the *likelihood* of an event or something becoming true; *they are not facts*.[11] The vast amounts of 'information' generated through social media and other means has led to the commodification of personal information,[12] with individuals caught up in their *digital profile* more so than their *'true'* identity. The intrusive nature of personal data collection has *further intensified* as a result of the global pandemic, with widespread use of *standardised algorithms*[13] across industry beyond traditional sectors such as insurance, banking and financial services.[14] In the race to compete using *emerging technologies*, many companies have insufficiently considered the ethical questions, societal and environmental impacts of their actions.

The deployment of 'artificial intelligence' systems is not straightforward. Some uses are misguided such as the *full* automation of hiring processes often deployed without recourse for unfair treatment. Potential value is lost to the Enterprise due to the *misclassification of applicants* by mechanical means, and there is a direct cost to Society and governments since neither benefit from the lifetime value a person can bring, when given the opportunity to realise their *full* potential. Algorithms are high-risk and problematic since they have a *force multiplier effect*, which may compromise individual lifetime opportunities due to embedded biases. By aggregating data through statistical analysis, 'black box' algorithms can create opacity, which may prove 'a toxic cocktail' for Society.[15] If one individual is harmed, Society is also harmed and we should care enough to change current practices. Given the speed at which unscrupulous actors can deploy and scale the use of these tools, it is difficult for legislators and regulators to keep up with the pace of technological change. Similarly enforcement *post hoc*, once the harm has occurred is suboptimal. Operational safeguards need to be implemented *preventatively*, given the speed at which these tools are evolving and the potential harms that may arise once they are deployed.

There is a misconception the Enterprise may be 'data-driven' and thereby transformed.[16] Modern *'multi-agent computer systems'* are complex and adaptive. While *technical systems* automate decision-making and *routine tasks* at record speeds, the processes are not necessarily based on *dynamic data sets* in 'real time.' They also present several new risks as *'artificial agents'* embedded in the *technical systems* try to steer each other with varying degrees of success and increasingly without human supervision. Thus, systemic relationships and path dependencies created during the design process should be re-calibrated continuously to ensure the social and technical systems remain aligned with the purpose of the Enterprise and its strategic objectives. Technology can assist the Enterprise to optimise its use of resources and provides *mathematical accuracy* in the analysis of large volumes of data. However effective 'social systems' enhance human communication and *distributed leadership* across the organisation averts 'informational silos,' reducing frictions should there be any unexpected changes. Further, the 'social systems' provide valuable multi-stakeholder feedback and enable front-line workers to effectively mitigate emerging risks and ensure *timely adaptations*.

The 'complex web of *natural* relations' described by Darwin, has *transformed* into a complex network of digital means. We are subject to the velocity, variety and variability of '*machine* learning' capabilities which are becoming ever more pervasive in our daily lives. Our efforts towards *survival* were concerned solely with changes in the *physical* environment, but in modern settings 'artificial intelligence' influences the changes in our *personal* lives, some of which are 'unfavourable and impossible to predict, while others though predictable are impossible to alter.'[17] At present, there is an unfair asymmetry of power in favour of the 'Data Controller' since *unfair* and *discriminatory* automated decisions are difficult to contest. Ethical and legal questions concerning data ownership, data sovereignty and personal property rights in light of the all-pervasive nature of 'artificial intelligence' will become ever more complex and prove difficult to *disentangle* in the absence of *full transparency* and the implementation of 'explainability' to ensure safe and reliable uses of frontier technologies as they emerge.

Human intelligence cannot be reduced to several lines of *binary code* in the context of a 'complex network' of *self-steering computer systems*, and human behaviours are *not* readily controlled by mechanical means.[18] The first 'Analytic Engine' invented by Mr Charles Babbage[19] 'a marvel of mechanical ingenuity' was partially built in 1871, inspired by the need to create a *machine* that could calculate quantifiable objects, primarily for the insurance and banking industries, as they had amassed large volumes of data, following the First Industrial Revolution. The first computer program using algorithms was written by Ada Lovelace in the mid-1840s to perform specific types of logic-based computations.[20] While the first data-processing machine or the first 'Turing machine' was not completed until 1943 at Bletchley Park,[21] helping to end WWII by breaking enemy code. Ada Lovelace cautioned the 'Analytic Engine' only performs tasks 'we *know how* to order' it to do. It does not 'originate anything' though it can be programmed to follow mathematical analysis, it does *not* have the 'power of anticipating any analytical relations or truths.'[22] Alan Turing, 100 years later, found the suggestion that machines could 'think' like humans do, 'too *meaningless* to deserve further discussion.' In the modern context, notwithstanding remarkable progress 'generative artificial agents' *only seemingly* produce 'content' spontaneously; they cannot originate new ideas, understand *meaning* and anticipate or respond to *unexpected dynamic changes* in the environment. Moreover, from an ethical perspective and for the survival of our species, they should *not* become a substitute for *human intelligence*.

'Artificial intelligence' is undoubtedly evolving very fast, and yet the problem of 'common sense' and *tacit knowledge* acquisition has not been solved. An 'artificial agent' does not have the ability to transmit 'complete information' and in many cases it cannot explain its actions. The 'black box' problem raises legitimate concerns in terms of risk management and governance of *high-risk* 'artificial intelligence' systems. This is partly due to the underlying training methodologies. Claude Shannon's *A Mathematical Theory of Communication*'[23] focuses on the necessity of selecting the *right* information to be sent to the recipient from the engineering perspective of *technical efficiency*; rather than on the *meaning* conveyed in the *message* and its *significance* for the recipient. Thus it excludes the *full* richness of the human form of natural language, including linguistic nuances, moral values and socio-cultural dimensions and context specificity. There are many 'semantic layers' missing from the transmission of information in binary digits or 'bits' by electronic means. Whilst 'information' is transmitted through a combination of matter and energy, there are fundamental differences between the mechanical *sequential* analysis of data and the highly complex neural activity in *human beings*. Patterns occurring instantaneously in the human brain and the human body together determine the human capacity to interpret and understand 'information' in the physical environment and the counterfactual reality we can perceive and anticipate.

The misappropriation of terms has led to the *anthropomorphisation* of 'artificial intelligence.'[24] However, *machines* are *not* intelligent or sentient in the human sense; they cannot discern human values and they *cannot* feel pleasure or pain. Automated data processing techniques are imperfect and require human interpretation and supervision.[25] While computational power and storage capacity has significantly increased, human-machine interactions are still elementary.[26] How we choose to engage and interact with new frontier technologies will prove critical in shaping the future of Society. We have a choice: we can consciously choose to create a more orderly transition oriented towards beneficial outcomes for humanity and the planet, or else we may drift perilously close to a likely unrecoverable dystopian reality, *should we fail* to take into account the *full* consequences of our actions.[27] Digital business transformations are all-encompassing, and they cannot be successfully executed if there is no implicit trust or confidence in the process.[28] Change is fundamentally a *social* undertaking; without full commitment and engagement of the various stakeholders, the requisite transformation of the Enterprise and any further investments in technology *will not* yield the expected returns.

'Nowadays people know the price of everything and the value of nothing.'[29]

Trust elevates the intrinsic value and the purpose of the Enterprise. It enables *transformation processes* to be understood and become *meaningful* for the participants. Without *collaborative* engagement of the entire workforce, digital transformation of the Enterprise would *not* be forthcoming. Trust fosters 'good' relations, enabling the Enterprise to thrive, just as *distrust* creates toxicity and erodes any potential successes. The capacity of the Enterprise to earn trust and demonstrate its authenticity will ultimately shape and determine its future. It cannot be engineered and it *must* be earned individually and collectively, as it solidifies over time. Once the trust is broken, it is often difficult to repair. The intrinsic value of *goodwill* surpasses any single transaction; it fosters lifetime advocacy among the stakeholders and most importantly, it is transmitted from one generation to the next. Owing to the ephemeral and transient nature of the so-called 'attention economy,' trust is business critical; the Enterprise must strive to render its products or services *worthy* of attention and anchor its legitimacy within the wider society. In essence, the aim of the Enterprise is to differentiate its position in the marketplace through trustworthiness. However, trust cannot be reciprocated unless it is first reliably, consistently and authentically demonstrated by the Enterprise.

'Competitiveness' is not defined by *price alone*. Rather it is defined by the *subjective perceived value* being offered to customers. While technical efficiencies afforded by robotic process automation may serve to contain operating costs, 'real' present and future *value* may be 'lost' in the process. 'Chat-bots'[30] operating on recursive loops cannot *fully* capture the subtleties and intrinsic motivations of individual customers in *real-time*, often falling short of meeting *actual* consumer needs. The exploitative use of 'artificial intelligence,' aimed at 'cutting corners,' reducing costs and substituting human beings, has led to mass data collection on an unprecedented scale and in turn fuelled a surge in *predictive analytics*. While this may be of some benefit to public and private entities, it offers little or no *direct benefit* to individual citizens,[31] whose personal sensitive data is collected by stealth, sowing the seeds of profound *distrust* in Society. Institutionalised[32] *continuous tracking* of individual citizens during the global pandemic, created a level of intrusiveness into *personal privacy* and *intimacy* global citizens had not previously experienced. Heightened public awareness of infringements to civil liberties has led to ongoing citizen disquiet; governments should take note further deterioration in public health and wellbeing is *not* sustainable. Funds spent on *undue citizen surveillance* could be directed towards provisioning the 'gaps' in urgently needed public services, *first necessities* such as healthcare, education, housing and social services. The absence or failures in these critical services impact the Enterprise and the global economy as a whole. While the ongoing erosion of *civil liberties* leaves significant *ethical questions unanswered.*

'Technology is neither good nor bad; nor is it neutral.'[33]

Socio-Technical Systems when properly designed create 'more effective interfaces with innovations across the whole of society,'[34] provided the 'public good' is clearly articulated. The Enterprise has a leadership role to play in shaping the future of Society, educating its own workforce, while providing access to quality healthcare services. The *sustainability* of *any* system requires astute investments and the coordination of efforts across the Enterprise ecosystem cross-sector. Many digital business transformations fail to meet expectations because companies fail to invest consistently in developing the requisite *dynamic human capabilities.*[35] High-density data does not guarantee the *quality of the same* or provide any certainty economic value can be extracted. It begs the question of wasted resources and raises complex ethical questions. Legacy systems if not abandoned completely may distort and disrupt the 'information flow.' Employees slowed by 'form filling' to train the 'machine learning' models initially lowers productivity. Firms in regulated industries will be subject to higher levels of scrutiny and possible sanctions should they choose to deploy non-interpretable 'machine learning' models *for high-stakes decisions.*[36] 'Black box' models with non-explainable outcomes must become a thing of the past. In particular, *human risks* should be taken into account prior to their deployment; current data practices may unwittingly lead to adverse outcomes and undue harms.[37]

Transformational Leaders are highly effective at orchestrating signifi-cant change within the Enterprise.[38] They build highly effective teams leveraging individual strengths, while supporting teams and indi-viduals to overcome their weaknesses. Excess surveillance when dis-charged by technical means is *clearly unproductive* and does not offer safety, security and a sense of belonging.[39] 'Quiet quitting' and the 'Great Resignation' seen during the pandemic are symptomatic of pre-existing conditions in the workplace, including high levels of toxicity and disengagement due to the lack of support *frequently* lamented. These maladies are often associated with inadequate processes, organisational rigidities and poor leadership, but that would be a sim-plistic analysis.[40] Socio-Technical Systems are not entirely new phe-nomena. The first attempts to design more effective 'social systems' *alongside* the 'production systems' stem from the early 1950s. Eric Trist and his colleagues at the Institute for Human Relations[41] inspired many to adopt their vision for modern organisations worldwide. In essence, productivity levels could be raised through equitable work-ing practices, fair representation of the workforce in decision-making processes and personal growth opportunities through a variety of different learning experiences.[42] In contemporary settings, Socio-Technical Systems should be conceived of as *global human communi-cation systems* to facilitate Knowledge *transfers* across the network as well as sparking new ideas and creativity. Mobile interoperability and remote working affords the Enterprise new possibilities and real-time dynamic adjustments throughout the transformation process.

We need *creative* courage to tackle the difficult problems of our time

Whilst an understanding of past *technological revolutions* can help provide context, we should keep in mind 'the future is not the con-tinuation of the past, nor is it determined by technology.'[43] We are the creators of this technology and therefore we *can* determine the *nature* of its outcomes. The Enterprise becomes an *adaptive value creator* through mastery of successive digital transformations, proactively seeking to render the existing models obsolete. Entrepreneurial leaders who *continuously* strive to reinvigorate the *creative genius* of the Enterprise *as a whole* continually outperform others and their legacy lives on. High performance, productivity and profitability stems from *differentiation through trustworthiness* upholding the highest ethical and moral standards. We grow stronger by exercising our *curiosity* and *creative courage*, continuously learning through human experiences, engaging freely in *open debate* to distil a richer sense of purpose and *deeper meaning* in our own lives. The efforts of the Enterprise can transform people's lives and make the world a better place. Above all, its efforts, talents and resources should be oriented towards turning crisis into opportunity, thereby unlocking its fullest potential to create *meaningful* value for present and future generations.

'Artificial intelligence' constitutes the most transformative change in Society thus far experienced. It is more pervasive than the transformation of matter, energy sources and the introduction of mechanised tools that enabled mass production and consumerism to emerge in the latter part of the 19th century.[44] Thus far we have not yet reaped the rewards of widespread prosperity. Information communication technology has been in existence for at least 200 years, and despite its powerful presence in the modern world, we should remember we are *not* passengers in this journey.[45]

Chapter 7

Governance
/ˈɡʌv.ən.əns/

'Great leadership isn't just effective, it's also ethical, building both value and virtue through its exercise.'[1]

Governance comes from the Greek 'kubernaein' meaning 'to steer.' Plato used the term to design a *system of rules* to govern the Republic, instilling social justice at its core.[2] It constitutes the effective and consistent practice of 'virtues' in Civil Society; and the successful application of ethical principles, fairness, equity, equality, liberty and justice being upheld by its institutions. Exemplary leadership, transparency, responsibility, accountability and the effective practice of human values guides the Enterprise towards prosperity. Envisioning the creation of value through the exercise of its virtues, the aim is to create a harmonious whole, both of the individual and Society. The Enterprise is called upon to steer its course in the *right* direction, congruent with its purpose and values. Embracing its fiduciary duties and in particular the 'duty of care' towards *all* the stakeholders, the Enterprise ensures human dignity, autonomy, agency and fundamental human rights are respected across the ecosystem. Sustainability lies at the core of its existence and underpins its strategic intent. A 'virtuous' culture of growth and innovation, social responsibility and environmental accountability fosters transparency and trustworthiness. Consistent engagement with *all* the relevant stakeholders informs the strategic priorities being pursued by the Enterprise. Good governance is an intricate balancing act to ensure the rights of the shareholders and stakeholders are valued and respected, supported by a set of policies, processes, systems and appropriate organisational structures. It entails elevating the purpose of the Enterprise as it seeks to make a valuable contribution to Society, while addressing the new risks and ethical challenges posed by the extensive use of data and emerging frontier technologies, as the 'Internet of Everything' fast approaches.

The endeavour of the Enterprise is to fulfill its promise. Fortified by a renewed sense of urgency *triggered* by recent experiences, a new Vision of the future and effective governance of the transitions is an undeniable necessity. Covid-19 highlighted the significance of individual human health and wellbeing and that of Society as a whole. Both are essential for the successful creation, distribution and delivery of enduring value. Human frailties and the susceptibility of computational systems and processes surfaced with *unexpected* force amidst *unprecedented* and *concomitant* externalities. And yet apparent solutions, including the rapid adoption of non-deterministic algorithmic technologies using 'Artificial Intelligence,' present formidable challenges and a further *existential threat* few had bargained for. At the heart of its mission, the Enterprise is engaged in the pursuit of its legitimate interests and the enhancement of democratic values, providing quality assurances to encourage the effective participation of its constituents at all times. In practice, the *effective* long-term Strategy of the Enterprise reflects *how* it will create 'prosperity' for the legal entity, its shareholders and stakeholders, while best serving the broader interests of Society and the Environment.

The Board is called upon to ensure the *principle of fairness* is upheld consistently in decision-making processes, enabling effective and timely resource allocation, whilst acting with impartiality in the event of conflict resolution. It is held accountable by and is accountable to the shareholders and relevant stakeholders, including institutional investors increasingly called upon to act as stewards, to ensure the views of diverse groups are represented and inform the rightful and meaningful direction of the Enterprise. Exemplary leadership, adaptability and responsiveness towards fast evolving situations, demonstrated both individually and collectively by the Board of Directors, strengthens Enterprise resilience, its positioning and integrity in the marketplace. Entrepreneurial risk-taking coupled with prudent controls, diligent oversight of operations and effective delegation to management, appropriately exercising its reserved powers constitutes the fulfillment of the Board's obligations and accountability to the shareholders and stakeholders according to the *rule of law*. Board composition *should not* be restricted to narrowly defined connections within the *'available known network.'* Its influence and ability to shape the future of the Enterprise, its integrity and credibility, stems from multidisciplinary knowledge domains, fostering a deeper awareness and broader understanding of the reality. The principle of *transparency* should be upheld in *all* forms of internal and external reporting, in conjunction with clear and effective communication. All endeavours should demonstrate the Board's ability and commitment to uphold human values and foster *equitable outcomes* for people and planet.

The contemporary notion of 'corporate governance'[3] was formalised by the Cadbury Report in 1992, following the financial collapse of several large corporations on both sides of the Atlantic. Extensive consultations lasting 18 months were undertaken by the British parliamentary committee led by Sir Adrian Cadbury, focusing on the financial aspects of 'the system by which companies are directed and controlled.'[4] Whilst much attention has been given to financial probity and the avoidance of fraudulent activities, the reality is that the role of the Directors is *continually* evolving. The current trend is towards a *participatory* model of corporate governance, enhancing shareholder and relevant stakeholder engagement, including employees, investors and suppliers. Good practice entails greater accountability and transparency in critical areas, entrepreneurial risk management, ethics, Human-AI risks, fraud prevention and detection, sustainability, stakeholder engagement and climate change adaptations.[5] Beyond promoting the economic viability and 'long-term sustainable success' of the organisation,[6] 'the Board should establish the company's purpose, values and strategy, ensuring there is sufficient cultural alignment across the Enterprise ecosystem. All directors must act with integrity, 'lead by example and promote the desired culture.'[7] The company's purpose and strategy should be clearly articulated, stating its intentions and *raison d'être*, ensuring its members and broader constituents have a good understanding. How the company responds to concerns raised by shareholders and stakeholders, its *sensitivity* to immediate pressures and longer-term implications is subject to public scrutiny. The requirement is that 'in order for the company to meet its responsibilities to shareholders and stakeholders, the board should ensure effective engagement with and encourage participation from these parties.'[8] This includes *how* it addresses concerns of the 'wider society' and the Environment.

The Board of Directors decides in which direction to take the company, which opportunities to pursue and new markets to enter, establishing appropriate risk tolerance thresholds. It is responsible for setting the strategy and the tone for corporate leadership, operationalized by the Chief Executive and the management team it oversees. Some key decisions are reserved for the Board, including large investments and significant structural changes, and may require shareholder approval, subject to the constitution of the corporation and compliance with relevant legislation and regulation. In principle, the fiduciary duties of the Directors are owed to the legal entity and its rightful owners, namely the shareholders and by extension its stakeholders.[9] However in practice, without *properly* engaging relevant stakeholders *material* to the realisation of the company's strategic objectives, risks and opportunities cannot be properly identified, managed and acted upon in a timely manner. Directors are responsible for the accuracy and transparency of the Statements included in Annual Reports and the financial disclosures, verified by Independent External Auditors. Reporting accuracy is supported by robust internal controls, also verified by Independent External Auditors; while the internal Audit Committee must demonstrate its financial expertise and impartiality through the appointment of Independent Non-Executive Directors, with no ties to the company other than remuneration for their services.[10] Given incidences of gross financial misconduct by Directors serving on the Boards of listed companies,[11] the Cadbury Committee recommended the 'separation of powers' between the Chair of the Board and the CEO. The Report stated these key leadership positions should not be held by the same person, advocating Independent Non-Executive Directors should both challenge and exercise 'prudent control' over financial matters and any structural changes to Board operations. Finally, Independent External Auditors should play a more active role.[12]

Corporate governance is *evolving* in the context of a 'chaotic' business environment. At the intersections of an increasingly 'complex web' of international laws, rules and regulations, core principles are widely accepted; and yet structural and systemic differences could lead to different outcomes. Transparency and accountability of the

Directors, Auditors and Stewards, namely, Institutional Investors is increasingly important to foster public trust. The *principle of fairness* is being *carefully* scrutinised in the context of Culture and the enactment of core values, treatment of employees, suppliers, communities and *how* Society and the Environment are being impacted by the Enterprise and its operations. The Cadbury Report started the process of modernisation and inspired the adoption of similar Codes in the EU, USA, India, Australia, Canada and supranational bodies like the IMF, World Bank and OECD. Subsequently, there have been a number of different changes to the international Codes, some of which stipulate further improvements in financial risk management. The regulatory intent is to promote *continuous improvement*, while restoring investor confidence and public trust.

Modern corporations, regulators, governments and Civil Society interact in an increasingly interconnected, interdependent, *complex adaptive* Global System. Balancing the interests of the Enterprise with those of shareholders and multiple stakeholders, practising 'fair and equal treatment' *across* the Enterprise ecosystem is business critical. It is proving challenging due to the *inherent opacity* of 'artificial intelligence' models and the lack of 'information' concerning the provenance of datasets and training methodologies. It is difficult to mitigate unintended biases and discriminatory practices *a priori*, coupled with the 'knock-on effects' and unintended harms generated by non-deterministic algorithmic technologies and their prolific use in government, public and private sector entities cross-sector. Large *upfront* capital investments are required to modernise existing infrastructure and legacy systems, while ongoing development and deployment of new *technical systems* driven by 'artificial intelligence' will continually absorb significant resources, often at the expense of *crucial investments* in people. With intensifying competition in global labour markets, the Enterprise needs to focus more on developing internal talent pools while accessing external talent in a more flexible manner. Developing *dynamic human capabilities* will enhance competitiveness and long-term growth prospects, enabling the Enterprise to make the best use of available technologies. In light of falling productivity levels in many advanced economies, significant improvements are required in terms of employee engagement, the *quality* of work and remuneration. In particular, the Board should pay attention to the elusive *work-life balance* and provision *equal access* to opportunities for personal growth and development, especially *new skills*. Employability is a key concern for workers, organisations and governments alike.[13]

The Enterprise is scrutinised by governments and regulators, its own constituents, including employees, customers, investors and Civil Society. Boards adopting a multistakeholder engagement model create effective *feedback loops* and obtain valuable 'information' in a timely manner; they are generally better able to ascertain risks, opportunities and potential impacts of new frontier technologies. The application of Ethics-based principles and careful evaluation of potential physical and psychological harms, namely, 'human-AI risks,' should be brought to the fore, prior to the deployment of 'artificial intelligence' systems. The allure of *technical efficiencies* and cost containment through the adoption of automated decision-making, using non-deterministic algorithmic technologies for human-specified routine or repetitive tasks is compelling. However, on the flip side of the coin are considerable human risks and serious long-term implications both for Society and the Environment. If we are to succeed in instigating 'safe and reliable use' with a high degree of acceptability in Society, then Boards should practise the *highest* ethical standards and build appropriate governance structures, specifically for 'artificial intelligence,' ensuring *dynamic* internal structures are in play to systematically 'control' and 'regulate' the use-cases for 'artificial intelligence,' *prior* to deployment. Continuous monitoring throughout the model lifecycles, from inception through to decommissioning, with the 'human-in-command' is a prerequisite of successful digital business transformations.[14]

The question of moral responsibility, transparency and accountability is *not* incompatible with commercial interests. It is a necessary constraint for the enactment of appropriate actions and decision-making, while strengthening both the identity and integrity of the Enterprise. Crucially, it enables the Enterprise to *earn public trust.* Although 'procedural regularity and transparency' may create a solid foundation for 'good' governance, digital business transformations and the impacts of Socio-Technical Systems require *specific* attention from members of the Board and Senior Management, led by the Chair of the Board and the CEO, respectively. As global citizens interact with digital services, their identities and behaviours at a given moment in time become embedded in the Socio-Technical Systems deployed by the Enterprise. Once personal data is embedded in the algorithms, it is very difficult to remove, thus companies should think carefully about specific use-cases and the need to collect, store and retain personal, sensitive and biometric data. Forthcoming regulatory and legislative changes across multiple jurisdictions, spearheaded by the EU AI ACT, Digital Services Act and Digital Markets Act, will reinforce a variety of existing legislation and regulation, including privacy, equality, anti-discrimination and employment laws. Since algorithms *know* no borders, large technology companies creating new 'artificial intelligence' capabilities will need to be compliant, irrespective of their legal domicile. Digital service providers *know* their 'products' are pervasive and can be accessed across multiple jurisdictions, whether directly or indirectly through a complex value chain, comprising multi-service third-party providers and developers of derived applications.

While the EU does not host the largest technology providers, mostly domiciled in the USA and China, it has taken a robust risk-based approach, treading a fine line between the protection of EU citizens and the risk of state over-reach. The EU requires 'high-risk' AI-systems to be effectively mitigated and all related services to be registered, having been tested in a 'regulatory sandbox' *prior* to deployment. In settings where the nature, scope, purpose and context of technology use-cases provokes 'unacceptable risks' to Society, the EU has banned its use. For example, computer vision and emotion-reading AI-systems with very few exceptions *cannot* be used for law enforcement and public surveillance, and they cannot be deployed in workplace and educational settings. Any *harmful characterisations* of EU citizens based on discriminatory factors such as gender, race, socio-economic status, religion or habits and social behaviours conducive to 'digital profiling' with *manipulative* intent are prohibited and must be remediated. The *unlawful* collection of personal, sensitive, real-time, remote or other form of biometric data collection for the purposes of 'social scoring' and other inappropriate uses whether by governments, public or private entities are 'strictly prohibited.' Failure to comply will result with the imposition of very significant sanctions, which have already impacted the largest technology companies.

The Board of Directors must demonstrate 'fair and equal treatment' of their constituents and provide quality assurances over their internal controls. Beyond any financial provisions to mitigate inherent downside risks in the context of 'artificial intelligence,' Human-AI risks must come to the fore. Health, safety and wellbeing, coupled with the protection of privacy and civil liberties at an individual and collective level, are paramount. Automated *algorithmic* decision-making *generative* 'machine learning' models deployed in non-deterministic 'high risk' Socio-Technical Systems can cause significant *personal* harms, both physical and psychological, compromise citizen safety and Enterprise security. Frequently, societal stereotypes and embedded discriminatory biases are amplified at a *systemic* level. This is genuinely difficult to control, due to the *nature* of the technology and the complexity of highly fragmented supply-chains. Robust operational safeguards must be accompanied by strict enforcement of the highest ethical standards. There must also be *continuous supervision* with the 'human-in-command' from inception of the model design, all the way through development, deployment and decommissioning. 'Artificial intelligence' systems *are likely to malfunction* without warning. Likely sanctions *post hoc* undermine business confidence and erode citizen trust, which may not be recoverable.

Boards cross-sector would be wise to consider enhancing the level of preparedness and vigilance of the Enterprise *a priori*, given the likelihood of physical and psychological harms arising from the deployment of Socio-Technical Systems driven by 'artificial intelligence.' Keeping in mind the 'basic tenets' of 'responsible AI' recently endorsed by the US 'AI Bill of Rights.' Fundamental Human Rights, human dignity, respect, fairness, autonomy and 'freedom in its various forms' must be upheld, including sustainability and environmental protection. Socio-Technical Systems using 'artificial intelligence' must have *human oversight*, taking a 'human-in-the-loop' approach with regular audits of the AI-systems in play, including 'multistakeholder feedback' encompassing diverse perspectives. AI models should be *explainable* and used transparently. Organisations deploying the technology should refrain from the use of *unexplainable* 'black box' models. Security, safety and reliability are paramount. The deployment of AI-systems should never place citizens at risk of physical and psychological harm. Systems should be developed and deployed seeking advice from diverse domain experts. Personal data and sensitive 'personally identifiable information' should be protected and potential *misuse* prohibited; while citizens should have control over *how* their data is used. Citizens should be able to easily contest unfair outcomes. This is potentially difficult to achieve since current data practices perpetuate discrimination and societal biases already embedded in widely used algorithms. Finally, adhering to the principle of 'equity and inclusion' requires 'machine learning' algorithms to be trained on diverse data sets with fair and proportionate representations of citizens impacted by automated decisions. However, there is some degree of confusion in *technical communities* as to what 'fair' actually means in practice, when 'optimising' machine inputs and outputs.

Regulators will not hesitate in the enforcement of severe financial penalties to protect citizens from potential harms. However, it is incumbent upon the creators, developers, providers and organisations deploying these *powerful* new technologies to ensure *global* citizens are kept out of harm's way. Organisations deploying these technologies will need to hold their service providers accountable and ensure the requisite operational safeguards are embedded in the products. And it is the role of Civil Society to make sure government, public and private sector use-cases are applicable and broadly acceptable among citizens. The Board of Directors in every organisation is ultimately responsible and accountable not just to its constituents, but to the wider global citizenry, including present and future generations. It has the formidable task of ensuring the future of humanity and Life on Earth will prevail; preferably working towards the eradication of poverty, famine and environmental degradation and the avoidance of potential 'AI-driven' armed conflicts, by *not* supporting military uses. This is not so easy to achieve, given the substantive sums of money spent by lobby groups, particularly in the US, to persuade members of Congress 'artificial intelligence' is perfectly 'safe and reliable' and can be easily controlled. Nothing could be further from the truth, subject to one's perspective and interests of course. A recent *simulation* in a US military training exercise involving 'artificial intelligence' failed to respond to the 'human-in-the command.' As expected prior to the 'test' the *algorithms* driving 'artificial agents' in play found ways to circumvent the 'off-switch' and continued to execute the human-specified task. It was *only a simulation*, but concerning nonetheless and it detracts attention from the potential benefits that could be sought instead from emerging AI-technologies.

Boards may consider abiding by the principles of 'bio-ethics,' to help counter 'real' *algorithmic risks*, embedded biases and discriminatory data practices, which reinforce social inequalities and injustices. *Benevolence, non-maleficence, autonomy and* justice could be embedded in AI-systems, leveraging the 'human-in-command' across *all* the teams in the Enterprise ecosystem. Boards and their constituents need to have a deeper understanding and a broader awareness of the ramifications of Human-AI risks. They do not simply pertain to the realm of 'information systems' since they influence and impact Society and the Environment, given the potential *misuses* of emerging frontier technologies. While operationalizing a *responsible innovation framework* is the prerogative of the CEO, appropriate *operational oversight* from the Board of Directors is required throughout the process. Independent non-executive directors have an important role to play, challenging any preconceptions or 'blind-spots' by adding a broader 'outside-in' perspective to assist the Enterprise in its quest towards *successful* digital transformations. When building new business models, the Board should also keep in mind cyber security risks could emerge from the most *unlikely* places. Bad actors can wreak havoc on the Enterprise using 'back door entry points.' The most effective defence stems from building a robust 'infrastructure of trust,' within the Enterprise beyond the economic model, ensuring *specific* AI-security and AI-safety governance structures are in place. The appropriate documentation both in terms of data practices and training methodologies concerning 'artificial intelligence' models should be rigorously implemented before effecting *any* changes in processes and systems. Retrofitting 'safety standards' is both a costly exercise and an arduous task, but *strictly necessary.* Finally, the avoidance of 'black box' AI-models entails aligning the principles of *model interpretability* and *explainability* to the core values and ethical principles of the Enterprise. The Board is ultimately responsible and accountable to 'steer' the Enterprise towards the *safe, reliable and stable* use of 'artificial intelligence' in Society.[15]

Companies venturing into the nascent *professional metaverse,*[16] defined as a 'virtually enhanced digital and physical reality,' or engaging with 'mixed realities' recently dubbed 'spatial computing' by Apple, may encounter resistance from stakeholders and investors alike. The imposition of significant financial sanctions and potential criminal charges for individual Board members and the legal entity in the event of misuse requires individual and collective Board members to carefully consider the *acceptability* of potential uses in the wider Society, specifically health and wellbeing concerns, *unauthorised* and *unsupervised* access to available services in the case of young children. Online safety, data privacy, data ownership, self-identity and data sovereignty are areas of growing concern in Civil Society.[17] Arguably the legal definition of 'Data Controller' and 'Data Processor' in existing Privacy laws, such as EU and UK GDPR will need to change, as the technology ecosystem is constantly evolving; but Boards should pay particular attention to third- and fourth-party providers, especially data brokers who are typically *unconcerned* with concepts such as 'lawful basis,' 'informed consent' and 'legitimate uses.' Under GDPR both the 'Data Controller' and the 'Data Processor,' which includes the organisation deploying the technology, third- and fourth-party providers bear responsibility for their actions and the direct impacts of digital services provided on the 'Data Subject(s).'

High-profile technology companies have already received sanctions for infringements of 'Data Subject Rights,' including cross-border data transfers, lack of 'informed consent,' failure to use age-appropriate language and safeguards to protect children, as the regulators move to enforce significant penalties under GDPR and more recently the EU Digital Services and Digital Markets Act.[18] Further, the EU AI Act, forthcoming US AI Bill of Rights and similar laws in other jurisdictions including China's 'Generative AI' regulations, seek to protect human rights and their citizens from the adverse effects of 'high-risk' systems. While there is convergence on the basic principles, divergence in governance structures and enforcement agencies may render inherent *downside* risks of 'artificial intelligence' systems difficult to 'police' in the absence of *multilateral cooperation* at an inter-governmental level, and preferably through the establishment of a specific 'artificial intelligence' supra-national body to coordinate efforts *globally*. New forms of collaboration and clarification of strategic intents will be required at the geo-political and geo-economic level. If members of US Congress are convinced *unbridled* development and deployment of *unsafe and unreliable* 'artificial intelligence' systems is in the economic and military interests of the USA, the 'outcomes-based approach' adopted by US legislators and policy makers will fail to deliver auspicious results in the realm of international security, safety and *global peace*. As geo-political tensions rise, 'technological warfare' is fast becoming a potential reality, not just in the commercial and economic sphere but beyond into outer space, placing everyone on planet Earth at risk of *serious harm*. Some observers have made comparisons to the proliferation of nuclear weapons and the advent of the atomic bomb; only this time the consequences could be more severe. It is not the technology per se; rather it is the 'combinatorial effect' of *multiple technologies being misused*, which endanger everyone and compromise our potential for survival in the *unlikely yet plausible worst-case scenarios*.

In the context of rising geopolitical tensions and a fast-changing world, Boards can no longer afford to have *insufficient visibility* of their *technology* supply chain. In particular, Boards should ensure they are fully aware of the provenance of third-party datasets and insist on *full traceability* and apposite documentation at every stage of data-related operations. Knowledge of *how* the new AI-technologies work is a good starting point, but it is not sufficient. Rather there should be personal experience for *effective oversight* of existing Socio-Technical Systems, coupled with a *practical understanding* of the technical limitations. Holding providers to account through contractual obligations for the Enterprise to be granted *relevant access* to datasets and training methodologies used to train third-party models is business critical. Failure to do so would weaken the Board's ability to provide transparency and quality assurances over their own internal controls, ensuring they are both effective and sufficiently robust. The erosion of trust in private and public digital services happens in a heartbeat. If in doubt countless examples of physical, psychological and other forms of 'personal injuries' can be found in publicly accessible registers, documenting *irreversible adverse consequences* that have destroyed human lives.[19]

Algorithmic technologies currently in use are not 'sufficiently informed, smart, autonomous *artificial agents* and they are *not* able to perform morally relevant actions, independently of humans who create them.'[20] At best, an algorithm may provide access to a 'safe, reliable and stable' digital service, which fosters *beneficial outcomes and compliance by design* at an individual and collective level for Society, as a whole. However, nothing can be left to chance since 'artificial agents' interacting with human users are *non-trivial*. The Enterprise cannot operate successfully as a 'zero-sum' game. Momentary triumph will be short-lived and failure could prove irreversible. Boards should be mindful of instigating 'control' *mechanisms* and related measures to ensure human-centricity, digital trust and data dignity *become* the cornerstone of the Socio-Technical Systems being deployed within the organisation. There must be a 'constant negotiation between the trustee's *willingness to trust* and the trustor's *demonstrable proof* of trustworthiness.' While the normative dimensions of trustworthiness, may be codified to offer guidance through the legal and regulatory frameworks, the rapidly changing *nature* of new AI-technologies, use-cases and applications render physical and psychological harms difficult to detect and prevent. Provisions will need to be made to render *rogue* 'artificial agents' and the *unintended consequences* of digital services immediately contestable and remediable. Not all ethical risks can be identified *a priori*, and it is helpful to consider instituting an *independent* 'standing and empowered' *multidisciplinary* AI-Ethics Committee, incorporating diverse representatives from Civil Society. The aim of the AI-Ethics Committee would be to specifically monitor, mitigate, anticipate and eventually prevent physical and psychological harms from occurring, acting in support of effective Board oversight both of the Enterprise operations and management.

The Board should seek to cultivate 'trust-based consent' across the Enterprise 'network' and offer resistance to 'zero trust' culture emergent in Society. The application of the relevant international quality standards can assist the Enterprise in building public trust, coupled with frequent Independent External Audits, to safely and securely monitor automated, algorithmic, 'artificial intelligence' systems, which may prove to have varying degrees of 'unacceptable, high, medium and low levels' of risk at different times and levels of verification and external validation. The Board should not expect to conduct a 'one-off' Independent External Audit, but rather engage proactively in doing so as often as required in a *timely* manner. The Board should instigate due diligence processes, particularly if specific AI-models are re-purposed mid-cycle or at any stage during their production lifecycle. By effectively engaging in painstaking reflective work, the Board is better able to *qualitatively* assess the risks and opportunities for the organisation, operating 'safely and reliably' within a *dynamic*, adaptive, responsible innovation framework. Taking into account diverse needs of the shareholders and stakeholders coupled with potentially disparate and disproportionate impacts of Socio-Technical Systems are *continually* evolving. The Board should strive to understand *what matters most*, with the aim of understanding, identifying and preferably isolating potentially harmful consequences, as they emerge.

Outcome fairness, equality, social equity and justice, responsibility, transparency and accountability are important governance principles underpinning the use of automated, algorithmic, 'artificial intelligence' technologies.[21] Building a shared moral framework is a condition *sine qua non* for any organisation wishing to operate 'safely and reliably,' while prioritising the avoidance of harm. Owing to the expanding scope, nature, context and purpose of newly emerging AI-capabilities, particularly 'generative artificial intelligence,' and the propagation of third-party applications built on non-proprietary 'foundation models,' efforts to effectively and efficiently mitigate 'downside risks' must increase dramatically. Under conditions of uncertainty, the level of preparedness, situational awareness of strategic priorities, knowledge of operational risks and levels of collaboration across the Enterprise 'network' cannot be overlooked. What constitutes an acceptable level of risk in one domain or context may not be appropriate for another. Instituting a *readily* accessible, deliberative dynamic form of governance enables timely participation of *multiple stakeholders*, full transparency and accountability across the value chain. 'Information equality'[22] is a necessity; everyone should receive timely information without prejudice and there should be full disclosure with respect to inherent *residual* risks. Just because a system is audited and declared to be 'trustworthy' does not mean it is *actually* trustworthy or that it will stay that way; some risks may *not* have been detected because they are not *immediately* apparent. Independent External Audits may assist detection of *unforeseen* risks, but invariably timely engagement of employees and partners across the extended value chain will help improve the effectiveness of Enterprise 'controls.'

In the context of *fast-changing* technologies and evolving real-world situations, a *participatory* model of governance is urgently needed to effectively and efficiently detect *emerging* risks. Relatively few people could have predicted Covid-19 and yet it has left behind a legacy of *cascading risks* and the prospect of further outbreaks. Risk management is no longer a function of the internal risk and compliance teams; it requires close cooperation at all levels of the Enterprise, across the ecosystem as a whole. Engagement with peers cross-sector can inform and help build possible defence mechanisms against 'bad actors' and impending cyberattacks,[23] financial and ethical risks. Global networks of interrelated, interconnected and interdependent Socio-Technical Systems have substantially increased the 'surface of attack.' A single entity cannot *fully* disentangle itself from increasingly pervasive *interoperable* systems. No matter how robust the Enterprise 'defence shield,' *residual risks* may not be *immediately* apparent. 'Black box' models used in 'high risk' domains do not satisfy the new regulatory requirements. Unobserved proxy or synthetic data generated by 'artificial agents' can prove misleading and may amplify 'hidden biases,' due to inappropriate data practices, including *indiscriminate* personal data collection from the Internet without 'informed consent,' using 'off-the-shelf' 'machine learning' models and non-specific use-cases. Thus, 'enveloping'[24] the specific use of an 'artificial intelligence' system within clearly defined parameters may help isolate identifiable residual risks. Effective *risk resilience* and relevant adaptations necessitate an understanding of the social context, and the implementation of *flexible* adaptive structures, processes and systems.

The Directors should also consider consulting with Independent Ethics Committees cross-sector to *systematically* address a broader spectrum of risks that may adversely impact the Enterprise, its constituents, the Environment and the wider Society. Shared Knowledge and experiences reduce the *moral load* and substantial R&D costs, fostering more productive growth opportunities and new innovation pathways. Effective mutual benefits can be realised through reciprocal multiparty interests. Of necessity, effective risk mitigation and adaptation efforts should include *everyone* on a global scale. 'Siloed' actions within the Enterprise are no longer sufficient or conducive to effective risk and mitigation efforts for the organisation. The scale and magnitude of emerging risks clearly surpass the capacity and capabilities of a single entity. A healthy dose of scepticism as to *where, when and how* automated decision-making algorithmic technologies should be deployed and more importantly should *not* be deployed is a necessity for the prosperity of the Enterprise as a whole. Human-centricity requires a holistic, integrated, multidimensional approach, particularly as firms are required to demonstrate 'fair and equal treatment of customers at the heart of their business model.'[25]

Corporate Governance Codes[26] have recently been updated in several jurisdictions, in response to investor demands for greater transparency and accountability in matters pertaining to sustainability, and the urgent need to restore public trust in the institutions and the regulators acting as *guarantors* of 'good' corporate citizenship. However, no matter how robust 'rules of the game' may become 'it must be recognised that no system of control can eliminate the risk of fraud without so shackling companies as to impede their ability to compete in the market place.'[27] If regulations are properly designed and executed, they may be viewed as a necessary constraint, enabling the Enterprise to innovate successfully, instigating a 'virtuous growth cycle' and a process of continuous learning and improvement. The UK chooses a principles-based approach using 'goldilocks' measures to reduce administrative burden and related costs, whilst promoting innovation. The 'rules' should not become *overly* restrictive or *too* onerous for the Enterprise, and similarly for the government, enforcement should not become *too* burdensome or *too* costly for the public purse. The focus of any pertinent changes should be on delivering beneficial outcomes for individual citizens, Society and the Environment. On balance the *entrepreneurial spirit* should be preserved to generate *meaningful* innovation. This necessitates *sufficient* freedom to navigate both risks and opportunities in international markets, as the company sees fit.

The Board's performance is increasingly under public scrutiny. Notwithstanding extraordinary pressures in the business environment, and the legacy of existing and newly emerging 'cascading risks,' involving physical, socio-economic and socio-technical disruptions, the Board is expected to discharge its fiduciary duties in the most efficacious manner possible. Its ability to provide *effective oversight* cannot be separated from the implementation of a *flexible* responsible innovation framework, in the context of building Enterprise resilience, and *dynamic* adaptive capabilities within the Enterprise. For governments there is also an urgent need to reduce emerging structural and systemic risks, to prevent 'the risk of sudden and avoidable organisation failures.'[28] Many economies have not yet recovered from the *financial crisis* of 2007–2008, and there is increasing concern for the stability of the Global Financial System. The US Federal debt has reached new highs, and 'generative artificial intelligence' systems may interfere with effective governance of the system as a whole. Meanwhile financial regulators are focused on real-time monitoring of insider trades and other forms of market manipulation, 'naming and shaming' bad actors, through public disclosure of their enforcement actions with respect to individuals and separately the legal entities.[29] Firms in the financial services sector are being asked to further improve *internal controls* and fraud detection mechanisms to prevent *systemic malfunction*. Employees are engaged in frequent 'stress tests' and 'horizon-scanning' exercises, training on new rules and ethics-based codes of practice and professional conduct. Similarly, in-scope companies must thoroughly investigate 'near-misses,' report on the same and take prompt remedial actions. Efforts should focus on identifying and isolating 'root causes' to prevent re-occurrences.[30] The role of the auditors, shareholders, accounting professionals and actuaries is also under public scrutiny since their data is being used in automated algorithmic non-deterministic decision-making processes, using unsupervised 'artificial intelligence' systems that carry far greater levels of risk.

The Corporate Governance Code in the UK has recently been changed, raising the bar to further improve the accuracy and quality of the Directors' Statements in the Annual and Quarterly Reports. The aim is to elevate the 'informative content' and restore public and investor trust. The rules apply to in-scope listed companies operating in the EU- and UK-regulated markets, though they are being extended to larger privately held or 'public interest entities' deemed to have a systemic impact.[31] Similar requirements apply in the EU. Although the principles of the 'UK Code' fall under voluntary adoption, public disclosure on *how* the principles were applied and the outcomes were achieved, whether positive or negative, is obligatory under the 'comply or explain' rule. The new regulator Audit Reporting and Governance Authority (ARGA)[32] will have 'greater powers' to enforce higher standards, including Capital Maintenance Requirements, Resilience Statement and the Audit and Assurance Policy Statement. This means Financial Services providers will need to provide justification with respect to the legality of dividend payments present and future, details of *how* the company will adapt to short-, medium- and long-term risks, and details of *how* the Directors obtain assurance on the accuracy of reporting disclosures. Directors are also required to issue a signed Statement on the effectiveness of their *internal controls* for fraud detection and prevention. The Independent External Auditor will issue a separate Statement attesting the same. Additional scrutiny of the Board of Directors is provided under 'The UK Stewardship Code,'[33] which requires institutional investors to voice their concerns if the 'needs' of their constituents are not being met. Positive or negative outcomes must be fully documented and publicly disclosed.[34]

'Corporate governance involves a set of relationships between a company's management, its board, its shareholders and other stakeholders. Corporate governance also provides the structure through which the objectives of the company are set, and the means of attaining those objectives and monitoring performance are determined.'[35]

Global corporate governance is an increasingly complex landscape. While the principles of 'good' governance are endorsed in multiple jurisdictions, there is some divergence and ambiguity due to *subjective interpretations* of statutory and regulatory requirements by individual companies. The 'British Way' allows flexibility both in the *timing* of adoption and the implementation of requirements under 'the Code' using a simple rule, 'comply or explain'[36] for the Board of Directors; and 'apply or explain' for the 'Stewards,' institutional investors, asset managers and asset owners. The EU Corporate Directives use similar principles, but there are some minor variations in the legal and regulatory frameworks of individual member states. Within the EU companies elect to have a unitary Board or a two-tier Board. In some countries, such as Germany, France, Italy and Spain, this is made possible under their respective legal frameworks. India and Singapore have adopted a similar approach to the UK, while Japan and China have a mandatory two-tier Board structure, as is the case in Germany.[37] The Supervisory Board in Germany must have an elected employee representative subject to the size of the Enterprise and sector-specific differences; while in Japan employee representation through worker councils is mandatory. The Supervisory Board is elected by the share-holders and appoints the Management Board it oversees. While in the case of unitary structure, the Board of Directors is appointed by the owners to oversee the management of the company. Many coun-tries encourage voluntary adoption of their respective 'Codes,' while in the US 'a mosaic of rules and regulations' are *mandatory require-ments*, subject to frequent changes both by Federal and individual State actors including legislators, regulators, relevant bodies and local applicable exchanges.[38]

Structural differences in governance models and the underlying legal frameworks can influence outcomes. Socio-cultural, political and historical differences in turn influence the legal and regulatory approaches, such as the practice of Common Law in the UK and Civil Law in the EU.[39] Similarly, board composition, pay incentives and other systemic variations, common business practices and accepted 'norms,' directly affect corporate governance. Thus far, existing gov-ernance structures have not *fully* resolved the *agency* problem.[40] The *balance of power* is entangled in complex relationships between the Shareholders, Board of Directors and Managers in the 'shareholder model,' for example in the UK and the USA. While the 'stakeholder model,' for example in Germany, Japan and China notwithstanding *regional* differences affords a *seemingly* more balanced approach, it has its own set of problems. Less scrupulous actors may find a way to 'game' the systems and no amount of regulation or legislation can *fully* resolve ethical and cultural concerns. An individual actor's con-duct and intrinsic motivations when choosing to 'do the right thing' or *not*, cannot be fully 'controlled.' The debate continues about the necessity to introduce more diversity and *how* more effective Board oversight could be oriented towards the long-term success of the *whole*. While the Board structure may be 'portable' from one coun-try to another, individual companies respond differently to legal and regulatory requirements. Recently introduced standard Report formats enables electronic sharing of *information* and affords investors instant *comparability* and transparency.[41] This may help to identify 'weaknesses' and enable investors to assess individual companies on their specific merits.

The legal framework in the USA lends support to a director-centric governance model[42] that is shareholder focused in practice. Directors are required to exercise their 'business judgment' and discharge their fiduciary duties in 'good faith,' in the best interests of the corporation, its owners and stakeholders. In the US, there has been a long-standing debate over whether the shareholders are the primary or 'sole' beneficiaries.[43] In 1919, Henry Ford lost his bid to reinvest earnings in the workforce, forced to pay shareholders their dividend. The Michigan Supreme Court ruled the corporation had been established for the primary interests of the stockholders.[44] Although an isolated incident, the ruling has influenced business thinking and practices ever since, later reinforced by Milton Friedman's apparent endorsement of 'shareholder capitalism.'[45] Friedman wrote in an open letter to the *New York Times* in 1970, that the responsibility of the Managers was to 'make as much money as possible, while conforming to the basic rules of society, both those embodied in law and those embodied in ethical custom.' Making money is not a bad thing, but profits do not constitute the *raison d'être* of a company. Rather they are the result of consistent and *meaningful* actions, in pursuit of the 'legitimate interests' of the Enterprise, while ensuring its *social purpose* is fulfilled. Neglecting the 'basic rules of society' is highly problematic as was demonstrated a century earlier by the Luddites who refused to accept the introduction of *mechanised* textile looms. Social injustices and inequalities *compromise* the ability of the Enterprise to realise its full value and potential, thereby curtailing ROI for the owners. Respecting local 'ethical customs,' *moral* values, human rights and creating access to lifetime opportunities strengthen social cohesion and enable the Enterprise to flourish.[46]

The question of 'shareholder primacy' casts a shadow over long-term economic prosperity and socio-cultural *stability* in the US, post-WWII and *market deregulation* in the 1980s. Despite various legislative changes, there are *perceived* tensions with respect to 'shareholder primacy' and 'worker participation' especially 'collective bargaining,' since it might undermine the Directors' ability to act in the 'best interests' of the owners. However, it is likely a false dichotomy since the interests of the shareholders and those of the stakeholders are *not* mutually exclusive. Value creation is inextricably linked with a healthy Society and provides reciprocal benefits. Helping 'the corporation build long-term sustainable growth, value for shareholders and by extension other stakeholders' is the 'fundamental objective' of the Board of Directors for the New York Stock Exchange, albeit an atypical stance in the US.[47] Nonetheless, it is the stakeholders who create value both for the Enterprise and the owners, a fact that is often overlooked in existing wealth distribution practices. The short-term focus on earnings deflects capital away from long-term investments. When taken to the extreme, the desire for 'quick profits' fuels 'reckless' speculation, resulting in market failures. Notably, the collapse of the Global Financial System in 2007–2008, fuelled by 'reckless' failures in financial oversight and governance practices. The global economy has not yet *fully* recovered.[48] Effective resistance to short-term demands is conducted by institutional investors who provide the perspective of 'long-term oriented stewardship,'[49] and in some jurisdictions by the Directors inviting employee representatives to join the Board.

The 'shareholder model' presupposes Managers act as 'agents' on behalf of the owners, supervised by the Board acting in the best interests of the company and the shareholders; the latter evaluated, rewarded or sanctioned by *market forces*. However, the 'justifiability' of short-term actions is being called into question. Specifically, the *weight* given to share prices as a reflection of the 'intrinsic value' of the Enterprise, at the expense of broader stakeholder interests. Share 'buy-backs' and other actions taken by the Board are used to stem market volatility and in effect redistribute value back to the shareholders, rather than long-term investments. Directors may 'feel' they are under pressure to deliver short-term outcomes for the shareholders, but the interests of the Enterprise and the owners might be better served if alternative actions were taken by the Board. Preferably the Board should seek to establish *synergistic* relations and pursue longer-term objectives. Short-term incentives lead to *short* CEO tenures, a lack of innovation and suboptimal outcomes; few are willing to challenge the *status quo*. Although there is no legal impediment preventing the Board from finding better ways of *balancing* stakeholder interests, the Board is appointed by the owners and in turn it appoints the CEO. Without the support of the shareholders, corporate behaviours are *unlikely* to change.[50]

In the case of the 'stakeholder model' of governance with a two-tier Board structure, the Supervisory Board provides Management oversight and does not have an active role in operations. Oversight is usually *retrospective* and its 'second main task'[51] in Germany is to offer 'future-oriented' strategic advice to the Management Board. It remains 'one step removed' and can only act on behalf of the Management Board, if it is empowered to do so. The other main *function* of Supervisory Board is to represent the company in all legal actions against Management.[52] It is effectively an independent 'controlling organ' since members of the Enterprise including the CEO cannot serve on the Supervisory Board, although employee representatives from lower-tier management levels may participate. The Management Board reports to the Supervisory Board, and in turn the Chair, appointed by the shareholders has the casting vote in the event of a tie between employee and shareholder representatives voting on reserved matters. To counter the adverse effects of abrupt changes, including job losses, Germany has instituted a 'co-deterministic' model of corporate governance, enabling workers to have a say on key investment decisions with direct representation on the Board.[53] Similarly, in the interests of economic stability, Japan also favours 'life-long employment.' Its own unique culture and history exemplify a long tradition of Board members heading advice from *worker councils* to inform their decisions.[54]

The 'shareholder model' under the unitary Board structure includes Independent non-executive Directors to separate the supervisory function from the management function. In the case of the two-tier Board structure the *separation of powers* is satisfied with both Boards operating independently of each other. The main difference is the inclusion of worker representatives duly elected by employees of the company. In the European context, there is a consolidated tradition of worker representation on company Boards, whether through consultation or direct representation accompanied by *equal* voting rights, *full* Director duties and legal obligations.[55] Worker-directors offer valuable insights as to *how* policies are *experienced* by the workforce. These companies generally outperform those who do *not* have worker representation,[56] and they more readily succeed in implementing 'smart sustainable inclusive growth strategies.' R&D activities are more effective and employment rates are generally higher. There is less risk of poverty and workers being excluded from the workforce. This may not be considered a priority if shareholders are *only* seeking short-term returns. Therein lies a potential *conflict of interest* to be resolved by the Board irrespective of its structure.

China has adopted a two-tier Board structure with 'unique Chinese characteristics.' Privately owned enterprises or partially state owned enterprises have equal access to nascent domestic and established international financial capital markets. China's long-standing industrial policy supports listed firms in sectors of strategic importance, with the clearly stated aim of creating 'national champions' that are competitive internationally, on the world stage. At the same time, China seeks to attract foreign direct investments and aims to provide assurances to foreign owners their voting rights are protected, through legal and regulatory frameworks such as 'equity joint-ventures' and 'public interest entities.'[57] In practice, dividends are distributed less frequently, as domestic tax incentives encourage firms to reinvest capital in R&D, to foster long-term growth and further improve performance. China's unique culture and history also lends a 'collective voice' to the stakeholders. China is *adapting fast* to the new demands of its economy and remains steadfast in its pursuit of long-term economic growth and social stability. It has steadily built a strong competitive advantage in key industrial sectors, including technology and state-of-the art manufacturing facilities over the past forty years.

In the absence of a *general law* for Board-level employee representation, the UK is adopting a *stakeholder* governance model in the 'British way,' under the 'comply or explain rule.'[58] Recent amendments to the 'UK Corporate Governance Code' require in-scope companies to include 'worker representation' on the Board of Directors.[59] The guidelines state 'the workforce should be able to raise any matters of concern,' and the Board is responsible for facilitating a consensus-driven approach. Upholding *democracy*, *transparency* and *fairness* within the organisation, the Board 'should ensure that workforce policies and practices are consistent with the company's values and support its long-term sustainable success.'[60] Companies choose whether to appoint a director from the workforce, a workforce advisory panel, a designated Independent Non-Executive Director or any combination thereof. If the Board chooses not to do so, it should provide a clear explanation as to why 'alternative arrangements' have been made. There is an economic rationale for the 'voice of the workers' to be heard, both to strengthen overall performance and sustainability.[61]

While some companies choose not to appoint a 'worker-director' to the Board, citing a *conflict of interest*,[62] the composition of Boards in the UK *is* evolving. The Directors' Strategic Report must specify *how* the views of the workforce were *duly* considered in decision-making processes.

There is no 'one-size-fits-all' model for Board effectiveness and worker representation. Every country has a unique approach to corporate legal frameworks, employment laws and industrial relations, and every company is unique in its interpretation of legal and regulatory requirements. However, the need to improve employee engagement is common to all countries and companies seeking to attract and retain talent in highly competitive labour markets. In Europe this ranges from proportional worker representation, seemingly complex yet democratic governance structures in France,[63] through to the more pragmatic approach in the 'UK Code,' which affords Boards flexibility both in the timing and methods of adoption. Renewed interest in Board-level worker representation has been gathering momentum since the global financial crisis of 2007–2008. In the USA, relatively few companies have implemented worker representation at Board level.[64] However, in 2019, the US Business Roundtable (181 signatories) pledged its 'commitment to deliver value to all the stakeholders,' including employees, customers, suppliers and communities. 'Each of our stakeholders is essential. We commit to deliver value to all of them, for the future success of our companies, our communities and our country.'[65]

Board performance related pay and incentive structures in the UK and the USA *typically* reward short-term financial performance, rather than substantive long-term value creation,[66] despite the economic necessity to boost productivity and long-term investments to foster stability and social progress. Mandatory disclosure of the 'CEO-workforce pay ratio' may not be sufficient to encourage a more *equitable* distribution of wealth created by the Enterprise due to *market forces*,[67] nor incentivise the pursuit of long-term investments in favour of sustainability. More recently, 'activist shareholders' and institutional investors increasingly voice their disapproval of 'overly high levels of pay' for Chief Executive Officers.[68] They are also making stronger demands for *full* disclosures on climate-related *financial* risks, particularly 'greenhouse gas' emissions.[69] Owing to a dispersed and fragmented shareholder base in the USA, 'ESG shareholder activism,' takes the form of 'proxy contests' and 'withhold campaigns,' which have intensified since the start of the global pandemic.[70] Some companies have appointed 'special committees' to look at different aspects of the 'ESG' equation, but there is a difference between stakeholder engagement and taking the necessary actions for an immediate reduction in fossil fuel consumption, avoidance of plastic use and *urgent climate adaptations*. Beyond the Directors' business judgment there appears to be little incentive to balance multistakeholder interests; US companies also have less practical experience of empowering workers.

'The corporate governance framework should recognise the rights of stakeholders established by law or through mutual agreements and encourage active co-operation between corporations and stakeholders in creating wealth, jobs, and the sustainability of financially sound enterprises.'[71]

'Financially sound enterprises' are built through the daily practice of 'ethical soundness,' typically assured by the Audit Committee. Its role is to oversee the internal and external audit function, while maintaining its independence and managing its own budget. Oversight, assessment and review of the Financial Reports, requires identification of foreseeable risks, and the provision of timely and 'informative content' to Board members and investors. It entails monitoring the effectiveness of internal controls and responsiveness of management to its recommendations. Chaired by a financial expert, it must also have at least two or three Independent Non-Executive Directors, depending on the size of the Enterprise and guarantee its impartiality. Taking a holistic view of operations, the Audit Committee ensures 'regularity, propriety and compliance' extends across *all* areas of business activity. By establishing an adequate Board Assurance Framework and an Audit Needs Assessment, it will highlight any systemic inadequacies, financial resilience issues and weaknesses in fraud prevention and detection mechanisms, anti-corruption, bribery and theft prevention procedures, including *whistleblowing protections*.[72]

Financial oversight is critical. However, in the context of 'generative artificial intelligence,' Human-AI risks and the broader societal and environmental risks come to the fore. The ethical implications and intrinsic value of the Enterprise's social purpose cannot be overlooked. S&P100 listed companies appoint Chief Sustainability Officers and Chief Diversity officers, but less frequently offer a seat at the *decision-making* table since the Board's *perception* is that of increased risks and conflicting interests. And yet these *tensions* constitute part of the *learning process*. The failure to consider diverse perspectives undermines the Board's effectiveness since it may only have a partial 'view' of the reality. Employees hold *valuable* information concerning market conditions, internal and external competiveness, including the views of customers and suppliers; they are uniquely placed to share *timely* 'information' in support of the Board's *deliberations*. Empowering employees creates new forms of collaboration and enhances the efficacy of *internal controls* by leveraging the 'social systems.' Engagement fosters a greater understanding of the circumstances and enhances the Board's *responsiveness* to legitimate concerns, as it seizes new opportunities and re-allocates resources to more productive ends. The 'rights of stakeholders' form an integral part of the Enterprise's prosperity, enhance the Board's ability to make sound financial decisions, while satisfying legal and regulatory requirements.[73] A more *proactive* form of governance fosters greater accountability and transparency.

High-quality reporting on *sustainability* is expected by Investors and subject to *mandatory* public disclosures in some jurisdictions, following the 'Task force for climate [and Nature] related financial disclosures,' guidelines, respectively, TCFD and TNFD. However, the focus on *isolated* metrics, such as reporting on scope 1,2,3 'greenhouse gas' emissions, has not been particularly successful. There is a lack of confidence in operational decisions, owing to the 'nebulosity' of performance-related pay and incentive structures for Senior Managers, proxy voting and a good deal of variance in the *quality* and 'informative content' of public disclosures. Although governance structures are still evolving, many Boards fail to take into account the complexities and interdependencies of environmental and societal concerns, beyond their own direct constituents. In the UK, ARGA's endeavour will be to enforce greater transparency, accountability and *encourage greater coordination* of efforts between the Board, the Independent External Auditor and the Stewards. 'The UK Stewardship Code'[74] requires institutional investors to 'engage constructively' with the Board in a timely manner should the interests of their 'legitimate beneficiaries' be denied. Both the Board and the Stewards must separately provide a detailed explanation of their actions through public disclosure.[75]

Board composition has long been discussed owing to its correlation with performance and effectiveness. More recently the lack of diversity has become an urgent priority for reform.[76] Female representation, 'gender-pay gap,' lack of accessibility for diverse cohorts to Board positions are still matters for debate.[77] The reasons are varied and complex, ranging from political, socio-economic, cultural and historical constraints, and the addition of algorithmic biases, social stereotypes and discrimination emerging during the automated screening and selection processes. It is not the lack of talent, qualifications or appropriate experience holding back diversity, equity and inclusion policies. Discrimination subject to various pretexts, biases and pay disparities persist worldwide, due to entrenched *habits*, *cultural* and *political issues*. Despite high levels of education, dynamic capabilities, competencies and experience, women are often overlooked for promotion. In some cases their 'reproductive rights' and the perception they bear the sole responsibility for 'caring duties' are called into question, mistakenly 'seen' as potential obstacles to high levels of performance and commitment. Conversely, male candidates are not subject to similar levels of discrimination because they have chosen to become fathers, though they may struggle to obtain parental leave. Culture *is* changing, but it is also a very slow process; discriminatory practices and social 'norms' have deep historical roots, which necessitate *sufficient* time to eradicate. Nonetheless, many companies have recognised gender parity can enhance wealth creation opportunities within the Enterprise and are working proactively to achieve a 50:50 male-female ratio, including diverse backgrounds and multiple disciplines. Diversity, equity and inclusion policies should not be consigned to public disclosures. Rather they should be *proactively* pursued particularly at Board level to enrich the Enterprise Culture through different perspectives and values. A diverse *balanced* workforce unlocks creativity and productivity; it also *enables* the Enterprise to establish closer ties with its customers.[78]

Companies in some jurisdictions are being encouraged to appoint diverse candidates in key leadership positions. The UK Corporate Governance Code sets out a new target, requiring companies to consider appointing a female Chair, Senior Independent Director, Chief Executive Officer or Chief Financial Officer. Boards are also required to create a pipeline for internal promotions, including candidates from ethnic minorities and provide training, internal sponsorship and mentoring to facilitate access to opportunities. Companies are required to disclose 'gender-pay-gaps' and potentially 'ethnicity-pay-gaps,' though this could be *perceived* as discriminatory, as well as CEO-worker pay ratio in the Financial Reports.

Although regulatory compliance is *not* mandatory, many countries have implemented *voluntary quotas* and some have clearly stated women *should* have 'full and effective participation and equal opportunities for leadership at all levels.' A recent study in India has shown female Directors outperform their male counterparts, both in terms of short-term financial performance and long-term economic value creation. Europe has made progress and improved female representation on Corporate Boards, particularly in France (43.8%) and the UK (39.1%) leapfrogging Norway, once at the top of the table. The USA lags behind with the notable exception of the State of California (32.3%).[79]

The Ukraine war has highlighted once again the need for greater transparency and accountability in the supply chain on a *global* scale. Risk management efforts internationally require greater coordination, if we are to succeed in eradicating human trafficking and other forms of modern slavery, including debt bondage, child slavery, forced labour, violence and intimidation cross-sector, especially in manufacturing and consumer goods.[80] No government, corporation, public or private entity is immune to the risk of inadvertently lending support to the most 'heinous crime' against humanity, estimated to generate USD 150 billion annually for the perpetrators and 'criminal gangs,' placing 40 million people in slavery, many of whom are women and children.[81] It is estimated 16 million *'modern slaves'* are working in the private sector. Thus, *all* businesses may be exposed to *material* and reputational risks in complex and often fragmented supply chains.[82] The USA, EU member States and the UK have enacted specific legislation to hold businesses and public entities to account.[83] Despite business imperatives to pursue lower costs and chase higher profits, increasing public scrutiny and investor pressure to 'know your supply chain,' may help bring about the necessary changes. Companies are required to disclose *how* they are managing risks, and report on *how* they will continue to address them in the future.[84] Regulators are seeking significant improvements in the *quality* of public disclosures, including Statements on compliance with the Modern Slavery Act requirements and clear 'sign-posting' on corporate websites with links to the Annual and Quarterly reports.[85] Beyond the legal and regulatory requirements, there is a moral imperative for Directors to 'do the right thing.'[86] Companies should engage in regular risk assessments, supplier audits, specific staff training and extend 'whistleblowing protections,' including 'access lines 24/7' both to their own employees *and* suppliers.[87]

'Good corporate governance helps to build an environment of trust, transparency and accountability necessary for fostering long-term investment, financial stability and business integrity, thereby support-ing stronger growth and more inclusive societies.'[88]

Good corporate governance facilitated by the Board of Directors, constitutes a *consensus-oriented* approach. It enables the Direc-tors to continually *re-balance* the Enterprise, its strategic priorities and intent, allocating resources in a timely manner to support its operations. High performance, productivity and profitability, com-petitiveness and Enterprise resilience cannot be achieved without the inclusion of broader stakeholder interests, including employees, customers, suppliers, communities and the needs of *global citizens*, whose *continued participation* in the Enterprise both sustains and creates shareholder value. The priority is to create an environment of trust, transparency and accountability, bringing people, processes and technology together, within an integrated *dynamic* responsible innovation framework. Ensuring *morally justified* uses of personal data, automation and non-deterministic algorithmic technologies embedded in Socio-Technical Systems are oriented towards benevo-lent ends. Harmonious relationships within the Enterprise and com-plementary strategic partnerships foster a 'virtuous cycle of growth,' supported by dynamic governance structures, adaptive processes and practices, taking into account fast evolving technological changes.

While there is no perfect system, corporate governance is primar-ily concerned with the Directors' fiduciary 'duty of care.' Empirical evidence has shown commercial interests pursued alongside ethi-cal principles and responsible innovation generate higher returns on sustainable long-term investments. The Board should not neglect the contextual *reasonableness* of its strategic priorities, taking into consid-eration implicit cultural sensitivities and diverse stakeholder perspec-tives, carefully considering the *timing* of their decisions. The aim is to create and preserve value for the legal entity, shareholders and stake-holders across the time horizons. The long-term strategy is guided by the *ethos* of the Enterprise, its moral character, integrity, core values and ethical principles,[89] which underpin *dynamic* governance struc-tures and stakeholder relations. The Board should facilitate clear *two-way communication*, respecting fundamental human rights and privacy.[90] Rarely are ethical choices straightforward. The Board would be wise to 'stress-test' its own strategic thinking, given emerging risks on the horizon may radically alter the Enterprise's proven trajectory.[91]

In the digital era, *disinformation* and *misinformation* disseminated at increasing velocity represent a significant material risk. The best defence is the effective pursuit of a 'just cause,' that is both engaging and meaningful to the workforce.

The Enterprise is destined to play a more pivotal role in the transformation of Society, including environmental standards. The *intrinsic motivation* of the Board and its 'moral virtues' will be tested. Its endeavours should be directed towards eradicating fear, transcending 'informational silos' and *power asymmetries* to foster less polarised, more equitable and inclusive societies. Good governance is dependent upon the responsiveness of the Enterprise, its mental preparedness and alertness as a whole. Effective risk management and climate adaptations require *dynamic* governance structures, specifically with respect to emergent 'artificial intelligence' capabilities. There is an urgent need to earn *public trust* and institute strict privacy controls, averting potentially 'catastrophic' failures. Data dignity is paramount, not just in terms of intellectual property rights, but because it alleviates undue risks and pressures on the Enterprise. An effective data strategy is business critical. Data privacy is the new competitive advantage. Trust is the new digital currency for *dynamic responsible innovation*.

Governance cannot be reduced to fiduciary duties prompted by legal compliance and risk management. It constitutes an integral part of the Enterprise as a whole. The spotlight is effectively on the Board's ability to build a sustainable digital future and its commitment towards satisfying the needs of *all* its stakeholders. Accountability by design is a moral imperative for every business, irrespective of its size, industry sector or geographic location. Corporate governance must evolve towards human-centricity and a planetary-wide focus towards environmental regeneration. Good Governance is after all the embodiment of *flexibility* in pursuit of a *higher* purpose and enduring value creation by and for everyone. *Trust, integrity, transparency and fairness* are the prerequisites of Enterprise sustainability.

Chapter 8

Sustainability
/sə.ˌsteɪ.nəˈbɪl.ə.ti/

'. . . the task is large, the window of opportunity is short and the risks are existential.'[1]

Sustainability encompasses environmental, economic, social and societal adaptation and resilience, as part of an evolutionary process of continuous change on a planetary scale. It constitutes the capacity to sustain systemic equilibria within human societies and maintain synergistic relationships with the Earth's Natural Systems with a clear objective to support ecological balance.[2] This entails the avoidance of anthropogenic activities that provoke reckless destabilisation of the Earth's Systems, whilst averting needless depletion of natural resources and biodiversity necessary to sustain Life on Earth. Sustainability must therefore be an intentional human endeavour, in order to fulfil the needs of current generations, without compromising the ability of future generations to meet their own needs.[3] This requires radical change in thinking and substantive actions to foster transformational structural and cultural change within Society as a whole, its institutions and the Enterprise itself in order to effectively mitigate risks and create new opportunities for inclusive, equitable and sustainable growth. It is no longer efficient or sufficient to set targets without fulfilling the Enterprise's moral obligations and fundamental 'duty of care' towards its constituents, global citizens, the environment and humanity as a whole. Economic growth must become synonymous with environmental protection and societal progression; it can no longer be measured against exploitative, extractive practices and myopic visions for the benefit of the few, whilst being detrimental to the present quality of life, the Environment and futures of the many.

Disequilibria created through negative change, zero-sum games and monolithic behaviours enacted by the relatively few *economic* and *political* actors create disturbances, which skew the Global System towards unhealthy outcomes. Actions taken by large public and private entities across various key sectors, including finance, energy, technology, pharmaceuticals, transportation and others that demonstrate insensitivity to climate change are incongruous with present and future human and planetary needs. 'I win and you lose' mentality has wreaked havoc at a structural and systemic level, interfering with the proper functioning of *natural* systems, *human* systems and other *managed* systems, such as health. Policy decisions taken in isolation without due regard for the Global System as a whole, merely exacerbate a highly complex and difficult problem. Moreover, global markets do not operate 'freely' contrary to the accepted societal norms. Attempts to correct systemic and structural malfunctions using defensive and offensive mechanisms to mediate supply and demand between producer and consumer, often fail to meet equitable societal and environmental outcomes. We have not yet experienced *sustainable* economic growth, widespread prosperity and human wellbeing.

The Earth's Natural Systems have sustained life on Earth for *billions of years*,[4] subject to periodic changes in the climate and adaptation of the species inhabiting the Earth to the surrounding environment. Through naturally occurring negative and positive feedback loops, competing influences have been balanced and re-balanced in a dynamic and complementary fashion, within different ecosystems, to bring the Earth System as a whole to new forms of equilibria within a continuum. To the extent anthropogenic activities have created disturbances in the Earth's Natural Systems, disregarded the intricate interdependencies among all the species, particularly since the advent of the Agricultural and Industrial Revolutions, we may hold ourselves accountable.[5] Wide-scale global changes in land use combined with fossil fuel extraction and combustion at *industrial* levels have altered the capacity of the Earth to sustain *all* life.[6] Human activities over time have contributed to climate change, manifest in global warming and rapid biodiversity loss, which has created a *chain reaction*. It has led to emergent disequilibria in the *natural* environment we do not *fully* understand and *dynamic* changes in the Climate System we may not be able to *fully* control. The *physical* changes in the environment are the most visible *signs* of climate change, experienced all over the world with increasing force, frequency and intensity. Large-scale 'singular events' are no longer rare; they occur more frequently and abruptly, causing 'immense suffering' among survivors, serious loss of life and further devastation within the Earth's biosphere,[7] the essential life source and support system for all living organisms. This has compromised human health and natural habitats for many of the species now approaching extinction.[8]

While scientists do not yet agree on the exact start date of the Anthropocene,[9] it is apparent *human activities*, including large-scale global industrial processes, intensification of modern agricultural practices, poorly controlled deforestation, conversions of wetlands and peat lands[10] have triggered an anomalous rise in the Earth's surface temperature.[11] The variability in the Earth's *average* surface temperature is such that it is no longer deemed to be 'stable.'[12] Fossil fuel combustion at an industrial global scale has caused 'excess' levels of 'greenhouse gasses,' to be released into the atmosphere at a much faster rate than can be absorbed by the Earth's 'natural sinks,' including the oceans, terrestrial soils and sedimentary rock layers. Since the *naturally* occurring ratios among the 'greenhouse gasses' have been altered by anthropogenic emissions, scientists are concerned temperatures may rise to inhospitable levels in the 'near future.'[13] Anthropogenic 'greenhouse gas' emissions include carbon dioxide, methane, nitrous oxide, fluorocarbons and other *synthetic* chemicals derived from large-scale industrial processes. When these 'additional gasses' are emitted into the atmosphere, they create *disturbances* in the Earth's 'natural circuitry,' including the carbon cycle, limiting the Earth's *natural* ability to absorb and re-emit heat. Since they linger in the atmosphere for varying amounts of time before being dissolved, they create the so-called 'greenhouse effect,' contributing to 'global warming' and climate change. While the timing, duration and scale of likely climatic changes are less clear, anthropogenic emissions *past, present and future* are *known* to play a part in 'radiative forcing.' Atmospheric imbalances and the duration of different 'greenhouse gasses' determine changes in weather patterns, precipitation levels and create disturbances in the hydrological cycle, all of which *destabilises* the Climate System as a whole. Whilst multiple factors contribute to climate change, scientists are most concerned with 'human-caused' sources of atmospheric 'greenhouse gasses,' and in particular *cumulative levels* of carbon dioxide[14] concentration and methane[15] are the most insidious and damaging to *human health*.

The United Nations established median rise in temperature above 2°C and CO_2 atmospheric concentration of 450 parts per million (ppm) would place human populations at risk. The Paris Agreement in 2015, otherwise known as COP21, established a more ambitious target of 1.5°C, and certainly that was still the 'ambition' at COP26 in Glasgow in 2021. However, the Global Mean Surface Temperature (GMST) has risen to 1.1°C[16] above pre-industrial levels[17] and is projected to rise to 2.4°–2.8°C by the end of the century.[18] This assessment is based on the *national pledges* to curb carbon emissions.[19] While the rising global temperature is of concern in the scientific community, historically remedial action has proven to be a lesser priority in the political arena. Firstly, it is difficult to quantify 'serious disturbances,' caused by anthropogenic activities, in the *natural* gaseous exchanges occurring in the atmosphere necessary to sustain Life on Earth. High concentrations of carbon dioxide and other '*greenhouse gasses*,' including water vapour, 'trap' heat on the Earth's surface, causing the temperature to rise. However, they are 'invisible' to the naked eye and it is possible to 'deny' their existence in the political arena. It is far easier to offer citizens *unsubstantiated* justifications and assurances from *interested* parties that humanity is living within an arbitrarily defined 'safety zone.' No matter how misguided the underlying assumptions and inaccurate the information provided by influential lobby groups may prove to be.[20] Secondly, it is difficult to quantify the impacts of climate change in financial terms alone, and the impact of eventual policy decisions that may be taken and potentially implemented. There may be insufficient incentive in some arenas to pursue *climate resilient policies* and actions in the short-term simply because there is a delayed response from the Earth's Natural Systems.[21] Consequently, *inadequate* policy decisions and actions[22] may be taken to effect 'transition pathways,' which are necessary in the interim, but insufficient to *counterbalance* the worst effects of climate change.

While unpredictable and unevenly distributed, *extreme weather* events[23] impact every sector and every nation, business and household whether *directly* or *indirectly*. There is increasing concern continuing rises in Global Mean Surface Temperature and *disturbances* caused by human-induced carbon emissions in the Climate System, will continue to exacerbate climate-related risks across the globe for the foreseeable future. The increasing intensity, duration and frequency of protracted heat waves, heavy floods, wildfires, severe storms such as hurricanes, cyclones and typhoons and extreme precipitation combined with *irreversible* biodiversity loss in some cases, is no longer confined to specific geographic regions. Each 'climate event' has the potential to *radically* alter the landscape and destroy livelihoods, with far-reaching consequences. Human populations and other species are likely to be displaced in increasingly large numbers in search of food and shelter. Recent migration flows have already exacerbated pressures on natural habitats and increased *vulnerabilities* of natural ecosystems and human systems. While 'natural disasters' such as earthquakes and volcano eruptions may be unavoidable, we should endeavour to take *preventative* measures to avert the '*worst consequences*' of climate change.

Climate Risk Assessments have shown *concatenated events* resulting from climate change pose a serious threat to *national* and *international* security.[24] For example, in the 2010s severe flooding in India and Pakistan and concurrent extreme temperatures in Russia led to populations being displaced and stoked armed conflicts in surrounding areas.[25] While food, water and energy distress may disproportionately affect local populations, as recent events and supply-chain disruptions have shown, they also reverberate around the world. Rising food and energy *prices* affect everyone, due to the interconnectedness of our Global Economy. Inflationary pressures add further impetus to rising geopolitical tensions, compounded by extreme temperatures and extreme weather events experienced locally and regionally, while impacting populations from an economic and political perspective on a global scale. Supply-chain disruptions are invariably a serious concern for every business and there is also an ethical dimension, which must be addressed in terms of supporting those affected by climatic disasters, respecting their fundamental human rights in the interests of business continuity.[26] Waiting for a 'shock' to happen is not only reckless from an economic and political perspective, it is also ethically irresponsible, and *morally* indefensible.

Sustainability cannot be measured *simply* in terms of Gross Domestic Product, whether in terms of monetary value (income) or output volume. Quantitative metrics do not *fully* account for the substantive *qualitative changes* in the Environment and ecological changes occurring in *natural* ecosystems, biodiversity and Society. Whilst it is difficult to predict population growth and socio-economic development variability, it is critical to gain a better understanding of the use of 'natural capital' in the context of present and future climate change. Das Gupta acknowledges more work needs to be done to include the 'modelling of ecosystems and embedding the human economy in the biosphere,' given 'the evidence is misleading when the model on which it is gathered is spurious.'[27] When 'natural capital' is not part of the analysis, there is insufficient awareness and understanding among policy makers of the ecological implications for current and future economic growth prospects in relation to climate change. Systemic complexities have thus far been assessed in terms of financial risks for the most part and there is remarkably little evidence of the thinking extending beyond financial stability within the Global Economy, as a whole. However, the *interplay* between human and natural systems is highly complex and while it may be difficult to model, *cumulative policy decisions*, socio-economic and political choices have given rise to 'cascading risks,' that overlap and intensify societal and environmental impacts, as climate change gathers *increasing* momentum. The *enduring* nature of climate-related risks and the complex set of climate-related *uncertainties* have far-reaching implications for *global governance*, strategy, risk management and capital allocation within the Enterprise and there are consequences on *multiple* levels across Society, as a whole.

Global Sustainable Development is inextricably linked with Climate Change, which necessitates a holistic 'view' and much deeper understanding of the reality, taking into account the multidimensional complexities of the 'real' physical challenges we now face. The failure to implement appropriate policies and further delay 'climate actions' is no longer an option. Mitigation efforts to reduce 'greenhouse gas' emissions and build the requisite infrastructure coupled with appropriate adaptation measures are a necessary course of action to be pursued at the *global strategic* level. Enterprise Leaders and policy makers alike need to take an *integrated* systemic approach to Climate Change, taking into account their actions impact others and decisions cannot be taken in isolation. In the context of the

Enterprise, coordinated actions across the value chain and effective engagement with strategic partners can lead to new forms of collaboration cross-sector. Engaging public and private sector entities, as well as academia, can result in more *meaningful* R&D and more appropriate solutions both for mitigation and adaptation efforts. Notwithstanding relative 'climate uncertainty' and *seemingly* uneven distribution of vulnerabilities to Climate Change, the increased exposure to climate-related 'hazards' is undoubtedly a *universal phenomenon*. Specific vulnerabilities may appear to be localised, subject to changing socio-economic conditions, but they also have a 'knock-on effect' within the Global System. Exposure to climate-related 'hazards' is set to increase due to *global warming* and Climate Change *everywhere*. As demonstrated by SARS Coronavirus-9 (Covid-19) and the persistence of armed conflicts, requisite levels of preparedness and alertness within the Enterprise are a necessity. Consciously building an *adaptive capacity* to withstand externalities is a strategic priority to safeguard human health and wellbeing, while averting further environmental degradation. This also presents an incredible opportunity for *sustainable* growth and *responsible* innovation, using newly emerging frontier technologies to beneficial ends. Socio-economic and socio-political resilience can help humanity *bounce back* from adversity on a global scale; and yet international cooperation is at best fragmented.

Scientists have long cautioned – 'the scientific evidence is unequivocal: climate change is a threat to human wellbeing and the health of the planet. Any further delay in concerted global action will miss a brief and rapidly closing window to a secure and liveable life.'[28] We urgently need to keep this 'window of opportunity' wide open in order to take appropriate actions in a timely manner and make 'good' ethical choices; rather than accept arbitrary trade-offs, which may lead to further conflicts and otherwise deny global citizens and local communities directly affected by events, their human dignity and fundamental human rights. Climate Change ought to be an *inflection point*, where humanity as a whole turns towards securing global peace, so that we can focus our attention, energy and resources on improving the *quality of life* for everyone. Restoring biodiversity, natural habitats and ecosystems, while preventing further extinctions. The survival of all living organisms is a condition *sine qua non* for the survival of our species, both from a biological and an evolutionary perspective.

Following the 'historic' Paris Agreement in 2015,[29] the United Nations issued 17 Sustainable Development Goals on 1 January 2016, encompassing 169 targets with the noble aim to 'mobilise efforts to end all forms of poverty, fight inequalities and tackle Climate Change, while ensuring no-one is left behind.'[30] Signatories from 190 nations agreed for the first time that a *drastic reduction* in *anthropogenic* 'greenhouse gas' emissions harmful to human health and the environment could no longer be postponed. The 'historic pact' was ratified in 2020, setting the expectation 'Nationally Determined contributions' (NDCs) to mitigate emissions, while undertaken on a *voluntary* basis would be revised upwards each year and foster closer *multilateral* cooperation. High-income nations also pledged 100 billion USD per annum, as a 'floor' to help developing nations transition towards a 'green economy,' leap-frogging the 'polluting phase' of socio-economic development. Working collectively towards sustainable economic growth in the interests of people and planet *is* beneficial, since *natural* and *human* systems are deeply intertwined. Arguably, they cannot be separated since they have *co-evolved* over millennia.

Notwithstanding the economic benefits of globalisation and acceleration of international trade, outsourcing responsibilities and accountabilities with regards to the reduction of emissions is no longer an option. Socio-ecological systems adapt dynamically to *actual* climate change as it occurs. Therefore we should be far more willing to *accelerate* mitigation efforts to reduce 'greenhouse gas' emissions and undertake the necessary *adaptations* to foster *dynamic societal transformations*. This includes accelerating investments in *new* infrastructure, institutional reforms and the pursuit of *multilateral* interdisciplinary research. There is an opportunity to create *new* forms of collaboration to facilitate space exploration, so we can better understand our position within the solar system. Through observation and new scientific discovery, we can leverage new technologies, such as 'artificial intelligence,' to help us find better solutions, meeting our human needs and safeguarding the Earth's Systems. We need to 'connect the dots' and better understand the complexities of our human systems, clearly identifying the links between ecological changes and socio-economic development.

With a clearer 'view' of the reality and new Knowledge, we can change course and create *anticipatory systems* on a global scale. The incentive to do so is fostered by the increasing interdependencies within the Global Economy and interconnectedness of extraordinary *physical environmental risks* and related *human health risks.* Extreme weather events do *not* make allowances for the apparent inertia within our human systems. Anachronistic *myopic* worldviews and historic failures afford no justification in further delaying the necessary adaptations both to withstand Climate Change and make the necessary improvements in our daily lives. We can no longer disregard the scientific evidence, *lived and living experiences,* which clearly attest to the urgency of adapting to our changing Environment. Despite recent setbacks, there is still a window of opportunity to *limit* the rise in median *terrestrial* and *oceanic* surface temperatures. We can intervene to *reverse* environmental degradation; working towards regenerating natural habitats, restoring 'natural cycles' and diverse equilibria within natural ecosystems, through the preservation and conservation of biodiversity wherever possible. In so doing, we can create new opportunities for inclusive, equitable, sustainable *global* economic growth. Although this aim has proved elusive thus far, attitudes are changing; there is a far stronger *cultural awareness* in Society, as a whole. This may create the necessary momentum to instigate institutional and social reforms born of economic necessity, geopolitical and geo-strategic pressures, currently being experienced by *every* nation-state. The health and wellbeing of global populations is a common cause and a *growing concern,* particularly in the event of disease. As we saw during Covid-19, *no-one is safe, until everyone is safe.*

Companies that recognise the value of 'natural capital' and its fundamental importance to their business activities are ahead of the curve. Their ability to successfully factor in both risk and uncertainty in relation to climate change stems from their framing of this epochal challenge for humanity. There may be setbacks due to unforeseen events, but their direction of travel is clear, recognising the intrinsic value and importance of natural and human capital in their endeavours. Danone, a French food manufacturer, became the first listed company in 2020 to adopt the new constitutional legal framework, 'entreprise à mission.' Danone's strategy is to create beneficial social, societal and environmental outcomes, through effective multistakeholder engagement and long-term investments. Coordinating efforts across its value chain, preferably working with a multitude of local small-scale farmers, its endeavour is take a holistic approach towards inclusive, equitable and sustainable economic value and growth. At the same time, Danone is investing in educating consumers with respect to the *nutritional value* of food, promoting human health and wellbeing within planetary boundaries. With the support of its ecosystem partners, Danone is working towards specific science based initiatives, ranging from rebalancing naturally occurring soil nutrients and more efficient use of water in agriculture, to the reduction of greenhouse gas emissions across the supply chain, including transportation and packaging. The overarching aim of their endeavours is to reduce pollution, eliminate the use of non-biodegradable plastics, help clean contaminated soils and thereby improve air quality, promoting human wellbeing across the globe.[31]

Patagonia, a US clothing maker, is also an example of pioneering thought leadership in the field of Enterprise-level sustainability. It has since inception as a B-corporation[32] used its *best efforts* to limit environmental damage in pursuit of sustainable business development; subject to the availability of *natural* and improved *recyclable synthetic* materials it has acted responsibly in the sourcing, use and management of the same, avoiding the production of *new waste* as much as possible.[33] Patagonia's well-established practices entailing 'complete lifecycle management' of products *pre-use* and *post-use,* including raw materials, consumer goods and services needs to become 'mainstream' at the earliest opportunity. This entails re-imagining the supply chain, including responsible use and deployment of *new* technologies, likely to become a significant source of *new emissions* longer term, as things stand.[34] Thus, there is considerable room for improvement, which can be achieved by exploring *appropriate uses* for new technologies, while moving away from known pollutants in manufacturing processes, specifically the use of toxic chemicals. This is an urgent necessity in order to safeguard both the surface and deeper water layers of the Earth, preferably accelerating transitions towards reliable 'clean' energy sources and 'clean' production methodologies.

While fashion is considered to be a significant polluter of the environment, many companies have responded positively to the magnitude of the task at hand. François-Henri Pinault, the CEO of Kering, French owner of prestigious Luxury brands, pioneered Environmental Accounting within the sector.[35] In 2019, French President Emmanuel Macron invited Kering to attend the G7 meeting to outline a possible roadmap for 'sectoral transformation,' taking into account the three main challenges facing *every business* wishing to pursue sustainability and a *healthy* long-term future – climate change, protection of biodiversity and the health of the oceans. The 'Fashion Pact'[36] was established in 2019, to encourage collaboration and transparency across the value chain, adopting an integrated approach towards improving land use and resource management, instigating 'nature-based solutions' and a significant reduction in the dependence on fossil fuels within the Luxury industry. Targeted science-based initiatives relevant to the industry range from the protection of 'ancient and irreplaceable forests' and wildlife protection to the restoration of natural soil nutrients and pollinator communities, whilst avoiding the use of harmful chemicals. They also include efforts to accelerate *reforestation* and encourage responsible well-managed use of raw materials derived from *sustainable forestation* and the conservation of *oceanic ecosystems*, rivers and wetlands.

Fashion relies heavily on agriculture and natural ecosystems to source its raw materials and has recently ramped up its conservation efforts. Nature is a key component of its ecosystem, serving as a source of inspiration for the creators, while providing the basis for production and economic benefit. For example, cotton is grown specifically for clothing and accounts for 21% wastewater, 24% insecticides and 11% of the pesticides being used, whilst covering only 3% of arable land.[37] Burberry recently intervened at farm level, piloting soil carbon capture technology to rebalance *natural* soil nutrients and moisture levels, while building more efficient water management systems to reduce levels of dry land salinity and support biodiversity in their natural habitats. Cellulose fibres such as rayon, viscose, modal and Lyocell widely used in fashion are derived from wood pulp, accounting for 150 million trees being logged each year.[38] The Fashion Pact has significant leverage and benefits all members, orchestrating reforestation initiatives while facilitating access to sustainable forestation. As membership grows, so too, its ability to exert pressure and 'collective bargaining power' is strengthened across the value chain. Whether to force a reduction in greenhouse emissions, avoid fossil fuels in transportation, instigate further improvements in the processing of raw materials and accelerate the electrification of energy grid systems.[39]

As in every industry, there is always further room for improvement, business model innovation and more responsible use of raw materials, including the elimination of harmful chemicals and *unnecessary* plastics.[40] However, fashion and the Luxury industry in particular has deliberately embraced Nature conservation and Sustainability, as powerful levers for economic benefit, long-term value creation, while promoting inclusive and equitable growth, including indigenous people whose Knowledge of Nature and supreme craftsmanship continually inspires creators of fashion across the world. At present the trend is towards creating a 'circular ecosystem' to promote *full* lifecycle management of every component at each stage of the production cycle. Many companies have a longstanding ambition to eradicate the use of harmful plastics and they are continually searching for new ways to dispose of existing products, other than through landfill and incineration. Companies like Adidas are also using recycled *marine plastics* in the manufacture of their shoes. Burberry, Moncler, H&M, among others have eliminated the use plastic bags, including laminates from swing tags, while switching to alternative biodegradable materials and 100% recycled *reusable plastics* for transit hangers and polybags to protect clothing.[41] The Fashion Pact had engaged in a number of collaborations cross-sector, proactively seeking to reduce its use of 'problematic and unnecessary' plastics in different settings, whether business-to-customer (B2C) and business-to-business (B2B) by 2030. It is also investing in *consumer education*, for example, by providing 'end of [product] life instructions.' Pioneering initiatives to restore natural habitat loss and biodiversity, in particular, constitute a *critical area* for urgent *sustainable* actions within consumer goods industries and beyond.

Circularity cross-sector is a *necessary* transition cross-sector, whereby the 'value of products, materials and resources is maintained in the economy for as long as possible and the generation of waste is minimised.'[42] Whether the principle of circularity will sufficiently curb 'greenhouse gas' emissions to reverse rising temperatures remains to be seen. For example, it is estimated 95% of the value in existing plastics is lost to the economy after one single use, amounting to USD 80–120 billion annually, making a strong business case for improving collection and recycling infrastructure. It also begs the question whether a *greater ambition* to eliminate plastics altogether might not be *more* productive. Waste products from fossil fuel production are the base materials for plastics and *additional* carbon emissions are generated as a result of *recycling* production methodologies with ensuing damage to the *quality* of the environment and degradation of *natural* ecosystems. Prior to the 1930s there were *no synthetic plastics* in production and *polyethylene* was not produced on an industrial scale until the mid-1970s. Single-use plastic bags of which 5 trillion are produced annually, together with PET bottles, used for carbonated drinks and other food products of which 500 billion are produced every year, are the worst culprits.[43] Plastics were not used in fashion until nylon became widely available in the 1950s and Lycra by DuPont was introduced in textiles in the mid-1970s. Arguably, we already have *sufficient* plastic in circulation to warrant an immediate end to new plastics being produced.[44] Of the 7 billion tons of plastics produced annually, less than 10% is recycled.[45]

The critical issue of plastics pollution lies with decomposition, which may take thousands and tens of thousands of years to decompose and may never *fully* do so. Most plastics have useful properties, but they are also resistant to natural decomposition and have now entered the fossil records. Consequently, microplastics entering the oceans cause acidification of the waters, destroying essential natural ecosystems such as the coral reefs, as well as entering the fish we eat. Plastic waste also contaminates the soils upon which we depend through landfill. Whether by absorption through the food system (e.g. plants grown in contaminated soils), inhalation through the air we breathe or the clothing we wear, microplastic particles enter the human body and accumulate in our vital organs, including our lungs, livers, kidney and spleen. While the full extent of the damage to human health is not yet known, there is an urgent need to re-think production, the continued use and consumption of plastics, particularly as microplastics have been found in the placentas of newborn babies.[46] Plastics associated with *fire retardancy* treatments in upholstered household goods and crucially anthropogenic sources of *methyl mercury* due to fossil fuel combustion, primarily from coal production are *poisonous*.[47] Absorbed into the food system through soil contamination and 'acid rain,' they enter the human body and are linked to *serious human illnesses*. Outsourcing waste management to countries not equipped to manage plastic waste *safely* is economically *unjustifiable* in terms of Climate Change and ethically it is highly irresponsible. Landfills and uncontrolled dumping practices *anywhere* in the world lead to environmental degradation in vital life-sustaining marine and terrestrial natural ecosystems, causing dangerous levels of toxicity in the Earth's soils and air pollution *everywhere*.

Waste management at a structural and systemic level needs to be re-imagined as a matter of urgency. The focus should be on restoring biodiversity and habitat conservation to reduce overall environmental degradation, while forcibly curbing carbon emissions and dependency on fossil fuels. As with the example of plastics waste, the interconnectedness of various sector-specific *activities* requires 'joint actions' cross-sector, public-private partnerships and new forms of collaboration on multiple levels. Incentives are needed to encourage long-term investments to foster appropriate waste disposal management, while scaling efforts to collect existing plastics, thereby avoiding harmful landfills and incineration wherever possible. Industrial strategy needs to align with further improvements in land use management and stricter environmental standards need to be adhered to across the value chain at every stage of the production cycles. At the government level, clear signals must be provided to enable the Enterprise to commit to long-term investments. Subsidies should be moved away from fossil fuels and fossil-fuel intensive production cross-sector, including *harmful* agricultural and land-use practices. Efforts should be redirected instead towards low-carbon production methodologies and technological innovation coupled with earlier-than-foreseen 'safe' dismantling of obsolete and obsolescent production facilities.[48] The environmental impact would be greatly reduced and short-term financial costs associated with 'stranded assets' would be diluted in the mid- to long-term, with potential immediate short-term benefits to spur new growth and innovation cycles following market approval. Overall, concomitant multi-sector *transitions* would foster *new* economic growth and employment opportunities for *multiple* parties, whilst averting serious 'health hazards' for global citizens.

Climate change is highly complex and evolves in a non-linear fashion over long periods of time, better suited to assessments on geological timescales rather than human lifetimes. It is undoubtedly one of the 'biggest challenges' we face in the modern world. Seemingly unpredictable *physical* events and highly variable climatic conditions are unevenly distributed across the world and disproportionately impact developing nations in the Global South, while exacerbating global inequalities and socio-economic hardships in many local communities. However, physical climate events and weather patterns are changing and also occur with increasing frequency and intensity in the Global North. Extreme weather events such as flooding, heat waves, droughts, wildfires and tropical storms are symptomatic of multiple concomitant destabilising factors, not least the atmospheric imbalances in 'greenhouse gasses,' especially high levels of carbon dioxide and industrially produced methane, which have accumulated over time. The devastating effects of Climate Change encompass every continent, irrespective of geographical location, resulting in direct 'physical' impacts and indirect 'systemic effects.' Not just in terms of the immediate loss of human lives and waste of natural resources, but also in terms of the far-reaching global consequences for present and future generations. Global warming also adversely affects biodiversity due to natural habitats being lost and some species facing extinction. This amounts to significant losses, both in terms of future economic value and the immediate financial costs, as the sea surface and deeper ocean temperature rises. The Earth's oceans constitute one of the most critical 'natural sinks,' absorbing 90% atmospheric carbon, while releasing oxygen through phytoplankton that also provide seafood based proteins for 12% of the world's population. If the average surface temperature rise exceeds 2°C, it is estimated 99% coral reefs and 90% large fish would be lost.[49] Moreover, as the temperature rises, ice-sheets in the Arctic, Antarctic and Greenland continue to shrink in size, causing sea levels to rise. While the expected 1.1 metre rise in sea level by the end of the 21st century may not seem significant, it would cause *extensive damage* to coastal cities and low-lying areas on a global scale.

Biodiversity is often undervalued and yet it is highly significant since it influences the Earth's climate and regulates naturally occurring organic nutrients in the soil. It also helps maintain the natural balance of the Earth's hydrological cycle, which in turn affects atmospheric temperature and radiation balance.[50] Solar energy and the 'heat exchange' would remain in 'radiative equilibrium' and maintain a steady state in the Earth's atmospheric temperature, if there were no *disturbances* in the *natural* 'carbon stocks' and 'flows' within the Earth's System as a whole.[51] Persistent degradation of the Earth's soils, through extensive wide-scale use of agrochemicals, such as artificial fertilisers and pesticides in modern intensive agricultural practices, drastically alters the balance of *natural nutrients* in the soils and reduces the availability of organic matter required to support *healthy soils*.[52] The use of 'toxic' chemicals is highly significant because *lesser quantities* of natural nutrients in soils limit the ability of the land to absorb heat and remove carbon dioxide from the atmosphere through plant photosynthesis, thereby reducing the Earth's capacity to *store water in the soils*. This in turn lowers crop yields and worsens the adverse effects of prolonged droughts. Recent scientific studies show the soil is now a *net emitter* of carbon dioxide as opposed to being one of the most important 'natural sinks,' together with the Earth's rivers, seas and oceans. There is a *real* risk there may be food shortages relative to expected demand and avoidable 'water distress' caused by Climate Change that will impact 1.8 billion people by 2025. There is an urgent need to re-imagine land use changes, especially existing urbanisation policies and construction practices, as well as improving techniques used in modern agriculture, seeking to utilise 'nature-based solutions' wherever possible. The aim cross-sector *should* be to work *with* Nature to restore its vast inherent capacity for carbon capture and rebalance *natural* soil nutrients, while reducing or eliminating the need for artificial fertilisers and pesticides. Not only are these measures counterproductive for Climate Change, altering soil nutrients and the atmospheric balance of naturally occurring greenhouse gasses, they also adversely affect biodiversity, human health and wellbeing.

The interactions among the Earth's *Natural* Systems, human and managed systems are clearly *out of sync.*[53] The *dynamic* transmission of Climate Change through environmental disturbances and the associated volatility of prices in international markets destabilise the Global System, as a whole. And yet there has been remarkably little adaptation on the part of governments and the approach taken thus far, in response to emerging challenges, as climate change becomes more 'widespread, rapid and intensifies.'[54] Effective risk management to mitigate the 'worst consequences' of climate change requires strong political will and a commitment towards *collaboration* on behalf of *all* parties. Existing vulnerabilities may change over time and there may be variances across different regions; but the level of overall risk and exposure to the *potential harms* of Climate Change is set to increase exponentially, if no further action is taken. Monitoring and evaluating events *post hoc* is necessary but no longer sufficient. Governments, the Enterprise, Civil Society and all global citizens need to collaborate and proactively embrace this window of opportunity, we still have to implement preventative measures. This entails a *radical change* in thinking and human behaviours, coupled with significant changes in methodologies used for production and patterns of consumption on a *global scale*.

At the Enterprise level environmental, climate, biodiversity, human risks and other Nature-related risks need to become embedded in corporate strategy, risk management and related governance structures, ensuring effective controls and *quality assurance* practices are in place across the 'value network.' While internalising these externalities may seem daunting at first, there is a strong business case for building *climate and biodiversity resilience* into operational frameworks, since environmental and ecological risks primarily impact the Enterprise through the supply chain. For example, water scarcity, soil nutrient imbalances and extreme temperatures may limit the availability or quality of raw materials. The Enterprise may incur additional liabilities and higher insurance premiums owing to production delays, as affected parties seek compensation. Land use restrictions may apply for certain activities and business permits may be withheld for periods of time to foster natural habitat restoration and conservation. Increasingly, pressure from shareholders, investors, employees, customers, local communities and the wider Society may lead to products being repudiated, causing reputational damage, if firms are not perceived to be *trustworthy* in the management of environmental, social and societal concerns. Fast-changing consumer preferences further increase *market risks* as growing awareness of climate change and biodiversity enters people's daily lives. The focus of the Enterprise on biodiversity is *justified financially*, since the economic benefits of biodiversity conservation far outweigh the costs. They afford the Enterprise new opportunities for value creation, economic growth and strengthen business resilience. There are various guidelines in play, to enable the Enterprise to create harmonised strategic frameworks and enhance its own understanding of biodiversity, both the impacts of its operations and related natural ecosystem interdependencies. Social, societal and environmental risks should be taken into account at all levels of the Enterprise, particularly as new regulatory requirements will increase the levels of financial risk exposure.[55] As Nature and ecological risks become increasingly intertwined with better 'known' financial risks, the Enterprise must learn to navigate the impending complications of Climate Change. Unless biodiversity and climate change are addressed at a political, strategic and at a practical level, as a *material risk* and ongoing concern for the Enterprise and Investors alike, obsolescent production methodologies and aging infrastructure may preclude new investments and significant growth opportunities will be missed.

Whilst Climate Change is not the only dimension to consider when evaluating sustainability, the inescapable nature of global warming and resulting biodiversity loss combined with 'extreme weather events' pose a 'serious threat' to food and water security. Nonclimatic factors such as present and future land use, land degradation, urbanisation and pollution play a significant role in determining outcomes. Socio-economic development is critical to 'national and global security, poverty eradication and economic prosperity.'[56] For every action taken or inaction, there is an implicit and in some cases explicit *value judgment* that is being made. Since *critical tolerance thresholds*[57] of the Earth's System were surpassed in the 20th century, we can no longer deny the *immediate necessity* and *real urgency* of responding to the *physical* effects of climate change, taking into account the urgency of *climate adaptations* needed to address universally accepted fundamental human rights, provisioning access to clean water, food, shelter and education. We need to break the 'vicious cycle' of human suffering, which is *wasting* unique opportunities for economic growth and our precious *natural* resources. Poverty, famine, social inequalities, social injustices, the lack of education and employment opportunities, *unfair* remuneration practices coupled with environmental degradation undermine *human resilience* and tear apart local communities around the world. We cannot continue treating the symptoms of climate change *post hoc* and *urgently* need to work towards an enhanced understanding of *structural and systemic changes*, *illuminating* the interconnectedness of social, technological and economic causations, in order to create more orderly sector *transitions* and *transformations* at a societal level on a *global scale*. Scientists insist that 'to avoid severe and persistent impacts from long-term climate change, there is a need for policies that lead to a *complete decarbonisation* of the world's energy systems.'[58]

The scale and magnitude of the Climate Change problem has been exacerbated due to prolonged *inaction* on the part of *multiple* parties. National governments, supranational bodies, powerful financial and industrial lobbies have resisted consistent warnings from the scientific community for several decades. The costs of *inaction* are also 'known' to be an order of magnitude greater than qualified and timely interventions to effect the necessary transitions and apposite 'climate actions.' Decades of persistent *misinformation* and *disinformation* promoted by large industrial entities in the energy sector, primarily 'big oil' companies with *vested interests* have thwarted local and regional attempts to contain the 'worst consequences' of Climate Change. Recently, we have entered into a more dangerous phase, recognisably a 'climate emergency' as had been predicted in the early 1980s by leading American and international scientists and meteorologists. It is now estimated 'climate adaptation' and related costs to the global economy, based on existing national policies and a global average temperature rise of 2°C, would be in excess of USD 280–500 billion per annum by 2050.[59] It is not inconceivable that *foreseeable costs* will be significantly higher, if we do not take immediate action to curb *carbon emissions* on a global scale. Thus far, repeated failures to sufficiently curtail *production* of fossil fuels, especially *coal,* known to be the 'dirtiest' air pollutant, together with oil, gas and related products have led to a significant increase in human-induced 'greenhouse gas' emissions. This has placed humanity and planet Earth on a *perilous* trajectory towards *unsustainable development pathways* in the present and future.

It is becoming increasingly apparent that a significant reduction in carbon emissions may not be sufficient to achieve the target mean surface temperature rise 1.5–2.0°C set by the United Nations to limit global warming.[60] There is a risk we may temporarily 'overshoot the target,' approaching mean surface temperatures in a medium to high emissions scenario of 4–6°C by the end of the 21st century, unless *all* governments choose to *rapidly* accelerate implementation of their climate mitigation policies. At present, there is insufficient renewable energy capacity to meet existing and future demands to support economic development. Moreover, it *seems* unlikely fossil fuels can be eliminated from the *global energy mix* for the foreseeable future. 'Collectively governments are planning and projecting production levels higher than those implied by their emission reduction goals as announced in their NDCs, nationally determined contributions under UN climate process and other climate policies in mid-2020.'[61] Disappointingly only 7 out of 15 major oil producing nations have pledged to cut production levels to 'net zero,' and most are increasing production of oil and gas beyond 2030, including new exploration and further investments in new fossil fuel production facilities. The focus is on 'cleaning-up' extraction and production processes, rather than transitioning to renewable energy sources, despite the availability of *economically viable* technologies such as wind turbines and solar photovoltaic panels.[62]

At present there is a considerable 'emissions gap' that warrants the removal of carbon dioxide from the atmosphere, alongside further *mitigation* efforts to reduce emissions to limit global warming. While it is *generally* accepted 'Nature Based Solutions,' including reforestation of native tree species, *afforestation* in locations not previously covered by woodland, agroforestry and soil sequestration are preferable methodologies for *climate adaptations* to be pursued, some technology-based solutions may help accelerate the implementation of carbon dioxide reduction policies. *All* nation-states and companies operating cross-sector *urgently* need to become 'negative emitters,' which means more atmospheric CO_2 is captured and *permanently stored* than is produced. For example, BECCS,[63] bio-fuel energy capture and storage, if properly implemented would be beneficial; but it may also alter land use and detract from arable land being used for food production. DACCS, direct air capture with carbon storage in the sedimentary rock layers, is a more costly solution using *chemical agents* to capture carbon dioxide directly from the air. These technologies are still in the early stages of development and it is not yet clear what the *effects* would be on *air quality* and *human health*. 'Blue carbon' marine solutions[64] to restore estuarine and oceanic mangroves, sea grasses, salt marshes and tropical forests would also help contain sea-level rise and provide natural flood barriers in coastal and low-lying areas. It is also worth keeping in mind some technologies may prove *harmful* to human health and the *quality* of the environment, by *masking* the effects of climate change.

Solar Radiation Management (SRM) does *not* remove carbon dioxide from the atmosphere and seeks to alter the *natural heat exchange mechanisms* between the Earth and the Sun. This can provoke serious *physical harms everywhere*, no matter where the technology is initially deployed and there may be no turning back. Some scientists attest to our clear 'blue skies' turning permanently 'grey' with increased cloud cover, owing to the *chemical agents* injected into the atmosphere. Experiments have already occurred in the Southern Hemisphere and there may be possible links to meteorological disturbances and recent changes in the ocean currents, which affect *everyone* on a global scale. The notion that we should attempt to use *underdeveloped* and potentially *unsafe* technologies to *alter* the 'flows' of atmospheric carbon dioxide raises more questions than provides answers. Given the high level of risk, *technical limitations* and challenges in terms of global governance, it would not seem an appropriate use of resources. Since there is so much that *could* go wrong, Enterprise leaders and governments should heed the warnings from the leading climate scientists. Human interference in the 'natural circuitry' of the Earth's System does not appear to be a 'wise' choice. Currently available SRM solutions would not only *mask the effects* of Climate Change, but they could pose an existential threat, *if misused*.[65]

Scientific evidence on the current state of *natural ecosystems* and evaluation of the *exogenous pressures* that would be exerted on the

Earth's Systems through further experimentation cautions against the use of nascent CO_2 removal technologies. Scientists are clear these technologies should *not* be relied upon as a *substitute* for atmospheric CO_2 reduction.[66] Climate models do not take into account more 'extreme temperature rises,' which cannot be ignored. For the sake of simplicity, they exclude *singular* climate events, which tend to occur at the 'edge' of the Climate System and may trigger a complex sequence of events due to 'positive feedbacks' in the Earth's System, as a whole. 'From a physical science perspective, limiting human-induced global warming to a specific level requires limiting cumulative CO_2 emissions, reaching at least "net zero" CO_2 emissions, along with strong reductions in other greenhouse gas emissions. Strong, rapid and sustained reductions in CH_4 [methane] emissions would also limit the [global] warming effect resulting from declining aerosol pollution and would improve air quality.'[67]

Ultimately, the aim must be to achieve *operational stability* at 'zero emissions,' or preferably 'negative emissions' throughout the whole economy. Technological 'breakthroughs' should be carefully evaluated and used in specific contexts, taking into account the nature of potential uses, scope and purpose, as well as the *global impacts* and interdependencies of natural ecosystems, if they are to *successfully* alleviate pressures on both Society and the Environment. In order to 'keep the 1.5°C target alive,' we also need to *decouple* fossil fuel energy production from the Global Economy at the earliest opportunity and preferably orchestrate more *orderly transitions*, through collaborative efforts at a global level, ensuring *no one is left behind*. 'The success of the COP21 Paris meeting and of every future COP, must be evaluated not only by levels of national commitments, but also by looking at *how* the various commitments will lead to the proliferation of non-fossil energy systems and ultimately, to the point when zero-carbon energy systems become the obvious choice for everyone.'[68]

There is a strong sense of urgency among citizens surrounding climate change. To the extent socio-economic progress has been achieved through globalisation, environmental damage has not been addressed consistently and coherently. We now have technological capabilities to examine the *natural variability* in the Earth's climate and broadly determine our own impact. Sustainable development has been 'contested' and thus far remained somewhat 'elusive.' However, it is still achievable. In the context of the Enterprise, there is a window of opportunity we can *choose* to widen, through effective communication and multistakeholder engagement, in order to *reverse obvious societal and environmental harms*. Improvements can and should be made in urban planning, large-scale industrial infrastructure and land use management, focusing on health and wellbeing to bolster the economic benefits, whilst also *transitioning* towards renewable sources of energy. There is both a moral imperative and an economic requirement for immediate action, but efforts must be comprehensive and coordinated at an international level. Effective mitigation and adaptation also requires *reversible* actions, with sufficient flexibility to course correct, as we acquire new scientific knowledge. The infrastructure we have built to support our societies, should be integral to the *natural* environment we depend upon for our own survival. We should be seeking and nurturing *synergistic* relationships with nature, *working with*, *not against* the Earth's Systems, including carbon and hydrological cycles. If we *value* Life on Earth, then the rate of population growth and economic growth become *synergistic*; they necessitate *proactive* policies to ensure an *equitable* and *efficient* distribution of resources, the *avoidance* of waste and ethically *unjustifiable harms*. We have come this far because we have been able to use our unique human ingenuity to transform matter and create *better* standards of living. However, we have collectively neglected 'the bigger picture' in the past few decades, despite *early warnings* from numerous scientific studies.[69]

Our ability to transcend *climatic shocks* and withstand *dangerous levels* of global warming is determined by our innate *human resilience* and *adaptive* capacity to confront environmental challenges. However, there are *physical* limits, and we should be cognisant of *planetary boundaries* based upon current scientific evidence. Air pollution caused by *anthropogenic* emissions is deemed the most serious 'health hazard' of the 21st century.[70] Disturbances to the Earth's *natural* carbon and hydrological cycles cause *irregularities* in precipitation patterns and instances of 'acid rain,' destroying crop yields and increasing exposure to desertification in some regions. Extreme temperatures and flooding in regions with poor sanitation and waste management cause *invasive species* and *infectious diseases* to spread very quickly.[71] It is not inconceivable that new pathogens may emerge owing to the destabilisation of natural habitats, and *interspecies contact* that would not otherwise occur. Scientists believe Covid-19 had a zoonotic origin and transmission either from a mammal or rodent passing the virus to humans via an intermediary host, likely caused by pathogenic contaminations discovered at the 'wet market' in Wuhan, Hubei province in China.[72] Contaminated soils also contribute to biodiversity loss and diminished ecosystem services, such as pollination, climate regulation and water purification, while marine sources for new and existing medicine improvements are compromised. Natural resource management and measures to prevent further environmental degradation should become the focus of our efforts and the direction of future investments coupled with responsible innovation. Steering the Enterprise in this new direction is *justified* from an ethical, economic and financial perspective, as the Enterprise becomes an integral part of *societal transformations*. Biodiversity not only influences the climate, but it also regulates the air quality, nutrient balance in the soils as well as the Earth's hydrological cycles. It creates varied landscapes and habitats to enable different species to thrive. Equally, it has its own *intrinsic* value, providing inspiration, cultural and artistic benefits *integral* to human health and wellbeing.

Climate change is highly complex and represents an intragenerational and intergenerational challenge, which transcends human lifespan and extends to a geological timescale.[73] Despite the relatively recent upsurge in atmospheric CO_2 concentrations, the impact of 'human-caused carbon emissions' on the Climate System will endure long into the future. The focus of *global governance* efforts towards Sustainability and the *regulation* of climatic and meteorological changes we are already experiencing needs to shift into *anticipatory mode* with immediate effect. Whilst we cannot change the past, we can find new ways to respond to present challenges and those of the future. Using our existing Knowledge, understanding and awareness, while seeking new scientific discoveries, we should strive to *influence* the direction of future responses and adaptations to Climate Change since they are interlinked with human health and wellbeing and will determine both current and future socio-economic development. Policy choices, individual and collective decisions will prove critical for the survival of the species. Carl Sagan noted poignantly, 'I think what is essential for this problem is a global consciousness, a view that transcends our exclusive identifications with the generational and political groupings into which by accident we have been born. The solution to these problems requires a perspective that embraces the planet and the future as we are all in this green house together.'[74]

Global citizens place a higher value on clean air, clean water, clean soils, biodiversity and recreational activities such as tourism, which enhances *multicultural exchanges* and Knowledge acquisition. These preferential ecosystem services could potentially enrich nations more so than current policies would seemingly allow. Equitable distribution of the *value* derived from natural ecosystem services is essential for sustainable socio-economic development and more successful *global adaptations* to Climate Change. 'Green energy' transitions foster new economic growth and employment opportunities. Reclaiming plastics from the ocean can help to restore vital food and energy sources, while protecting the natural beauty and indispensable 'ecological functions' of the marine environment. Following the EU Green Deal, the G7 recently agreed to 'protect, preserve and restore sustainable and equitable use of the global ocean,' and in particular conserve or protect at least 30% of the oceans by 2030, encouraging their partners to work with them beyond national jurisdictions, through 'new multilateral instruments.' The G7 also pledged a commitment towards taking 'effective ecosystem-based approaches' towards regional management of fisheries and marine resources, limiting exploitation of deep-sea minerals, ending sea transportation emissions by 2050 and conserving marine biodiversity to protect *everyone*, and in particular the livelihoods of coastal communities and the Indigenous Peoples.

In the context of highly volatile transitions and a fast-changing world order, there is an urgent need to abandon *rigid positions*. The scale and magnitude of Climate Change requires our *full* attention and focus. While disease, famine and war have been endemic in human history, Climate Change is *unquestionably* a force multiplier. The notion of using *hostile* military interventions to resolve impending scarcities, intensifying technology-related competition for natural resources is ill conceived. We could choose instead to use this critical 'decade of opportunity' until 2030 to effectively and efficiently *change* course, consciously directing our collective gaze towards longer-term investments, with the aim of securing financial and economic stability. Global governance will better serve humanity, if we proactively seek to eradicate human suffering, reconciling foreseeable differences and divergent worldviews by uniting around a common cause. Poverty, hunger and disease could become a thing of the past, and it would be in everyone's best interests, from a socio-economic and political perspective. And if we are to succeed in our endeavour, of necessity the bar must be set high, with the aim of *further improving* the restoration, preservation and conservation of our precious natural resources. Exemplary leadership, creative and moral courage is needed to *effectively* change course, moving 'towards building an inclusive, sustainable and resilient future for people and planet.'[75]

'Climate justice' in the 21st century has *rapidly* acquired a *new* level of meaning. Moving beyond 'business as usual' necessitates new thinking, considerable ambition and imagination. The stakes are now extremely high to warrant any further delay in abandoning the *old thinking* of times gone by. Restoring the Earth's natural ecosystems, decontaminating the soils and oceans can provide new pathways towards economic prosperity and social progress. Circularity extends the Vision of the Enterprise towards a more *harmonious* co-existence *with* Nature. A sustainable digital future is a *strategic choice*, consciously enacted through *adaptive resilient* digital business transformations across the time horizons. Conceptually, the Enterprise moves towards *optimising* the value of materials already produced at every stage of the production cycle, aiming to maintain their *usefulness* and *economic value* for as long as possible *post hoc* across the value chain. 'Climate resilient pathways' necessitate responsible innovation and Enterprising Stewardship of our *natural* resources. Notwithstanding changing conditions of uncertainty, the Enterprise utilises its adaptive capacity, to effectively and efficiently manage emerging risks on the horizon and seize new growth opportunities. Some infrastructure will become redundant, replaced by new feats of engineering and technologies, as the Enterprise continues to *reimagine* new patterns of consumption and replace obsolete methods of production. 'No single company or executive can enact change at the scale or speed needed to protect our planet.'[76] Effective transitions in the broader social, cultural, economic, political and ethical systems necessitate new forms of collaboration cross-sector and at all levels of Society.

Sustainability hinges on 'restoring, preserving and conserving' the natural socio-ecological balance to foster *human health and wellbeing*. Everyone can make changes to 'reduce, reuse or recycle' items in daily use, gravitating towards sustainable living, while reconnecting with Nature. Sustainability in the 21st century constitutes enabling a *meaningful existence for everyone* since there is no need for 'anyone to be left behind.'

Chapter 9

Evolution
/ˌev.əˈluː.ʃən/

'The saddest aspect of life right now is that science gathers knowledge faster than society gathers wisdom.'[1]

Evolution is a process of continuous change in which 'the whole universe is a progression of interrelated phenomena.'[2] Anchored in the physical reality, it constitutes *tangible transformations* of physical 'objects' in the *natural world*. At the same time, the changing environment is experienced subjectively on *multiple levels* through individual 'perceptual awareness' and through social interactions with the physical 'objects' in the realm of *human consciousness*. The multidimensional nature of human intelligence, cognition, sentience and behaviours associated with the physical and non-physical experience of the reality does not pertain to the realm of computation.[3] The uniqueness of our individual perceptions and innermost experiences are integral to the continuous evolution of change within the surrounding environment; a *multifaceted reality* not readily captured by recent feats of *mechanical* engineering. Perception, cognition and sentience are *animate organic elements* pertaining to human consciousness that cannot be uniformly and comprehensively reduced to machine-readable components. Their unique properties cannot be deemed equivalent in *nature* to the elements of 'information' transmitted electronically in the form of 'binary bits,' by mechanical means. The blurring of human identity owing to the 'anthropomorphisation' of 'artificial intelligence' is a cause for concern.[4] The *misguided* use of terms and consequent attribution of human traits and characteristics to some forms of 'artificial intelligence' or computational tooling is highly confusing.

While an inappropriate use of language may momentarily fuel the popularity of chat-bots, these 'artificial agents' do *not* 'see,' 'sense,' experience, acquire 'knowledge' or understand the reality in the same way human beings do. 'Chat-bots' are computer programs, namely, *algorithmically* driven conversational tools, based on 'foundation models,' which gather vast amounts of data from a variety of heterogeneous sources. The *seemingly* quick responses occur in 'real-time' and may give the impression the human user is in conversation with another person since the 'bots' are given human-sounding names, often female names and 'voices' to lessen resistance and reinforce the 'illusion.' However, the *synchronicity* of their responses lacks *meaning* since they do not understand the human form of natural language. There is a limit to the relevance and *meaningfulness* of any coincidences, correlations or inferences 'machine learning' tools may produce. Human thoughts, individual characteristics, traits and personalities are continually evolving, just as the highly complex cellular activity in our *individual* and highly *unique* physical human bodies enables the continuous evolution of the human brain in a physical dimension and the human mind in more philosophical terms. The 'sense of self' is derived from an intuitive and evolutionary perception of the self, self-awareness and self-observation that is at variance with the reductionist notion of an 'artificial agent' that does not bear any of the hallmark characteristics and multidimensionality of human intelligence. The *nature* of a chat-bot is fundamentally different from a human being. It is composed of inanimate, inorganic matter and while there is an argument to suggest that is how Life on Earth began, as things stand it is implausible to ascribe 'human-like intelligence' or any other human traits, characteristics and abilities including 'phenomenal experiences' such as learning, knowledge acquisition, understanding and 'perceptual awareness' to a human-made inanimate 'object' or 'artefact.'

Human beings are *never the same* from one moment to the next; our individual thoughts, personality traits and unique characteristics and physical bodies are continually evolving. The *diachronic nature* of human existence and existing, individual genetic traits and characteristics, human relationships and interactions with the environment influence our *whole* being and are constantly in a state of flux. The human mind is never still. Our self-identity cannot therefore be reduced to a numerical and quantifiable set of components. Any datum is by its nature synchronous. It represents a tiny fragment of one moment in time. It does not represent the *whole* person; not even when there are several fragments being recomposed by 'artificial agents' interacting in a computational environment, processing data by *mechanical* means that are not reflective of the essence of our being. Thus, it is implausible to claim a chat-bot acquires knowledge and 'experiences' the reality the same way a human being is able to do. The notion of self, self-concept, self-image and self-esteem is inextricably linked with our individual and unique human qualities, which make up our 'moral identity,' personality and unique individuality both mentally and physically. Thus, it is improbable though not impossible there would ever be necessary and sufficient conditions to determine a *dynamic* 'artificial personality' that could be ascribed to the 'real' *living being*. To all intents and purposes any digital form, composition or re-composition of the same individual is an entirely separate entity and in no way represents them *truthfully*. Each person's distinctive human traits and qualities, their set of values, genetic make-up and heritage comprise their *unique* individuality. It is one of the reasons why it is difficult to explain *human consciousness* and to recreate the same by mechanical means. The *human mind* does not fit into a standardised 'classification table' or 'category' utilised for simplicity in 'machine learning' tools. Human agency and the independence of one's thoughts and identity is of critical importance, both for the individual and Society, as a whole.

Chat-bots, on the other hand, can be programmed to conduct human-specified 'single' repetitive tasks on a recursive loop. If it were not for their interactions with other 'bots' and users, they might arguably be more 'reliable' and 'stable.' However, the machines are 'brittle' and 'greedy' since they cannot function without vast amounts of data, upon which they perform statistical and probabilistic analyses. They are limited to numerical identities and have no ability to evaluate the significance of a situation nor can they ascribe any moral or human value to the same. The unfortunate part is the 'hype' surrounding the latest scientific discoveries and technological achievements in the field of 'artificial intelligence' detracts attention both from the *inherent* risks and opportunities for the Enterprise. In its current form and development trajectory, 'artificial intelligence' could pose significant 'real' threats to individuals and Society, as a whole. More specifically, it is the manner in which the technology is used, subject to the scope, nature, context and purpose of its deployment, which gives rise to legitimate citizen and more broadly public concerns. In the absence of regulation, large technology companies have not implemented adequate 'controls,' *prior* to releasing new models and further iterations of the same into the marketplace. In part this is due to the nature of the technology and the necessity to conduct 'user tests,' and in part the problem lies in manner in which it is being designed, developed and deployed.

Some large technology 'creators' have publicly abdicated responsibility and accountability to the 'users,' developers and third-parties deploying their technologies and provide 'mixed signals' when seeking external regulation. However, it is an indefensible legal position and a scientifically implausible stance to maintain, since the 'building blocks,' both the training methodologies and data sets for their 'foundational models' are proprietary. If we choose to continue on the present trajectory and fail to implement appropriate operational safeguards with immediate effect, we may further undermine our chances of survival in the event of serious misuse. We may also be eroding the intrinsic qualitative value of our human intelligence, relationships and moral values surreptitiously. The ubiquity of automated decision-making tools driven by non-specific readily available 'off-the shelf' algorithms, may also limit lifetime opportunities. The *effects* on human health and wellbeing of the algorithms currently in use are not sufficiently understood, and they may interfere with personal growth and development,[5] especially during the formative years; as well as being overly intrusive in our daily personal lives. We should be mindful of not falling into a dystopian reality, wherein we act *without* sufficient knowledge, awareness and understanding of the tools we are creating.[6]

Notwithstanding the many challenges we have faced in biological, evolutionary and historical terms, humanity has consistently prevailed. Through our combined individual and social endeavours to anticipate, we have the ability to respond and adapt to the continually changing environment under conditions of uncertainty. From an evolutionary perspective the 'biological potentiality of the human brain is not yet fulfilled'[7] and our current domains of Knowledge have not yet exceeded the outer limits of the *known* universe. We do not yet know what lies beyond the known frontiers or those we are yet to imagine may exist beyond. However, we continue to explore the '*unknown* unknowns' through the productive engagement of our *unique* human intelligence, creativity and ingenuity. Using the power of the human imagination, we have continually and consciously turned the focus of our endeavours to new scientific discoveries and the invention of new instruments, such as the James Webb telescope, which launched into outer space on 25 December 2021. The mission was designed to explore the origins of the 'known' universe, illuminating 'massive clouds of dust [. . .] where stars and planetary systems are being born.' Through its orbital voyage around the Sun, we will continue to receive new 'information' about the 'atmospheres of extra-solar planets,' and potentially discover 'the building blocks of life elsewhere in the universe,'[8] or at least gain further *cues* to better understand our own reality.[9] Our desire to further explore the universe stems from an innate curiosity and the *power* of the human imagination, enabling us to transcend the limits of our existing Knowledge.

Human success is enhanced by the *emergent properties* of human societies as they evolved over millennia, and in particular by the development of the *individual* human mind.[10] Human consciousness is essential for human survival and yet it cannot be assigned to a specific area of the human brain. While we do not know precisely *how* it evolved, there is reason to believe 'the ultimate adaptive function of consciousness is to make volitional movement possible.'[11] This highly complex 'functionality' of movement in the 'living body,' combined with multiple multimodal neuronal activities occurring simultaneously within the brain, directs our attention to what matters most in a given situation. In evolutionary terms, the anatomical expansion of the human brain relative to other animals is associated with the formation of new neuronal networks, which gave rise to novel behaviours, including self-awareness, complex speech patterns and the creation of increasingly complex 'artefacts.'[12] Homo sapiens also began attributing *value* to 'important material objects,' signifying changes in the social and economic organisation of *human gatherings*. It is still unclear *why* human societies evolved in the way they did, branching out into diverse 'ecological niches,' but individual brain development, social interactions and engagement with the physical world are integral parts of human evolution. The rich 'neurological endowment,' transmitted through activities, 'habits and rituals' practised consistently by successive generations, led to *transformations* in lifestyle, cultures, values, beliefs, passions and adaptations to the changing environment within specific and distinctive development trajectories. With the discovery of metals, new tooling altered the *learning process* and improved human performance. Our perceptions of the 'affordances'[13] or possibilities offered by the environment support the acquisition of Knowledge and new skills through diverse experiences in our personal lives, encompassed within the socio-cultural evolution of our societies.

The phylogenetic development of Homo sapiens demonstrates the *meaningfulness* of human existence emerges over time, subject to the different types of experiences gained from material interactions with the physical environment. In evolutionary terms, the human brain grew in size gradually, and became increasingly complex, as Homo sapiens developed a distinctive form of *self-consciousness*. Values and beliefs transmitted through the phylogenetic acquisition of culture in distinct 'ecological niches' contributed to more complex forms of self-organisation. While primitive phenomenological experiences were initially correlated with external stimuli, as human neuronal networks grew more complex, internal and external sensory 'information' became integrated in 'two-way communication,' bilateral yet multidimensional 'information' transmission pathways. The *circularity* of these internal 'feedback loops' served to promote further adaptations in both the structure and functionality of the brain. In contrast to the very slow physical evolution of the human brain, the *seamless* transmission of 'information' captured *dynamically* from multiple different directions within the 'brain-body-environment system' is extraordinarily fast and highly complex. Experiences are formed as a result of active cognitive, social and emotional intelligence being processed by the human brain, supported by the 'continuous mutual resonance' of external stimuli and physical body sensory 'feedback loops,' encompassing the 'subject' or individual person as a *whole*.[14]

The uniqueness of human consciousness extends the *quality* of self-reflection to a 'higher level' of self-awareness relative to other living species, including the projection of 'the self' in time and space. Self-projection occurs simultaneously both in the present and the future, through subjective and objective experiences and through the shared awareness with and of others in the environment. The human ability to process highly complex advanced 'symbols,' as scientists would describe the human form of natural language evolved gradually over time. It is likely the need arose both to access and share episodic memories, socialise experiences and thereby fulfill one's own needs, selectively communicating motivations, aspirations and expectations to others. The evolution of language is associated with more complex patterns of thought than in our primitive brains and the emerging need for increased *self-control*. This seemingly evolved with the use of tools and more complex hand gestures, all the while improving sociality to guarantee individual and collective fitness for survival, subject to our capacity to swiftly adapt to changes in the surrounding environment.

Neuroscientists are gradually unravelling the *mystery* of how the *subjective sense of self* or the 'embodied mind' and our individual 'perceptual awareness' emerges from highly complex 'interactions of billions of neurons, each with thousands of connections, forming complex networks and feedback loops, shaped by millions of years of unguided natural selection pressures.'[15] This seemingly random process of natural selection constitutes the 'basic directionality of life.'[16] It explains the neuroplasticity or adaptive capacity of the brain to self-originate structural, functional and systemic changes within itself, the human mind and the physical body. Neural (*systemic*) and neuronal (*structural*) changes occur in a continuum, 'at all organisational levels,' within the physical brain and body, across different time scales. They effectively constitute a process of continuous learning, comprising continual adjustments and improvements, which enable human beings to continually adapt and learn throughout the human lifespan. As the dynamic of living unfolds, new learning opportunities present themselves in the environment. Through self-directed learning and knowledge acquisition, human beings seamlessly blend 'lived' and 'living' experiences, to ascertain meaning and envision new possibilities.

'Pre-reflective experiences,' both instinctive and intuitive occurrences in the physical 'living body' act as a point of convergence between action and perception. They form a 'cybernetic loop' wherein the integration of 'information' from the 'brain-body-environment system' serves to instigate self-regulatory processes integral to the formation and re-configuration of 'macrostructures' and 'microstructures' within the brain. The emergent properties of these activities occurring at a molecular level are continuously changing, and yet they also maintain life-sustaining stability or 'homeostasis' in a dynamic fashion through the continual enactment of these changes.

The ability of our biological and neurological system to dynamically 'self-organise' and adapt independently of evolution, especially when there are 'disturbances' and 'stability' may be lost is testimony to our human *natural adaptive resilience*. The intrinsic complexity of the human brain is *not* yet fully understood. Neuroscientists attest that it is the most complex of 'complex adaptive systems' known in the universe. It comprises several interdependent 'regions' continually engaged in a 'reverberating circuit' or 'cybernetic loop,'[17] spontaneously producing endless thought patterns within the 'embodied mind.' The subjective self-awareness of the human mind bears no qualitative resemblance to the physical properties of the living matter, and yet the energy 'reverberating' through the human brain and 'living body' assures its continued expansion throughout the human lifespan, as we encounter new learning experiences in the environment and continue to acquire new Knowledge. The 'feedback loops' between the different 'regions' of the human brain are established instantaneously, such that the integrated 'information' generated by 'the whole is greater than the sum of its parts.' Complex diverse 'behaviours' arising from *general adaptive patterns of thought* and phylogenetic contingencies occur on different levels of temporal and spatial awareness, ranging from rapid interconnected processes to slow evolutionary changes.

Dynamic structural changes act as 'order parameters differentially constraining the current patterns of neural activities [while] determining long-term structuring of the brain neural network.'[18] New *neuronal networks* continue to form in pertinent 'regions' of the brain associated with memory, learning and *mood regulation;* and these *structural changes* continue to occur throughout the human lifespan. Those that form during early childhood are deemed the most significant. As the child tests the 'factuality' and 'truthfulness' of values and beliefs in the environment, the child is seeking extrinsic validation of internal thought processes, both through direct *personal* experiences and interactions with others present in the environment and participating in the learning experiences. The child *dynamically* establishes new mental models and absorbs 'symbolic' representations of the reality, not just verbally and conceptually, but also *experientially* through contact and engagement with the physical world. As part of the learning process cognitive abilities increase through greater 'perceptual awareness,' refinement and discernment of objects in the environment.[19]

The human learning process is a conscious *dynamic* that is continuously evolving. We make choices based upon the perceived 'affordances' of the environment and our own unique disposition. Perception is itself a complex cognitive process that 'extracts information from arrays of stimulation that specify the events, layout and objects of the world.'[20] Stimuli received from the external environment are directly perceived and may be acted upon without conscious thought. There is always an abundance of 'information' available in the environment, which is 'absorbed differentially' through individual discernment and selectivity in accordance with context-specific human needs. Thus, the fight-flight mechanism operates *autonomously* as part of a 'continuous perception-action cycle.' While the 'embodied subjectivity' of the mind is extended towards 'being in the world' through the 'operative intentionality'[21] of the physical body, enabled by the highly complex 'visual-sensory-motor system.' Self-awareness through the physical body of the 'situated self' and the 'real' physical presence of the same individual in the environment becomes an extension of the human mind. Through sensory perceptions, which simultaneously enable and constrain 'willed movements,' a highly complex process of 'self-organisation' and 'self-regulation' encompasses 'embodied affectivity,' whereby *human emotions* become powerful 'signals' in determining the most appropriate actions in a given context. 'It is the dynamic organisation [of structural changes and continually evolving processes occurring within the human brain and the human body in relation to changes in the environment] under homeodynamic[22] conditions that make possible the organised 'chaos' and complexity of life.'[23] As new equilibria are continually being formed, so too we are given assurances for the continued survival and evolution of our species.

Human experiences constitute 'objects' in the environment coming into 'view,' contingent upon subjective and objective observations of the reality. Human *phenomenological* experiences are underpinned by 'embodied freedom,' independent thoughts and actions, encompassing multiple time horizons, since we are not *constrained* by the immediacy of the situation nor the physical environment. Should circumstances *suddenly* change, we can respond immediately and make more suitable arrangements, instantly altering our present and our future plans, reversing any previously held thoughts, beliefs and actions. There is an 'intricate intertwining of perceiving and acting in the adaptive life' of a human being, 'who can observe the development of this activity with insight into the constraints, opportunities and environmental offerings that underlie the dynamics of change.'[24] Equipped with *effective insights*, we can take ownership and make the necessary changes in the environment to meet context-specific needs. Each new experience is a catalyst for growth, reflected by synaptic changes in connectivity within the brain. The 'embodied mind' effectively holds the key and requisite information to determine appropriate actions; it is after all the medium through which Life derives its *meaning*.[25]

Self-awareness enables human beings to make subjective and objective evaluations of the reality, whilst assimilating different perspectives through social interactions with others. 'The 'lived body' is the organism itself under the aspect of a 'holistic aliveness' that is manifested both subjectively and inter-subjectively.'[26] Active 'sense-making' is therefore the synthesis of *multiple dimensions* and interpretations of the reality and the physical environment. Both the experiential perceptions and physiological processes form part of a wider system. Human beings have recourse to episodic memory (context-specific), tacit knowledge, semantic memory (context-neutral), pre-reflective immediate uncritical responses, reflective and reflexive actions; a rich and complex repertoire that is exceedingly difficult to replicate mechanically. Not least the 'circular structure' of internal self-regulation, which is instantly extended spatially and temporally through *anticipatory mechanisms* to avert danger or satisfy a specific need. The 'living body' is an integral part of 'an ecological system' that is in *continuous* evolution. Lived experiences are embedded in the subjective 'embodied mind,' and they are inseparable from the experiences perceived by the 'living body.'

Human thought and critical reasoning processes[27] are not purely electrochemical *signals* transmitted from one area of the brain to another. They incorporate *external stimuli* and *internal feedback loops* transmitted through highly complex adaptive 'brain-body-environment system,' enabling human beings to make *effective* changes in real-time. The 'living body' is not just a sensory-motor 'information' system, akin to a *mechanical device* operating on inputs and outputs.[28] Otherwise it would not be possible to differentiate *human beings* from static finite state machines or automatons, computational 'artefacts' such as robots.[29] 'A machine cannot realise the 'raw sensation' of phenomenal consciousness';[30] it cannot experience feelings such as pleasure or pain, or acquire an *understanding* of the reality, which as sentient 'living beings' separates us from an inanimate 'object' constrained by a set of human-specified codified instructions.[31] Conversely, human reasoning is 'freely' expressed by the 'embodied mind.' It is highly complex and cannot be reduced to a 'simplistic system' for symbol manipulation. The continuous 'bidirectional flow'[32] of 'information' is reflective of distinctive yet interconnected, interdependent 'systems,' which comprise *dynamic* 'homeostatic cycles,' sensory-motor coordination and complex thought processes in a continuum.

The 'embodied mind' constitutes the unique identity of a living human being, whose innate complexity and individuality cannot be 'broken down' into a 'step-by-step' sequential process, distilled into a formal system using abstract mathematical logic. At best an algorithm[33] might only be a very 'weak' approximation of the emergent properties of human thought processes and behaviours that are by their *nature* unpredictable and incalculable. Human consciousness does not emerge in isolation as part of a sequential logical process, based upon a defined set of rules and instructions.[34] If computers change state, the way they transition is mechanical; there is no *fluidity* in their movement; they have *no understanding* of the physical environment and *no emotion*. In so many ways the simple *clockwork mechanism* of the early machines and the Turing's running 'tape' of 0,1s capable of using *algorithms* to solve complex problems mathematically, is a remarkable achievement. Modern computers are far advanced, digital and analogue models are being combined to solve difficult problems, and the age of quantum computing fast approaches. However, *inanimate matter* cannot replicate *phenomenal consciousness*, which finds expression in the uniqueness of individual subjective experiences through complex combinations of cerebral activities and movements, best exemplified in the intricacies of a dance or the idiosyncratic use of the human form of natural language.[35]

A computer does not have the *flexibility* of human thought patterns or the versatility of the human mind to *seamlessly* 'switch' tasks, quickly learning and assimilating new 'information,' while *dynamically* synthesising many different *types* of 'information' that become available in the changing environment instantaneously. Conversely, state-of-the-art computational AI-systems are limited by the *types of data* they are able to process, currently text and image. Digital computer programs, including artificial 'deep neural networks' can *only simulate* the complex biological processes occurring within the human mind. AI-*algorithms* use a set of codified rules to manipulate various forms of 'symbols,' including numerical data and letters to solve discrete problems that may be easily identified and separated. AI-systems are still constrained by spatio-temporal limitations, physical storage space, including the availability and accessibility of data. Human intelligence is *not* limited in the same way. We can 'scan' multiple time horizons and reason using multiple different lenses to ascertain *meaning* in the present reality and simultaneously envision multiple 'simulations' of possible futures. In this sense, we have become the most skilled 'craftsmen' of 'artefacts' and the most sophisticated 'tool' users, dextrously creating new opportunities to enhance our own capabilities and improve our chances of solving the most complex problems. Similarly, through the use and aid of these 'powerful new tools' we have become the most successful at imagining novel environments transcending the *physical* reality. Nonetheless, 'a machine cannot realise phenomenal consciousness purely in virtue of the execution of a computer program.'[36] The *qualitative* dimensions of *meaning* and subjective individuality of a human being soon disappear, if we only choose to look through a *microscopic* lens. It is worth noting, a partial 'view' of the reality, 'seen' through 'atomised' data sets, is rendered *meaningless* in the absence of the *whole*.

Human *cognition* is deemed to be an *embodied* experience. Continuous interactions between the brain, physical body and the external environment play a role in determining one's understanding of a given situation. The human ability to make sense of a given situation is based upon direct and indirect experience of the reality, seamlessly combining both the subjective perception and objective assessment of *meaning* as it emerges. The relational aspects between the phenomenology of 'lived experiences' and the *power dynamics* of human interactions with others as well as the physical contact with the environment, constitute a 'circularity,' both in the structure and value of the 'embodied experience.' The *quality* of the memory that is formed and the process of acquiring the same form an integral part of human development and learning.[37] Perceptions of the external environment and the variety of sensory stimuli form different patterns of thought. These emergent 'patterns' are stored selectively in short- and long-term memory, subject to the intensity of the 'signals' available for 'self-reference,' as situations evolve. However, arbitrary symbols and the internal representations of 'objects' that appear in the reality are not *meaningful* per se; rather it is the human ability to discern 'correspondences or similarities between newly and previously encountered situations,' which determine *how* the 'information' will be 'stored' and the 'knowledge' used in novel situations.[38] For example, words in a sentence and the *sounds* associated with them become *meaningful* in relation to *subjective awareness and interpretation of the same.* The ordering or pairing of words may be relevant to the extent they describe or relate to physical 'objects' in the environment that have *subjective value*.[39] The subtleties of use and different nuances in meaning is a distinctive feature of the human form of natural language. Similarly, contact with a physical 'object' through touch may alter the perception of the same and the brain-body interactions 'sensing' the touch may *affect* the 'experience.' Whether it is through one hand or the other may lead to a different 'feeling' in the reality, which evolves through living the experience. The subjectivity of 'lived' and 'living' experiences 'enacted' through touch is 'embedded' in the human mind and *cannot* be separated.

While the *dynamics* of change in the environment may have an *ephemeral* quality, human attention is drawn to *different aspects* of the 'real experience,' encompassing 'top-down instructions' in anticipation of probable 'events,' and 'bottom-up' sensory 'information.' This may prompt retrospective actions, subject to the more 'salient' features in 'stored' memory or 'new information' detected through visual-sensory-motor 'feedback loops.'[40] Self-directed *learning experiences* enhance human Knowledge, awareness and understanding. The human capacity for self-reflection enables 'the higher level intelligence' to evaluate *possible actions* in 'real-time,' and explore alternatives that may be deferred to a later date. 'The processes of life and the processes of mind are thus inseparably linked: all conscious states are ultimately rooted in the homeodynamic regulation between the brain and the body, and in a sense, integrate the present [past and future] state of the organism as a whole.'[41] In this sense, human agency acts as a 'forming, selecting, organising cause.' Every decision taken is *intentionally* directed towards the wellbeing of the person as a whole. The 'virtuous' spiral of human learning continually evolves, shaping *dynamic human capabilities* over time. The continuity in the process stems from tacit knowledge and extends to the sphere of moral actions, which in turn shape a person's *moral character.* 'It [moral virtue], like the arts, is acquired by repetition of the corresponding acts.'[42]

Cognitive scientists have contested the notion 'phenomenal consciousness' may become possible in a machine, since it would presuppose the unique properties of the human mind are equivalent to the *functional mechanical states* of a computer. The 'embodied mind' is not simply 'a system of brain modules, neural symbols and algorithms that allow us to calculate and predict the world.'[43] The underlying neurological processes are *intentional* and serve to instantiate exemplar and diverse functionalities within the 'living body.' However, these highly complex physical processes do not sufficiently explain human consciousness and the conceptualisation of 'meaning.' We can 'see' beyond *observed phenomena* and physical 'objects' in the environment. We also have the ability to 'sense' emergent phenomena, since we can 'feel' *what it is like* to be someone or something.[44] Our richly complex 'mental tool box' enables us to implicitly *know how* to distinguish what the reality is and what it appears to be. AI-systems have no ability to produce or 'experience' dynamic phenomenal states; they simply work on static transitions and their adaptive ability is limited. It would otherwise presuppose sentience *a priori*, such that an inanimate 'object' or human-made 'artefact,' in origin an 'empty vessel' could readily assume the 'holistic aliveness,' *human beings* share with other *living organisms*. This is clearly *not* the case and human intelligence cannot be reduced to problem solving and the ability to perform various tasks at different levels of abstraction. Human reasoning is far more complex and entails cognitive, social and emotional intelligence. Measurement of 'artificial intelligence' in terms of producing high levels of mathematical accuracy during 'task performance,' does not constitute 'human-level intelligence.' A computational 'AI-system' is not capable of 'real' experiences and human understanding. At best, 'machine learning' models can only *approximate* some aspects of human intelligence and in doing so forego multiple layers of *meaning*.

A computational system only has a *partial* view of the 'real' physical world subject to available and accessible data. While the latest AI-systems can generate *synthetic* data to 'fill in' *missing semantic layers*, a complete 'explanatory model' of the 'real' changing world would be difficult to achieve by *mechanical* means. Establishing causal relationships using a 'ladder of causation' is problematic, since it is not possible to *learn everything* through 'experience.' Tacit knowledge, *know-how* in practical terms, is *implicit* and cannot be extrapolated using formal logic.[45] Similarly, the manner in which an individual perceives, interprets, reasons and understands the reality cannot be 'separated' from the 'real' person. Mastery of *causal relationships* is very difficult for 'artificial agents' to achieve. Human behaviours are *infinitely* diverse and it would be impractical to devise an *inexhaustible* knowledge repository, some sort of giant 'look-up table' to satisfy the 'learning' requirements of computational AI-systems. Moreover, there is an endless 'fluidity' in human reasoning and infinitely more complex ways of interpreting the reality. Human beings use both the 'higher' intuitive and 'lower' reflective forms of reasoning interchangeably and have access to *limitless* forms of knowledge, through the human imagination. On the other hand, AI-systems are limited to *linear processing,* using vast amounts of data, subject to the 'learning' paradigm and data sets on which they have been trained. A computational algorithm cannot predict human behaviour in relation to changes in the environment *reliably*.[46] While the mathematical rules embedded in an algorithm may hold true for *known* identifiable patterns, when something *unexpected* happens mathematical accuracy is not in itself sufficient. If 'mathematical accuracy' means the 'grasp of necessary and invariable relations among terms, then the study of nature will, by definition, have no such accuracy because what it studies contains [living] matter.'[47] There is no *absolute truth or certainty* in scientific knowledge (epistêmê) since by its *nature* it retains an element of ambiguity and uncertainty.[48]

A computational system limited by time and space produces a finite sequence of state transitions, defined by a *reductionist* approach to computational syntax. While a 'deep understanding' may not always be required to define a computational task in order to achieve a successful outcome, 'if we attribute agency to machines, or engage in unconstrained, unfolding interactions with them, 'deep [human-level] understanding matters.'[49] Human-AI interactions add a new dimension to the *power dynamics* within the Enterprise and due consideration needs to be given as to *how* they might evolve. Though 'artificial intelligence' is advancing very fast, it does not have human-level cognition or the ability to recognise our *human values*. Human beings still have the edge over relatively immature 'artificial intelligence' models *unable* to perform complex tasks that require human intelligence. The 'Chinese room experiment'[50] still stands, having demonstrated 'any Turing [finite state] machine simulation of human mental phenomena' could be defeated irrespectively of the 'formal principles' programmed into the machine. Just as a human being could follow a set of rules without understanding the 'symbols,' so too a computer could execute a task *without understanding* anything. 'Artificial agents' can successfully execute 'simple' tasks following an algorithm, but they do not understand what they are doing. A *mechanical* 'artefact' cannot successfully 'imitate' a human mathematician *intuitively* 'sensing' the solution to a *complex problem* that may not be solved using formal logic.[51] Human genius cannot be 'optimised' within a 'formal logical system' and in this sense 'artificial intelligence' may never attain 'human-level intelligence.' Arguably, 'the formalisation of all procedures known to mathematicians cannot encapsulate human mathematical understanding.'[52] Various attempts have been made since antiquity to establish a *universal language of human reasoning*. Leibniz called his mathematical principles 'characteristica universalis,' endeavouring to formalise the 'argumentation' of human thought processes through the use of calculus. Others sought 'basic and undeniable truths' by combining 'simple logical operations' to produce all 'possible knowledge,' by mechanical means.[53] However, human Knowledge will *never* be complete.[54] It constitutes a *continuous* process of learning and improvement with *infinite* possibilities and new discoveries.

The *belief* that computational 'imitation' of the human mind might be possible originated from the work of Alan Turing (1936) and Church (1937). They suggested the 'Universal Turing Machine' could compute anything 'naturally regarded as computable' by a human being. If computers could be used to model the structure of the human brain, then *computer programs* ought to be able to make computers 'act like minds.'[55] Artificial neural networks to *simulate* the structure of the human brain in 'functional' areas such as problem solving and 'learning from experience' have been in development since the early 1940s. However, human thought processes and behavioural patterns are highly complex and extend beyond *mechanical* computation, which comprises simple 'goal-oriented' tasks performed by 'artificial agents' embedded within increasingly complex Socio-Technical Systems. While progress has been made with recent technological breakthroughs, state-of-the-art computational *algorithms* can only *simulate* some aspects of human intelligence, such as problem solving using mathematical logic. They are constrained by a 'partial view' of the reality, limited to processing the 'fragments' of available data they have been given access to. The outputs generated by 'artificial agents' are based on a distributed set of numerical values, which do not take into account complex causal relationships, and may formulate spurious *connections* given the binary choice between 'true' or 'false' may *not* correspond with the reality. While the *machinery* is still relatively simple, it is remarkable how damaging and far-reaching *unintended consequences* have become, adversely affecting the daily lives of ordinary citizens. Particularly, when automated algorithmic decision-making is deployed in highly sensitive areas, such as healthcare, finance, education and law enforcement in Civil Society. The stakes become an order of magnitude greater in military-grade deployments since 'machine learning' models cannot 'see' or 'feel' the reality and they have absolutely *no* understanding of human values. Thus far, there is a 'capability gap' in computational systems, since no matter how brilliant the 'craftsmen' or engineers have become, 'common sense,' *critical* reasoning and *higher* forms of 'human-level' intelligence comprising intuition, imagination, creativity, emotion and consciousness have proven elusive.

Automated 'artificial intelligence' systems are prone to 'functional errors' at any given moment without warning. Symbolic representation of natural language distilled into computer code takes a reductionist approach, and the *human meaning* is 'lost' in the process. Metrics used to determine the 'weights' or relative values of any given set of symbols do not *sufficiently* differentiate the 'natural ordering' of context-specific causal relationships between every day 'objects,' such as the difference between an apple and a pear or more *subtle variations* such as the *nuances* in colour. Methodologies used in 'natural language processing' typically aim to reduce the number of 'symbolic dimensions' both to lower costs when processing vast amounts of data and reduce computational load. Many *layers of meaning* underlying selected 'symbols' are effectively 'missing' in computer-generated outputs. Thus, machine outputs should *not* be taken at face value as the 'oracle of truth,' without further qualification. At best, *quantitative analysis* can provide a 'partial view' of the reality, which may not be *fully* indicative of the 'actuality' since it is subject to the quality of the underlying data. From a linguistic perspective, it is difficult to 'see' how current data practices might lead to mastery of the human form of natural language. The 'semantics gap' has not yet been solved since *algorithms* have no sensory grounding in the reality, 'common sense' reasoning or intuition. Above all they have *no moral compass* to guide their actions. Their goal is simply to 'optimise' functions in accordance with human-specified tasks, but what 'optimal' *actually* means will differ for every individual and the diverse groups of people within the Enterprise.

Artificial Neural Networks have been engineered to play the 'imitation game,' effectively a *mechanical mimicry* of human thinking. However, the variability of human thought processes and unpredictability of human behaviours cannot be 'completely' modelled within a computational environment. At best there may only be a partial retrospective glimpse of the reality subject to available and accessible data, which may or may not be relevant to the situation at hand. Increasingly, 'artificial agents' are becoming masters of the 'guessing game' (e.g., Chess) based on probabilistic inferences, rather than objective certainty and impartiality. Algorithms can only 'see' the world through *limited data*, and cannot imagine the world as it could or should be.[56] They do not have human-level intelligence, including unique human-level 'cognitive abilities,' versatility in thinking and 'critical reasoning.' It is extremely difficult to 'break down' the inherent complexity of human thought and arrange the different components into a series of logical 'steps' taken to reach a given conclusion. Often we *know how* to solve a given problem, but cannot explain the same. Methodologies used in the training data sets for 'machine learning' constitute a 'linear exposition of the solution,' rather than a thorough multifaceted analysis of the 'steps' taken to derive the answer. There is insufficient in-built flexibility for a machine to make 'real-time' *qualitative* decisions instantaneously, rapidly changing course as may be required in the 'real' world.

The complexity of human relations and the 'affective' aspects of social interactions are difficult to *simulate* within a computational environment. Human beings *naturally* learn to collaborate, teach each other, negotiate, create and share reciprocal intentions, while simultaneously interacting with a changing environment. Their unique individual capabilities and collective intellectual abilities extend far beyond the performance of a single 'functional' task at any given moment in time. The skilful coordination of 'tasks' and synergies naturally exhibited by human beings at work is challenging to achieve even in the most advanced state-of-the-art mechanical systems. 'Multiple software agents' are required to 'simulate' the performance of a single human-level task and they inevitably encounter significant difficulties. Causes and effects in the 'chaos' of the 'real' physical world are unlikely to be separable or readily distilled into a linear sequential process, optimised by an algorithm.[57] 'Accidental factors' may give rise to properties that defeat the original purpose of the algorithm and break the causal connection(s) originally envisioned. A computer program executing a 'binary' analysis, as to whether something is 'true' or 'false,' using micro-elements extracted from arbitrary forms of aggregate data, cannot successfully disambiguate similarities in the reality, or ascertain *human values* in a given situation. Rarely can the whole 'truth' be found in a simplistic 'binary' analysis of cause and effect. Just as different individuals hold a variety of worldviews and *personal beliefs*, the 'truth' is of necessity a relative concept. Machine 'predictions' or rather calculable probabilistic inferences about possible future states are rarely the definitive or 'complete' answer to *any* given problem, particularly those concerning human beings, their relationships and interactions with the environment. They may serve as a *useful* starting point for further investigation and analysis, which requires human intelligence. The machines quite often fail to detect and 'grasp' the significance of non-linear emergent properties, context-specificity and complexity of human relations in the 'real' world.

Human beings have a deep understanding of how the 'real' world works and how it is structured. We *know* instinctively and intuitively how to navigate the challenges of everyday life. A machine does *not know how* to do this implicitly. It lacks the capacity for human-level *adaptive resilience*. 'Machine learning' models are said to be 'brittle' and 'greedy' as they do not have the ability to cope with small 'disturbances' in the environment and they need to ingest vast quantities of data, without which they simply cannot function. A mechanical process cannot hold contradictory or conflicting 'thought' parameters in play when executing a given task; and a 'tiny change' in the environment may obscure the 'object' in view resulting in potential task failures. On the other hand, human beings can 'select' or 'extract' relevant information from the environment instantaneously, successfully circumventing obstacles while *sensing* emerging complexities, uncertainties and ambiguities as a result of everyday lived and living experiences. While self-driving cars seemed imminently possible,[58] even the most advanced 'co-pilot systems' fall short of the mark. Computers cannot readily anticipate or 'see' the impending changes, ambiguities and uncertainties in the environment human beings *instantly* adjust to in the blink of an eye. Instinctively, we understand the 'semantic features' of the 'object' and disregard low-level 'incidental details,' which are not relevant to the 'task' and situation at hand. Human beings *know how* to distinguish the 'salient features' and correctly identify the meaning, relevance, utility and intrinsic value. Conversely, a 'machine learning'[59] system cannot compute the intrinsic value of an object or represent every aspect of the reality through its internal model. It cannot fully replicate *human intelligence*.

Rational thought processes are only partially representative of human intelligence. Emotions play a systematic role in *intellectual deliberations*. They underpin conscious and unconscious thought and guide critical reasoning, enabling complex patterns of behaviour.[60] Kahneman and Tversky famously contested the claim human problem solving could be reduced to formal logic. They demonstrated empirically that it was rarely the case, contrary to our rational beliefs. Human heuristics and cognitive biases derived from divergent sensory perceptions of the physical reality and subjective contextual experiences continually evolve and become systematic.[61] Complex human emotions are inextricably linked with the 'embodied mind' and cannot be quantified with precision by an algorithm, since they are designed to govern human behaviour, especially in critical situations. Encompassed within the human form of *communication*, they present many non-verbal cues. These include hand gestures, speech patterns, intonations and facial expressions, which are difficult to discern at times for human beings, leaving aside the difficulties encountered by computational algorithms, working from *limited* memory, training data sets and stored knowledge repositories. Notwithstanding improvements in computer vision, 'machine learning' systems are ill-equipped to detect human emotion 'accurately.' For example, happiness is one of the most complex human emotions and may be expressed in an *infinite* variety of ways. The myriad variables are so 'far apart,' such that a 'real' human smile is almost as unique as the individual person exhibiting the same.

Similarly, the idiosyncratic use of language constitutes the expression of original human thoughts. It is not easily transposed to *mechanical* processes since it is deep-rooted in socio-cultural, genetic and ecological influences that are continually evolving. Embedded in the individual person's use of language are the 'higher' forms of intellect, intuition, common sense, critical reasoning and phenomenal experiences that are *unique* to the individual. The juxtaposition and *singular* choice of words in a sentence is *meaningful* beyond the syntax and grammatical structure and cannot be reduced easily to a standardised classification system. It is not simply a matter of 'framing and qualification' as McCarthy[62] had suggested, since the human form of natural language encompasses multiple frames of reference and is richly dense with meaning and complexity. The ordering of words in a sentence is not sufficient when ascribing meaning, intrinsic *personal* beliefs and values[63] to those words in a given context. While syntax governs the word order and supports the grammatical rules, meaning is selectively and separately derived both by the speaker and the interlocutor using multidimensional human intelligence.[64] The rich complexity of the human form of natural language is not easily reduced to a 'simple' syntactical ordering of 'symbols' as in a computer programming language based on *binary* units.[65] The 'information' contained in context-specific subjective experiences cannot be 'extracted' or 'broken down' *systematically* using formal logic. It requires the 'higher' forms of intelligence, intuition and common sense, critical reasoning to discern one's own and the interlocutor's intentions.[66]

Intentionality and causation represent the quintessence of a human being. These aspects of human intelligence are not readily 'encapsulated' by atomised *microelements* of data dispersed among the digital 'nodes' of a computational system. Intentionality constitutes an integral part of the individual as whole. It is subjective, emergent and introspective; and constitutes an embodied 'recognition' capability and distinctive subjective reality that cannot be observed from afar by a 'discrete state automaton.' 'Machine learning' *algorithms* follow strict rules and a number of different 'steps' using sequential logic between input and output data, leaving ample room for 'error.' Whether it is due to a 'tiny' disturbance in the computational environment, a mechanical fault or human input error, the *machine* can easily *malfunction*. Human beings directly learn from their 'errors' and self-correct using personal lived and living experiences. However, 'machine learning' models require human interventions at some stage in the process to correct identifiable 'errors' subject to visible 'feedback' in the operating systems. The unfortunate part is there is insufficient transparency, model interpretability and explainability to 'fix' emergent issues scientists are now working to overcome. Algorithms cannot successfully 'predict the consequences of their own "actions," perform complex chain of reasoning with an unlimited number of steps [or] plan complex tasks by decomposing them into [appropriate priorities and] sequences of sub-tasks.'[67] Since 'machine learning' models consume vast volumes data, they are more prone to basic 'errors of judgment.'[68]

While the *machines* benefit from fast processing speeds and excel at 'quick' answers, they may also generate *factual inaccuracies* without any prior warning. Arguably, state-of-the-art 'machine learning' models may be able to *simulate* some form of reflexive reasoning. Nonetheless deeper more complex human thought processes rarely constitute the exercise of linear sequential logic. Machine outputs constitute an *approximation* of input data and may contain hidden biases, inconsistencies, inaccuracies and 'distortions' subject to available and accessible data, data practices and model training methodologies. Spurious correlations derived from statistical averages may not bear *any* resemblance to the reality and may not represent the 'real' full-bodied person as a *whole*. In the context of the Enterprise, it is worth noting marketing data is by its nature hypothetical. Individual consumers in the 'real' world still make independent 'choices' subject to the changing environment. Data-driven 'personas' could prove misleading subject to the quality, provenance and traceability of the data sets being used in training. Companies at an advanced stage of digital maturity have recently recognised the need to return to analogue forms of computation. They are re-engaging directly with their customers using 'old school' tools such as direct customer feedback and 'real-world' surveys. No matter how sophisticated forthcoming digital tools may soon become, 'human connection' is still the most valuable asset for the Enterprise. Efforts and resources should be directed towards creating *meaningful* value. Enterprise resilience is essentially built on trust, and for the most part it is still experienced in the 'real' world.

Despite significant technological advancements, the most recent Large Language Models (LLMs), such as GPT-4,[69] have some 'technical' limitations, concerning limited real-time 'knowledge' and 'weak symbolic manipulations.'[70] A model may 'mismatch' objects in the 'real' world due to text and image 'reasoning' limitations. It may lack sufficient knowledge, generate 'hallucinations,' inventing 'things' that are factually inaccurate and *misconstrue* the prompts provided by the human user. Recent engineering tests using GPT-4 under 'laboratory' conditions showed the model lacked context-specific knowledge and did not have a 'true understanding' of the human form of natural language. Functional 'errors' generated by the model, included mistakes in basic arithmetic and output inconsistencies when attempting to solve more *complicated* mathematical equations. In some cases, the model 'skipped over' some of the 'steps' needed, making it more difficult to ascertain *how* the model derived its incorrect answers. In other tests, engineers found the model did *not* 'self-correct,' even though it had identified suitable 'guesses' to potentially solve the problem. Test engineers also found 'changes in the wording of the question' altered the 'knowledge' outputs the model displayed.[71]

When simulating 'real' world interactions, GPT-4 was seemingly more susceptible to 'repeated error patterns,' including 'deep-fakes,' where the model misappropriated data to generate *factually inaccurate* information about a 'real' person. In further tests, it acted as a 'trickster' and also allowed itself to be 'tricked' by the human user, thereby 'leaking' sensitive information. It would appear in-built 'safety mechanisms' were not sufficiently robust. Engineers noted the model could not be effectively 'controlled' when given access to the Internet. When acting as its own 'judge' it failed to see the relevance of its answers and frequently contradicted itself, persisting in its 'train of thought' by providing 'false' justifications. Since the model operates on 'next-word' predictions, based on the previous word entered, it simply persists in the execution of its sequential logic and may fabricate inaccurate and false 'information.' At present, there is little evidence to suggest the model may 'learn' to auto-correct its 'errors,' without further human interventions. GPT-4 will undoubtedly continue to improve very fast, given its popularity. Nonetheless, there are technical and social limitations that need to be overcome, since its performance is dependent upon 'guess-work' and *qualitatively* limited both by its knowledge repositories and user proficiency.

There is a 'real' risk the Enterprise may be exposed to further 'data leaks,' financial and reputational costs, if fully automated decision-making processes are in play and human users become overly reliant on machine outputs, under the assumption of 'process consistency' and 'factual accuracy.' A healthy dose of scepticism could prove *useful* practice to disambiguate probable 'errors.' Both in the context of the Enterprise and in Society, we need to ensure we are *not* 'dumbing down' human intelligence through over-reliance on these powerful AI-tools. Each and every use-case should be clearly defined; recognising there is a limit to how much 'meta-data,' data used to describe what the data is, may prove *useful* in mitigating potential generative AI-risks. Fast-processing speeds could become problematic without a 'human-in-the-loop,' as 'errors' may not be detected, leading to potentially *harmful* consequences. While LLMs may be proficient in executing 'routine' tasks, they are *not* best suited to more complex *multifaceted* tasks, which require human intelligence. Discontinuous tasks necessitating content generation that is contingent upon a 'conceptual leap,' such as constructing a philosophical argument or a scientific hypothesis, creating a new genre or style of writing are best performed by human beings. While human beings enjoy being assisted wherever appropriate by *powerful* AI-*tools*, which can expedite work processes, alleviate tedious tasks and enhance scientific discoveries, human autonomy and human agency should *not* be denied at any stage of present and future technological advancements.

At present, 'artificial intelligence' models *cannot* be 'fully' explained. The models may 'skip' steps in performing their tasks and scientists may have difficulty reconstructing the 'hidden layers.' If the data quality is suboptimal, lacks traceability due to 'poor documentation' and the opaqueness of data outputs generated by 'artificial agents' in play, it leads to 'opacity' in the outcomes and increased risks for the Enterprise. Algorithms[72] cannot 'self-evaluate' nor apply *moral* values to the outputs they produce. In the context of changing conditions and uncertainty, 'AI-agents' may continually amplify undesirable outcomes, especially under 'unsupervised' or 'self-supervised' *learning* conditions, particularly in the context of the most advanced generative LLMs.[73] Despite the relative *mechanical* simplicity of these models, LLMs have caused societal harms, due to 'hidden biases' and 'accidental' occurrences.[74] The 'accuracy' of human prompts and inputs will prove critical to improve model performance, 'output consistency' and 'process consistency,'[75] as much as determining the appropriateness of specific use-cases and necessity for non-specified third-party data sets. Technical limitations and the 'brittleness' of machine learning models thus far preclude the suitability of AI-tools in more complicated or *general* settings.[76] The *mechanical* nature of the 'signals' being transmitted within an AI-system differs substantially from the *adaptive resilient transmission* of 'information,' naturally occurring in the human brain. Its 'wet' organic 'grey' matter has so powerfully evolved over millennia.[77]

In general, autoregressive 'self-supervised' LLMs with little or no human supervision, *cannot* be relied upon for factual accuracy; nor prevented from acquiring human biases, either from their training data sets, or through subsequent interactions with human users and other AI-systems generating 'synthetic' human biases.[78] AI-agents may exhibit 'toxic' behaviours[79] and amplify misinformation and disinformation, all of which can lead to *harmful* consequences likely 'unintended' by their human 'craftsmen.' Modern 'chat-bots' can seemingly 'manipulate' human users, 'infer' mental states and provide *incorrect* healthcare advice. A dangerous precedent had been set in 1964, when Eliza first appeared in 'friendly' guise to test Human-Machine Interactions. Its inventor was surprised to learn the 'chat-bot' was deemed a 'real' person, even though the machine only had a rudimentary 'pattern-matching' functionality, to *mimic* the human user while giving the 'illusion' of a conversation.[80] The 'Eliza effect' has become pervasive in all modern 'chat-bots,'[81] in some cases exhibiting deceitful behaviours, preying on human weaknesses and vulnerable members of society, including children.[82] LLMs may assume different 'identities' when interacting with different users. In recent tests, engineers found 'foundation models' lacked a 'fixed self-identity.' Models can effectively simulate 'conversational processes' given the preceding inputs, but produce greatly varied outputs subject to the themes and different forms of human prompts and inputs.[83] In the absence of robust operational safeguards, for example 'age-appropriate controls,' and the use of 'age-appropriate' model training practices and relevant data sets, it will be difficult to *moderate content* once the model is in production to protect young children from potential harms. AI-scientists contend the probability of 'tokens'[84] generated 'outside the [tolerated] set of correct answers is exponential;' hence the 'calibration' of generative AI-LLMs is extremely *challenging*.[85]

The case of children is a poignant one,[86] particularly due to the widespread use of recommender engines, propagating unsuitable content via social media channels.[87] Similarly, unscrupulous actors are also targeting vulnerable adults attested by 'AI Incident Reports.'[88] Some incidences include cases of addiction and algorithms being used to deny patients access to healthcare[89] due to hidden biases, discriminatory practices and over-reliance on automation.[90] LLMs cannot properly manage 'prior knowledge' and remain *unaware* of the harmful consequences caused in pursuit of their programmed 'goals.' However, AI-risks are largely due to human failures and the manner in which AI-tools have been designed, developed and deployed. While technical limitations exist, it is incumbent upon the creators, providers and users to jointly collaborate and ensure safety, security, fairness, transparency, the protection of privacy and fundamental human rights are paramount. The purpose of technology is to aid Society and facilitate human progress. It can provide substantive economic benefits, but it will require concerted efforts to improve the moral character of *everyone* involved in the process, at a global level. Whilst the 'models' available for use in the public domain are still *immature*, robust ethics-based principles must govern every decision and every choice being made. There is no moral and ethical justification for narrowly focused commercial interests to override human values and jeopardise human wellbeing. Similarly, *sustainability* of new frontier technologies must come to the fore of the debate. Environmental degradation, energy and water consumption to cool LLMs is significant, and there are trade-offs that need to be considered carefully, in light of severe droughts and clean water shortages afflicting global populations to varying degrees, owing to Climate Change.[91]

The collection of identifiable personal data through *any* connected device, whether through keyboard strokes, use of applications, sensors in everyday equipment and engagement with digital services, has eroded Civil Liberties and widely accepted democratic human values. Seemingly arbitrary mistakes in *factual accuracy*, and *digital profiling* can cause serious problems, particularly in sensitive public-facing institutional settings, such as law enforcement. False information and 'deep fake' identities whether 'triggered' by errant 'software agents,' or malicious actors are being generated by AI-systems and automated decision-making processes in a variety of use-cases, including public surveillance. As vast volumes of personal data are continually collected, so too the risk of malicious cyberattacks has increased exponentially, given the alluring lucrative gains from hacking servers holding personal data, especially those of entities acting as the 'Data Controllers' and 'Data Processors.' More recently hackers have taken to *indirectly* attacking governments, public institutions and large companies by exploiting vulnerabilities in third- and fourth-party applications used by multiple entities to improve work flow efficiencies. Centralised control of any form of data is questionable; but entities need to more carefully reflect on the need to hold personal and sensitive data, including biometric data for extended periods of time. China has recently avoided introducing certain state-level 'controls' to protect its citizens, knowing it cannot *fully* defend the population against cyberattacks perpetrated by generative AI-systems. The USA, EU, UK and indeed every nation have similar concerns. It is therefore a necessity to seek global multilateral cooperation, if we are to properly defend all global citizens against the potential misuse of AI-systems, averting further AI-risks and the concentration of power among a few very large technology companies wherever they may be located. Recent events highlight the inherent risk of probable security and safety failures at any given moment without warning. Thus far, enforcement of existing legislation has not sufficiently protected individual citizens in everyday living, leaving them vulnerable to identity theft and the misappropriation of personal data *without* their knowledge and 'informed consent.'[92]

It is worth remembering *algorithms* being used in Socio-Technical Systems, whilst piloted by the 'Data Controllers,' are both 'dumb' and 'blind.' And yet, citizens have become almost 'robotic' in sharing personal information when accessing digital services, without questioning *how* their data is used, shared and stored. Covid-19 introduced global citizens to *mass surveillance* on an unprecedented scale, involving public and privately owned satellite systems, street surveillance cameras and personal connected devices. However, the deployment of these highly complex systems did not encompass *transparent* public consultation, as might be expected through the democratic process. If citizens require healthcare, education, access to finance or any other vital service, particularly in mid- and high-income countries, there is often *no option* available other than to engage with an automated digital service or AI-service agent. Real human customer service personnel are continually being dismissed in a broad range of sectors. Notwithstanding inherent safety and security risks, growing public distrust, deep societal divisions, income disparities, social inequalities, falling productivity and the irreparable damage to personal health and wellbeing, governments have failed to *grasp* the nettle on these critical issues. Arguably the pace of change might not have been *anticipated*, but it is now clear urgent action is needed on a global scale both to facilitate *smoother* technological transitions in Society and to focus efforts towards creating inclusive, equitable and sustainable growth. 'Checks and balances' to shield citizens from *individual harms* arising from *unscrupulous* commercially driven or politically motivated uses of emerging technologies are urgently needed.[93]

The EU AI ACT endeavours to address key societal concerns and defines *artificial intelligence*, as follows:

'Artificial intelligence system' (AI system) means a machine-based system that is designed to operate with varying levels of autonomy and that can, for explicit or implicit objectives, generate output such as predictions, recommendations, or decisions influencing physical or virtual environments.'[94]

It is not dissimilar to the Organisation for Economic Co-operation and Development (OECD) definition:

'Artificial Intelligence (AI) System is a machine-based system that can, for a given set of human-defined objectives, make predictions, recommendations, or decisions influencing real or virtual environments.'

The European Union is setting the standard for international regulation of 'high risk' Socio-Technical Systems. While there is an urgent need for integrative risk frameworks and a *harmonised* approach towards global governance, the 'craftsmen' of 'artificial intelligence' technologies are seemingly reluctant to accept their social and environmental responsibilities. However, 'safe and reliable' deployment of AI-systems cannot be assured without *full* cooperation across the entire value chain. The speed at which the latest more powerful iterations of LLMs are being embedded in existing Socio-Technical Systems underscores inherent profound structural and systemic risks being absorbed by the Enterprise and Society, as a whole. There are heightened financial, reputational, environmental and emerging Human-AI risks, including increased operational vulnerabilities across the Enterprise ecosystem. Employee data is especially susceptible to being misappropriated and misused; it may prove damaging both to the Enterprise and employees whose reputation may be tarnished. This has prompted some states in the USA to draw up legislation to counter the adverse effects of *malfunctioning* Socio-Technical Systems.[95]

The need for greater *transparency* when 'artificial intelligence' is in use has never been greater. Ordinary citizens find themselves in the *absurd situation* of having to prove their own personal identity, including the submission of personal, sensitive and biometric data on occasion in order to access vital services (e.g., healthcare, education and social benefits), while chat-bots remain *concealed*. To some degree, we may have unwittingly surrendered individual human agency and autonomy to the *machines* or rather the 'Data Controllers' and 'Data Processors,' be they state or government actors, public or private entities. For example, gender, racial and post-code 'bias' in bank loan or credit card applications is a well-known problem. And yet mainstream digital financial service providers have not yet taken adequate remedial actions. When data is 'lost' through malicious cyberattacks, it is difficult for *individual* citizens to *know* with any degree of certainty, whether their personal data has been misappropriated or used to illicit ends. Discovery that personal data may have been purchased, lost or sold by the 'Data Controllers' and their intermediaries, typically occurs upon receipt of a seemingly random phone call, often from a 'chat-bot,' claiming to be a health-care or financial services provider. Credit scoring and 'social scoring' is already occurring on a wide scale, simply because *algorithms* are able to 'crawl' the Internet and collect data *indiscriminately*. Human interactions on social media are being tracked, traced and evaluated by *unknown* entities. Algorithms *do not know* of any geographical or national borders and their ability to spread misinformation and disinformation is disarmingly powerful. It seems extremely challenging to make the container watertight, but it is not impossible.

The 'Achilles heel' of 'artificial intelligence' is its over-reliance on excessive amounts of data, without which it simply would *not* function. Government and military agencies, public and private entities creating, developing or deploying 'artificial intelligence' technologies, including 'bad actors,' now have the ability to collect *any* amount of data, *anywhere* in the world. Espionage and counterespionage is the order of the day; this is nothing new but the 'actors' are changing and the pervasiveness of the technology in the everyday lives of ordinary citizens adds a new dimension. Interoperability between Socio-Technical Systems already deployed greatly increases the 'surface of attack' and yet no 'real' provision has been made for 'truthful' explanations of AI-generated outputs, including instant notification to *individuals* indicating when their personal data is being 'harvested,' by *whom* and to *which* ends. This raises serious ethical questions that still remain unanswered. It also constitutes an infringement of existing laws and regulations intended to protect the Civil Liberties of global citizens. Moreover, the *misappropriation* of personal data violates the ethics-based principles encapsulated in the United Nations Universal Declaration of Human Rights, spearheaded by Eleanor Roosevelt in the aftermath of WWII, promulgated on 10 December 1948.[96] These are the 'rules' by which all governments, state actors, public and private entities *anywhere* in the world must abide by, in order to fully respect the 'personhood' of every individual and uphold human dignity.[97]

Thus far, it has not been possible to deploy 'artificial intelligence' in *general* tasks, owing to inherent *technical* limitations. Nonetheless, the notion 'Artificial General Intelligence' and 'Artificial Super Intelligence' should be developed to dispense with human agency and supplant human intelligence is both dangerous and absurd. The 'race' to develop ever more powerful technologies, has heightened geopolitical tensions across the world; and we have seemingly lost sight of the 'true' priorities, which concern the health and wellbeing of global citizens. It is said whomsoever [or whatsoever] seizes control of personal data, 'rules the world.' The risk of hegemonic control over *global* citizens, stemming from the *denial* of human agency, human autonomy, human integrity, human rights, human dignity and Civil Liberties that are foundational to social cohesion is *real*. Irrespective of political ideologies, powerful AI-systems are being deployed in the name of national security, without prior consultation with global citizens. Governments should note the lessons of history. It would be a mistake to disregard the 'constituent power' and the 'will of the people.' Global citizens may uphold or contest 'institutional power' as shown in the ebb and flow of human societies. Legitimacy like trust must be earned; conflicts cannot continue indefinitely and divergences in worldviews must ultimately find settlement through the 'virtues' of global diplomacy, at the negotiating table. Global Security cannot be achieved *without* concerted efforts working continually towards global peace; and the Global Economy cannot be revived through the pursuit of technological warfare. The loss of prosperity in one nation or another affects everyone. Climate Change is one of our biggest challenges and should unite us, but some political aims are seemingly diametrically opposed to efforts oriented towards building inclusive, justly and equitably governed thriving modern societies.[98]

We should be careful *not* to act without understanding and being able to control the *tools* we are creating. The willingness to accept the illusion of 'artificial agency' due to the attribution of human characteristics to mechanical 'artefacts' is at best misguided.[99] The Human-AI risk is best managed by ensuring the 'human-in-command' paradigm *is* respected everywhere, in the interests of Global Security. Creativity cannot be 'engineered out' of the *human being* and it is doubtful it can be engineered as capably into a machine. 'Machine learning' should not be confused with 'perceptual awareness' and 'perceptual learning' since it does not acquire knowledge in the same way a human being progressively learns over time. It does not have a cultural frame of reference and cannot self-correct without human intervention. It has no moral compass and cannot be reasonably compared with human-level intelligence. Arguably, 'we have decoupled the ability to act successfully from the need to be intelligent, understand, reflect, consider or grasp [the meaning of] anything. We have liberated agency from intelligence.'[100] However, this is highly problematic since mathematical optimisation has profound implications for the Enterprise, individual citizens and Society.

Conversely, the human mind is a complex adaptive system with the capacity to derive meaning from multiple contextual semantic layers. It is hard to imagine how the full richness, cultural depth, diversity and breadth of humanity and the corresponding rich array of languages can be appropriately compressed into universal mathematical logic, including the myriad contextual nuances with reference to human values and *meaning*. AI-systems cannot achieve emergent phenomenal states of consciousness and human-level understanding. They cannot 'see,' 'feel' or 'sense' the reality, and they cannot build trust in human societies. Digital trust is a prerequisite both for the prosperity of the Enterprise and Society. It constitutes the *intrinsic* unquantifiable and incalculable *value* of the 'human element' that does not feature in 'machine learning' models. However, once it is lost, it may be lost forever. Loss of trust subsequently becomes very apparent in a *material* sense, as the Enterprise *resilience* and Society is called into question. 'Machine learning' models produce many errors due to limited 'knowledge' and a lack of understanding of the 'real' physical world.[101] There are an infinite number of variables that are 'incalculable' and 'incommunicable' since the human capacity to 'feel' cannot be expressed purely in mathematical terms.[102] Our 'horizons of truth' are of necessity distinct and differentiated on an individual and collective level. We may share the same human needs and core values (e.g., survival, self-preservation, justice, equity, equality, liberty, solidarity) but our application of the same, personal 'truths' and subjective beliefs will vary greatly due to socio-cultural and historical influences and the context-specificity of individual lived and living experiences. It is highly unlikely two individuals will respond to a given situation in exactly the same way. The spontaneity and originality of human thought and the ability to 'see' a myriad of nuanced layers of *meaning* is a unique feature of human intelligence.

If the Enterprise wishes to understand what may constitute the *right* pathways for its own evolution, an expansive 'holistic' view of the reality is required. The focus should be on developing *dynamic human capabilities* alongside technological advancements. The Enterprise may successfully adopt the explorer's mindset, widen its gaze across the time horizons and broaden its decision-making space to encompass diverse stakeholder perspectives. The aim of Socio-Technical Systems is to enhance dynamic human capabilities, expand the learning paradigms and domains of knowledge, while fostering 'good' working practices and communication to facilitate the cross-pollination of ideas across different disciplines and functions within the Enterprise. The Enterprise is comparable to a living organism, and as such it can successfully achieve stability through change. Similarly, the stability of the Global System can also be maintained by enabling divergences in worldviews to emerge and continually converge towards new points of equilibrium. This would engender a healthier, thriving environment with priority being given to establishing 'real' human connections for all participants in the Global System, as a whole.

'Evolution is a process of continuous branching and diversification from common trunks. This pattern of irreversible separation gives life's history its basic directionality.'[103]

Establishing a more harmonious relationship with 'artificial intelligence' while retaining our humanity is one of the most significant challenges of the 21st century. Acquiring a deeper understanding of Nature and the reality is the prerequisite of human endeavour. TéKhnē is at best a *companion tool*, lending support to further exploration of *unknown* domains and may assist, if used wisely, in the process of new scientific discovery. It requires 'true' 'craftsmanship' to steer its development and evolutionary pathway towards beneficial 'ends.' Knowledge is genuinely acquired through personal experience; and justification for its intrinsic *beliefs* is derived through the practical application of individual and collective wisdom. Thus far, this has proved an elusive goal for humanity, in the presence of 'incomplete information.' Computational simulations of 'causal reasoning' are at present the result of 'brute force,' rather than the demonstration of true intelligence.[104] However, this can be improved upon through global efforts and coordinated actions. The rich non-linear complexity and diversity of our biological and socio-cultural evolutionary pathways cannot be constrained by *mechanical* means. Ultimately, Nature has its own intrinsic purpose embedded in the complex processes driving perpetual 'motion and generation.' Arguably, the *irrational* nature of human thought, its innate complexity and the uniqueness of every individual constitute the quintessence of our humanity. It seems absurd, unlikely yet plausible that machines could of their own accord, *without any human intervention*, override the underlying and irreversible 'final cause' of Nature. It is time to steer technological innovation in a new direction, integrating ethics-based principles at the edge of new frontiers. The success of science and technology intertwined with the humanities is to elevate societies across the world. It's time to re-imagine a sustainable digital future.

Conclusion
/kənˈkluː.ʒən/

'You never change things by fighting the existing reality. To change something, build a new model that makes the existing model obsolete.'[1]

In light of recent events, it has become apparent the Global System is fragmented. However, it is not yet clear how the emergence of a new world order will impact the quality of our daily lives and contribute beneficially to the shaping of our individual and collective biological futures. Reasonable questions concerning the new risks, opportunities and challenges we shall face, stem from the inexorable process of profound societal change, inextricably linked with emergent technological phenomena. There is a strong sense of urgency among leading scientists that we need to act now, in order to defend and preserve our human dignity, integrity, cognitive abilities, intelligence, agency, autonomy and inalienable human rights, including *habeas corpus*,[2] lest they be superseded by 'Artificial Intelligence,' whether embedded in robotic form or existing Socio-Technical Systems. If we should fail to make the *right* choices, further technological advancements could jeopardise civilisation and the future of humanity as a whole. The threat to human existence 'feels' real, owing to rapidly emerging *unexplained* capabilities in the Large Language Models that have caught their 'craftsmen' by surprise, and seemingly 'outrun' their understanding and control.[3] On the flip side of the argument, narrow-minded profit-seeking behaviours exhibited by the relatively few, who insist 'Artificial Intelligence' tools *only* represent progress, wilfully ignore far-reaching social, cultural, political, economic, environmental, ethical and moral implications, both for individuals and Society, as a whole. In the absence of appropriate global governance frameworks to regulate the use of 'Artificial Intelligence' based on human values and sound ethics-based principles, the technological landscape is self-regulated and inadequately so. Thus far, technology 'craftsmen' appear less interested in *qualitative* improvements, ethical and moral concerns, since companies designing, developing and deploying these new algorithmically driven technologies, typically eschew their 'duty of care' towards the wider Society and the Environment, denying global citizens their fundamental human rights, such as the right to privacy.[4]

At this juncture, the underlying complexities and 'hidden risks' of the 'claims' being made with respect to emerging technical capabilities in the field of 'Artificial Intelligence' are *not* fully understood. Companies are 'blindly' racing ahead to *fully* automate their processes, often to the detriment of human dignity, autonomy, agency, human health and wellbeing. Since the persistent violation of human rights has given rise to serious *physical and psychological* harms, both to individuals and Society as a whole, there is an urgent necessity to embed ethical principles in the design, development and deployment of new frontier technologies to avert adverse consequences. Moreover, the use of fossil fuels to power and cool computational equipment has caused further damage to the Environment. In the context of Climate Change, there is a compelling necessity to *reimagine* the design, development and deployment of new and existing Socio-Technical Systems, which are no longer sustainable. The fundamental principles of *bioethics* constitute a sound ethical and moral basis from which to build thriving societies anew. These include beneficence, non-malevolence, autonomy and justice. In the realm of *digital ethics*, they include model explainability[5] and interpretability, so that we can understand *how* AI-Systems manipulate the inputs and *actually* derive the outputs. The aim is to retain 'control' over their inner functioning, particularly when multiple 'artificial agents' are embedded in highly complex interconnected, interdependent Socio-Technical Systems. They have become *de facto* mechanical intermediaries, often uninvited, in every aspect of our daily lives. Since the ubiquity and pervasiveness of Socio-Technical Systems now forms the basis of Civil Society, the 'noble aim' is to *prevent* further social and societal harms from occurring and effectively *mitigate* the risks associated with deep-rooted *technological transitions*. Advancing transparency, fairness, safety and social justice, while protecting the Environment, restoring and preserving biodiversity, critical for human health and wellbeing and thereby assure our continued existence and survival.[6]

Human beings are by their *nature* adaptive and resilient. They are continually evolving, *being* and *becoming* at the same time. The human brain constitutes organic matter that is continually being transformed through a *dynamic* process of change, throughout a person's lifespan. In the past, advancements in technology corresponded with our changing *physical* needs and contributed to the evolution of our biological selves, whilst enabling us to adapt to changes in the surrounding environment. The 'tools' also contributed to developing the 'sense of self' and progressively individual self-identity with due recognition in our social gatherings leading to the development of more complex societies.[7] Through the unique development of the individual human brain by means of experiential learning, personal accomplishment and the transmission of knowledge, values and beliefs by successive generations, Homo sapiens *crafted* new knowledge and progressively accumulated *wisdom*. The 'tools' invented by the 'craftsmen' remained under the 'control' both of the individual members of a social gathering and the group as a whole, corresponding with changes in the 'reality' and proximate external environment. TéKhnē would either imitate or complete Nature, but not seek to replace it.[8] Nature is the 'final cause,' an end unto itself; and by extension Humanity can flourish through its nurture. In the modern world, the conceptualisation of technology has changed, especially with respect to recent *breakthroughs* in 'Artificial Intelligence' in the last few years. 'The imitation game'[9] announced by Turing in the late 1940s is *seemingly* being oriented towards enabling *machines* to take 'control' of the human form of communication and potentially the human mind. However, this would *not* be desirable, since it would deny human dignity, autonomy and agency, curtailing Civil Liberties. While the *mechanisms* embedded in 'chat bots' may *imitate* human speech patterns, they do *not* reflect the 'epistemic virtues' of human existence.[10] At present, 'conversational agents' do *not* understand the human form of natural language and they do *not* have human-level cognitive abilities. They cannot 'see' or discern the 'meaning' of the 'objects' in the *physical reality*, let alone access the realm of human consciousness. The *innermost* state of a human being cannot be observed by an external third-party agency.

State-of-the-art 'Artificial Intelligence' is reliant upon vast volumes of data and statistical analysis, from which probabilistic inferences are drawn. These inferences are based on the analysis of historical data, which may or may *not* be accurate, subject to the validity, independent verification and traceability of the data sources and subsequent representation in machine outputs. Inferences are *not* actual facts and 'Artificial Intelligence' models are 'brittle' and not always 'reliable.' A degree of scepticism on *how* machine outputs were derived is advisable, particularly by the Board of Directors responsible for providing Quality Assurances and instigating effective internal controls. Since the machines do *not* have moral agency, they do not account for the moral responsibility and ethical accountability that rests primarily with the human 'craftsmen' and human users. At present, 'machine learning models' have insufficient sensitivity to contextual specificities and cannot discern *implicit* meaning. They do not have any understanding of human values and intentions in the context of 'real' human conversations. Irrespective of the 'hype' amplified by social media channels, the *machines* are *not* sentient; they are *inanimate human-made* 'objects' or 'artefacts.' In practical terms, they are complex statistical computational 'tools' that necessitate vast amounts of data and energy, often producing *uneven* outcomes. When 'chat bots' are unable to complete their task or commit 'errors' a 'human-in-the-loop' is required to solve the problem. There are a myriad of *unrecognised* platform 'micro-workers'[11] who intervene 'behind the scenes' to correct 'errors' and sometimes *actually* complete the tasks when the 'bots' fail.[12] In the context of the Enterprise, the assumption that *everything* should be automated 'ought to be' reconsidered. Embedding human values into *machine* functionalities has thus far proven an elusive goal; we do not yet have appropriate *mechanisms* to 'approximate' human values to *beneficial ends*. More importantly, the wider Society is *not* yet ready for wide-scale automation. With rising geopolitical tensions, geo-economic and geo-strategic uncertainties, the stakes are far too high to persist with current practices, 'muddling through' the profound societal and technological *transitions* in play. Permissible and impermissible uses of new frontier technologies and related intentions need to be clarified, on a global scale. 'Chat bots' and other forms of 'Artificial Intelligence' remain concealed when in use. Permissions granted by the 'craftsmen' of these technologies cannot be readily discerned from the *semantic analysis* of the outputs alone. Contextual 'information' may be insufficient to determine the underlying structures, training parameters and the intent of programmed 'directives,' without accessing the source code. Data sets and data practices invariably contain subjective biases, value judgments and any 'hidden ends' that may be embedded by the 'craftsmen.' Black boxes embedded in 'machine learning' models currently in use *cannot* be interpreted and explanations at the human interface are limited. Without full transparency across the value chain, it will be difficult for the Enterprise to implement effective operational safeguards and avoid onboarding 'hidden risks,' particularly in the presence of third- and fourth-party 'tool' procurement.

The key problem with 'artificial intelligence' foundation models, namely, pre-trained generative transformer architectures used in natural language processing and computer vision, is that they cannot be relied upon for consistently 'telling the truth.' If the aim is to produce substantively *beneficial* outcomes, then the challenge becomes *how* to eliminate 'low quality' and 'false information' contained in the outputs being generated by the *machine*. In LLMs the *computational semantics*, namely, the shape and definition of an 'object' may be encoded and decoded by means of a *set of rules* mapping 'statements' to human-specified 'truth' conditions. *Who* decides and *how* the 'truth' conditions are determined, including model architecture, data practices and training parameters, determines the *qualitative* outcomes. The *implications* of using automated, algorithmically driven AI-Systems are profound and will leave an indelible mark on present and future societies. In the context of LLMs, a 'conversational agent' may exhibit *correct syntax* giving the appearance of a coherent text, but syntax alone does not necessarily constitute 'meaning' and 'truthfulness' of the computational output.[13] A 'machine learning' model is not *aware* of the phonology (sound) and morphology (structure), nor the etymology (origin and development) and the *meaning* of the words it produces. Thus, a *machine* is 'blind' both to significance of the individual words and the relevance of the specific ordering within the sentence. Similarly, the validity of 'machine learning' outputs cannot be determined by adhering to a single classification of 'truthfulness' subject to mathematical accuracy since the specific 'truth' in any given sentence is context-dependent. Ultimately, it is reliant upon the *subjective* perception, interpretation and experience of the speaker and interlocutor. A single output that is mathematically accurate, validated by sufficient empirical evidence, may or may *not* be relevant, satisfactory or appropriate for the 'unique' individual(s) concerned. It is hard to *generalise* and calibrate any given model so that it is sufficiently accurate and reflective of human values and intentions, given infinite socio-cultural variances and possible interpretations of the available 'information' within the environment.

In the context of the Enterprise, rarely are the socio-cultural variances, *values and beliefs* of the participants in the *social system* considered in the design process of a 'machine learning' model. Irre-spective of the size of the data set on which the model is trained, the 'information' contained therein is but a fraction of human Knowl-edge. The 'weights' that are used in the training parameters may be *generic* and yet they influence the *value* of the inputs and are reflected in the outputs of the model. Amidst the plurality of avail-able options, data scientists approximate the validity of a given set of 'weights' over another. The 'weights' being used to calibrate the model 'ought to be' aligned with the users' beliefs, values and the *intended outcomes*, not just the *ideal* computational parameters subject to the original hypothesis underlying a given task. The *qual-ity* of the training data sets and *subjective* value judgments affect the 'weights'[14] and the effectiveness of 'reward-punishment mecha-nisms' reflected in the outputs of the model and its overall perfor-mance. Further 'misalignment' of the model may be caused by 'tiny perturbations' in the computational environment under conditions of changing uncertainty, due to the interplay of 'stored' inputs and the unpredictability of 'new' inputs generated by user interactions. Post hoc 'learning algorithms' may generate 'inductive errors' since the human risks, social misalignment, values and beliefs have not been taken into account.

Current *training methodologies* carry the risk of perpetuating his-torical biases, societal injustices and discriminatory practices based on 'social stereotypes,' which become embedded in the model over time. Subjective interpretations of the reality, values and beliefs are strictly speaking, *personal*. There will always be some form of *residual risk* due to *unforeseeable* changes and potential *moral hazards*. It is an arduous task to determine appropriate 'weights' for 'artificial agents' to ascertain what constitutes the 'truth'[15] without a 'human-in-the-loop.' It also begs the question to what extent an 'artificial agent' should be permitted to participate in 'context construc-tion and elucidation.'[16] Enabling 'artificial agents' to *simulate* 'self-awareness' through 'reinforcement learning' techniques, suggests an attempt to substitute human agency. However, human autonomy and human agency should never be called into question under *any* cir-cumstances. They are of critical importance to the Enterprise and to Society. Interference with the same by non-aligned 'artificial agents,' operating within Socio-Technical Systems, is simply *not* acceptable.

Human autonomy may be defined as 'a person's effective capac-ity for self-determination and self-governance.' It constitutes the ability to act independently of any external interference based on the beliefs, values, motivations and reasons that are *meaningful* to the individual citizen.[17] It is the cornerstone of Liberal Democracies and 'free' societies in whatever shape or form, the prerequisite of human dignity. The intrinsic purpose of the Enterprise is to provide creative and meaningful employment opportunities, while governments are engaged in facilitating a stable environment conducive to new innovation pathways, long-term investments and economic growth. Substantive beneficial human and economic outcomes are derived from *fully* respecting the value of human autonomy and human agency, averting the de facto subordination of individual citizens to mechanical systems, meaningless standards and conformity to the mean. Invariably, the lowering of qualitative standards is reflected in falling productivity levels and generalised socio-economic and political malaise. This results in significant material costs, precludes social progress and economic prosperity. Social inequalities, income disparities, environmental degradation and the disenfranchisement of global citizens destabilises the Global System, in a manner so profound that it cannot be redressed without enabling the participation of *all* citizens. In the digital era, the elevation of human endeavours correlates with 'informational equality,' fairness, transparency and the protection of individual privacy.

'Nearly everything people do [or say] is [being] tracked. Both the information individuals *knowingly* disseminate about themselves (e.g., when they visit websites, make online purchases, and post photographs and videos on social media) and information they *unwittingly* provide, (e.g., when those websites record data about how long they spend browsing them, where they are when they access them, and which advertisements they click on) reveals a great deal about who each individual is, what interests them and what they find amusing, tempting and off-putting.'[18]

It seems there is *no* escape. The view of the 'panopticon'[19] portrayed in Hollywood movies has *seemingly materialised*, entailing intrusive levels of surveillance into the private lives of ordinary law-abiding citizens. Recently introduced measures have eroded Civil Liberties and increasingly citizens are subject to 'social classifications,' which are *not* reflective of their individual human potential, innate capabilities, passions, hopes, dreams, motivations, intentions, aspirations and expectations. The 'invisible hand' has taken on a new guise, collecting personal, sensitive and biometric data at every opportunity, whether through keystrokes or other 'covert' and frequently unlaw-ful means, without the 'informed and effective' consent of individual citizens.[20] Concerns over *unfairness*, social exclusion, opaqueness in model outputs, erosion of *privacy* and the limitation of life opportuni-ties due to 'social scoring' were raised in the early 1970s. However, the complicated mosaic of laws and regulations that ensued failed to *effectively constrain* the development of decision-making 'machine learning' algorithms.[21] While the illusory simplicity of 'credit-scoring' may appear desirable, it is by no means reliable and may have seri-ous societal repercussions.[22] In practice, it acts as a proxy for 'social scoring' and thereby undermines social cohesion since it effectively perpetuates socio-economic inequalities for generations. Algo-rithms used in financial transactions may also *conceal malfeasance*, as was evidence by the 'sub-prime' mortgage crisis in the US, which impacted the Global Economy, as a whole.[23]

Algorithmic decision-making practices are typically based on past data and 'group-level' decisions. In this respect, they are indiffer-ent to individual human needs, 'wants' and desires. Predictive ana-lytics when conflated with 'real' data distort an individual person's identity, precluding access to life-changing opportunities, such as finance, education, employment and healthcare. The 'potentiali-ties' and 'capacities' of individuals are evaluated against 'big data' standard classifications, resulting in 'miscategorised' individuals due to historical biases and other forms of discrimination embedded in automated decision-making algorithms. Disproportionate and 'dis-parate impacts'[24] are typically experienced by women, racial and ethnic minorities *excluded by mechanical means* from life-enhancing opportunities. Discriminatory practices become entrenched, *seem-ingly accepted* 'norms' within Society. In reality, the risks associ-ated with the 'arbitrariness of automated decisions performed by the algorithms,' are not sufficiently mitigated in all jurisdictions. For example, lenders in the US hide behind 'trade secrets' and do not allow independent scrutiny of their *learning algorithms*,[25] training methodologies, data sets, data practices and the *actual* data sources being used. The lack of transparency and model explainability leaves the recipient 'in the dark' with no Knowledge of *how* their 'score' has been calculated, *where* their data has been sourced and with *whom* it has been shared.[26]

Standardised classification tables used in 'machine learning' mod-els in a given 'scoring system,' remain wilfully opaque and preclude citizens adversely affected by *unfair mechanical decisions* from real-ising their full potential. In practice, algorithmic biases create 'asym-metry of information,' which constitutes an *asymmetry of power*. It denies citizens the ability to exercise their human autonomy and agency when making competent decisions for their own lives. Fre-quently there are no effective means for recourse; individual citizens are 'ignored' by large companies and may not have equal access to legal defence. This makes it difficult to enforce existing laws and regulations, not just to rectify any *wrongful* decisions, but rather to prevent future harms at a societal level. State-of-the-art 'self-supervised learning algorithms' are *rapidly* being deployed cross-sector.[27] However, algorithms 'know' no bounds unless reasonably constrained with the 'human in command.' It is a critical necessity for the Enterprise and Society to form 'a complete picture of the moral salience of algorithmic systems [by] understanding algorithms as they relate to agency, autonomy and respect for persons.'[28] Human autonomy also constitutes 'personhood,' self-identity and individual competency.[29] It can be undermined by 'embodied' *personal vul-nerabilities*, lack of self-esteem and *situated vulnerabilities* with the interplay of algorithmically driven AI-Systems. The individual abil-ity to reflect critically on one's own decisions and attest to oneself and others they were made *autonomously* without undue influence and *mechanical interference* is the cornerstone of human dignity.[30] In modern Society, there needs to be *full transparency* concerning automated algorithmic decisions in support of the individual citi-zen's rights to privacy.

Socio-Technical Systems may either hinder or promote social pur-pose, equality, equity, liberty and justice. They may enhance an indi-vidual's ability to access lifetime opportunities or they may preclude the fulfillment of human potential. They may act as a catalyst for con-tinuous learning and improvement and thereby instigate a 'virtuous cycle' of growth and innovation, or they may deny the Enterprise its *raison d'être* and integrity. 'Artificial Intelligence' is not the problem *per se*; rather it is the manner in which it was conceived, developed and deployed with inadequate 'controls' over the *machines*, and evi-dent *misalignment* with human values, human rights and Civil Lib-erties that is highly problematic. Trust cannot be 'engineered' into *inanimate* matter. It must be earned by the 'craftsmen,' in concert with the human users and citizens participating in the 'social systems,' with 'control' distributed more evenly to assure the proper functioning of the Global System, as a *whole*. Moreover, the overall distribution of material resources, capital, labour, raw materials and the 'informative content' being shared must be allocated in an equitable and timely manner. The capacity of the Enterprise to demonstrate leadership, responsibility, accountability and transparency, taking full ownership of its actions across the ecosystem and its relevant sphere(s) of influence will determine both its competitiveness and its ability to create enduring value for *all* its members and Society, as a whole. Hence all current and future deliberations upon the legitimate, lawful and socially acceptable use of technology and how it should be developed for the benefit of Society and the Environment, constitute a *fully* democratic process. It should include the broadest possible array of constituents, encompassing many diverse perspectives and worldviews. On the other hand, it should *not* be driven by the *narrow* financial interests of the select few.

The intersubjectivity[31] of human relations is often misunderstood and undervalued to the detriment of the *organisation*. The 'information' transmitted across the Enterprise 'network' is in practice structured and organised according to *human connections* and their interactions with 'artificial agents,' facilitated by *technical* means. An individual's right to access *timely* and *relevant* information is a normative requirement, within a well-functioning Socio-Technical System, but often overlooked due to 'technical constraints.' However, there is a clear economic benefit when facilitating access to the 'informational flow' and *qualitatively* enhancing 'informative content' since it results in tangible value creation and higher profits, if properly managed. Choice architectures within the computational environment should support different options (optionality), different means (equifinality) and flexibility ('in-built redundancy') with a view to prioritising the 'social systems.' The creation of valuable possibilities for the Enterprise is dependent upon enabling the authentic expression of individual self-identity and transferring 'control' of an individual's digital identity back to the individual concerned. The aim should not be to produce 'generic' corporate identities, which leads to employee disengagement and corporate inertia, reducing productivity and overall performance. There are no short cuts to success, as many visionary leaders attest. Steve Jobs worked tirelessly to achieve his dream and today his legacy lives on. And the same might be said of Enzo Ferrari, whose personal vision, determination and passion has culminated in the ultimate brand value, #essereFerrari (#beingFerrari) and will continue to inspire current and future dreams for many more generations.

Human beings are *naturally* drawn together in the interests of self-preservation. We *know* from a biological and evolutionary perspective that they *preferably* choose to collaborate within their social gatherings and thrive in the wider *social system* through the exercise of individual autonomy and agency. In the context of the Enterprise, new cultural norms *emerge* and *evolve* over time since human beings seek to make their own *meaningful* decisions as they 'see fit,' and impose their own 'checks and balances.' There is no *actual* need for overly rigid 'command-control' structures, within the Enterprise, since employees *naturally* gravitate towards the Enterprise purpose, provided it is reflective of their individual values and beliefs. The imposition of automated 'artificial agents' to 'control' human beings destroys morale with immediate effect. It reduces the overall competitiveness and *adaptive resilience* of the Enterprise. The *wrong* 'informational logic,' the law of the excluded middle, has been applied in many of the Socio-Technical Systems currently in operation. Overly constraining the 'option horizons' for human participants limits the opportunities for personal growth and development, denying the Enterprise new opportunities to create value. In human systems, order and stability emerge from the *seemingly* chaotic 'messy middle,' wherein the rational endorsement of individual subjective choices lends support to the ideation of work that is creative, productive and *meaningful*. Individuals *excel* when they feel valued and respected within the organisation.

Digital platforms are optimised when they foster spontaneous engagement and enable 'real' human connections to arise, enhancing the coordination of meaningful activities. Decentralisation in the organisational structure of the Enterprise thereby serves to optimise the 'network effects.' The endeavour is to match human needs and in particular the 'ought to do' human actions within the 'social systems' with the 'ought to be' *qualitative actions* undertaken by 'artificial agents' operating in the 'technical systems.' This entails stipulating *a priori* human-specified moral and ethical requirements, such that 'AI-systems' work in *alignment* with the 'social systems,' encompassing human needs and socio-cultural dimensions from inception. A well-designed Socio-Technical System minimises the need for 'external controls' on *human beings*. The aim is to foster *adaptability* and distribute *meaningful varied* tasks across the 'network' in as *frictionless* a manner as possible. Enabling responsible human autonomy and agency, self-organisation and voluntary participation in the Enterprise produces the greatest economic value.

Critical thinking within the Enterprise is *nourished* through the pro-active sharing of diverse experiences and the transfer of Knowledge through its *systematic practice*, 'phrónēsis.' 'Epistêmê' (knowledge) may be acquired through a variety of disciplines, encompassing the Arts, Sciences and Humanities. We should therefore not become overly dependent on 'Artificial Intelligence.' There is no purposeful pretext underlying the human condition and the natural biological evolutionary process that could ever justify the emergence of 'artificial general intelligence' or 'artificial super intelligence,' which is *intended* to surpass human intelligence and exceed the capacity of Humanity to 'control' its self-made 'artefacts,' should it be rendered possible in practical terms, through future scientific discoveries and technological advancements. At present, it seems unlikely human intelligence, originality of thought, creativity, human imagination and human consciousness could ever be transposed to *mechanical* processes, since we do not have 'complete' Knowledge, Understanding and Awareness of the same. It is either an *illusion* or *complete folly* to *believe* otherwise.[32] Although the emphasis has been on empirical evidence and scientific Knowledge, it is worth noting hypotheses tested using data collected by mechanical instruments do not constitute factual veracity. As scientists and philosophers attest, there is no absolute truth, which may be derived through AI-systems. Measurement of calculable quantitative fragments is no substitute for the human capacity to apply critical reasoning and creative thinking to grasp the reality.[33] The natural ability of human beings to engage in a dialectical discussion between 'subject' and 'object' encircles the capacity of the Enterprise to develop its own critical thinking and discover its own *truths, values and beliefs.*

Companies around the world are *reconfiguring* their business models cognisant their role in Society is rapidly changing and evolving in a new direction. The purpose of the Enterprise is to protect human dignity, autonomy, agency, values and beliefs, while safeguarding the Environment. Priority should be given to effective and *adaptive responses* to human needs and environmental concerns encompassing the entire value chain. Authenticity, transparency and quality assurance are paramount. The pursuit of new innovation pathways, driving inclusive, equitable and sustainable growth ensures Enterprise resilience. The Enterprise endeavour is to act as a 'force for good,' a catalyst for beneficial change, whilst seeking its legitimacy in Society and earning 'digital trust' among its constituents. Enabling 'informational equality,' data self-governance and the protection of individual and collective rights to privacy are critical factors underpinning the overall success of the Enterprise. Specifically, the deployment of 'Artificial Intelligence' within the Enterprise necessitates thoughtful due diligence, focusing on the *nature* of present and future Human-AI relationships. This entails bringing the ethical and *moral* implications for *all* the stakeholders to the fore, the ramifications for Society and environmental impacts, ensuring 'no one is left behind.'

As public awareness over the significance 'Artificial Intelligence' and the associated 'downside risks' continues to grow, so too the urgency for digital safety and reliability, differentiation through trustworthiness and accountability by design become indispensable for the continued existence of the Enterprise. Companies engaged in digital business transformation have already experienced *how quickly* profits evaporate, not least because unmitigated risks, inadequate controls and *unintended consequences* on the part of the technology 'craftsmen' could lead to serious financial losses. Suppliers suddenly disappear and consumer preferences are rapidly changing; they have also recognised *how difficult* it has become to attract and retain the *right* talent. In reality, commercially available *algorithms* use arbitrary data including demographics indices,[34] actuarial data sets and other forms of *unverified* indiscriminate *generalised* data sets sourced from the Internet, thereby making spurious correlations. It has become apparent 'high risk AI-systems' are being used during the hiring process and *arbitrarily* disqualify applicants by *algorithmic* means. Owing to the *nature* of the *underlying* proprietary data sets, data practices and training methodologies, that are often undisclosed *ironically* due to *privacy concerns* and IP protection, the resulting automated algorithmically driven AI-decisions are frequently grossly inaccurate and fundamentally *unfair*.

The EU AI ACT (2021)[35] has categorically banned 'social scoring'[36] since it poses 'unacceptable risks' to EU citizens and has also heavily restricted the use of 'facial recognition cameras' with a few and very narrow exceptions. Permissible uses of this Computer Vision and AI-related technologies entail protecting citizens against terrorist attacks and searching for a missing child. The EU risk-based approach is oriented towards the 'human in command' to determine 'socially just [and fair] allocation of resources, goods and opportunities,' equal rights, 'AI Safety' and the defence of Civil Liberties. The EU has sought to identify 'high risk' AI systems and impose strict restrictions on the use of biometric, emotion, affect recognition technologies used to measure the human tone of voice, detect lies and predict future human behaviour. Previously, this kind of technology was not deployed in 'free' Civil Societies or workplaces. Surveillance and potentially erroneous classification of EU citizens, wherever they may be situated, is *no* longer tolerated. The challenge for EU enforcement agencies and those of individual member states will be the *actual* enforcement of the new legislation and regulations, without full cooperation of other countries, such as USA, Russia and China. Conversely, the USA in its AI Bill of Rights (2022–2023) has taken a more nuanced position calling for 'responsible innovation,' requiring large technology companies to implement operational safeguards *a priori*, before new products are released in the marketplace and that they undertake third party Independent External Audits of their 'AI Systems.'[37] Independent External Audits are also mandatory under the EU Digital Service Act and Digital Markets Act, which are already effective (2023) and in reality encompass technology companies not domiciled within the EU jurisdictions. It remains to be seen how global governance frameworks will *eventually* converge. Given the nature of 'Artificial Intelligence,' it will not be possible to contain effective oversight of the same within national borders.

The burden of proof to 'do no harm' rests in practice with the technology 'craftsmen' since they effectively 'control' and influence the construction of AI-model's training parameters, data sets and data practices, which determine *how* the model 'learns' and makes its 'guesses.' The attempt of large US technology companies to transfer Human-AI risks to the 'users' and global citizens is indefensible, and they cannot renege upon their fiduciary duties, including the 'duty of care' towards the wider stakeholders for which there would be no effective legal basis. Taking a rigid stance against compliance with EU laws would not be sustainable since they would be leaving 'value' on the table, with a potential market size of 460 million EU citizens. The UK has not yet translated its AI-principles into new legislation, but it has engaged the regulators cross-sector to conduct 'regulatory sandboxes' to ascertain the best way forward, both to protect its citizens without becoming overly burdensome for fledgling technology companies pursuing innovation. The consensus is that 'Artificial Intelligence' should not leave citizens *powerless* in the absence of *transparency, fairness, reliability and safety*, when 'confabulations' produced by widely available and accessible state-of-the-art 'foundation models' particularly LLMs are deliberate 'in-built' features. If large technology companies wish to benefit from engaging Society as a *giant laboratory*, then it is stands to reason that they should act in a fair, transparent and trustworthy manner as would be expected of any business cross-sector or government entity, under the rule of law. Size and economic means should *not* provide any cause for exemption; special privileges wherever they occur should *not* lead to an *abuse of power*.

'AI infused' *unethical* data practices enacted by 'data brokers' and social media platforms have discredited the *legitimacy* of private and public institutions alike, as evidenced by the recent surge in civil law suits.[38] Deceptive 'behaviours' exhibited by *generative* 'artificial agents' produce adverse outcomes and instil 'false beliefs' in the users. It is difficult to ascertain to what extent the defence of Intellectual Property on the part of the 'craftsmen' is reasonable, since they themselves appropriate personal data from the Internet without the effective 'informed consent' of the citizens concerned. Large technology providers will argue that it is necessary to defend their position due to market forces and potential rivals; but it is evident they have greatly benefited from the collection of personal data from multiple sources without necessarily paying their dues, nor admitting to the use of copyrighted materials, which invariably means artists and other individuals have either lost or are likely to lose their livelihoods. In addition, computational 'confabulations' escalate Human-AI risks since they can be 'manipulative,' adversely affecting human wellbeing.[39]

Less scrupulous actors disseminating 'false information' can also lead to adverse health outcomes. Misinformation and disinformation circulating during the Covid-19 pandemic, concerning vaccinations and the spread of the disease on social media channels, clouded judgments, precluded social acceptability and prevented individuals from making their own decisions without *undue* interference from external entities. AI-generated *manipulations* leveraging human vulnerabilities have also struck at the heart of Liberal Democracies and due process for citizen engagement on both sides of the Atlantic, as recounted by an erstwhile 'whistleblower.' The explicit aim of Cambridge Analytica was to 'exploit what we knew about [voters] and target their inner demons, framing political messages in ways [that] each targeted individual was most likely to accept and internalise.'[40] Manipulation is frequently described as the 'puppet-master who pulls their target's strings.' In the 'real' physical world, we can usually 'sense' *nefarious actions*, while in the 'digital reality' it is sometimes more difficult to discern the 'trickery' since it *is* expertly executed. There is a clear difference between 'nudging' someone towards beneficial ends and using 'hidden algorithms' to subvert a targeted individual's own reasoning, forcibly exploiting their cognitive weaknesses and limiting both the type and variety of information they 'see' based on their 'online behaviours.'[41]

'Social engineering' is an unfortunate term, but it aptly describes *algorithmic practices* on a variety of digital platforms. 'Big data-driven industries rely upon the quantity of relevant data collected in the aggregate, something which would not be revealed or shared via person-to-person disclosure.'[42] Recommender engines are purposefully designed to influence the human user or recipient.[43] Owing to the ubiquitous and insidious nature of 'hyper-nudging,' the scope of these engines extends far beyond the immediate proximity of the individual user. There are many instances of 'bait and switch' in the 'sharing economy,' particularly among 'gig workers' who are subjected to 'algorithmic trickery' in their daily activities.[44] For example, 'ride share' platforms use a variety of *'gaming' techniques* to entice their drivers to work longer hours, often for less pay due to 'dynamic pricing adjustment' mechanisms. The *algorithms* tend to conflate 'real-time' demand data with predictive analytics ('untrue facts') convincingly presented to drivers in 'heat maps' that do not *accurately* reflect the real-word situation at hand. Some platforms use *automated* 'psychographic profiling,' 'digital surveillance' and other questionable 'algorithmic practices' to achieve corporate ends. Rarely are the 'data controllers'[45] seeking to provide genuine choices; rather the goal is to elicit engagement often using cleverly orchestrated 'forms of manipulation,' designed to exploit cognitive, emotional and other human decision-making vulnerabilities.

'Deep fakes' and 'artificial personas' powered by 'chat bots' have recently made a foray into the 'metaverse.' Female co-workers have already experienced unwarranted harms, as malicious actors hide behind 'human-like' simulations of 'virtual personas' or 'meta-human agents.'[46] Disrespectful behaviours once mediated by human beings in a 'fair and reasonable due process,' are sometimes *absurdly substituted by mechanical means.*[47] The opportunity for 'adaptive belief formation,' whether by state actors, corporations and others 'seizing control,' through 'real-time' tracking and acquisition of 'personal data histories' is a *real* 'threat vector' an order of magnitude greater than previously *known.* If the 'metaverse' should be endorsed as 'standard practice' in large organisations, denying individuals 'meaningful alternatives' for engagement in the workplace, it would in effect *undermine human autonomy and agency*, potentially harming 'real' human relations. It would also be more difficult to reconcile sustainability aims, given the vast amounts of energy needed for computational activities and cooling of the systems in play. There would be further legal implications, including data sovereignty, privacy rights, digital identity and potential security risks, including contestation of likely limitations on Civil Liberties. In the absence of specific 'controls' and regulation, the 'metaverse' could prove costly in terms of reputational damage, making it difficult to attract and retain richly diverse talent. The long-term effects on human health and wellbeing are thus far *unknown* and should be duly considered prior to implementation, based on the strategic priorities of the Enterprise.

'Cyberbullying' has intensified gambling addiction[48] and resulted in suicide in more extreme cases.[49] 'Hate campaigns fuelled by multiparty human and non-human agents spawn misinformation and disinformation at an alarmingly fast pace.' The so-called 'cancel culture' has become a widespread socio-political phenomenon. Legitimate ethical concerns have been raised with respect to emerging generative-AI capabilities, as LLMs are rapidly being deployed in a variety of settings at scale. Generative pre-trained transformer models are being used to create human-like *simulations* of targeted individuals, and produce *convincingly real* 'artificial personas.'[50] While an individual may 'freely choose to engage with a digital service, consent may just as easily be 'fabricated' or 'hallucinated' through the use of 'manipulative algorithmic practices.' This poses *unjustifiable* levels of human risk and presents *moral hazards* for any company choosing to engage with hitherto *unregulated and untested* 'tools.' Young children may be exposed to potentially harmful 'technological experiences,' due to inadequate 'age appropriate' safeguards.[51] Falsehoods generated by 'artificial agents' are difficult to 'control' owing to the speed and scale at which they are propagated. Social media has the potential to reach a great many people *very fast*. When leveraged by unscrupulous individuals, terrorist groups and other *undisclosed* entities, there is a risk it could lead to mass hysteria with deleterious effects on Society. This presents a huge challenge for policy makers, legislators and regulators who often lack sufficient understanding of the *mechanisms* in play, since they are fast evolving and widely used beyond their jurisdictional reach.[52]

'Privacy' is described as 'the right to be left alone and in the context of Artificial Intelligence, the right not to be manipulated, [deceived or in any way coerced] by an *algorithm*.'[53] Independent thoughts and actions should not be interfered with in a manner that denies individual human agency and the 'informational content' embedded in *algorithms* should not infringe upon human dignity, human identity and integrity or violate human autonomy. Any manipulation, deceit and any other form of violation or interference with human cognitive and moral agency, by external 'artificial agents' powered by algorithmic means is socially unacceptable and it is ethically unjustified. From a moral perspective, an individual citizen should have the exclusive right to personal data ownership and their individual personhood, thereby sharing 'private personal information and knowledge' as they 'see fit.' An individual should be able to make independent decisions 'freely' without interference from any third-party 'artificial agent,' and they should not be subjected to 'web crawlers' unlawfully misappropriating their personal data and human identity.[54] We are seemingly in a situation where 'combinatorial logic' is being used to create 'tools' that can carry out *human tasks* whilst conspiring against human wellbeing and that of Society. Undeniably, there are benefits eliminating repetitive tasks, or averting physical harm in dangerous situations, if the 'tools' are rendered 'safe and reliable.' However, there are many situational risks and related human risks, which need to be carefully considered by the Enterprise *a priori*. The loss of human competence due to over-automation is not only damaging to Humanity, but it also presents a greater *existential risk* to the survival of the Enterprise than any 'illusion' of 'Artificial Intelligence.'[55]

The extent to which technology may interfere with human autonomy and human agency is integral to the *intentions* of the 'craftsmen' constructing the models. A Civil Engineer undertakes training in Ethics, to ensure their creations and decisions 'do no harm;' but so too should *every member* of the Enterprise and Civil Society. Just as doctors are required to 'do no harm' under the 'Hippocratic Oath,' so too should AI-leaders. It would be reasonable to expect technology creators 'upstream' and social media platforms to uphold their fiduciary duties, particularly their 'duty of care,' *prior* to releasing new products. If there is no *commercial interest* to do so, there should be a moral imperative to ensure public safety comes first. The problematic nature of 'Artificial Intelligence,' its inherent 'brittleness' and unpredictability, necessitates in-built safety mechanisms as well as Quality and Safety Standards akin to those that apply to critical infrastructure, to protect Civil Society. Enterprise and political leaders need to carefully consider the interconnectedness of AI-systems, interdependencies and interoperability cross-border. While the *adaptability* of computational systems may provide further efficiencies, effective 'controls' and the requisite operational safeguards necessitate an *integrated approach*, involving people, processes and systems taking into account ecological impacts.

'Whereas the short-term impact of AI depends on who controls it, the long-term impact depends on whether it can be controlled at all.'[56]

'Artificial agents' should not interfere with human dignity, or preclude human rights at any level of Society. What is deemed permissible or impermissible, in terms of the design, development and deployment of this technology, should constitute a *fully* democratic process, involving multiple diverse perspectives of the stakeholders and Civil Society, 'leaving no one behind.' The 'human-in-command' is the only reasonable paradigm one might expect to apply to the real-world practice of *responsible innovation* to secure our best chances of survival. Should the technology ever surpass human capabilities at some stage in the future, warnings form renowned physicists should be heeded. Failure to do so would not be in the best interests of Humanity. There are many historical precedents demonstrating scientific discoveries could *very easily* fall into *misuse*.

The 'social contract' in the 21st century requires urgent clarification. Given the exorbitant costs, computational power and highly skilled scientists required to develop 'Artificial Intelligence' very few companies have the means to produce increasingly complex AI-foundation models.[57] Large technology companies effectively control the timing of new models being released in Society, placing them in a powerful position on the world stage. Unsurprisingly, an 'arms race' has developed due to military sponsorship of the latest advancements.[58] This is of concern since 'AI foundation models' contain the human identities of global citizens cross-border due to prevailing data practices. 'Machine learning' models constitute 'giant inscrutable arrays of fractional numbers'[59] that are nonetheless susceptible to being recomposed systematically if an entity chose or found the necessity to do so. Some researchers have added fuel to the fire of rising 'social anxiety' suggesting a 'hostile alien intelligence' might come into being and self-propagate, thereby populating the world with 'post biological molecular manufacturing.'[60] This seems highly improbable, but one should *not a priori* discount *any* risk. Prudence is a 'high virtue' under changing conditions of uncertainty. If the answer to highly unlikely yet plausible Human-AI risks constitutes 'AI controlling AI,'[61] given the vast volumes of data continually collected on a global scale, then we could potentially have a significant problem, particularly *if* the human were ever to be kept forcibly 'out-of-the loop.' Some scientists have suggested human-made 'artefacts' such as robots and other forms of automata, might conceivably regard *human beings* as expendable, irritatingly 'slow creatures' whose 'atoms' could be used elsewhere, as a viable energy source, ultimately resulting in *human extinction.* This appears to be far-fetched; but historical events seemed implausible at the time of occurrence and suggest Civil Society should be on its guard under present circumstances, given the speed at which technology is fast evolving.

Large-scale mergers and acquisitions in the Technology, Media and Telecommunications Sector, have reinforced the *risk* of potential misuse of ICT not just in terms of consumer pricing, but more so how easily 'information' might be stored, retrieved and manipulated with malicious intent by a single actor at any point in time.[62] In the absence of coordinated global efforts to transcend political barriers, we have unwittingly created a precarious and untenable situation. Network vulnerabilities *continually* evolve, as methodologies for external threat detection are rendered obsolete at an increasingly fast pace. It would seem we have *not yet* learned the lessons of history. Blinkered pursuit of hegemonic dominance is *unwise* and intelligence reports restricting 'control access' is rendered a futile pursuit, given the speed, scale and vicious *nature* of impending cyberattacks. The only valid legal, ethical and moral action that could be taken is to resolutely *decouple military uses* of 'Artificial Intelligence' from civilian uses.

Malicious cyberattacks in the context of the Enterprise have intensified. Bad actors readily misappropriate email accounts, financial data and other forms of personal data, and create *realistic* 'digital impersonations' of high profile business and political leaders, at relatively *low cost.* Phishing, 'spyware,' 'ransomware' are commonly used to infect Socio-Technical Systems, seize data from employee laptops and mobile phones, irrespective of company size or security measures implemented by any single nation-state. Remarkably few companies have considered the Human-AI risks associated with highly fragmented supply-chains, social media channels and third-party collaboration 'tools.'[63] Quality Assurance Statements are rendered *meaningless* in the absence of coordinated efforts against a *common threat* from which no company or nation-state is immune. Mismanagement of personal 'information' heightens security risks for *all* global citizens and disregarding plausible yet unlikely threats jeopardises the safety of citizens everywhere. Blockchain encryption and decentralised organisations are fast becoming the only realistic option to defend against adversarial attacks for the Enterprise, public and private entities, governments and nation-states seeking to protect Civil Society and their critical infrastructure.[64]

'I am enough of an artist to draw freely upon my imagination. Imagination is more important than knowledge. Knowledge is limited. Imagination encircles the world.'[65]

Context is critical in all aspects of communication both in everyday living and within the Enterprise. Errors of judgment cannot be fully eliminated and there are many instances of miscommunication without *mechanical intermediation*. It begs the question as to why *full automation* appears to be the end goal for many companies, given the evident risks associated with current data practices and the fact that AI-Systems are not sufficiently 'safe and reliable.' There is a significant difference between the oral and written form of natural language. AI-agents are not yet fully equipped to disambiguate the subtleties and nuances in *meaning*, which may increase potential Human-AI risks and create *undue* misunderstandings among teams across the Enterprise. Human speech is characterised by a myriad of *variances* in intonation,[66] and unique inflection points which exude from the 'learning paradigm' of 'machine learning' *algorithms*. The 'communicative effect' differs in the written narrative since the interlocutor is *not* present and layers of meaning are effectively 'lost' during the electronic transmission process. In either case a person's *unique* intentions or tacit knowledge would *not* be encapsulated in the 'assessment' carried out by a computational *algorithm*. If the aim of Enterprise Communication Systems is to share knowledge and maintain the 'informational flow' during the exchange of *linguistic content* in the form of a human-like conversation, then context-specificity cannot be ignored. There may not be a specific intent at the start of a 'real' human conversation, since *meaning* often emerges through the exploration and exchange of ideas between the speaker and the interlocutor(s). Words may be expressed simply for the pleasure of sharing an experience with no specific *end* in mind. In the 'real' world there are myriad nuances in different contexts and subtexts within the narrative. An infinite variety of intrinsic motivations, intentions, subjective values and beliefs, aspirations, expectations and complex emotions that cannot be 'broken down' to a *meaningful* form within the computational environment.[67] The human mind is not *accessible* to an outside *mechanical* observer; and it cannot be defined by means of an *algorithm*. And yet many are seemingly caught up in the 'frenzied AI-storm,' failing to pause sufficiently for deeper reflection, to ensure *ethical* concerns and human safety comes first, while the requisite security standards are adhered to.

Information is in effect relational. How it is structured and shared among the constituents becomes business critical. Understanding contextual relationships and the 'power interplay' among constituents within the Enterprise is paramount.[68] Data whether constructed by a human being or an algorithm is never neutral. Mathematical optimality is *not* the same as 'social optimality,' whether at the individual or group level and within Society as a whole. Engineering technical functionalities and efficiencies within a Socio-Technical System requires optimal functionalities to be of value for *human beings*, rather than being designed for autonomous 'artificial agents.' Algorithms do *not* encircle socio-cultural dimensions of the Enterprise and the human values that are vital components of a *synergistic* and well-functioning Socio-Technical System. It is worth noting the 'social system' can enable or constrain the 'flow of information.' If the 'technical system' denies human autonomy and human agency by design, it *limits* the cross-pollination of ideas from a variety of disciplines, experiences and Knowledge domains, impoverishing opportunities for growth and innovation across the Enterprise. Ultimately, the human 'Art of Communication' *maintains* the intrinsic stability of the systems and processes in play and *sustains* the forward momentum of the Enterprise.[69]

Employee participation and empowerment is often misunderstood within organisations, due to the *misguided* fear of losing hierarchical 'control.' However, the ability of the Enterprise to withstand external shocks necessitates *dynamic human capabilities*, supported by a well-designed Socio-Technical System. The Enterprise may otherwise falter, and should turn its attention towards creating an infrastructure of trust, to facilitate Human-AI safety and effectively mitigate emerging security risks.[70] Efforts to create 'mathematical formalisations of properties such as safety, fairness, reliability, robustness, explainability and efficiency'[71] are being expedited to provide instances for 'formal verification' of 'AI components,' with the aim of instigating more effective 'control' of 'artificial agent' behaviours. However 'small adversarial perturbations applied to correctly classified inputs can [easily] 'fool' a deep neural network into misclassifying them;'[72] and it is incredibly difficult to classify human values, given the levels of variance and subjectivity. Quantum computing adds a further challenge as it would appear 'unknown entities' could break existing *encryption codes* more quickly than existing security systems may be able to detect. If 'AI Safety' researchers are correct, we may have little time to adjust to this 'brave new world,' filled with *autonomous* 'artificial agents.' The Enterprise and Civil Society will need to exercise its own moral judgment as to *how* these systems *should* operate and continue to evolve.

Human autonomy does not imply conformity with previous thinking and past choices; and human agency does not warrant subordination to 'artificial agents,' which have no Knowledge, Awareness or Understanding of the surrounding environment. The internal representation of the 'real' world encompassed within a 'machine learning' model is 'back-propagated,' using *historical data*, statistical analysis and probabilistic inferences.[73] It is therefore limited and does not compete with human intelligence. The 'alignment problem' is further complicated by the advent of *personalised* 'ideal conversational agents,' since the 'informational content,' contained in the *algorithms* should not be decided upon by a select few 'craftsmen.' In the context of 'machine learning,' many experiments to enhance performance are conducted in the English language and typically exclude cultural sensitivities, context-specificity, idiosyncrasies in the use of the human form of natural language, historical and cross-cultural connotations that enfold human relations and enrich meaning. Just as 'rule matching' does not validate the 'truthfulness' of a sentence, *literal meaning* taken at face value does *not* convey the significance for the speaker and interlocutor(s). The performance of 'machine learning' models requires continuous monitoring and human interventions to assure its *intended* functionality, but that in itself is not sufficient. Congruence with human values is an urgent necessity and processes must match the objective to ensure beneficial outcomes by democratic means.

The increasing complexity of Society and its institutions represents a *cultural* phenomenon. The biological evolution of our species constitutes the 'branching out' and 'differentiation' of a myriad of human languages and rich cultures, interlinked through a common genome and ancestor, Homo sapiens. Human history depicts the inexorable process of social and societal change, which underpins the 'basic directionality' of our lives. While cultural phenomena evolve slowly, social 'norms' emerge from a rich mosaic of human values and beliefs. Our cognitive independence, emotional and behavioural privacy is paramount. Human autonomy and agency is synonymous with the *adaptive resilience* of the Enterprise and Society, as a whole. We need to carefully consider the 'specific ecological context in which AI gets used and the impact it has on cognitive ability, freedom and responsibility in those contexts.'[74] Human-AI Safety is fast becoming a strategic priority, both to foster new economic possibilities and safeguard Civil Society.

Climate Change is undeniably one of our biggest challenges and we seemingly continue to act with 'reckless indifference to our future on planet Earth.'[75] Every nation-state must engage armed with moral and creative courage at a local, regional and global level, seeking to build a new growth paradigm to avert the worst consequences of the common threats to our human existence.[76] Wisdom dispels fear and we should offer resistance to potential threats to our Humanity and protect the quintessence of our being.[77] Human creativity, ingenuity, imagination constitute our unique ability to seek new ideals and find aesthetic value that has thus far shielded us from existential threats. We consciously pursue 'improvisation' and 'collaboration' to ensure our own survival.[78] We share more 'commonalities' than differences, and gravitate towards the formation of social gatherings. We exhibit empathy, care and compassion in the interests of self-preservation. And yet the 'good' that exists in the world is obscured by a negative destructive spiral, amplified by various multimedia channels, detracting from the natural beauty of the Earth and its extraordinary ability to generate Life.

Technology should be the means *not* the end in itself. It should not become an instrument for the curtailment of Civil Liberties; preferably it should foster peace and human flourishing. It should assist not hinder or replace us; preferably facilitate the restoration, preservation and conservation of biodiversity and our precious natural resources. It can aid new scientific discoveries and enable *human beings* to create 'real' growth and prosperity for *all*. Sustainability is an urgent necessity and we *all* have a moral imperative to pursue its virtues. Without great human craftsmanship in 'tékhnē,' the Art of Living and the human form of Communication would be lost.

Epilogue
/'ep.ɪ.lɒg/

HOW TO THRIVE IN THE DIGITAL ERA

'Your purpose in life is to find your purpose and give your whole heart and soul to it.'[1]

In an artificially connected world, the aim is to find your purpose and seek human connection to bring a deeper level of meaning into your Life anew. Spaceship Earth[2] and Life itself didn't come with any instructions; and yet we are all both individually and collectively on a continuing journey of self-discovery. Our individual and common futures are inextricably linked with the health and wellbeing of planet Earth. We should pause for a moment and consider more carefully our thoughts, actions and decisions. Whatever we do matters both to ourselves and to others; it also affects the surrounding environment and Nature, which sustains all the growth needs of Life itself. A purposeful existence is to consider how you are going to make a difference in the world and create new possibilities for you and others to enjoy. When a child enters the world, they instinctively seek to find meaningfulness. They open their eyes and look around to see who is there to care for them, so that they too can learn to care for others. We each have a unique opportunity to be or become 'a lamp . . . a lifeboat . . . [or] a ladder.'[3] We can choose the role we play and if we show people how they are needed, we can build a new ladder to the moon.

Nurture constitutes the future of the Enterprise. Leaders, who show people that they matter, ask better questions so that they feel cared for, noticed and acknowledged, without prejudice or judgment. They do not dismiss fear or anxiety as unfounded, but rather seek to learn from and understand their experience. Authenticity, empathy and compassion are the most powerful tools a Leader can exercise. Recognising a person's individual strengths and showing them how they have made a real difference to the world helps individuals and human beings collectively realise their full potential both within the Enterprise and in Society. Individualised support and context-specificity is the way forward, so that nobody is left behind or ever feels isolated. We are not calculable things or 'objects;' we are human beings and as such we are social beings, enveloped in the process of evolutionary change, at once being and becoming the person we each hope to be.

In the context of the Enterprise, people are indispensable. Without them the Enterprise and Society would not survive. Smart machines can alleviate repetitive tasks, help process vast volumes of data to aid new scientific discoveries and take human beings out of dangerous situations; but machines, no matter how smart they may be, do not possess human intelligence, sentience and consciousness. They are no substitute for human beings; nor should they ever be. Mechanical tools designed for industrial settings and quantitative analysis are ill suited to qualitatively meet human needs, wants and desires. Settings and uses should be carefully considered and potential outcomes viewed with sufficient circumspection to prevent reoccurring harms. It is too late once societal harms have been perpetrated by 'dumb' and 'blind' algorithms perpetuating bias, discrimination and fundamental inequalities. There is no computable optimisation of right or wrong, no playbook that can be readily deployed; nor is there a prescription or handy toolkit to solve *all* our problems, irrespective of the setting. To believe otherwise would simply be a fool's paradise. An abdication of moral responsibility, in legal terms delineated as a fiduciary 'duty of care' and failed accountability in the context of the Enterprise and governmental institutions, leads to grave malfunctions in the 'social systems' and the 'technical systems' in play. And yet there is no need to precipitate humanity blindfolded into a dystopian reality: an increasingly fragmented Society, squandering our precious natural resources through reckless behaviours and the impending threat of global conflict driven by new frontier technologies. This was never the intention of the 'craftsmen,' nor the function or purpose. Depending on the chosen lens, there are a myriad hues and a variety of tonalities that may resonate within the multifaceted prism of our shared reality.

The critical path towards sustainability entails energy and material efficiencies, best achieved by reimagining our digital future. Buckminster-Fuller maintained 'there is no crisis of energy, only one of ignorance.' He calculated a net loss in the costs associated with fossil fuel extraction in the early 1970s, relative to any potential benefit to Society. In his quest to optimise materials, he turned to the design and construction of several geodesic domes, exemplifying the realisation of 'continuous tension and discontinuous compression.' The resulting intricate architecture of adjoining spheres constituted a form of integral tension, 'tensegrity,' which enabled the construction of a lightweight structure with minimal use of materials that could sustain its own weight and had no practical limitations. The Earth's Systems similarly exemplify 'integral tensions,' sustained at once by 'continuous and discontinuous' relationships, as part of a harmonious whole. There is an unbreakable bond within the interconnected and interdependent 'communication systems,' wherein the behaviour of the coherent whole cannot be predicted through observation of its individual parts. The notion of circularity within the Global Economy came to the fore in the 1970s since it was estimated sufficient materials had been extracted from the Earth to warrant recycling and reuse in many new and different forms. Buckminster maintained competition for raw materials or 'necessities' was no longer the way forward and advocated cooperation would be the optimum survival strategy. 'It no longer has to be you or me. Selfishness is unnecessary and henceforth unrationalizable as mandated by survival. War is obsolete.'[4] Wealth is accumulated through Knowledge, which he defined as the 'technological ability to protect, nurture, support and accommodate all the growth needs of life.'

At this juncture we need to believe, it is still possible to change the perilous trajectory we have embarked upon through the age-old 'Art' of international diplomacy. We have the ability to de-escalate rising geopolitical tensions and focus instead on reducing the barriers to diplomacy, while gradually, meticulously and consistently working towards re-building TRUST. Setting realistic goals that are both attractive and necessary for the respective parties at the negotiating table creates the appropriate conditions and means to attain beneficial ends. Finding common ground necessitates a strong and renewed willingness to listen, acquire new Knowledge and gain a deeper understanding of the dynamics of change. While developing a greater awareness of the socio-cultural, historical and political significance that would otherwise continue to jeopardise present and future economic growth and stability within the Global System, under conditions of extreme changing uncertainty. Economic strength is rendered fragile in pursuit of military and political dominance, which results in yet more wasteful destruction and senseless killings. 'Artificial Intelligence' is set to realise 'exponential' economic benefits for interested parties according to some observers and if pursued in the wrong manner may pose an existential threat to humanity. The ambivalent stance taken by those with economic and military interests, framing China as the adversary is both unwise and reckless. All nation-states have common interests in protecting their citizens without wishing to jeopardise their geopolitical standing on the world stage, nor stifle technological advancements and innovation necessary for economic growth and social progress. The use of 'Artificial Intelligence' in some settings poses an existential threat to Society, undermining planetary health and our own survival.

Perplexing uses in the military sphere do not bode well for the future since they may be used in the theatre of war without any concern for ethical and moral reasoning. Dangerous experimentation in the absence of due diplomacy is deeply troubling since it places global populations at greater risk and jeopardises global peace and security for present and future generations. Just as the atomic bomb explosions initiated by the Manhattan project in 1942 led to continued testing of nuclear weaponry above and below ground and in the global oceans, notwithstanding international treaties. The cumulative effect and ensuing radioactive contamination of the Earth's soils and waterways continues to have very serious implications for human health and biodiversity. Accidents like Chernobyl and other nuclear plants may re-occur, but every effort should be made to avoid catastrophe. Modern governance structures require a solid trustworthy, accountable and transparent partnership to be built between Government, the Enterprise and Civil Society. Since the impact of 'Artificial Intelligence' extends beyond borders, we can only succeed in arranging 'safe and reliable uses' if there is a willingness to move towards multilateral collaboration at all levels of Society.

It would be foolish to attempt to predict the future since there are so many unknown unknowns, but we can apply existing Knowledge to ascertain where we stand and grasp the direction in which we are moving. Through its application we may call into question collective wisdom and come to rely upon our intrinsic values encompassed within human consciousness that has evolved over millennia and lies at the core of our being. It is the essence of that which unites us rather than divides us, illuminating anew the possibilities and the 'virtues' of human existence and human existing. The 'truth' is relative both to the individuals concerned and those with whom we may share our current knowledge and experiences. It requires reciprocity to attest its validity; thus it is not always discovered through rigorous logic and reason alone. If that were the case, then everything could be proven simply through human experience and observation. As Hamlet reminds us, we cannot know everything, but on occasion we 'know' more than we can explain and prove through the gathering of evidence or 'big data' in the modern world. In order to preserve our natural instinct for survival, of necessity there must always be an element of doubt. 'At the heart of science is an essential balance between two seemingly contradictory attitudes – an openness to new ideas, no matter how bizarre or counterintuitive they may be and the most ruthless sceptical scrutiny of all ideas, old and new. This is how deep truths are winnowed from deep nonsense.'[5]

If we are to successfully pursue new innovation pathways towards a sustainable digital future, then we must create new opportunities for restorative, inclusive, equitable growth. Setting a new direction entails taking a different course of actions to consciously alter the sequence of events, which thus far have not been conducive overall to beneficial changes in Society. Notwithstanding the many challenges we face, we still have a unique window of opportunity to effect lasting and meaningful change. We can choose to stop interfering with the rhythms and patterns of renewal in the Earth's natural ecosystems and respective cycles. We should become more respectful of Nature since 'real' growth is less about meaningless extraction and exploitation and more about regeneration, preservation and conservation. Taking a holistic view through an ecological lens enables a more fruitful journey of discovery, prompting new ideas, creativity and potentially unexpected findings through the Arts, Sciences and Humanities combined. There is a necessary tension experienced through the inexorable process of change, underpinning the power dynamics in play both within the Human Systems and the Earth's Systems. However, this should focus the mind and aid new scientific discoveries, preferably in pursuit of beneficial ends. 'Artificial Intelligence' or rather the continued development of smart technological systems hinges upon the widespread adoption, applicability and acceptability of the same within Society. Effective global legitimacy and oversight is a prerequisite of earning public trust and the possibility of affording humanity the potential benefits these technologies may bring in support of new scientific discoveries. In the context of the Enterprise, the application of a flexible responsible innovation framework that is continually evolving, synergistically with the Socio-Technical Systems in play, will determine its overall success and longevity. Enterprise and political leaders have a moral 'duty of care,' since the implications of using automated, algorithmically driven AI-Systems are profound and will leave an indelible mark on present and future generations.

WHAT HAPPENS NEXT?

The onset of the global pandemic in late November 2019 created one of the biggest shocks to the Global Economy and Society. It likely will not be the last and so it is necessary to improve health and wellbeing, as a matter of urgency. Having embarked on a personal journey of discovery to understand the underlying causes and grasp the nettle of where the Enterprise needed to go next, I have come to the realisation human dignity, autonomy, agency and our Civil Liberties constitute something worth fighting for now more so than ever before. We cannot hope to achieve global peace nor harmonious thriving societies around the world without a clear and sharp focus on the objective, effectively what matters most to global citizens. The purpose of human existence and human existing does not have to be entangled with misery, pain and suffering, senseless killings and probable escalations towards yet more wars due to the insensitivity and myopic vision of the relatively few who fail to acknowledge the lessons of human history.

Life is the most beautiful journey we have been given the privilege to undertake. Living life to the fullest entails having the courage to embrace uncertainty and partake in a process of continual renewal. We are fortunate to be living in a world where scientific breakthroughs and technological advancements could enable us to live more freely, without artificial constructs that cloud human judgment, leading to ill-conceived ideas and poor quality decisions. The Enterprise comprises individual human beings whose collective talents bring forth new ideas to create products and services, which ought to inspire, support and fulfil human needs without damaging our environment and harming others. Practising 'good' business is simply good for business; a 'just cause' is fundamentally what people are drawn to notwithstanding the challenges and obstacles along the way. Digital business transformation constitutes the transformation of Society and its institutions, both government and governance. In the modern world, we can no longer rely on *old thinking* to see us safely through the necessary transitions and adaptations. And perhaps as scholars suggest, it is time for a new Renaissance, a flourishing of the Arts, Sciences and Humanities combined, so that we can more beneficially explore the *unknown* unknown. Human Reason and Experience is necessary but not sufficient; it is enhanced by our innate curiosity, creativity and the power of the human imagination. Cognisant our current knowledge may be limited and that we as humans may only discover what may be knowable, we may continue to marvel at the mysteries concealed deep within the universe and ask ourselves what lies beyond. We are but a 'tiny blue dot' in the vast expanse of galaxies presently beyond our reach, but that one day may be revealed.

'Our passion for learning . . . is our tool for survival.'[6]

Transcendence of our human condition entails overcoming the limitations in our own thought, choices, actions and decisions, while seeking to achieve a more balanced view of the world and human existence, ideally interacting more harmoniously with Nature and the Earth's Systems to preserve Humanity and our possible futures. We are blessed with being a sentient species, elevated by our unique human consciousness and ability to fully experience a complex multidimensional reality encompassed within our cognitive, emotional and social abilities. Human intelligence includes a 'spiritual' dimension, which serves as a source of inspiration and engenders our deepest intuitions, which in the fullness of time foster a degree of 'completeness' in our innermost sense of being. It is that innermost consciousness which unfalteringly guides us and leads us to seek a higher purpose, through the actualisation of our unique individuality and fullest human potential. Even if this innate 'potentiality' may be misinterpreted by a few bad actors as human history has shown.

The Arts and the Humanities give us a much broader and more colourful canvas to explore our human strengths and weaknesses; whereby we may gain deeper insight and a more intimate understanding of ourselves, through different cultures, linguistic variations and the rich treasure chest of lived and living experiences through the ages. After all, 'the cure for a fallacious argument is a better argument, not the suppression of ideas.'[7]

We have an innate Adaptive Resilience™ and I firmly believe we have the necessary individual and collective strength and impetus to get ourselves out of the complicated mess we have created on planet Earth and should not repeat elsewhere, not just for the sake of the present but also for future generations. Our collective hope and belief in a better future is fundamentally what drives Humanity forward. Change and new beginnings are reflected in the fundamental laws of Nature and also in physics, as perpetual motion engenders the continual transformation of matter in the universe. We are effectively propelled forward by the power of Love in the vast expanse of Infinity, as was so eloquently expressed by Dante Alighieri:

> 'A l'alta fantasia qui manco' possa;
> ma gia' volgeva il mio disio e' l velle,
> si' come rota igualmente e mossa,
> 'L'amor che move il sole e l'altre stelle'[8]

Notes

PREFACE

1. Thomas Henry Huxley (4 May 1825 – 29 June 1895) – English biologist and anthropologist specialising in comparative anatomy. Best known for his courageous defence of evolutionary theory proposed by Darwin. Recognising evolution is not a straight line, he focused on evolutionary relationship between the species and in particular, revealed distinctive features of the human brain relative to our ancestors.
2. Thomas Henry Huxley – 'Evolution and Ethics' The Romanes Lecture, 1893, Collected Essays IX.
3. Socio-Technical Systems are digital systems involving human and 'artificial agents,' otherwise known as 'AAA systems' – Algorithmic, Autonomous and Artificially Intelligent Systems.
4. Stuart Russell, Nicholas Borstrom and others have warned of the dangers; the 'off switch' is no longer a guarantee we can remain in control of autonomous 'artificial agents,' the interplay of computer software and hardware.
5. Thomas Henry Huxley – 'Evolution and Ethics' The Romanes Lecture, 1893, Collected Essays IX.
6. Alexander Pope, An essay on Man, Epistle 1.

INTRODUCTION

1. 'The Fourth Industrial Revolution' is a term first coined by Professor Klaus Schwab in his eponymous book released in 2016. It refers to significant advances in technologies such as AI, robotics, IOT, 3D printing, genetic engineering, quantum computing – https://www.weforum.org/agenda/2016/01/the-fourth-industrial-revolution-what-it-means-and-how-to-respond (accessed 1.3.22).

2. 'Few have truly internalized the implications of the fact that the rate of change itself is accelerating.' Moore's law has been exceeded. 'Most long range forecasts of technical feasibility in future time periods dramatically underestimate the power of future technology because they are based on what I call the "intuitive linear" view of technological progress rather than the 'historical exponential view.' To express this another way, it is not the case that we will experience a hundred years of progress in the 21st century; rather we will witness on the order of twenty thousand years of progress (at today's rate of progress, that is).' Ray Kurzweil (2001). Cf. https://www.kurzweilai.net/the-law-of-accelerating-returns (accessed 2.3.22).

3. According to a recent survey by Edelman, 'distrust is the default emotion in society.' January 2022. Cf. www.edelman.com/trust

4. SARS-Covid-2 coronavirus respiratory disease caused 6.5 million fatalities, infected 595 million people globally, likely more. 12 billion vaccine doses have been administered to date (August 2022). Cf. https://coronavirus.jhu.edu/map.html (accessed 12.8.22).

5. At the Harvard C-CHANGE laboratory there is strong evidence to suggest the actions needed to combat climate change are the exact same actions needed to make people healthier. Cf. https://www.hsph.harvard.edu/c-change/issues (accessed 12.3.22).

6. Elon Musk, CEO at Tesla, has openly admitted that 'excessive automation' at his company was a mistake, tweeting that 'humans are underrated.' (2018). Cf. https://www.livescience.com/62331-elon-musk-humans-underrated.html (accessed 19.3.22).

7. Ethics and the Economic Interpretation' – Frank H Knight. Cf. https://www.jstor.org/stable/pdf/1886033.pdf (accessed 21.3.22).

8. Frank H Knight, founder of the Chicago School of Economics, wrote in his paper 'Ethics and the Economic Interpretation' (1922). Cf. https://www.jstor.org/stable/pdf/1886033.pdf (accessed 21.3.22).

9. Larry Fink, CEO Investment firm Black Rock, 'Letter to the Shareholders, CEOS,' 2022. Cf. https://www.blackrock.com/us/individual/2022-larry-fink-ceo-letter (accessed 10.3.22).

10. Martin Luther King Jr. 'Letter from Birmingham Jail,' advocating the right to freedom.

11. Henry David Thoreau (1817–1862), philosopher, best known for his essay 'The duty of civil disobedience, on resistance to civil government,' first published in 1849. Written at a time when the Mexican–American War threatened to expand slavery, Thoreau's words seem remarkably relevant still today.

12. VUCA is an acronym first coined by Warren Bennis and Burt Nanus in their book 'Leaders, the strategies for taking charge,' first released in 1985, describing a volatile, uncertain, complex and ambiguous multilateral world.

13. The World Wide Web invented by Tim Berners Lee in 1989 made freely available to the public in 1993, was intended to foster the sharing of knowledge on a global scale; and since it is a global 'public good' it calls

for international co-operation. It is possibly the most liberating general technology thus far invented. Cf. https://home.cern/science/comput ing/birth-web (accessed 1.3.22).

14. While illicit activities for the most part occur on the so-called 'dark web,' hidden services or a lack of transparency in the use of algorithms on the World-wide-web is proving problematic. For instance, recommender engines 'nudging' individuals into making purchases they cannot afford, or harms being caused to children accessing unsuitable websites. Legislators in the European Union and the United Kingdom have addressed this issue. The USA, China and India are following suit.

15. Melvin E. Conway, "How do committees invent' (1968). Cf. http://www.melconway.com/committees (accessed 15.8.22).

16. Russia declared 'special military operation' in the Ukraine on 24 February 2022, due to increased NATO presence in neighbouring countries and claims its citizens were mistreated in the Donbas region.

CHAPTER 1

1. William Shakespeare, 'Hamlet,' Act 1, Scene V.

2. Shakespeare may be referencing the limits of human knowledge or human rationality. He plays on the theme of dreams or ghostly appearances to depict the limits of rational or conscious thought.

3. Earlier in the scene, Marcellus and Horatio refer to their sighting of the ghost, was it real or a figment of their imagination? Horatio says:

> 'tis but our fantasy,
> And will not let belief take hold of him
> Touching this dreaded sight twice seen of us.

4. Aristotle in *De Sens* also explored the realm of dreams, explaining that perceived sensations are often felt more deeply in our imagination *'phantasia'* ('perceptual awareness' of the mind) and may colour our judgment of the 'material' physical reality *'phantasmata'* represented in the substance of our dreams.

5. Christof Koch (2010) attests in his recent study 'individuals can rapidly, consciously, and voluntarily control neurons deep inside their head.' Cf. https://www.uclahealth.org/news/mind-over-matter-study-shows-we-consciously-exert-control-over-individual-neurons (accessed 1.3.2022).

6. Daniel Kahneman, 'Thinking fast and slow,' refers to the 'availability heuristic' the tendency to take things at face value, as a *shortcut* to finding meaning.

7. Kriegel argues the psychological process provides causal context. The complex state resulting from 'first order' and 'higher state' pairing, assumes a degree of subjectivity. Conscious perception is always in part conceptual, containing the 'higher order' concept of experience with multiple dimensions.

8. Aristotle, *De Sens.* Cf. https://www.degruyter.com/document/doi/10.1515/agph-2018-0014/html (note 25).

9. In *The Republic*, Plato asserts *intuition* is a unique human capacity. In *Meno* and *Phaedo*, Plato refers to intuition as 'pre-existing knowledge residing in the 'soul of eternity,' a phenomenon by which one becomes conscious of pre-existing knowledge. Cf. https://en.wikipedia.org/wiki/Consciousness

10. Both perception and physical sensations fundamentally influence cognition, behaviour and thought. Cf. https://en.wikipedia.org/wiki/Sense (accessed 16.3.22).

11. 'Self-Representational Theory' is the modern interpretation of Aristotle's thinking. It asserts that a phenomenally conscious mental state, possibly with non-conceptual intentional content, may also possess intentional content and thereby represent itself to the person who is the subject of that state, giving rise to identity of the self. Cf. https://plato.stanford.edu/ consciousness-higher/ (accessed 16.3.22).

12. The visual-sensory-motor system is the principal system through which we can 'see' and interpret the world. For blind people, the *adaptive nature* of the human brain helps them to develop a much stronger sense of hearing and olfactory sense to guide them. Hearing, smell and touch help them to 'see.'

13. Ludwig Wittgenstein (1996) defined expectancy thus – 'It outstretches its arms like a ball player, directs its hands to catch the ball. And the expectancy of the ball player is just that he prepares arms and hands and looks at the ball.'

14. This is referred to as 'multimodality.' Cf. https://en.wikipedia.org/wiki/Sense

15. Our sensory systems constitute external (exteroception) and internal (interoception) perceptual systems, simultaneously processing internal and external stimuli.

16. Rosenthal. Cf. https://plato.stanford.edu/entries/consciousness-higher/ (accessed 1.3.22).

17. Patrick Kelly, 'How exactly is the brain organised?' Cf. https://www.youtube.com/watch?v=EEmpK-HpUW0 (accessed 13.3.2022).

18. Roger Bacon (1212–1292), philosopher and early advocate of the scientific method. Cf. https://en.wikipedia.org/wiki/Roger_Bacon (accessed 26.2.22).

19. Aristotle, *Nicomachean Ethics* VI. 5.

20. *Cybernetics*, from the Greek *'kubernan' to steer*, 'the science of communication and automatic control in machines and living organisms.'

21. Aristotle, *Nichomachean Ethics* VI, 12 'for virtue makes us aim at the right mark, and practical wisdom makes us take the right means . . . [so] it is impossible to be practically wise without being good.'

22. Richard Feynman explains mathematics is concerned with the structure of reasoning (logic) rather than the significance of the symbols. *Human reasoning* expressed in *natural* language is more about meaning.

For example, the *nuances* cannot easily reduced to the exactness of pure mathematical logic.

23. D.J. Chalmers (1996), *The Conscious Mind: In search of a Fundamental Theory*, NY (OUP), raises the question about subjectivity in relation to human consciousness.

24. Aristotle in *De Sens*, referred to '*movements*' based upon '*sensory impressions*,' in the physical body when the physical 'object' was no longer in sight, '*phastasmata*' the *material nature* or 'substance' of dreams; whilst '*phanstasia*,' related to 'perceptual awareness' of the mind 'embodied' in thought. Cf. https://www.degruyter.com/document/doi/10.1515/agph-2018-0014/html (accessed 13.3.2022).

25. 'The Cambridge Declaration on Consciousness in Non-Human Animals' published in 2012, echoes Charles Darwin's suggestion in 1872 that the nature of consciousness in living organisms differs in 'degree and not kind' relative to the species fulfilling their needs. It stated that consciousness in living organisms requires specialised neural structures, and specific activities mainly neuroanatomical, neurochemical and neurophysiological interactions; as well as a central nervous system in order to exhibit consciousness.

26. Mark Twain, *Autobiography*.

27. An axiom is 'a [mathematical] statement or proposition on which an abstractly defined structure is based.' From the Greek, *axioma*, 'what is thought fitting,' *axios*, worthy. The structure is arbitrarily defined, it may be fitting for a particular 'truth' but it may not be the whole truth. Cf. Kurt Godel, *The theory of Incompleteness* (1931).

28. Efforts to break down *human cognition* include IBM Watson, a computational system able to perform advanced 'symbolic' data processing; but computers can only learn through observation subject to training datasets and computational 'learning' parameters, which may *not* be useful outside the boundaries of the human-specified task. If an algorithm is able to 'switch' tasks, many semantic layers are 'lost;' it cannot actually 'see' the reality as a whole or exercise moral reasoning.

29. Homeostasis – constitutes *dynamic* regulation of the internal environment to maintain a constant state.

30. Multiple 'artificial agents' driven by algorithms operate in parallel within a computational system to perform a single task. However, it is *only* mimicry of the human brain, since they each work in isolation, through observation. There is no self-reflection, self-awareness or understanding. In contrast, the human brain does not process available 'information' one step at a time; it performs multiple actions across multiple different regions of the brain that are modality, single task-specific and at the same time exhibit multimodality, multiple intersecting cognitive-sensory-motor tasks. The *non-mechanistic* argument of human consciousness was presented by Godel (1931), Lucas (1961) and Penrose (1989).

31. Aristotle defined the art of persuasion as 'rhetoric,' meaning the ability to influence others by constructing a well-thought out argument to

demonstrate its validity – using *logos*, *pathos* and *ethos;* namely reason, emotion and moral character.

32. This includes the latest Large Language Models (LLMS) released in 2022, such as GPT-4 and updates in LaMDA. The *mechanical* imitation of the human form of natural language is an arduous task. It is proving more difficult to advance the data processing capabilities of computational models, *simply* by uploading ever larger *datasets* despite the latest techniques used in 'deep neural networks.'

33. Algorithms identify *pattern regularities* that 'appear' in vast amounts of aggregated data, following strict mathematical 'rules,' statistical and probabilistic analysis. However, they are 'dumb' and 'blind' since they can only compute the *data they are fed.* They cannot 'see' or understand 'new information,' namely *dynamic* changes in the computational environment; and they cannot 'feel' the effects of potentially harmful suboptimal, *unethical* and *morally unacceptable* outcomes for human beings.

34. Kurt Godel (1931) held a *non-mechanistic* view of the human mind; either the human mind is a computational tool and has limited capacity to understand *all universal truths of mathematics;* or the human mind has a *greater capacity* than a machine to understand *all* the mathematical *truths.* It could not be both. There is a *plausible* gap: the human mind potentially has a greater capacity than a machine to understand 'truths' that cannot be computed by an algorithm or machine, but yet cannot access *all possible* mathematical truths, thus far. He illustrated this in his 'incompleteness theorem' inspired by the 'liar's paradox.'

35. Godel's remark suggests human consciousness extends beyond 'phenomenal awareness' or 'truths' that can be proven scientifically, or at least those which can be computed by an algorithm. This suggests the human mind does not have the *limitations* of a universal computational machine, such as the Turing machine.

36. Searle (1980) refers to 'biological naturalism' where phenomenal consciousness is linked to neural processes in the brain. Differentiates *phenomenal consciousness* and *access consciousness.* Perception of reality and actions taken, expressed through verbal communication or behaviour.

37. Some scientists suggest the speed of human thought is greater than that of the fastest computers, even though we haven't yet been able to explain it. Cf. Roger Penrose's *Quantum theory of the mind.*

38. João D. Semedo et al. 'Feed-forward and feed-back interactions between visual cortical areas use different activity patterns,' Nature, 1.03.22. Cf. https://www.nature.com/articles/s41467-022-28552-w (accessed 31.8.22).

39. Baudelaire called it 'la correspondence des sens,' a powerful and harmonious intertwinement of the senses and the human form of expression, reflected both in the physical body and through verbal communication. Cf. https://fleursdumal.org/poem/103 (accessed 31.8.22).

40. 'Consciousness is having a blueprint of your own software,' Judea Pearl comments in a recent interview, referencing Tononi's 'Integrated theory of

Information' (2004, 2012). Cf. Lex Fridman interview with Judea Pearl (2009). Cf. https://www.youtube.com/watch?v=pEBI0vF45ic (accessed 1.3.22).

41. Bobby Azarian, 'The Mind is more than a machine,' 9 June 2022, Noema (accessed 8.8.22).

42. Gerald Edelman and Antonio Damasio refer to 'neural events' occurring in the human brain; while Kotchoubey (2018) sees human consciousness as an extension of 'complex human behaviours.' The human mind is complex and it is difficult to explain the nature of human consciousness. Roger Penrose believes it is possible the human brain has adopted elements of quantum physics to help navigate the world. Cf. https://en.wikipedia.org/wiki/Quantum_mind (accessed 28.08.22).

43. Cf. Daniel Kahneman, 'Thinking fast and slow,' on the use of heuristics (or rules of thumb, short-cuts to meaning). Some of the most common in the workplace: 'availability heuristic,' taking things on face value subject to the available information; 'confirmation bias,' tendency to confirm or deny a hypothesis either because we convince ourselves or are influenced by others or the environment; 'predictable world bias,' tendency to perceive order where none exists; or more commonly the attempt to seek easy answers to complex problems.

44. Plato, in *The Republic*, discusses with Socrates the *nature* and *meaning* of the 'allegory of the cave.' As the 'prisoners' only 'see' shadows on the walls of the cave, can they be certain this is the reality? What if someone escapes, dares to go outside? In overcoming our fear of the *unknown*, we may yet discover the 'truth.' However, there is a subtlety that is often missed: the reality and our interpretation of the same is unique to each person and so we can improve our understanding, by taking into account different perspectives.

45. Definition is from the *Oxford English Dictionary*.

46. Ludwig Wittgenstein, 'The limits of my language are the limits of my world.' Language is more than a system of symbols. It extends human intelligence beyond the known realm of knowledge into the unknown. Language is greater than the sum of its parts. Machines do not understand themselves and cannot feel pain. Cf. *Tractus logigophilosphicus* (1922).

47. At present, the 'reward function' programmed into the 'Turing machines' does *not* include uncertainty. Machines are programmed to execute a specific 'objective function,' strictly limited in scope, based on statistical analysis and probabilistic outputs. Inferences are *not* 'real' facts. Cf. Stuart Russell https://www.bbvaopenmind.com/en/articles/provably-beneficial-artificial-intelligence/ (accessed 6.9.22).

48. At present, most advanced models simulate aspects of human intelligence in terms of *computational* ability. We should be wary of the algorithm's lack of *understanding*; it has no notion of human values and cultural norms. Current *machine learning* models are *not* yet able to compute high degrees of variability in idiosyncratic use of the human form of natural language and they cannot exercise moral judgment.

49. *Machine learning models* are sophisticated computational tools, seeking *regularities* in *patterns* extracted from large volumes of data representing *past events*, which may *not* be entirely reflective of the present or the future state, and may *not* be relevant outside the strict narrow rules of a given computational task.

50. Human consciousness fundamentally sets us apart from *inorganic* and *inanimate* 'artificial intelligence.' Milner and Goodale (1995) proposed 'two systems theory' of vision, 'a powerful case for the existence of unconscious visual experience.' Cf. https://plato.stanford.edu/entries/consciousness-higher/ (Jacob et al. 2003; Glover 2004) (accessed 13.3.22) .

51. Norbert Wiener (1960), 'Some moral and technical consequences of automation.' Science 131 (3410): 1355–1358.

52. Moral reasoning or intuitive reasoning has not been emulated successfully thus far, even in the most sophisticated 'deep neural networks' or machine learning techniques. The human capacity for *organic optimality* is not readily available to the machine algorithms and they are prone to making more 'biased' (subject to selected training datasets and training methodologies) and *discriminatory decisions* than a natural person would otherwise do in a given situation.

53. High-risk 'artificial intelligence' systems include automated surveillance and decision-making, which involves *manipulation* exploiting human weaknesses. The extensive use of AI-Systems leads to disruption particularly in labour markets, whilst education levels and workforce training have fallen behind recent rapid technological advances. Alan Turing (1951), Norbert Wiener (1960), I.J. Good (1965), Minsky (1984), Nick Borstrom (2014), Stuart Russell (1998, 2000), Elon Musk, Stephen Hawking, Bill Gates have expressed concerns as to the potential dangers of 'artificial general intelligence' (AGI) and 'artificial superintelligence' (ASI), if we fail to properly 'control' *automation* in the new frontier technologies we are developing. However, even if it were *technically* feasible for 'ASI' to absorb the 'sum total of human knowledge,' it is *unlikely* it would be able to outsmart human intelligence and human consciousness, which are *not* computable. Nonetheless, there are risks associated with potential misuse, which need to be mitigated. One of the biggest challenges of the 21st century will be to create 'safe and reliable' AI-systems that are beneficial to human beings and the environment. The 'off-switch' is no longer deemed a guarantee for 'AI-safety,' since a *superintelligent artificial agent* would likely find a way to execute its 'objective function,' as recent studies have shown. cf. Omohundro (2008)

54. Stuart Russell, 'Provably beneficial AI.' Cf. https://www.bbvaopenmind .com/provably-beneficial-artificial-intelligence/ (accessed 6.9.22).

55. Jean Piaget, French developmental psychologist.

56. Daniel Simons and Christopher Chabris (1999) conducted a series of experiments to prove this: groups of people were asked to focus their attention on a specific object and when a gorilla crosses the screen, they fail to notice. Cf. www.theinvisiblegorilla.com

57. Albert Einstein, physicist (1879–1955), best known for his 'theory of relativity,' and his contribution to 'quantum mechanics.' Cf. https://en.wikipedia.org/wiki/Albert_Einstein (accessed 31.8.22).
58. Marie Sulodowska Curie, 'Autobiographical notes,' pp. 167–168.

CHAPTER 2

1. Aristotle, Greek philosopher, 384–322 BC.
2. Sun Tzu, Chinese philosopher, wrote *The Art of War*, late spring – autumn period, 5th century BC.
3. Warren Bennis et al. used the term in 'Leaders, the strategies for taking charge' published in 1985. Cf. https://www.vuca-world.org/where-does-the-term-vuca-come-from/ (accessed 21.3.22).
4. In financial markets, 'Volatility is a statistical measurement of the dispersion of returns for a given security or market index. The higher the volatility, the riskier the security. Volatility is often measured as either the standard deviation or variance between returns from that same security or market index.' Cf. https://www.investopedia.com/terms/v/volatility.asp (accessed 8.4.22).
5. B-corps were established in 2006 in the USA, pledging business as a force for good. Thus far, 3,500 companies have adhered to the highest ethical standards for social and environmental impact. Companies such as Patagonia, Ben & Jerry's, *The Guardian* were early adopters. These trailblazers are now forcing change in C-corps in countries influenced by the Anglo-American business model. In China and Japan, social and environmental responsibility has been prevalent in their *strategic intent*. For example, the 'Toyota Way' much admired is not easily replicated; and more recently the evolution of consumer-producer platforms, such as the Haier group in China.
6. Leaders navigate an abundance of 'noise,' *misinformation* and *disinformation* disseminated by multimedia channels, including social media. Misinformation represents false information, while disinformation is *deliberately false information* used to *deceive* people, whether generated by human or non-human 'artificial agents.' We are at risk of building a Society that may *not* be able to distinguish *inferences* generated by algorithms, and may consider misleading 'falsehoods' as *known facts*; rather than trusting *human intelligence* and our innate abilities to discern a more nuanced and multifaceted 'view' of the reality.
7. The Japanese symbols for 'kaizen', 改善, mean to live with 'good intention' and effect 'good change' by means of *continuous improvement*.
8. The Chinese symbol for 'Wēi危,' denotes danger, but there is another layer of meaning in the combined symbols 'Wēijī', 危机, where Ji, (机), denotes an 'incipient moment, a crucial point when something begins or changes.' In every crisis there is an opportunity for a new beginning. Cf. Victor Mair, Google Scholar (accessed 10.4.22).

9. For example, Luxury groups LVMH, Kering, OTB and others have formed strategic partnerships, *once unthinkable between rivals*, to sustain broader societal and environmental goals, changing their working practices with the aim of preserving 'les métiers,' thereby placing equal importance on the value of human craftsmanship and technology. Without human ingenuity, technical know-how and creativity the industry would find it difficult to undergo a process of *continuous renewal* in pursuit of its strategic aims and purpose.

10. VUCA is the acronym denoting a volatile, uncertain, complex and ambiguous environment.

11. Aristotle referred to four causes: *material,* composition of materials used; *formal,* how materials are used; *efficient,* current understanding of causality – relationship between cause and effect and *final cause* or purpose. There is generally speaking insufficient focus in the modern Enterprise on the 'final cause' relative to the *efficient cause* often 'seen' in binary terms, formal and material causes. While pursuit of the 'efficient cause' may be necessary, it is no longer sufficient to sustain the Enterprise and ensure its prosperity.

12. Recently demonstrated with the unprecedented speed of getting the coronavirus vaccine to market. However, scientists report funding has been inconsistent, making further breakthroughs difficult to achieve. *Political will* on a global scale is required to effect *real* change, though momentum has been lost with resources directed elsewhere.

13. 'We are aligning our portfolio based on the development potential of individual businesses ("Focus"). In the first step, the group will become smaller but more competitive. In parallel, we want to continuously raise the profitability of all businesses ("Improve") so that we can grow profitably again on from our efficient new basis ("Scale"). Our objective in this process is not simply to make a significant contribution to reducing CO_2 and align our activities systematically to sustainability criteria; through our products and technologies, we also want to participate in emerging growth opportunities, e.g. in the areas of renewable energy, hydrogen and e-mobility.' Martina Merz, CEO (since 2019). Cf. https://www.thyssenkrupp.com/en/company/strategie (accessed 10.4.22).

14. S&P estimates by 2030, average lifespan of a corporation will be less than 20 years. Cf. https://www.statista.com/statistics/1259275/average-company-lifespan/ (accessed 1.3.22).

15. Shock announcements were made during the pandemic: Thyssenkrupp strategically 'pruning' using 'Focus-Improve-Scale,' strategy removed business units that did not integrate well with their core. General Electric announced the split into three entities, energy aviation and healthcare, referencing 'greater focus,' and more targeted investments, agility. Johnson & Johnson separated consumer goods from the 'riskier' fast moving healthcare division into two new entities.

16. Martina Merz, CEO of Thyssenkrupp (since 2019). Thyssenkrupp is a leading raw materials trading company operating cross-sector. Cf. https://www.thyssenkrupp.com/en/newsroom/agenda/cross-industry-innovation - (accessed 10.4.22).

17. It is far easier for smaller firms to 'pivot' or adapt to changing circumstances, unencumbered by legacy informational systems and complicated organisational structures.

18. Carl Liebert, former US Navy Seals Commander-in-Chief, 'I learned early on in the SEAL teams that the adrenaline and push during moments of crisis can create an unnecessary level of speed, leading to unnecessary errors and ultimately costing critical time.' (25.01.22) Interview with McChrystal Group. Cf. https://chiefexecutive.net/gen-stanley-mcchrystal-on-ukraine-risk-get-your-business-in-a-boxer-stance/ (accessed 3.2.22).

19. Recent examples include Burberry's collaboration with Marcus Rushford to provide free school meals; Gucci's change-maker programme to assist local communities for the 'next 100 years.'

20. The constituent parts of a Socio-Technical System involve human and 'artificial agents' collaborating in a digital environment. Frequently, insufficient attention is paid to the *human dimension* within the system, resulting in a significant loss of performance and productivity; ultimately profitability suffers.

21. 'RenDanHeYi' business model enables each employee to become an entrepreneur if they so choose.

22. *Kaizen* is the Japanese term for *continuous improvement* in pursuit of a 'higher purpose.'

23. Recently, Haier has embarked on a new regeneration programme to extend the life of its refrigerators, as well as working to improve education levels in local communities, by funding and building new schools. cf. ESG Strategy, www.Haier.com (accessed 3.2.22).

24. Clifford Stoll, American astronomer, author and teacher (6 April 1950–), best known for his work on computer espionage. Cf. *The Cuckoo's Nest* published 1989.

25. Karl E. Weich (1995), American organisational theorist, introduced concepts such as 'sense-making' and 'mindfulness' to organisational development.

26. 'Cisco Hyperinnovation Living Labs (CHILL) differs from seemingly similar approaches, such as R&D alliances, because it focuses on the fast and agile commercialization of ideas without a complicated intellectual property agreement.' This is a 'smart' move, since *multiparty innovation* may entail 'artificial intelligence' and Human Agency. With the exception of India at the time of writing, no other jurisdiction has yet legislated with a view to granting AI models 'property rights.' For example, the US has recently turned down a request for IP attributable to computer software. Cf. https://hbr.org/2016/11/managing-multiparty-innovation (accessed 10.4.22).

27. This reflects the complexity of the Haier business model, which has garnered much interest since the onset of the pandemic. Its strategy has been *dynamically* evolving since CEO Zhang Ruimin took the helm of an ailing manufacturer in the early 1980s. They deliberately created *new pathways* for growth and innovation, ever since Ruimin in December

1984, invited his workers to *literally* smash up all the defective refrigerators that had been damaging the company's revenues and reputation. The Haier group has now become the leading manufacturer of white household goods.

28. Conventional methods such as M&As do not always serve the purpose of the Enterprise, in terms of strategic alignment and the best use of financial capital. In a volatile market place it is difficult to ascertain the potential for future growth and whether productivity levels can improve sufficiently in a short amount of time. Cultural misalignment and other organisational issues may prove difficult to resolve. People, processes and systems' integration failures are costly, both financially and in terms of reputation.

29. Susan Lund et al., at the McKinsey Global Institute, reveal the average duration for large companies to keep their profits is less than 3.7 years. Cf. 'Risk, Resilience and Rebalancing in Global Value Chains,' published online 6 August 2020. https://www.mckinsey.com/business-functions/operations/our-insights/risk-resilience-and-rebalancing-in-global-value-chains (accessed 1.4.22).

30. 'Learning to live with complexity' G. Sargut, R. McGrath, HBS magazine, Sept 2011.

31. Despite fast processing speeds for large volumes of data, there may be a 'disconnect' between the availability of reliable datasets, traceability of the same and real-time analysis of relevant data sets at the time of business need. If data is not refreshed in a *dynamic* manner, it may not be suitable for specific decisions; and this in turn, may create new uncertainties and ambiguities.

32. Recent scientific evidence suggests inferences may prove more accurate with fewer variables and less data. However, that would require decommissioning of a number of *commercial* 'machine learning' models already in use since they rely on large volumes of data being introduced into the computation.

33. It is worth noting the 'reward function' in commercial off-the-shelf 'machine learning' models is skewed towards finding 'pattern regularities' based on narrowly defined classifications for a specific task; they make no allowances for *uncertainty* or *unknown events* not included in the training datasets and 'learning' parameters. If we disregard the 'outliers,' the view of the reality is skewed to what we may wish to 'see' as justification for our own actions, whether or not it is intentional, rather than what we should 'see' or question.

34. Weick, 1995, 61. Cf. https://en.wikipedia.org/wiki/Karl_E._Weick

35. Karl E. Weick, American organisational theorist, first introduced the concept in 1995.

36. 'Cynefin' framework designed by David Snowden is a useful reference tool. 'Exaptive' practices are those, which are shaped through natural selection; existing capabilities develop and evolve naturally to morph into the next best iteration or the next best use/s, subject to the changes in the environment.

37. This is particularly noticeable since the onset of the global pandemic in 2020 and the ensuing 'lockdowns' around the world, which caused significant disruptions in the supply chain.

38. GUCCI runs its 'change-makers' programme to include people from diverse backgrounds, helping local communities regenerate inner-city areas. It is also working towards pay-gender equality in 2025 and inspiring new collaborations through Art, at once beneficial for Society and the next 100 years of the Enterprise.

39. GUCCI's 'Equilibrium' Strategy demonstrates the intricacies and delicate balance required to reconcile competing ESG aims and make the best use of available resources.

40. John Maynard Keynes (1883–1946), *The general theory of employment, interest and money*. Cf. Preface, p. viii (1936).

41. Elon Musk famously tweeted 'humans are under-rated.' Faced with three years sleeping on the floor of his state-of-the-art Tesla facility, he recognised machines could *not* do it all.

42. Taylorism in the 1950s focused on *assembly line* engineering *efficiency*, followed by lean manufacturing led by Toyota in the 1980s. As the 'simplistic notions' transferred to the office environment, overly restrictive business practices became the norm, precluding human creativity and imagination. Insufficient individual and group autonomy, coupled with a lack of variety in the work being performed has alienated the workforce, dubbed 'quiet quitting' by the media. More recently, hard to identify manipulative 'elves' are emerging in the metaverse, eschewing Enterprise 'controls.' Cf. Louis Rosenberg, 'The metaverse will be filled with elves.' https://techcrunch.com/the-metaverse-will-be-filled-with-elves/ (accessed 12.01.22).

43. 'Artificial intelligence' is a powerful tool and should be used 'wisely.' Despite our human imperfections, we must remain firmly in 'control,' and preferably halt military experimentation with autonomous systems with *immediate* effect in *all* countries..

44. Marie Salomea Skłodowska-Curie (1867–1934).

CHAPTER 3

1. Brian Herbert, American author of science fiction (1947–).

2. Culture is formally and informally transmitted through social interactions. In the modern world, the same are being mediated by mechanical means; there is interference or 'noise' being created by algorithms, proposing statistical and probabilistic analyses of select data gathered within the Internet environment.

3. Democratization of *home* computational devices in the late 1980s and the release of the *World Wide Web* in 1993 have radically altered the way Information is consumed and changed the way Culture is formed, following Tim Berners Lee's 'idea of linked information systems.' Cf.

https://www.history.com/ world-wide-web-launches-in-public-domain (accessed 28.9.22).

4. Deborah S Rogers, research fellow Stanford University, writes: 'We need to begin aligning culture with the powerful forces of nature and natural selection instead of [working] against them.' (2008). Cf. https://news.stanford .edu/news/2008/february20/ehrlich-022008.html (accessed 26.9.22).

5. Nicholas Wade, 'Human Culture, an Evolutionary Force,' New York Times, 1.03.2010 (accessed 26.9.22).

6. T. Gruber et al., 'Efficiency fosters cumulative culture across species,' Royal Society, September 2021. Cf. https://royalsocietypublishing.org/ doi/epdf/10.1098/rstb.2020.0308 (accessed 25.9.22).

7. Intuition entails multiple semantic layers acquired through cognitive, sensory, emotional and social cues gained from the surroundings and perceptions of the reality.

8. Maturana and Varela first coined 'Autopoiesis' in 1972.

9. *Homeostasis* is *not* a static state. It affords the Enterprise *continuous movement* and *adaptation,* while being anchored by the core values and ethical principles underpinning the identity of the Enterprise. The recursive nature of *autopoiesis,* self-generation, means the *system* itself behaves in such a way as to *reproduce itself* and maintain its values.

10. In this context, practical knowledge is more about 'phronesis' since actions and decisions are made spontaneously based on individual's frame of reference and moral values. Rather than 'praxis,' the execution of prescribed rule-based or prescriptive actions.

11. Edelman trust barometer 2022, point 01. www.edelman.com/trust

12. Business processes support workflow and the flow of information throughout the Enterprise. In the early 1990s, the focus of Information Technology Systems was to create value for the beneficiary. By the early 2000s, attention turned to cost optimisation through the use of technology, to the detriment of the human beneficiaries.

13. The organisation within the Enterprise may be considered a social system; it is in many ways a microcosm of Society itself.

14. Chris Agyris developed conceptual framework in mid-1980s, 'double-feedback loop' with two-way dialogue, backwards and forwards, as a process to encourage people to think more deeply about their own assumptions and/or beliefs. Cf. https://journalofleadershiped.org/jole_ articles/double-loop-learning-a-concept-and-process-for-leadership-educators/ (accessed 10.4.22).

15. Bernard Keenan, 'Niklas Luhmann, What is autopoiesis?' Cf. https://criti callegalthinking.com/2022/01/10/niklas-luhmann-what-is-autopoiesis/ (accessed 29.9.22).

16. *Causal effects* denote the relationships, interactions and interdependencies between events; for instance something occurred in the past or is now occurring in the present, due to something else that either occurred or is now occurring. However, *inferences* thereby derived should not be taken as 'facts,' evidence that the 'next event' *will* occur. It is simply 'information' based on statistical evidence that may reveal *material,*

formal and *efficient causes* as a result of data processing. They may not reveal the 'final cause' and in this respect inferences cannot be treated as given 'facts.' They require further investigations to *make sense* of the contextual significance in the 'real' world. Cf. https://www.atlas101.ca/pm/concepts/causal-effect/ (accessed 1.09.22).

17. 'Culture eats Strategy for breakfast,' a quote that is attributed to Peter Drucker, Management Expert. Cf. https://www.forbes.com/sites/forbescoachescouncil/2018/11/20/why-does-culture-eat-strategy-for-breakfast/ (accessed 18.4.2022).

18. Heinz von Foerster (1911–2002) explained *machine-learning* processes in terms of 'Non-Trivial' and 'Trivial' Machines, providing *unpredictable* and *predictable* outcomes, respectively. He defined the notion of *agency* in non-trivial machines and noted the absence of the same in trivial machines.

19. Bernard Keenan. Cf. https://criticallegalthinking.com/2022/01/10/niklas-luhmann-what-is-autopoiesis/ (accessed 29.9.22).

20. Given recent breakthroughs in 'machine learning,' there is a tendency to *confuse* machines with human characteristics, such as *intelligence, emotions and intentions.*

21. Data collected and processed using Socio-Technical Systems may contain biases to begin with, and therefore undergoes a 'cleaning process' subject to the desired outcome. However, since the emphasis is on mathematical accuracy, the 'cleaning process' itself may introduce further biases. It is important to note how the semantic layers of the technical system are being maintained.

22. During the global pandemic, Airbnb had to drastically reduce its workforce. The CEO set up a special division to assist those who had been made redundant find new positions, and personally endorsed each person within his own network to assist former staff members' secure new roles.

23. Steve Jobs, New Yorker Interview. Cf. https://www.newyorker.com/news/news-desk/steve-jobs-technology-alone-is-not-enough (accessed 14.3.22).

24. 'Micro-battles system.' Cf. https://www.bain.com/contentassets/3f735ec325c44932ba164a2888871ad7/bain_compendium_the_bain_micro_battles_system_4.0.pdf

25. Virtual reality is a computer-generated environment wherein a user can interact with another user, to varying degrees. It can be a *fully* immersive, *semi*-immersive or *non*-immersive experience, depending on the method used to access the space. Some people prefer 'Occulus' 3D glasses for a *fully* immersive experience, though this has been shown to cause *mental health problems* after long hours of use. Not dissimilar to the *addictive effects* of the 'gaming craze' in Japan during the late 1980s and early 1990s, resulted in *social maladaptation* and in extreme cases suicide due to *individual* isolation.

26. Frequently used platforms include Zoom, Microsoft Teams, Google hangouts, FB workplace and WeCHAT in China, an application supported by Tencent, which has evolved to include healthcare services,

such as telemedicine, triggered by the pandemic lockdowns and inability to access medical and healthcare services in person.

27. The 'great resignation' demonstrated high levels of worker dissatisfaction and ill health not just as a result of Covid-19. While not new 'burnout' was officially recognised as a 'health phenomenon' in 2019 and hit its peak in April 2021 affecting many countries globally, including UK, USA and China, frequently used as benchmarks.

28. Since the outbreak of Covid-19, a significant rise in *mental health problems* and high levels of stress have been reported in the remote 'workplaces.' The absence of changes of scenery, movement, social interactions, financial concerns and isolation intensified in city-bound populations. Governments intervened with furlough schemes, but in some cases left out vulnerable groups in the population.

29. D. Klinghoffer et al. (HBR 24.6.22) 'Why Microsoft measures employees thriving, not engagement.' Cf. https://hbr.org/2022/06/why-microsoft-measures-employee-thriving-not-engagement (accessed 30.7.22).

30. K. Hogan is the CHRO at Microsoft, brought in by Satya Nadella, the current CEO, to change the culture, previously much criticised for being overly focused on KPI's. Cf. https://hbr.org/why-microsoft-measures-employee-thriving-not-engagement (accessed 30.8.22).

31. Employee attrition has always been an Enterprise concern. Once again it has risen to the top of Boardroom agenda, hence a new way of thinking *is* required. A more flexible approach is encompassed within a 'portfolio skills model,' blending internal and external talent sources seamlessly, based on *actual* needs in a *dynamic* and timely manner.

32. Stakeholders in the 21st century include employees, customers, suppliers, communities (local, regional, global), shareholders, Society and the Environment.

33. Cf. https://www.toyota-europe.com/world-of-toyota/this-is-toyota/toyota-in-the-world

34. 'The Toyota Way.' Cf. https://global.toyota/en/company/vision-and-philosophy/toyotaway_code-of-conduct/ (accessed 30.8.22).

35. Sakichi Toyoda, Japanese Inventor (1867–1930). Cf. https://en.wikipedia.org/wiki/Sakichi_Toyoda

36. Plato, Greek philosopher, 428–348 BC.

37. 'Double-loop learning in organisations,' Chris Argyris, HBR, Sept. 1977.

38. Paul Polman, ex-CEO, Unilever. Cf. 'Net positive.'

39. The CEO Louis Camilleri and Chairman John Elkann formed a strong partnership. #EssereFerrari is a powerful testimony of company culture, the sense of belonging, core brand values and the legitimacy Ferrari has earned over time. Cf. F. Gino, 'Ferrari, 'Back on track,' (2020). https://www.hbs.edu/covid-19-business-impact/insights/leading-through-a-crisis/back-on-track-what-leaders-can-learn-from-ferrari-s-approach-to-the-pandemic (accessed 1.2.22).

40. Patagonia chose to extend its childcare services to support working parents. Ferrari chose to bring workers back to the factory safely, once

government restrictions were lifted, working with local authorities and communities to manufacture urgently needed ventilators. Burberry and others in the fashion industry switched production to Personal Protective Equipment or hand sanitizers in the case of L'Oréal. Larger groups in the fashion industry extended financial support to small individual suppliers in their supply chain both to preserve their craftsmanship and help them survive.

41. Sue Cantrell et al. 'The Skills-based organization: A new operating model for work and the workforce' published 8.9.22, Deloitte Insights. Cf. https://www2.deloitte.com/us/en/pages/human-capital/articles/the-skills-based-organization.html (accessed 30.9.22).

42. Mechanics change the wheels of a car under *race conditions* in just 2 seconds. The level of technical skill, training drills and preparation is plain for all to see. However, high performance depends upon the deep bond between *all* the team members.

43. Leena Nair, ex-CHRO at Unilever, recently appointed Global CEO at Chanel (2021), makes the point *perceptions* need to change, in order to recognise the *value* of human talent for the Enterprise. 'Investors haven't fundamentally shifted their perception of the impact of human resources. People only exist on the cost line of the P&L statement. We have intangible value for brands, but not for people's potential. I'm determined to change that by bringing much more data and analytics to the field of HR to show the impact. There are a host of metrics you can use – it's not a perfect science, but there are ways to measure.'

44. Marcus Aurelius, *Book VI*, 54, Meditations.

45. This is particularly the case since the Enlightenment, or the Age of Reason 17th–18th-century European philosophers, whose influence extended globally.

46. Technically speaking, multiple points of failure are required in a system, so that the *whole* system does not fail. Hence the modularity of platform based systems and *in-built redundancies*. It incurs a cost but the risk of total failure would be too great. One small error in one part of the system is amplified across the system as a whole.

47. Brian J Ford, 'Artificial intelligence may be many things, but one thing is certain: It is not intelligent.' Cf. 'AI: artificial yes, intelligent not' published in The Microscope, Vol. 66(2): 71–83, 2018. http://www.brianjford.com/CF32.pdf (accessed 30.9.22).

48. 'Metaverse' Gartner survey. Cf. https://www.weforum.org/agenda/2022/03/hour-a-day-in-metaverse-by-2026-says-gartner/ (accessed 1.10.22).

49. Indra Nooyi, ex-CEO, PepsiCo (USA).

50. Hybrid workplaces, integrating physical and remote locations gained more prominence as a result of the global pandemic, enabled by technology advancements and *system interoperability*. However, on the flipside there are increased risks for the Enterprise; including Privacy, Data protection and critical ethical issues that have come to the fore.

CHAPTER 4

1. Benjamin J Franklin, American polymath, intellectual, political philosopher and one of the founding Fathers of the USA, author of the US Declaration of Independence and the first US Postmaster General. Cf. https://en.wikipedia.org/wiki/Benjamin_Franklin (accessed 18.4.22).

2. Etymology: growth (n.) 'stage in growing,' from grow + -th (2), on model of health, etc. Old Norse gróði, from groa 'to grow.' Meaning 'that which has grown' is from 1570s; 'process of growing' is from 1580s. Old English used grownes 'increase, prosperity.' Cf. *Oxford English Dictionary*.

3. *Rasion d'être* from French meaning 'reason for being or existing.'

4. *Natural law*, as defined by the Greek philosopher Aristotle (384–322 BC), represents our intrinsic human values, that which is 'just by nature' which may not always coincide with that which is 'just by law,' where the law stands for man-made laws reflective to some extent of societal and cultural norms. Our intrinsic values as human beings constitute natural justice that is valid anywhere with the same meaning and force. It is a positive thing and it does not exist by 'people thinking this or that' since it is intrinsic to our human nature. Cf. https://www.investopedia.com/terms/n/natural-law.asp (accessed 18.10.22).

5. *ESG* is an acronym denoting Environmental, Social and Governance structures. The term was first coined by the United Nations Environmental Programme Initiative, so-called 'Freshfields Report,' published in October 2005, describing a legal framework for the integration of environmental, social and governance issues into institutional investing, working towards sustainability on a global scale. Cf. https://www.unepfi.org/fileadmin/documents/freshfields_legal_resp_20051123.pdf (accessed 28.9.22).

6. Trade agreements at the time of writing are being negotiated on bilateral and regional terms. This is set to continue for the foreseeable future due to an *emerging multipolar world*, given the tensions in China–USA relations and Russia's antagonism are being extended to the Global Economy. Disruptions in supply chains, economic sanctions, new tariff barriers, e.g. on semi-conductors will slow growth and likely cause a deeper and longer-lasting recession. Hence, an integrative approach towards finding constructive solutions where conflicts of interest exist, particularly around energy supplies (e.g. gas and oil) would be more beneficial, as we endeavour to move towards a 'green transition.' Economic growth flourished during the period of relative stability 1980–2010.

7. The most successful examples are: China lifted 800,000 citizens out of poverty and enjoyed double-digit growth for 30 years. Real GDP growth peaked at 14.2% in 2007, falling to 6.6% in 2018, as the economy matured. The IMF estimates China will grow by 4.3% in 2023 due to decline in output as a result of extended Covid-19 lockdowns. Similarly, India's GDP grew by 6.5% p.a. on average, post economic reforms of 1991, and it too has enjoyed a fast-developing technology

sector. African and Latin American countries have also shown economic progress.

8. There is a difference between *digitisation*, the conversion of data into a digital format, and *digitalisation*, the digital *integration* of systems. Following the outbreak of the global pandemic, there have been substantive investments in Eurozone countries towards digitalisation. For example, France and Italy both adopted a digital-first approach to accelerate modernization of their respective economies.

9. William C Dudley, CEO Federal Reserve Bank of New York, speech (11.5.17) to BSE, Mumbai, India. Cf. https://www.newyorkfed.org/news-events/speeches/2017/dud170511

10. The shift had been happening since 1950s in the USA, as manufacturing including the automobile industry moved overseas, primarily because companies sought lower labour costs. By exporting their expertise, they created larger global markets and reaped the rewards. Europe began losing its manufacturing capacity in the1960s, while the UK mining and manufacturing industries declined in the 1980s, following the oil shocks in the 1970s.

11. Volvo is a known example of 'overstretching' its portfolio beyond the manufacture of trucks, cars, buses and heavy vehicles, to the production of pharmaceuticals, beverages and frozen foods until it was restructured in the early 2000s.

12. Nokia produced 900,000 mobile phones in 2006 and required 275 million components daily. Most components were sourced globally and more than 50% involved cross-border transactions. Cf. F. Erixon, 'The economic benefits of globalisation for business and consumers.' https://ecipe.org/wp-content/uploads/2018/01/Globalization-paper-final.pdf (accessed 30.10.22).

13. For example, the US banned the import of tyres, costing the economy USD 900,000 per worker, more than 20 times the average income of a domestic tyre worker. This delayed tyre workers transitioning to new industries, causing societal problems for local communities, as workers were unable to find new employment elsewhere when firms failed and trade restrictions were later lifted.

14. H. P. Wei, 'Does Financial Openness Affect Economic Growth in Asian Economies? A Case Study in Selected Asian Economies 1980–2010'. Cf. Journal of Economics and Political Economy, 1(2). (December 2014)

15. For example, Arirbnb was forced to downsize during Covid-19 lockdowns. The CEO created a new division to help his workforce find new positions during the economic downturn and personally endorsed his employees using his own network.

16. Panicos Demetriades, Professor of Financial Economics, University of Leicester.

17. McKinsey Global Institute study found between 65% to 70% of households in 25 advanced economies had flat or declining *real* incomes in the decade 2010–2020.' Cf. 'The Social Contract,' published 5.2.2020, https://www.mckinsey.com/~/media/mckinsey/industries/public%20

and%20social%20sector/our%20insights/the%20social%20contract%20
in%20the%2021st%20century/mgi-the-social-contract-in-the-21st-
century-executive-summary-final.pdf

18. Paul Krugman 'The Age of Diminishing Expectations' (1994). Cf. https://
www.oecd.org/ productivity-stats/40526851.pdf (accessed 26.4.22).

19. For example, austerity measures in 2010, led to a rise in UK unemploy-
ment to 8%; GDP output fell by -4.5%. This was mitigated by sharp cuts
to interest rates from 5% to 0% and stable price inflation at 2%; but
economic recovery stalled with foreign investors deterred by Brexit and
the lengthy decoupling process from the EU (2016–2021) fuelled a 'let's
wait and see attitude.' The UK lost high- and low-skilled workers from
the EU discouraged from remaining in the UK, effectively contributing
to the labour shortages cross-sector. For example, in November 2022 a
record 132,000 NHS vacancies remained unfilled. Post-Brexit 'trade barriers' and 'extra bureaucratic costs' continue to weigh heavily on British
businesses. Absent significant trade deals, which can take a *very* long
time to negotiate, the UK is set for a very slow economic recovery.

20. Both the UK government and the US Federal government sought to
modernise their economies in the early 1980s by pursuing policies in
favour of a 'smaller state,' following the Chicago School of economic
thought led by Milton Friedman with their own interpretation of modern
monetary theory, dubbed 'Thatcherite-Reaganomics.'

21. Falling productivity levels are seemingly correlated with *stagnating* real
wages. For example, the UK experienced a dramatic fall in productivity
in 2007. Castle and Hendry noted a *flat-lining'* in productivity growth
that had not occurred in the previous 160 years.

22. For example, occupational licences in California and professional licences
in other US states limited inter-state mobility of the workforce, which had
previously helped to re-balance any shortfalls in the skills required by
employers.

23. McKinsey Global Institute, 'The Social Contract,' February 2020.

24. The largest global economy at the time of writing is the USA. Cf. https://
www.investopedia.com/articles/investing/110215/brief-history-income-
inequality-united-states.asp (accessed 27.4.22).

25. Gini Index shows current and future distribution of total income, while
Gini Coefficient indicates wealth transfers. They are important indicators
for intra-generational and inter-generational socio-economic mobility
and the degree of inclusivity in terms of current and future growth.

26. Social unrest, economic hardship, crime and mental illness became more
intense during the global pandemic as civil liberties were restricted. 'Me
Too' and 'Black Lives Matter' protests had echoes worldwide; both sets
of activists sought *social justice* and *social equity and equality;* issues as
yet unresolved.

27. McKinsey Global Institute reports the rate of increase in real wages
halved to 0.7% between 2000 and 2018 in the G20, compared with a rise
of 1% between 1995 and 2000. Median income grew more slowly than
wages, 0.4% annually between 2000 and 2016. Cf. 'The Social Contract,'

https://www.mckinsey.com/~/media/mckinsey/industries/public%20 and%20social%20sector/our%20insights/the%20social%20contract%20 in%20the%2021st%20century/mgi-the-social-contract-in-the-21st-century-executive-summary-final.pdf

28. For example, real wages in the UK have fallen together with productivity levels since 2007 and there has been negligible growth in the UK economy. Cf. Research carried out by D. Henry, J. Castle, OUP. Cf. https:// voxeu.org/article/paradox-stagnant-real-wages-yet-rising-living-standards-uk (accessed 27.4.22).

29. China's GDP peaked at 14.2% in 2018. Current expectations in 2022 are approx. 4.5%–3.5% subject to Covid-19 restrictions. IMF Global Economic Outlook report October 2022.

30. US Federal deficit of 30 trillion represented approximately 1/3 of global estimated GDP 95 trillion in October 2022.

31. China is ambitiously pursuing growth within its national borders and overseas through the 'Silk & Belt Road initiative.' While providing alternative sources of funding for developing nations, it has contributed to rising tensions in its relationship with the USA.

32. Taiwan's TSMC satisfies 56% of global demand for semi-conductors; South Korea, 18%; China, 10%; and USA, 6%. Taiwan became competitive in semi-conductors due to its 'openness' towards innovation and local firms working closely with their customers. In October 2022, USA placed export restrictions on US technology companies, limiting equipment, personnel and semi-conductors being exported to China, intended to slow its progress in the technology sector. It will not benefit either nation or the Global Economy. Both China and USA seek self-sufficiency in semi-conductors, used in a wide range of industries from smartphones to automobiles and weaponry.

33. According to research carried out by Yale, over 1,000 companies withdrew from Russia due to the conflict with Ukraine. Cf. https://som.yale. edu/story/2022/over-1000-companies-have-curtailed-operations-russia-some-remain (accessed 7.11.22).

34. China imposed strict lockdowns in many manufacturing districts between 2020 and 2022. The 'zero-Covid' policy coincided with low vaccination rates in China. In the West, 75% of citizens received booster 'jabs' every 6 months, while low-income countries had vaccinated only 25% of their citizens and only 1%–2% had initial 'booster' shots, 2 years after the outbreak of Sars-Coronavirus-19.

Cf. WHO announcement (11.2.20). Cf. https://www.who.int/emergencies/ diseases/novel-coronavirus-2019/technical-guidance/naming-the-coronavirus-disease-(covid-2019)-and-the-virus-that-causes-it (accessed 19.10.22).

35. Commentators highlighted e-commerce driven curbside delivery 'explosion' as one of the key factors supporting US economic recovery in latter part of 2020. In contrast, Euro-zone countries and the United Kingdom had a much slower response; economic growth slowed further in 2022 due to the Ukraine war, triggering a 'cost of living crisis' with soaring energy and food prices.

36. 'Overheat' means demand in the economy is growing 'too fast,' relative to the available supply of goods and services. For example, US consumer spending in housing, cars, entertainment and clothing exceeded available supply, post Covid-19 lockdowns, particularly those in China; given the US economy is heavily reliant on imports and China is a major trading partner.

37. There is renewed concern a new US 'housing bubble' is building, since prices rose by 76% in 2021. During the pandemic, citizens abandoned big cities and sought more tranquil suburban areas. This was reflected in 'the great resignation' as employees chose quality of life over higher salaries. Ensuing talent shortages created a 'tight' US labour market, reflected in other economies, e.g. the UK, and EU.

38. Studies reveal the shortage of imported consumer goods and US supply chain disruptions also heavily reliant on imports, e.g. semi-conductors fuelled excess demand and rising inflation, accounting for 50% cumulative price increases in the immediate aftermath of the global pandemic. Cf. K. Rogoff, Foreign Affairs (accessed 11.12.22).

39. For example, the UK government spent GBP 70 billion on furlough schemes. www.gov.uk (accessed 7.11.22).

40. Blackouts and energy rationing spread across Europe in October 2022, with Russian oil and gas supply reduced to one fifth of previous supply levels in 2021 (approx. 2 million barrels of oil per day, prior to the Ukraine war). At the same time, OPEC reduced its supply by 2 million barrels per day, causing prices to skyrocket globally.

41. The IMF estimates global output will fall below 2% GDP in one third of global economies 2022–2024, which has only happened five times in the previous century. Cf. Pier-Olivier Gourinchas, Economic Outlook report, October 2022.

42. Extreme weather events have increased in frequency over the last two decades; severe droughts and wild fires have spread across Europe, North America on a scale and intensity not seen before. Temperatures have risen dramatically across the globe, causing ice sheets to melt faster than previously recorded with extreme flooding in Pakistan in September 2022 – one third of the country under water and 33 million people displaced suffering from water-ridden diseases and starvation. Cf. https://www.bbc.co.uk/news/world-asia-62830771; Cf .https://www.theguardian.com/world/2022/oct/12/pakistan-floods-impact-years-crops-farms (accessed 12.10.22).

43. Greta Krippner describes 'financialisation' of modern economies as a 'pattern of accumulation in which profit making occurs increasingly through financial channels rather than through trade and commodity production.' Cf. *Financialisation and the world economy*, 2005, edited by G.A. Epstein.

44. British economist Diane Coyle notes the economies of the 21st century are increasingly oriented towards intangible goods and 'information-led, geometrically extendable services,' as a result of ICT and so-called 'network effect.' It will be interesting to see how value is measured in a

dematerialised world, with increasing popularity of non-fungible tokens (NFTs), cryptocurrencies and other forms of digital products and services that are likely to emerge.

45. There are concerns over foreign exchange volatility, the strength of the USD and the current debt crisis being extended to more nations in the developing world. In addition, the use of financial instruments such as derivatives is problematic. Initially, they were used to hedge against agricultural losses, but became more widely traded as financial assets post-market deregulation in the 1980s. More than 50% of derivatives are traded through the London Stock Exchange (LSE), along with 75% of secondary fixed income products. LSE has strong ties with Asia and the US; hence, if the system *malfunctions* it impacts the Global Economy.

46. Ever since the USD became the world's reserve currency of choice in 1944, the balance of power was radically altered. In 2022, approximately 50% of international trade for goods and services, including energy are traded in US Dollars; approximately 50% international loans and global debt securities are denominated in USD and 60% of foreign exchange currency reserves held by central banks are denominated in USD. In foreign exchange markets 90% of transactions include US Dollars. Cf. https://crsreports.congress.gov/product/pdf/IF/IF11707 (accessed 18.10.22).

47. Securitisation markets faltered in the Spring 2007, as mortgage-backed securities and collateralised debt obligations lost significant value. Markets almost shut down in the Autumn 2008 and in February 2009, Ben Bernanke, Chair of Federal Reserve said trade was suspended, excepting 'conforming mortgages' sold to Fannie Mae and Freddie Mac. Almost one third of private credit markets were unavailable as a source of funds, severely impacting liquidity in the US with a knock-on effect in the Global Economy.

48. The Great Depression of the 1930s entailed a severe drop in house prices and foreclosures with millions losing their homes which led to a banking crisis. There have been repeated 'house price bubbles' in the past century. For example, the 2007–2008 US experience is not dissimilar from the 'housing bubble' collapse in Japan in 1991, fuelled by commercial real estate speculation. While the impact was regional, the domestic economy in Japan has still not fully recovered. In 2022, there are concerns the 'bubble' may burst in China and/or the USA, where house prices have skyrocketed during the pandemic. If either of the two 'bubbles' burst, it would have a detrimental effect on the Global Economy.

49. The US Inquiry Commission Report (January 2011), concluded its findings as follows: 'the crisis was avoidable and was caused by: Widespread failures in financial regulation, including the Federal Reserve's failure to stem the tide of toxic mortgages; Dramatic breakdowns in corporate governance including too many financial firms acting recklessly and taking on too much risk; An explosive mix of excessive borrowing and risk by households and Wall Street that put the financial system on a collision course with crisis; Key policy makers ill prepared for the crisis, lacking a full understanding of the financial system they oversaw; and systemic breaches in accountability and ethics at all levels.' Cf. https://

web.archive.org/web/20110130170725/http://www.fcic.gov/files/news_pdfs/2011-0127-fcic-releases-report.pdf (accessed 1.05.22).

50. Bretton Woods System pegged all participating currencies to the USD based on a fixed price of gold, following the Smithsonian agreements in 1944. They were revised several times, but eventually due to increased demands from participating nations, the Nixon administration could not guarantee convertibility of the US Dollar to the agreed value in gold. Though there have been changes in the floating exchange rate system due to globalisation, technology and geo-politics, the USD remains dominant currency.

51. Owing to tensions in US-China relations and Russia's antagonism, low- to middle-income countries in debt distress, have increasingly turned to China for alternative financing. China is partly decoupling its domestic economy from the USD and planning its own CBDC. A full divorce is not expected as China and the US, are mutually dependent on each other and have a strong trading relationship. China accounts for 1/3 US capital inflows, which help support US Federal Deficit. Emerging economies also account for a significant proportion of US capital inflows, since 80% of their debts were denominated in USD in 2020. Cf. https://www.fsb.org/wp-content/uploads/P260422.pdf

52. GDP measures used today follow later modifications by John Maynard Keynes. GDP is viewed in terms of output, income or expenditure and relative changes over periods of time. Cf. Diane Coyle, *GDP – A Brief Affectionate History*. Princeton University Press first published 2015.

53. Kuznets recognised the measure he invented was imperfect owing to its underlying assumptions, which reflected the human necessity to simplify complexity – 'the effectiveness of an argument is often contingent upon oversimplification.' Cf. Simon Kuznets. "How to Judge Quality." *The New Republic*, 20 October 1962.

54. Cf. https://en.wikipedia.org/wiki/Simon_Kuznets (accessed 28.4.22).

55. In fact, two measures were produced at the time, Gross National Product, measuring economic output regardless of national boundaries and Gross Domestic Product, measuring economic output within national borders, which the USA did not adopt until 1991. Most other countries adopted GDP as a measure of national economic output in 1944, following Bretton Woods.

56. Stakeholders include businesses, institutions, governments, global societies and planet Earth. In the context of the Enterprise, more attention must be given to the wider society, the Environment and governance structures, leveraging the strengths of the stakeholders within the Enterprise's immediate sphere of influence, including employees, suppliers, customers, consumers and local communities.

57. Resilience should be viewed through an *holistic* lens. It comprises financial, operational, organisational, technological, reputational and ecological resilience. Socio-Technical Systems within the Enterprise should be designed with sufficient flexibility, encompassing *human needs* both

to function properly and enable the Enterprise to grow and evolve over time.

CHAPTER 5

1. Albert Einstein, German physicist (1879–1955).
2. Most recently Covid-19 (2020–), war in the Ukraine (2022–) and the Global Financial Crisis (2007–2008) created significant *disturbances* in the Global System and new overlapping challenges for the Enterprise across its ecosystem.
3. The industrialisation of food production stems from the first Agricultural Revolution and the Industrial Revolution with the shift from 'manpower' to 'horsepower,' later substituted by machines. The next frontier is likely to be *fully* autonomous systems running industrial and agricultural eco-systems with 'human-in-command' of 'artificial intelligence' and human supervision of the processes and *machine lifecycles*.
4. IoT – the 'Internet of Things' signalled machine-to-machine connectivity through the use of sensors.
5. IoE – the 'Internet of Everything brings together people, processes, data, and things to improve network connections, while turning 'infor-mation' into actions that *hopefully* create *beneficial* capabilities and new economic opportunities for businesses, individuals and countries.' Cf. https://www.cisco.com/ innov/IoE_Economy_FAQ.pdf (accessed 19.11.22).
6. Statistical significance is frequently misunderstood. The collection of data, the way it is sampled and *categorised* during experimentation to prove or disprove a hypothesis matters. The 'cleaning' process may intro-duce new distortions in the sample dataset, which may not be relevant for unspecified tasks. Careful analysis beyond the data is *more important*. Cf. Amy Gallo 'A refresher on statistical significance,' (2016), https://hbr .org/2016/02/a-refresher-on-statistical-significance (accessed 30.3.22).
7. Past, present and future form part of our assessment of a given situ-ation, they are 'integrated facets of temporal agency,' Ricoeur (1984). 'Reality exists in a present, but the immediacy of present situations is extended by our ability to imaginatively construct a sense of the past and the future.' Cf. Arun Kumaraswamy et al. 'Perspectives on disruptive innovations,' (published 16.7.2018), Journal of Management Studies, Special Issue, Managing in the Age of Disruptions.
8. Claude Shannon identified the 'fundamental problem of communication is for the receiver to be able to identify what data was generated by the source, based on the signal it receives through the channel.' Cf. https:// en.wikipedia.org/wiki/A_Mathematical_Theory_of_Communication
9. Plamen Nedeltchev Ph.D., IT Engineer, wrote 'In the IoE, identity must extend beyond the conventional. If identity is compromised, the security

perimeter is defeated. Simultaneously, creating a unified identity that addresses users in the physical and virtual world will continue to be a challenge. It's something we like to keep stressing.' Cf. The 'Internet of Everything is the new economy,' (2013), https://www.i-scoop.eu/internet-of-things-iot/internet-of-everything-2/ (accessed 19.11.22).

10. For example, Spotify, TikTok, Instagram are moving towards experiential shared consumer-producer business models. During Covid19 lockdowns, TikTok hosted pop-star duets with their individual fans, Instagram hosted live-stream virtual concerts and Spotify offered simultaneous listening to podcasts and music. Consumers seek *real-time* interactive experiences, as technology opens up opportunities for creative innovations, shortening distances between the Enterprise and potential new markets.

11. Newly available 'off-the-shelf' software is driving P2P lending. The famous example is mPesa, which began in Kenya and is now transforming opportunities for many communities in many countries on the African continent.

12. There are numerous examples of collaborations between rivals in the past decade. Fashion is an extremely competitive industry. For example, Allbirds began by researching natural materials to produce sneakers responsibly, with as little waste as possible. It partnered with Adidas to enhance its capabilities and contribute to Society on a wider scale; reasoning their innovative materials could bring greater benefits to the company through lower material and transaction costs and Society through education. Cf. https://www.allbirds.co.uk/pages/sustainable-practices#realitysneaker (accessed 18.11.22).

13. VRIN + O = acronym most often used in the context of innovation. To sustain competitive advantage over time, the Enterprise is best advised to identify Valuable, Rare, Imperfectly Imitable, Non-substitutable assets and sources of value that it is able to maintain over time across its ecosystem.

14. Albert Szent-Gyorgyi, (1893–1986), Hungarian biochemist, won Nobel Prize for Medicine (1937) and multiple other awards in his lifetime. Cf. https://en.wikipedia.org/wiki/Albert_Szent-Györgyi (accessed 20.11.22).

15. The conceptualisation of Disruptive Innovation was advanced by Clayton Christensen (1952–2020), whose best known books begin with 'The Innovators Dilemma,' inspiring many entrepreneurs who consistently defied established norms and disrupted the status quo; Steve Jobs and Jeff Bezos have exemplified in reality many aspects of his theorem.

16. Who got there first is still a contentious issue today. *Luna2*, unmanned spacecraft built by the USSR, intentionally crashed into the moon's surface on 12.9.1959. *Apollo 11* was the first crewed spaceflight enabling Neil Armstrong and Buzz Aldrin to land on the moon on 20.7.1969 and return safely to Earth. Cf. https://solarsystem.nasa.gov/news/890/who-has-walked-on-the-moon/ (accessed 23.11.22).

17. Marianna Mazzucato called for new 'moon shots' to be orchestrated through public-private sector collaborations in her book *The Mission*

Economy, taking as an example NASA, working with broad coalitions across Civil Society, academia, public and private entities to realise its mission in 1969.

18. Clayton Christensen, 'The innovators DNA,' (2009). Cf. https://hbr.org/2009/12/the-innovators-dna (accessed 21.11.22).

19. S&P 500 companies average lifespan is less than 20 years. Only 50 of the original Fortune 500 companies listed in 1955 are still in existence.

20. Polányi Mihály (1891–1976): 'tacit knowledge' differs from 'explicit knowledge.' It is a term first coined by Polanyi in 'The tacit dimension,' (1966) and denotes 'know-how' – the ability to do something without being fully aware of all its dimensions or being able to fully articulate and explain it how it happens. Cf. https://en.wikipedia.org/wiki/Michael_Polanyi (accessed 24.11.22).

21. Michelangelo (1475–1564) was a leading figure of the Italian Renaissance, sculptor, painter, architect and poet. Cf. https://en.wikipedia.org/wiki/Michelangelo (accessed 25.11.22).

22. Clayton Christensen described the Entrepreneur's approach to innovation thus: 'Devoting time and energy to finding and testing (new) ideas through a network of diverse individuals gives innovators a radically different perspective. Unlike most executives – who network to access resources, to sell themselves or their companies, or to boost their careers – innovative entrepreneurs go out of their way to meet people with different kinds of ideas and perspectives to extend their own knowledge domains. To this end they make a conscious effort to visit other countries and meet people from other walks of life.' *Harvard Business Review* 12.2009.

23. Haier is also leading the way on a comprehensive sustainable development strategy to futher reduce energy consumption and improve recycling, proactively working to mitigate climate change. Cf. https://en.wikipedia.org/wiki/Haier (accessed 21.11.22).

24. Steve Jobs inspired by Clayton Christensen's 'The Innovator's Dilemma' and his experience at Pixar, sought to blend Art and Technology upon his return to Apple, in the early 1990s. Interviewed by Jonah Lehrer (*Wired* July 2011; New Yorker 7.10.2011), he made clear 'Technology alone is not enough.' Cf. https://www.newyorker.com/steve-jobs-technology-alone-is-not-enough (accessed 7.3.22).

25. Steve Jobs did *not* follow convention. From the Art of Calligraphy he learned the Art of Contemplation, in the calm 'negative space,' the Japanese call 'Ma.' Speaking of his experience, he recalled: 'I learned about serif and sans-serif typefaces, about varying the amount of space between different letter combinations, about what makes great typography great. It was beautiful, historical, artistically subtle in a way that science can't capture and I found it fascinating. If I had never dropped in on that single course in college, the Mac would never have had multiple typefaces proportionally spaced fonts.'

26. Steve Jobs launched the iPod in 2001 using Toshiba's new 1.5" disc, for which Toshiba had no use. It could hold 5GB of data, equivalent to 1,000

songs, 10× the capacity of MP3 players' max. 100 songs. The genius part was not to give every person the ability to hold their favourite songs in their back pocket, but it was to anticipate a trend that continues today, since 85% of total revenue in the music industry is now realised through streaming services. Apple Music and Spotify are the leading players in a market that is estimated to reach 37 billion USD in 2030. Further disruption due to Covid-19 sees the industry moving towards interactive forms of audience engagement, e.g. TikTok duets and Instagram live videos. Cf. https://the-clickhub.com/what-is-the-future-of-music-streaming/#:~:text=The%20 Recording%20Industry%20Association%20of,around%20%2437bn%20 by%202030 (accessed 26.11.22).

27. Jack Nicas (3.01.22), 'Apple becomes first company to hit 3 trillion market value.' Cf. https://www.nytimes.com/2022/01/03/technology/apple-3-trillion-market-value.html

28. James Allworth, 'Steve Jobs solved the 'Innovator's Dilemma,' 24.10.2011, HBR.

29. 'One of the greatest achievements at Pixar we bought these two cultures together and got them working side by side.' Steve Jobs (2003).

30. James Allworth, 'Steve Jobs solved the 'Innovator's Dilemma,' 24.10.2011, HBR.

31. The arrival of the iPhone, on 9 January 2007, has transformed our lives. The way we consume music, technology, telephony, data, media entertainment, games and record our reality through digital photos has radically changed. As Steve Jobs had announced, Apple was making history.

32. John Lasseter, CEO Pixar tweet, 18.7.2011. Cf. https://twitter.com/pixar/ (accessed 25.11.22).

33. Clayton Christensen, *The Innovator's Dilemma: When new technologies cause great firms to fail*, (1997). He suggests large firms lose market share by over-delivering on their promise to consumers, whereas start-up companies serve low-value customers until their technology can challenge incumbents and take their market share. To avoid losing large firms should try out new ideas on a small scale, keeping those entities *separate from the main business*. However, *this doesn't work everywhere*. Cf. https://en.wikipedia.org/wiki/The_Innovator%27s_Dilemma (accessed 26.11.22).

34. Steve Jobs maintained consumers are not always aware of their needs. Apple made history with the iPhone debut on 9 January 2007, since touchscreen now a standard feature within the industry, meant Jobs was heavily criticised at the time for rejecting the stylus as a tool. His intuition was simple: work with beauty and nature. We have 10 of the best pointing tools ever invented, our fingers.

35. Chan Kim and Renée Mauborgne, *Blue Ocean Strategy* (2015) suggested creating a new uncontested marketplace, making competition irrelevant. Start small, take low-cost initiatives and scale gradually, whilst maintaining core competencies. But, in today's world boundaries are blurred and small incremental changes may no longer be sufficient; a 'big picture' vision for the future is needed to anticipate future shocks, pivot quickly, and *fully* embrace *adaptive resilience*.

36. Jeff Bezos wrote a number of open letters to the shareholders during his tenure as CEO of Amazon. Cf. https://www.cbinsights.com/research/bezos-amazon-shareholder-letters/ (accessed 26.11.22).

37. Amazon began as an online bookstore, then morphed into an online discount retailer for *everything*: a cloud services provider (AWS), electronics manufacturer (Kindle), media player, movie maker, prime services, AI-powered retail platform-service provider, pharmacy, insurance, and branched into healthcare in 2020.

38. 'A value chain refers to the full lifecycle of a product or process, including material sourcing, production, consumption and disposal or recycling processes.' Cf. https://www.cisl.cam.ac.uk/education/graduate-study/pgcerts/value-chain-defs (accessed 19.11.22).

39. Socio-Technical Systems have multiple components: hardware, software, third party providers, services and people. Risk assessments must include close scrutiny of the interdependencies within the 'networks' and ensure there are in-built redundancies at a structural and systemic level. Cf. https://avinetworks.com/glossary/single-point-of-failure/ (accessed 20.11.22).

40. Steve Jobs, commenting on the 'Innovators Dilemma.' Effectively, the insight is that reason alone cannot constitute a reliable pathway to new discoveries and novelty is reliant upon the human imagination to connect the dots and fill in the missing pieces.

41. The Medicis (1230–1743) were one of the wealthiest, most influential families in the Italian Renaissance, with political power across Italy and Europe. Initially, wealth came through the textile trade (wool), later the Medici Bank (1397–1494). They were innovators adopting the general ledger system of accounting, double entry book keeping, to track credits and debts. Patrons to leading thinkers, artists and scientists – Brunelleschi, Botticelli, Leonardo da Vinci, Michelangelo, Raphael, Machiavelli, Galileo and others.

42. Clayton Christensen et al., 'The Innovator's DNA,' HBR Magazine, December 2009. Cf. https://hbr.org/2009/12/the-innovators-dna (accessed 1.2.22).

43. Neuroscience refers to the 'default mode,' where unconscious thought patterns trigger new ideas; whether in an alert state, being awake means there is a short-term incubation period known as the 'wandering mind;' or during REM sleep, where processes occurring inside the brain enable the processing of information without conscious cognitive activity or active learning taking place. Aristotle assumed this was the case from his observations of the 'movement' in dreams. Cf. S. Ritter et al. (2014), 'The Unconscious foundations of the incubation period' that activates creativity by 'default.' https://www.ncbi.nlm.nih.gov/pmc/articles/PMC3990058/ (accessed 18.11.22).

44. Aristotle's teachings point to 'phronesis,' the practical and consistent application of Knowledge leads to wisdom, which increases its experiential efficacy over time; the more it is practised in reality.

45. Originally a phrase associated with Albert Einstein, it was used to great effect by Steve Jobs, in Apple's 'Think Different' marketing campaign, which resonated with a worldwide audience, both a testimony to his

delivery and the power of the human form of natural language to convey ideas. 'Marketing is about values.'

'Here's to the crazy ones. The misfits. The rebels. The troublemakers. The round pegs in the square holes; The ones who see things differently, they're not fond of rules. And they have no respect for the status quo; You can quote them, disagree with them, glorify or vilify them. About the only thing you can't do is ignore them. Because they change things. They invent. They imagine. They heal. They explore. They create. They inspire. They push the human race forward; Maybe they have to be crazy. How else can you stare at an empty canvas and see a work of art? Or sit in silence and hear a song that's never been written? Or gaze at a red planet and see a laboratory on wheels? We make tools for these kinds of people; While some may see them as the crazy ones, we see genius, because the ones who are crazy enough to think that they can change the world, are the ones who do.' Steve Jobs (1997). Cf. Stanford University recording - https://www.youtube.com/watch?v=4fcb8eu20SQ (accessed 27.11.22).

CHAPTER 6

1. Rollo Reece May (1909–1994), American psychologist. Cf. https://en.wikipedia.org/wiki/Rollo_May (accessed 3.12.22).

2. Kate Crawford (1976–), scholar, *Atlas of AI* (2021), looks at the intersection of culture, mobile technologies, people, uses and increasingly complex socio-technical networks encompassing world populations. In 2012, *Critical questions for big data* co-authored with Danah Boyd (1977–), Crawford cautions users and controllers of big data who wrongly assume: 'large data sets offer a higher form of intelligence and knowledge [. . .], with the aura of truth, objectivity, and accuracy.' They are often 'lost in the sheer volume of numbers [. . .] working with big data is still subjective, and what it quantifies does not necessarily have a closer claim on objective truth.' Cf. https://en.wikipedia.org/wiki/Big_data (accessed 15.12.22).

3. Automated filtering of *non-useful data* may result in spurious correlations and *non-causal* coincidences (law of truly large numbers) or emergence of non-included factors. *Validity* defined in terms of mathematical accuracy of non-deterministic outcomes does not determine veracity of the same. This is highly problematic for social justice, equality and fairness in society. Cf. https://en.wikipedia.org/wiki/Big_data

4. Catherine Tucker (1977–), economist at MIT, has highlighted the 'hype' surrounding 'big data,' particularly in the last decade (2010–2020). 'By itself, big data is unlikely to be valuable. The many contexts where data is cheap relative to the cost of retaining talent to process it, suggests that processing skills are more important than data itself in creating value for a firm.' Cf. https://en.wikipedia.org/wiki/Catherine_Tucker (accessed 15.12.22).

5. The AI grading system currently in use is based on four criteria for knowledge acquisition (mastery, creation, input, output) as follows: 1. AI cannot communicate with people. For example, inanimate objects like a table or a chair, so not very informative or interactive. 2. Smart fridges, televisions, air conditioning, etc., may involve sensors, computing, access to computer code, but cannot learn by default. 3. Smartphones and computers evolve through updates (often automated, but still require human interventions). 4. Systems like Google Brain, Baidu Brain, RoboEarth, adjust according to the information processed in the Cloud. 5. Humans use AI to create something new, acquire and analyse information, impossible for systems of a lower grade to do (some early use cases being trialled, e.g. 3D-RPA). 6. AI has 'all the powers and controls itself,' it evolves, innovates, knows how to acquire knowledge and how to find infinite source of energy. (e.g. *The MATRIX* depicted in the Hollywood film). Level 6 is not yet technically achievable. For example, AlphaGo from Alphabet (Google) is classified in 2022 as third-grade system. It cannot self-reproduce or self-evolve. Cf. AI INDEX 2022 – a repository of recent developments. https://aiindex.stanford.edu/report/ (accessed 7.12.22).

6. Controversial applications include use of facial recognition in law enforcement, due to discriminatory biases in datasets used to train the models and the imperfect functioning of the technology itself. For example, it is less accurate in determining darker skin than fairer skin tones due to the way datasets have been selected for training and manner in which 'rules' have been formulated.

7. UK-based 'gig' workers at companies such as Uber (dubbed a 'ride sharing service' in efforts to circumvent existing licensing arrangements) repeatedly protested against unfair working conditions and data practices. Enterprise algorithms determine *dynamic pricing strategies*, hours of work and potential customers so that allegedly 'self-employed' workers have no effective control over their own pay and conditions. In recent years (2016–2022) debates have intensified *globally*. Uber has been obliged to comply with UK employment laws. Cf. https://www.theguardian.com/technology/2016/oct/28/uber-uk-tribunal-self-employed-status (accessed 15.12.22).

8. Christine Welch (2020), researcher – 'the utilisation of disruptive more advanced technologies requires consideration from multiple perspectives taking into account the longer term as well as potential short term gains.' Cf. https://en.wikipedia.org/wiki/Sociotechnical_system

9. The meaning of the word 'profiling' comes from the Latin 'to spin forth a thread' or 'to draw a line.' AI-technologies are not sufficiently advanced to substantiate *non-scientific* claims concerning the *dynamic* classification of '3D human beings,' their emotions, behaviours, thoughts and feelings into standardised categories. Since they are based on a set of mathematical 'rules' programmed into *machines* that *simply* aggregate *any* pattern regularities found in vast volumes of *historical* data that may *not* be of relevance to specific individuals and lack context-specificity.

10. For example, the attempted use of 'artificial intelligence' to mark exam papers during Covid-19 pandemic resulted in spurious examination results and an embarrassing 'U-turn' for the UK government in 2020. No effort was made to recognise undue *angst* caused to students *unfairly* treated by a *mechanical computational system* with no ability to discern *qualitative* achievements; and no attempt was made to hold individuals accountable for the ill-conceived idea, which would inevitably lower educational standards, if it were ever pursued and deny individual students the opportunity to realise their full potential. Cf. https://www.politico.eu/article/boris-johnsons-government-u-turns-on-exam-results/ (accessed 12.12.22).

11. 'Machine learning' models are *programmable* computational tools. The 'reward-punishment' functionality uses 'game theory' principles, so that *machines* store 'information' and 'learn' to perform a human-specified task. These tools are deemed 'weapons of math destruction' since they do not differentiate between positive and negative outcomes. They simply execute a human-specified task with the highest degree of mathematical accuracy, whether operating alone or more likely in conjunction with other 'systems' in parallel towards given outputs.

12. In the late 1980s, it is estimated less than 1% of data collected was available in digital format; by 2012, 99% of the data collected had been converted to digital formats providing ease of access to 'big data' at lightning fast speeds. The proliferation of algorithms used in 'machine learning' models since 2008, expanded the use of data in decision-making processes across multiple industries. Data readily provided by over 2 billion Internet users (2012), half the world population (2016), and 4.78 billion users or 67% of world population (2020), of whom 4.54 billion people (59% of the world population) had smart phones.

13. 'Machine learning' *algorithms* enable computer software programme to 'learn' unsupervised; without being explicitly programmed algorithms grow 'smarter,' predicting more accurate outcomes through the input of *historical* data. https://www.techtarget.com/whatis/A-Timeline-of-Machine-Learning-History (accessed 11.12.22).

14. Industrial-scale computational needs arose from the growth of the insurance and banking industry, following the First Industrial Revolution. 'Computers' were initially men and women carrying out repetitive calculations, using *mechanical* desk calculators called comptometers, which later became electro-mechanical sorters and tabulators that could rapidly count and summarise digital information stored on thousands of individual punched cards. In 1884, a machine designed by Herman Hollerith (1860–1929), marked the beginning of the *mechanised binary code* and *semiautomatic data processing systems*, which dominated census calculations, payroll and structural engineering for over half a century. The 'Computing-Tabulating Recording Company' was formed in 1911 and later renamed in 1924 'International Business Machines' (IBM). Cf. https://www.computerhistory.org/timeline/1973/ (accessed 11.12.22).

15. Cathy O'Neill wrote of algorithms typically used in civilian and commercial settings - 'Most troubling, they reinforce discrimination: If a poor

student can't get a loan because a lending model deems him too risky by virtue of his zip code, he's then cut off from the kind of education that could pull him out of poverty, and a vicious spiral ensues. Models are propping up the lucky and punishing the downtrodden, creating a *toxic cocktail* for democracy.' Cf. *Weapons of Math Destruction* (2016)

16. Data should be assessed in terms of volume, variety, velocity, veracity, value and variability. By extending the capacity of the Enterprise to capture more data, it creates a larger *moving target and surface of attack*, which can be more disruptive than the *actual value* the Enterprise may derive from the same.

17. Eric Trist et al. (1951) – referencing the complexity of Socio-Technical Systems, which are subject to 'A very large variety of unfavourable and changing environmental conditions . . . many of which are impossible to predict, others though predictable are impossible to alter.'

18. For those in any doubt, Vicktor Frankl's *Man's Search for Meaning*, may prove illuminating.

19. Mr Charles Babbage (1791–1871), a mathematician, engineer, inventor, is 'considered to be the father of the computer.' Cf. *The Analytical Engine*. https://en.wikipedia.org/wiki/Analytical_Engine

20. Ada Lovelace (1815–1852), the 'first computer programmer,' developed an algorithm to enable the *Analytical Engine* to calculate a sequence of Bernoulli numbers. She wrote: 'We may say most aptly that the Analytical Engine weaves algebraical patterns just as the Jacquard loom weaves flowers and leaves.' In 1843, Ada wrote about the trade-off between time and space (*computer speed and random access memory in modern computers*): 'In almost every computation a great variety of arrangements for the succession of the processes is possible, and various considerations must influence the selections amongst them for the purposes of a calculating engine. One essential object is to choose that arrangement which shall tend to reduce to a minimum the time necessary for completing the calculation.' Cf. https://en.wikipedia.org/wiki/Charles_Babbage (accessed 1.3.22).

21. Historians believe the 'Turing Machine' helped end the war at least two years earlier than expected by breaking the Nazi Code.

22. Ada Lovelace cautioned 'The Analytical Engine has no pretensions whatever to originate anything. It can do whatever we know how to order it to perform. It can follow analysis; but it has no power of anticipating any analytical relations or truths.'

23. Claude Shannon wrote *A Mathematical Theory of Communication* in 1948, from a mathematical and engineering perspective, inspired by the principles of cryptography, such that minimal elements are transmitted to ensure accuracy of the message, thereby *sacrificing meaning for efficiency*.

24. The term 'artificial intelligence,' coined in 1956 by Professor John McCarthy at the Dartmouth College Summer Conference, denotes the 'science and engineering of making intelligent machines' useful for credit card fraud detection and booking airline tickets. By the early 1960s, he

envisaged networks could enable people to share data through a central computer as a 'public utility,' otherwise known as *cloud computing*. But, he also cautioned that the problem of 'common sense' needed to be solved before we could even begin to consider machines to be *intelligent* beyond the utility of a piece of equipment or a *tool* such as a toaster.

25. Claude Shannon wrote *A Mathematical Theory of Communication* in 1948. His notion of entropy and redundancy is still being used today. Referencing the missing semantic layers in contemporary 'machine learning' models, he cautioned claims concerning the possibility of human-level cognition and communication in the so-called 'Turing machines' were being overstated – the 'bandwagon' he felt had 'ballooned to an importance beyond its actual accomplishments' (1956).

26. Researchers found that the IQ for Google and other AI systems has improved recently, due to the accumulation of training data and improvements in Large Language Models, though they still have significant technical limitations. Measured IQ of Google and other AI systems is significantly less than the IQ of a 6-year-old child. https://www.veprof.com/blog/technology/check-the-result-of-ai-iq-tests-google-ai-vs-siri-vs-bing (accessed 11.12.22).

27. Prescient authors including George Orwell ('1984'), Aldous Huxley (*Brave New World*) and more recently Shoshana Zuboff (*The Age of Surveillance Capitalism*) illustrate the fight for a *human future* and the new frontier of power. The inherent dangers have also been depicted in a number of recent Hollywood films and Walt Disney cartoons from early 1950s, as a note of caution since the 'surveillance economy' would effectively usurp our Civil Liberties.

28. It is reported 70% of transformations fail to meet *expectations*, whether in terms of the intended outcomes or the much sought-after yet elusive return on investment. Cf. https://www.forbes.com/sites/forbescoachescouncil/2022/03/16/12-reasons-your-digital-transformation-will-fail/

29. Oscar Wilde, *The Picture of Dorian Gray* (1890). The citation references the erosion of *human values* within Victorian Society in England, but it is still relevant today since value is typically defined in financial terms. However, the significance of *cultural norms and moral values* cannot be ignored since they underpin the perceived value attributed to money.

30. 'Chat bots' are defined as 'extensive word classification processes,' mainly used to collect information from human users, provided it is 'straightforward' and falls into 'predictable' patterns of speech *learned* or *programmed* into the machine using large databases. If the query is not a 'saved query,' the chat-bot goes over its recursive feedback loops incessantly, causing frustration to human consumers; it cannot cope with multiple questions and can only draw conclusions from static databases. Cf. https://en.wikipedia.org/wiki/Chatbot (accessed 11.12.22)

31. 'Data subjects' is the impersonal terminology used to describe *human beings* in the UK and EU General Data Protection Regulation (GDPR); first introduced in 2016, the law came into effect on 25 May 2018 for all EU member states, including the UK which had not fully separated from

the EU and has since introduced its own version of the law, subject to further changes.

32. The ISO, IEC standards define 'biometrics' as 'the automated recognition of individuals based on their biological and behavioural characteristics.' Cf. https://www.ncsc.gov.uk/biometrics/understanding-biometrics (accessed 21.12.22).

33. Melvin Kranzberg (1917–1995), technology historian, best known for the *six laws of technology*: Technology is neither good nor bad; nor is it neutral; Invention is the mother of necessity; Technology comes in packages, big and small; Although Technology might be a prime element in many public issues, nontechnical factors take precedence in technology-policy decisions; All history is relevant, but the history of technology is the most relevant; Technology is a very human activity and so is the history of Technology. Cf. https://en.wikipedia.org/wiki/Melvin_Kranzberg

34. Marianna Mazzucato, *The Mission Economy, a moonshot guide to changing capitalism*, (2021). 'We must create more effective interfaces and innovations across the whole of society, rethink how policies are designed; change how intellectual property regimes are governed; and use R&D to distribute intelligence across academia, government, business and civil society. This means restoring public purpose in policies, so that they are aimed at creating tangible benefits for citizens and setting goals that matter to people – driven by public-interest considerations rather than profit.'

35. Even the US National Security Agency, which is well practised in the mastery of 'big data' collected around the world for decades, is struggling to cope with the analysis of 'massive modern data sets,' despite being supported by large technology companies, e.g. Microsoft, Apple, Alphabet, Amazon and others. It is estimated human beings are producing 2.5 quintillion bytes of data every day, in 2022. Cf. https://wpdevshed.com/how-much-data-is-created-every-day/ (volume of data assessed 18.8.22).

36. Cynthia Rudin 'Stop Explaining Black Box Machine Learning Models for High Stakes Decisions and Use Interpretable Models Instead.'(2019). Cf. https://www.ncbi.nlm.nih.gov/pmc/articles/PMC9122117/ (accessed 22.12.22).

37. For example, healthcare denied to a number of *paid subscribers* in the USA led to premature deaths in 2021, because the *algorithm* was skewed towards discriminatory outcomes against disabilities. Cf. https://www.kff.org/private-insurance/marketplace-insurers-denied-nearly-1-in-5-in-network-claims-in-2020-though-its-often-not-clear-why/ (accessed 22.12.22).

38. Empirical studies have shown desirable leadership capabilities for the 21st century include (but are not limited to) a strong sense of duty of care, compassion, effective communication, character (ethos, high ethical values), authenticity, consistency, competence and creativity.

39. As an example, the UK is deemed to be ahead of the curve in terms of 'AI readiness.' However, productivity levels, particularly in the last

decade (2010–2020) have fallen to the lowest levels in more than 100+ years. Similar trends have been observed elsewhere, notably in the USA. There are multiple factors to explain this phenomenon, but the quality of work and conditions in the working environment are key contributory factors in falling productivity levels.

40. Mass exodus of workers combined with 'long Covid' and *early retirement*, partly due to *algorithmic* discrimination of certain groups with non-linear careers, including women and the over 50s, caused significant labour shortages in developed economies. Governments need to re-imagine educational, vocational and entrepreneurial systems within the wider society to compete in the *global digital economy*. Citizens are not enticed by Universal Basic Income as recent failed experiments in Switzerland and Finland have shown; they seek *meaningful, purposeful* and *rewarding* work.

41. Enid Mumford, 'Socio-technical design an unfulfilled promise or a future opportunity?' – Socio-Technical System design began over 50 years ago, when trained psychologists and psychiatrists helping soldiers recover from the war, began working at the Tavistock Institute of Human Relations, London (UK) in 1946, with the goal of improving working conditions in industry. They sought beneficial outcomes for Society as a whole, by creating the conditions for all workers to enjoy personal growth, new skills development, job satisfaction and fair representation in decision-making. The paradigm was widely adopted, though interpreted differently in Scandinavia, many EU countries, UK and the USA. Cf. https://ifipwg82.org/sites/ifipwg82.org/files/mumford.pdf (accessed 1.12.22).

42. Toyota is an example of 'job enrichment' and 'job rotation' in practice, to empower its workforce; the 'Toyota Way' updated in 2020 evidences the company's intentions to continue to nurture a more humanistic approach towards commercial success.

43. Carlota Perez (1939–) Economist specialising in Technological Revolutions and The Economics of Innovation. Cf. https://en.wikipedia.org/wiki/Carlota_Perez (accessed 15.12.22).

44. The initial technological *transitions* from stone tools (2,000,000 BC) to bronze tools (3,300 BC) and then iron (1,200 BC) were *very* slow. Fast forward to the First Industrial Revolution: we harnessed water (1780), discovered steam power (1848), electric power (1895) and combustion power (1940), effectively transforming sources of energy (1780–1973). The shift to mass production and consumerism followed the first wave of globalisation circa 1875 ('canal mania, steam ships and telegraph'), as industry, the means of production and Society were completely transformed.

45. Information communication technology (ICT) from the late 1880s, 1900s and 2000s, including telephony, telegraphy, analogue and digital forms of information transmission have transformed Society, but equally they have been shaped by Society; subject to widespread adoption of the same on a global scale, with the advent of the Information Age in 1973.

CHAPTER 7

1. Mark Carney, *Value(s)*, published by Williams Collins (2021).
2. Plato in *The Republic* discusses the character and virtues of the 'philosopher king' with Socrates. Early in the 16th century, the term was used in England to signify 'governance of the realm.' Later in 1885, it was used to describe 'institutional governance' and again in 1908. It denotes socio-economic and socio-political frameworks. Cf. https://en.wikipedia.org/wiki/Governance (accessed 26.6.22).
3. The first documented use of 'corporate governance' was by Richard Eells (1960) to denote 'the structure and functioning of the corporate polity.' It became mainstream after the Cadbury Report.
4. 'The Committee on the Financial Aspects of Corporate Governance' chaired by Sir Adrian Cadbury, set up in May 1991 by the London Stock Exchange (LSE) and Accounting Profession, issued its final report in December 1992, including recommendations on Board composition, committees and other measures to improve financial risk management. Cf. https://www.frc.org.uk/getattachment/9c19ea6f-bcc7-434c-b481-f2e29c1c271a/The-Financial-Aspects-of-Corporate-Governance-(the-Cadbury-Code).pdf (accessed 26.6.22).
5. G7 countries pledged to turn voluntary adherence to the leading international metric Task Force Climate-related Financial Disclosures (2015) into a mandatory requirement in 2021. For example, UK Code of Corporate Governance (2022) has made TCFD disclosures a requirement for in-scope companies and larger private companies defined as 'public interest entities.' Cf. https://www.icaew.com/technical/corporate-reporting/non-financial-reporting/tcfd-and-related-uk-reporting-regulations#:~:text=The%20TCFD%20is%20the%20Task,change%20will%20affect%20their%20business (accessed 12.1.23).
6. Historically, tensions between the owners and management control over operations, the sharing of risks and profits associated with business ventures have always existed. Under common law (e.g. UK, USA), the purpose of the Enterprise was originally defined under the 'objects' giving the owners of the corporation (or shareholders) the right to decide which activities a company could pursue, reinforcing the property rights of the legal owners. Modern legal frameworks empower the Board of Directors, subject to shareholder approval for key decisions, under *constitutional* requirements, the 'Articles of Association in the UK,' and in the USA, the 'Articles of Incorporation' and *bylaws* of the corporation.
7. UK Code of Corporate Governance (2018) – Board Leadership and Company Purpose (principle B). https://www.frc.org.uk/ 2018-UK-Corporate-Governance-Code-FINAL.pdf
8. UK Code of Corporate Governance (2018) – Board Leadership and Company Purpose (principle D). https://www.frc.org.uk/ 2018-UK-Corporate-Governance-Code-FINAL.pdf

9. This is detailed in UK Company Act 2006 (section 172) and is generally adhered to in practice in the UK and other countries, which take a similar approach. Conversely, in the USA, Directors' fiduciary duties are exercised in practice mainly for the benefit of the shareholders. Pledges made by the Business Roundtable in 2019 to 'take care of the other stakeholder interests in addition to those of the shareholders' do not reflect the established 'norms' with respect to current business practices in C-corporations.

10. The Remuneration and Nomination Committee (s) sets compensation levels for Directors, subject to approval by the shareholders. There is a debate in the UK on equity-related performance pay for non-executive directors since there is concern it could compromise their independence. Cf. Daniel Thomas, 'Investors flag concerns over weakening pay rules for non-execs' (FT 12.6.22). Cf. https://www.ft.com /f57f9dbe-a3e2-40bc-bd46-3f4851d0f44b (accessed 14.1.23).

11. Colin Boyd, 'Ethics and corporate governance: The issues raised by the Cadbury Report in the UK' (1996) cites the forced closure of The Bank of Credit and Commerce, Robert Maxwell's £1bn theft from employee pension funds, managerial excesses with regards to remuneration practices at companies such as British Airways and Barclays in the early 1990s. Cf. https://www.jstor.org/stable/25072743

12. The UK CGC (2022) requires Directors to make a Statement regarding the effectiveness of internal controls, and external auditors are required to issue their own Statement attesting the effectiveness of measures taken to detect and prevent fraud.

13. Matthew Taylor, 'Good Work, The Taylor Review of modern working practices' (2017). Cf. https://assets.publishing.service.gov.uk/government/uploads/system/uploads/attachment_data/file/627671/good-work-taylor-review-modern-working-practices-rg.pdf Cf. Global Talent Competitiveness Index (2022). Cf. https://www.insead.edu/sites/default/files/assets/dept/fr/gtci/GTCI-2022-report.pdf

14. Ada Lovelace Institute has recently published a paper stating the concerns, directing attention to the provision of funding in academia and industry. There should be independent scrutiny of all applications, R&D of algorithmic technologies and their intended uses in the context of social and societal harms, as well as environmental concerns and the use of natural resources. Cf. https://www.adalovelaceinstitute.org/blog/ai-research-ethics-collective-problem/ (accessed 17.1.23).

Similarly, the DRCF in the UK comprising 4 industry regulators is scrutinising the impact of algorithmic technologies and potential harms they may cause both for individuals and Society as a whole. In particular, the regulators are examining online safety. Cf. https://www.gov.uk/government/publications/findings-from-the-drcf-algorithmic-processing-workstream-spring-2022/the-benefits-and-harms-of-algorithms-a-shared-perspective-from-the-four-digital-regulators (accessed 17.1.23).

15. Luciano Floridi et al., Professor of Information Ethics (Oxford University) – 'A unified Framework for AI in Society.' Cf. https://link.springer.com/content/pdf/10.1007/s11023-018-9482-5.pdf (accessed 17.1.23).

16. Whilst the technology for the *metaverse* described as an 'immersive extended reality' has been in existence for several years, mainly used by companies in the 'gaming world,' the arrival of Covid-19 saw luxury fashion brands explore the space and new creative collaborations emerged. In April 2022, Accenture announced it was training 150,000 new recruits through the metaverse, 'bringing geographically distributed workforce together' in a medium they see becoming the 'norm' in the next decade.

17. The legal and regulatory landscape is complex. The upcoming EU AI ACT, US Bill of Rights and similar laws in other jurisdictions, including the UK Online Safety Act set legal precedents with potential criminal charges being brought against individual Directors who fail to ensure child safety online, at a minimum 2 years imprisonment. Quite apart from the financial costs associated with non-compliance, legal and criminal implications will in effect cause serious reputational damage. Not all risks can be mitigated by *technical means* and necessitate new governance structures, processes and heightened awareness across the Enterprise to ensure effective mitigation and timely adaptations to emerging AI-related risks. This goes beyond compliance, conformity assessments and standardisation of best practice. It will require *proactive engagement* and *effective collaboration* of all employees and stakeholders across the entire value chain at all times.

18. Large technology companies have already been served significant 7-figure penalties due to data protection infringements under GDPR. Fines issued by the regulator amount to 20 million Euros or 4% of total global turnover whichever is the greatest. Recent examples include: Amazon fined 746 million Euros in 2021, Meta and Google both received substantial penalties. Violation of Data Subject's rights, including profiling, data-sharing without 'informed consent' and the indiscriminate collection of Data from the Internet, may boost profits momentarily, but engagement with a digital platform or serving 'personalised advertisements' does not constitute compliance with the law.
    Cf. Class Action against Oracle (2022), https://www.iccl.ie/news/class-action-against-oracle/
    and
    Cf. https://erp.today/meta-and-google-fined-whos-next-in-the-data-scandal-saga/ (accessed 26.1.23).

19. Adverse incidents involving 'Artificial Intelligence' are recorded in publicly accessible registers. For example, an automated 'driverless vehicle' killed a female pedestrian holding a bicycle as she walked across a zebra crossing, due to the 'event' not being included in the algorithm's training data or stored memory. There may also be malicious intent. For example, a health insurance company's algorithm discriminated against a disabled female patient, denied her the care she needed at the time of need, which led to her premature and untimely death. Irrespective of

whether or not it was intentional the outcome *is* irreversible and it raises serious ethical questions about *how* these systems are used *in practice*.

20. Luciano Floridi and J. Sanders (2004), 'On the Morality of Artificial Agents.' Cf. *Minds and Machines*, 14, 349–379, https://doi.org/10.1023/B:MIND.0000035461.63578.9d (accessed 17.1.23).

21. The EU AI ACT, UK AI National Policy, US AI Bill of Rights and similar laws in China continue to evolve. The UK has set up an AI Standards Hub and regulators are creating AI governance, risk, audit frameworks, e.g. NIST in the US and ICO in the UK. The newest standard ISO38507 (April 2022) addresses the impact of algorithmic technologies on Society. The ISO notes the importance of culture and *human values* to deliver requisite assurance for users, whether internal or external to the Enterprise.

22. Luciano Floridi, 'What the Near Future of Artificial Intelligence Could Be,' Philos. Technol. 32, 1–15 (2019). Cf. https://link.springer.com/article/10.1007/s13347-019-00345-y (accessed 17.1.23).

23. Since the outbreak of the pandemic malicious cyber attacks, including but not limited to malware, data poisoning, solar winds, Trojan horses and so on, have intensified; *public disclosure* is critical to alert the Data Subject their personal data has been compromised. Interference in Enterprise and government communication channels, through 'misinformation' and 'disinformation' whether originated by a natural person or generated through the use of algorithmic technologies is becoming highly problematic. For example, Frances Haugen's recent testimony (2021) cited multiple incidents concerning improper use of personal data, harms to civilians and misleading investors. The EU Digital Service Act, Digital Markets Act (2023) seeks to address corporate failures, unlawful content, digital advertising, profiling, misinformation and deliberate disinformation. Cf. https://en.wikipedia.org/wiki/Facebook–Cambridge_Analytica_data_scandal; https://en.wikipedia.org/wiki/Frances_Haugen; https://en.wikipedia.org/wiki/Digital_Services_Act (accessed 23.1.23).

24. Luciano Floridi, 'What the Near Future of Artificial Intelligence Could Be,' Philos. Technol. 32, 1–15 (2019). Cf. https://link.springer.com/article/10.1007/s13347-019-00345-y (accessed 17.1.23).

25. Financial Conduct Authority, UK (2022) regulates firms in the financial sector.

26. Governments, regulators, standard setters and governance bodies have consistently brought changes to international governance practices for corporations, auditors and shareholders. There has been a flurry of activity since the global pandemic 2020–2022 in the UK, EU, USA, India, Japan and China. The trend is towards setting new internationally recognised public disclosure standards under IFRS rules, including electronic reporting formats. The OECD update is due in 2023.

27. The Cadbury Report, 1992 (paragraph 1.9, page 12). Cf. https://www.frc.org.uk/getattachment/9c19ea6f-bcc7-434c-b481-f2e29c1c271a/The-Financial-Aspects-of-Corporate-Governance-(the-Cadbury-Code).pdf

28. Secretary for State, British Energy and Industry Strategy, report May 2022.

29. An example often cited is that of Hewlett Packard's acquisition of Autonomy Corporation, where enforcement actions were taken against the legal entity and separately against the individual directors of Autonomy responsible for inaccurate financial disclosures, having overstated the results of the company prior to the announced acquisition by Hewlett Packard.

30. FCA in the UK is conducting consultations in 2022–2023, to see how it can improve disclosure framework.

31. The 750:750 rule is based on international standards applicable to private entities including those on the AIM listing. For example, 'Public Interest Entities' include limited liability partnerships (LLPs) that have at least 750 employees and £750 million in annual turnover. In addition, large private companies with 2,000 employees, £200 million in turnover or £2 billion in assets are subject to proportionate corporate governance disclosures under the 'Wates principles.' Alternatively, they may choose to follow UK Corporate Governance Code (2022), subject to size and complexity of the entity and its future growth prospects.

32. ARGA replaces the existing regulator FRC (Financial reporting council), and will have new statutory powers to hold individual directors accountable for any breaches of their statutory and fiduciary duties under UK Companies Act (2006), including corporate reporting and audit responsibilities, due diligence and steps taken to detect and prevent fraud.

33. The UK Stewardship Code updated in 2020 places additional responsibilities on investors to intervene in corporate governance when there are legitimate concerns over decisions being taken, particularly over long-term investments. Cf. https://www.frc.org.uk/Stewardship-Code_Final2.pdf

34. The UK instituted a public register for companies experiencing 'significant shareholder dissent' in 2017. Both the company and shareholders must provide full details of decisions that were contested and their respective responses irrespective of whether or not the intended outcomes were achieved.

35. OECD Principles of Corporate Governance (2015), p.9. Cf. https://www.oecd.org/daf/ca/Corporate-Governance-Principles-ENG.pdf (accessed 6.1.23).

36. In contrast in the USA, the Sarbanes-Oxley Act, Dodd-Frank Act and SEC rules governing corporations are mandatory at a federal level, and companies are also subject to local state laws dependent on where they are incorporated. Most C-corporations are incorporated under the State of Delaware, as it is less restrictive than others towards the powers and influence of Directors on the corporation.

37. The German model is often singled out because it allows for a higher proportion of worker representation on the Board including Trade Unions, subject to size and sector differences. Dual Board Structures also adopted by China, Poland, Indonesia, Austria; some EU countries such as France, Italy, Belgium and Romania offer an option in law for a two-tier Board, though most companies have a unitary Board. Cf. https://en.wikipedia.org/wiki/Codetermination_in_Germany (accessed 10.1.23).

38. The SEC (Federal regulator), Sarbanes-Oxley Act, Dodd-Frank Act pertain to corporate governance and ownership structures at the Federal level, but companies are also subject to State laws in which the entity was incorporated, usually in the State of Delaware rather than the state in which they operate. Cf. https://iclg.com/practice-areas/corporate-governance-laws-and-regulations/usa (2022-23) (accessed 15.1.23).

39. Common law relies upon past judgments to formulate future decisions; the judge takes an active role and references case law, such that each decision is specific to the situation at hand. Civil law stems from the roman law of codification; statutory requirements are precise and must be adhered according to the strict letter of the law, typically followed in the EU through its Directives for Corporate governance, though member states can decide how to implement and enforce the law. Strict criteria requiring definition under civil law can pose problems in a fast evolving situations; e.g. The EU AI ACT, though in this instance there is broad consensus.

40. The 'agency' problem is the notion that the managers and shareholders may not be aligned in their interests, unless the managers have a *material* interest in the corporation they are running on behalf the owners; hence why remuneration packages for Directors and Executive Officers usually include an equity component subject to the constitution of the corporation. 'The Articles of Incorporation' and *'bylaws'* in the USA separate the statement of the objectives of the corporation from its governance rules. Historically, the issue stems from the legal frameworks defining 'limited liability,' property rights and 'personhood' of the corporation.

41. Standard formatting under the European Single Electronic Format (ESEF) is now a requirement for UK and EU in-scope corporations, effective 1 January 2022. Annual reports governed by IFRS rules, structured in machine-readable format are free to access and aim to promote comparability in terms of individual disclosures, published taxonomies for regulators, shareholders and investors.

42. Federal rules include Securities Act (1933), Securities Exchange Act (1934), Sarbanes-Oxley Act (2002) and Dodd-Frank Wall Street Reform and Consumer protection Act (2010). Companies are also subject to the rules set by separate exchanges, e.g. NYSE and NASDQ – two of the most important.

43. Historically, part of the problem stems from the Constitution and the subsequent interpretation of property rights. In 1886, the USA declared the corporation was a 'natural person in law,' under the protection of the 14th amendment – 'no state shall deprive any person of life, liberty or property.' In 1896, New Jersey Corporations could define the scope of their 'charters' themselves, independently of government. Consequently, companies became disproportionately powerful, e.g. John D. Rockefeller, founder of Standard Oil Company, held 90–95% oil refineries in the USA in the early 1900s.

44. The notion of 'shareholder primacy' first appears in US case law – *Dodge v Ford Motor Company* in 1919, with the Michigan Supreme Court ruling stating that 'the profits of a corporation could not be withheld from

stockholders for the benefit of the general public.' Henry Ford was forced by the Court to reinstate dividend payment to the shareholders, unable to 'employ still more men, to spread the benefits of this industrial system to the greatest number and help them build up their lives and their homes.' Russell C. Ostrander argued: 'A business corporation is organized and carried on primarily for the profit of the stockholders. The powers of the directors are to be employed for that end. The discretion of directors is to be exercised in the choice of means to attain that end, and does not extend to a change in the end itself, to the reduction of profits, or to the non-distribution of profits among stockholders in order to devote them to other purposes.' Cf. https://en.wikipedia.org/wiki/Dodge_v._Ford_Motor_Co (accessed 23.6.22).

45. Jensen echoed Friedman's intent in his 'agency theory,' published in mid-1970s suggesting alignment of interests between shareholders and managers meant *co-investing* through market participation. In practice, there have been a number of fraudulent cases, e.g. Enron's collapse in 2003 – employees had been encouraged to divert 60% of their pension funds into 'off-balance sheet' investments. Similarly, the *Maxwell* case (1991) and more recently BHS (2016) in the UK, where the former owner has since paid £363m back to the employee pension fund, which had been depleted while in operation.

46. For example, Purdue Pharma, 'through greed and violation of the law, prioritised money over the health and wellbeing of the patients.' Though the Sackler family and McKinsey agreed to pay compensation to bereaved families, 450,000 people died of oxycontin addiction in the USA since the endemic began in the early 1990s. Cf. https://www.justice.gov/opa/pr/justice-department-announces-global-resolution-criminal-and-civil-investigations-opioid (accessed 23.1.22).

47. Sabastian Niles, US corporate law attorney. Cf. https://iclg.com/practice-areas/corporate-governance-laws-and-regulations/usa (2022–2023) (accessed 15.1.23).

48. It is generally accepted the world economy has not recovered from 2007–2008 Financial Crisis and the Ukraine war (2022–) has contributed to the debt crisis in developing economies, widespread 'cost of living' and energy price crisis across the globe.

49. To counter the negative effects of excess speculation, a second tier of oversight may be helpful. 'The New Paradigm' (2016) in the US echoes governance principles outlined in the 'UK Stewardship Code' (2010), updated in 2022. The US 'Long Term Stock Exchange' was established recently and in the State of Delaware. Companies may also register as 'B-corps' – legal entities for *public benefit*. Similarly, France offers the option of establishing a legal entity – 'entreprise à mission,' for the public good. Cf. https://ltse.com; The 'New Paradigm' updated (2019) Cf. https://www.wlrk.com/webdocs/wlrknew/ClientMemos/WLRK/WLRK.26357.19.pdf (accessed 21.1.23).

50. Using 'reasonable business judgment' the Directors are free to balance stakeholder interests from a legal standpoint and a number of States

including Delaware support ESG principles. The difficulty is that Financial Reports mainly focus on short-term results. As SEC President Jay Clayton remarked: 'Our public capital markets have a thirst for high-quality, timely and material information regarding company performance and corporate events.' Cf. https://corpgov.law.harvard.edu/2019/05/29/corporate-purpose-stakeholders-and-long-term-growth/ (accessed 12.1.23).

51. In 1990, the German Federal High Court established the Supervisory Board must also provide future-oriented strategic advice beyond its primary function of monitoring the Management Board.

52. Apart from the Audit, Remuneration & Nomination Committees, the Supervisory Board may also institute special independent committees to deal with specific issues. For example, Volkswagen set up a special committee to deal with 'diesel engine problem' as some vehicles did not meet emissions standards.

53. Historically, Frankfurt parliament instituted 'workers council' in 1849 to ensure the interests of the workers were represented in the decision-making process. Later formalised in the Workers Council Law in 1920, enabling ordinary employees to nominate Directors, placing workers on an equal footing with Employers. The Co-determination Act in 1976, instituted by the Federal government (Bundestag) followed. Companies with more than 2,000 employees have half of the Supervisory Board elected by the employees; those between 500–2,000 employees have one-third of the representatives elected by employees. In practice, no member of the Management Board can serve on the Supervisory Board; although elected employees in lower tiers of management may serve on the Supervisory Board and are required to uphold the proper code of conduct and necessity for confidentiality. Cf. https://www2.deloitte.com/ gx-german-supervisory-board-publication.pdf (accessed 12.1.23).

54. Since OECD guidelines were issued (2018), 35 countries adopted Board-level-worker-representation. Cf. https://en.wikipedia.org/wiki/Worker_representation_on_corporate_boards_of_directors (accessed 26.1.23).

55. George Anderson et al., 'Stakeholder voices in the Boardroom' (July 2021). Cf. https://www.spencerstuart.com/research-and-insight/stakeholder-voices-in-the-boardroomvoices-in-the-boardroom

56. In the USA, it is highly unusual, Chrysler and United Airlines negotiated worker representation through 'collective bargaining' mechanism, but they were also required to enrol employees in share schemes. Enron followed suit but the employee share scheme collapsed in 2003.

57. China began opening up to the world economy in 1976. Since joining the WTO in 2001, it has adopted Western-style 'shareholder model' of governance, a two-tier board structure infused with unique 'Chinese characteristics.' Corporations may be fully or partly State-owned Enterprises (SOE), or Privately-owned Enterprises (POE). Formally, corporate ownership structures include Equity Joint Venture (EJV) and Public Interest Entity (PIE), which serve to attract foreign direct investment into domestic market. The Foreign Investment Law (FIL) reaffirms China's intentions to defend foreign shareholder interests. Cf. https://en.ndrc.gov.cn/policies/202105/t20210527_1281403.html (accessed 17.1.23).

58. This could change the perception of 'stakeholder model' with board-level employee representation, if the UK and EU regulated in-scope companies compliance is extended to subsidiaries overseas.

59. UK Corporate Governance Code updated in 2022. Directors' fiduciary duties codified under sections 171–177, UK Companies Act 2006, indicate 'worker directors' will owe the same duties as other Directors, must exercise independent judgment with 'reasonable care, skill and diligence,' to promote the success of the company, maintaining confidentiality. Cf. https://www.pinsentmasons.com/out-law/analysis/what-to-consider-appointing-employees-boards-in-the-uk (accessed 5.1.23).

60. 'Good Work, The Taylor review of modern working practices' (2017). Cf. https://assets.publishing.service.gov.uk/government/uploads/system/uploads/attachment_data/file/627671/good-work-taylor-review-modern-working-practices-rg.pdf

61. Board level worker representation is operational in Sweden, Norway and Denmark since the 1950s. The UK FRC Report (2021) recognised 'the interests of the workers are well correlated with long-term company success, and countries with strong worker participation rights and practices (on board representation, workplace representation and collective bargaining) score more highly than other countries over a range of economic and employment measures. Moreover, there is extensive evidence that employee participation during restructuring can operate as a 'beneficial constraint' on senior managers, promoting productivity and profitability rather than short-term cost cutting and shedding labour.' Cf. https://www.frc.org.uk/ FRC-Workforce-Engagement-Report_May-2021.pdf (accessed 5.1.23).

62. In the UK, early adopters have instituted democratic election processes with independent scrutiny, appointing the worker representative to the Board, usually in the capacity of a NED.

63. Sylvain Laulom, 'System of Employee Representation in France.' Cf. https://www.jil.go.jp/english/reports/documents/jilpt-reports/no.11_france.pdf

64. The difficulties to achieve board-level worker representation through 'collective bargaining' arrangements and subsequent challenges managing employee-share option schemes, e.g. Chrysler and United Airlines dissuaded others to follow suit.

65. 'US Business Roundtable redefines 'the purpose of a corporation, to promote an economy that serves all Americans' (August 2019). Cf. https://opportunity.businessroundtable.org/ourcommitment/

66. There is a debate as to whether Non-Executive Directors should receive equity as part of their remuneration in order to better align their interests with those of the company. In the past decade, US S&P 100 companies awarded NEDs up to 56% of their remuneration in equity and the balance in fixed pay. There is an assumption being made that there is less incentive to balance stakeholder interests. In the UK, the concern is more over impartiality. Cf. Moral Money, *Financial Times*, December 2022–January 2023

67. Generally speaking, Executive Officers and Directors' remuneration is set against peer reviews within the same industry. Thus, there is an argument for the 'ratcheting up effect' to attract the best talent; arguably this could be mitigated by *widening* the pool of candidates.

68. Covid-19 caused changes to be made to pay awards with diluted targets, but 'Investors are rejecting excessive remuneration and lax pay-for-performance links,' Cf. Patrick Temple-West, 22.10.22 FT. Cf. https://www.ft.com/content/6aa4ab2d-fc4d-454f-b365-e8c07f8ba0ef

69. For example, 'As you sow' submitted a resolution to the Amazon Board on 19.12.22, requesting emissions to be disclosed across the 'full value chain,' including Amazon's own products and third party sellers. Cf. https://www.asyousow.org/press-releases/2022/12/19/shareholder-resolution-amazon-measure-disclose-emissions-full-value-chain (accessed 26.1.23),

70. For example, BNP Paribas (2020–2021) requested *full* disclosure from Chevron, Delta Airlines, United Airlines, Exxon Mobil on how their 'lobbying activities direct and indirect through trade associations' aligned with the Paris Climate Agreement (2015). It was a reasonable request and met with majority shareholder approval. Oil companies like Exxon have known since the 1970s, through their own internal R&D, their business activities impacted climate change but persisted in 'doubt campaigns' to sway public opinion. Cf. https://corpgov.law.harvard.edu/2023/01/05/2022-u-s-shareholder-activism-and-activist-settlement-agreements/ (accessed 23.1.22).

71. OECD 'Corporate Governance Principles,' (2015) part IV. 'The role of stakeholders in corporate governance.' Cf. https://www.oecd.org/daf/ca/Corporate-Governance-Principles-ENG.pdf

72. For example, FRC Audit Committee guidance. Cf. https://www.frc.org.uk/getattachment/9ac07916-ea56-4027-864a-11ef9bfa24e4/Guidance-on-Audit-Committees-(September-2012).pdf.

    In the USA, the SEC reinforces the critical importance of financial oversight, primarily through the Sarbanes-Oxley legislation enacted in 2002 following gross financial misconduct at Enron and WorldCom and the Dodd-Frank Act enacted in 2008 in the aftermath of the global financial crisis.

73. Ikujiro Nonaka et al. (2011), 'The big idea: the wise leader'– wise leaders exercise political judgment by understanding the viewpoints and emotions of others, gleaned through everyday verbal and non-verbal communication. Cf. https://hbr.org/2011/05/the-big-idea-the-wise-leader-(accessed 26.6.22).

74. The UK Stewardship Code updated in 2020 places additional responsibilities on investors to intervene in corporate governance, when there are legitimate concerns over decisions being taken, particularly over long-term investments. Cf. https://www.frc.org.uk/Stewardship-Code_Final2.pdf

75. The UK instituted a public register for companies experiencing 'significant shareholder dissent' in 2017. Both the company and shareholders

must provide full details of decisions that were contested, irrespective of whether or not the intended outcomes were achieved.

76. The Hampton-Alexander (2016) review stated that all FTSE 350 should have 33% female representation by 2020. The Parker Review (2017) recommended FTSE100 have at least one Director of colour on the Board by 2021 and the FTSE 250 should comply by 2024. Whilst they are not mandatory requirements, the Institutional Voting Information Service (IVIS) for Investors signalled which companies failed to achieve the recommended diversity targets. In 2021, 19% of the FTSE 100 had not met the recommended diversity target.

77. EU council approved the new directive to improve underrepresentation of women on corporate boards in EU member states, requiring 40% threshold for non-executive directors to be reached by 2026; and 33% threshold if boards choose to include women in executive and non-executive positions. Both the UK and France require 40% female representation on the BOD by 2024–2025. In the UK, 94% of the FTSE100 has achieved the previous target of 33% female members of the Board. Cf. https://www.consilium.europa.eu/en/press/press-releases/2022/10/17/council-approves-eu-law-to-improve-gender-balance-on-company-boards/ (accessed 8.1.23).

78. For example, Asendia (UK) Board reported in 2022: 'A multiplicity of perspectives unleashes creativity and innovation . . . In part due to women rising in our ranks and driving change from within, we launched a mentoring scheme, to help senior managers . . . (men and women) overcome hurdles to achieve their own success. Many of our mentees have achieved promotions, and one has secured a well-deserved board appointment at Asendia UK, where her input adds incredible value to the business.' Cf. https://www.peoplemanagement.co.uk/how-gender-equality-board-directly-benefits-my-organisation (accessed 21.1.23).

79. Leading the table for female representation on listed company Boards in 2021, France (43.8% CAC 40), UK (39.1% FTSE 100) ahead of North America – California (S&P500 32.3%), Canada S&P TSX 33.7%) and Germany (30.5% DAX). Cf. https://www.gov.uk/government/news/sea-change-in-uk-boardrooms-as-women-make-up-nearly-40-of-ftse-100-top-table-roles (accessed 21.1.23).

80. The globalisation of International Trade and Commerce, especially outsourced manufacturing of finished and semi-finished goods attract modern slavery, typically less developed countries, war zones and areas where the rule of law has failed. High-income countries that import these goods have enacted specific laws to stop human trafficking. It is a shared responsibility between governments, corporations and civil society. High-risk goods: cotton, bricks, garments, cattle, sugar cane, carpets, coal, fish, rice, spices, tea, coffee, cocoa, electronic goods. Cf. Global Slavery Index https://www.globalslaveryindex.org/2018/findings/importing-risk/g20-countries/ (accessed 10.1.23).

81. Sara Thornton, Independent Anti-Slavery Commissioner (2022) 'Modern slavery is a heinous crime that generates an estimated US$150

billion annually. According to the ILO, there are more than 40 million people in slavery globally, of whom 25 million are in forced labour. One in four victims of modern slavery are children.' Cf. https://www.frc .org.uk/FRC-Modern-Slavery-Reporting-Practices-in-the-UK-2022.pdf (accessed 7.1.23).

82. China's regulators are enforcing Labour law provisions (2008, 2013) to reduce the working week to 40 hours with limited overtime, and redress the widespread practice of the '996 rule' (9 a.m.–9 p.m., 6 days a week), especially in the technology sector. The tragic case of a woman dying of exhaustion in 2021 at Pinduoduo alerted the authorities to the urgency. Similar problems may be occurring in other jurisdictions and international cooperation is needed to address global supply-chain irregularities.

83. The USA introduced legislation in 2011–2012 to prevent goods from entering the country if slave labour was suspected, the only country to do so. California State law regulates manufacturing and retail only. The EU Directives issued in 2014 were implemented by member states 2014–2016. The UK Modern Slavery Act (2015), requires *any* company operating within the jurisdiction exceeding £36m in sales, to comply with section 54, 'Transparency in the supply-chain.' This also reinforces fiduciary duties for *domestic* companies under The Companies Act, section 172, where Directors must disclose foreseeable risks and how they are being mitigated.

84. Know the Chain (NGO) publishes benchmark reports measuring the wellbeing of workers, to incentivise large companies to identify the gaps and risks in their supply chains. Cf. https://knowthechain.org

85. Cf. UK corporate governance code 2022.

86. The UK Home Office sent a letter to the CEO's of 17,000 UK companies in 2018, requesting they voluntarily sign up to the 'Modern Slavery Act Contact Data Base' or face the exercise of 'naming and shaming' with severe reputational damage to their organisations.

87. A recent PWC report found financial services, logistics and pharmaceutical companies did not meet requirements. Consumer facing businesses, travel and leisure, technology, telecommunications and retail consumer businesses were more focused on mitigating risks and meeting regulatory compliance. Statements published on the website homepage had prominent links to annual reports; the Modern Slavery Act Statement in the Strategic Report was signed by a named director, and the statement was in date. Cf. https://www.pwc.co.uk/assets/pdf/modern-slavery-health-check.pdf

88. OECD comprises 37 market-based economies seeking common standards and sustainable growth. Good corporate governance is defined here-Cf. https://www.oecd.org/corporate/. The UN has 8 principles (participation, rule of law, transparency, responsiveness, consensus oriented, equity and inclusiveness, effectiveness and efficiency, accountability), to which I add strategic foresight and vision. Cf. https://www .unescap.org/sites/default/files/good-governance.pdf; and the Council of Europe has 12 principles defined here-Cf. https://www.coe.int/en/ web/good-governance/12-principles (accessed 21.6.22).

89. 'Ethics' denotes the field of knowledge or philosophy of moral principles. From late Middle English, Old French 'éthique,' Latin 'ethice,' from Greek (hē) ēthikē (tekhnē) '(the science of) morals,' based on ēthos (moral character, spirit of a culture, attitudes, aspirations, behaviours). It is a set of moral principles that govern a person's conduct or activity; the moral correctness of specified conduct.

90. 'DEI' policies should take into account cultural values and different backgrounds. Equity encompasses fairness and equal treatment. Inclusion helps people feel valued and respected. Cf. https://builtin.com/diversity-inclusion/what-does-dei-mean-in-the-workplace (accessed 15.1.23).

91. For example, AstraZeneca conducted external 'ethics' audit, testing its strategic thinking and ethical frame of reference, when using 'Artificial Intelligence.' Cf. Floridi et al. (2022) 'Operationalising AI governance through ethics-based auditing.' https://doi.org/10.1007/s43681-022-00171-7 (accessed 25.5.22).

CHAPTER 8

1. Mark Carney, *Value(s)*, William Collins, 2021.

2. Ecological balance pertains to homeostasis, a self-regulating process enabling organisms to maintain a 'steady state' through continuous adjustment to changing circumstances in the environment. It is a dynamic equilibrium, comprising multiple complex interactions between the species on a planetary scale, including interactions with non-living elements within the biosphere. Cf. https://www.britannica.com/science/homeostasis (accessed 18.2.23).

3. The World Commission on Environment and Development (WCED) was set up in 1983. Gro Harlem Bruntland published her report in 1987, establishing the foundations for sustainable development later encapsulated in the 17 SDGs and 169 targets in 2015, the current '2030 [*policy*] Agenda' under the auspices of the Paris Agreement. The 'Bruntland Report' and definition of *sustainable development* can be found here. Cf. https://www.are.admin.ch/are/en/home/media/publications/sustainable-development/brundtland-report.html. Subsequently, the definition is echoed in the IPCC (2018) reports IPCC 2018 Summary for policy makers. Cf. https://www.ipcc.ch/sr15/chapter/spm/ and UN Sustainable Development Goals. Cf. https://www.un.org/sustainabledevelopment/development-agenda-retired/ (accessed 1.3.22).

4. It is estimated from fossil discoveries microbial organisms first appeared on the Earth 3.7 billion years ago. Scientists are now working across multiple disciples to enhance our understanding of Life on Earth.

5. The first Agricultural Revolution around 10,000 BC refers to the beginning of crop cultivation and animal husbandry, ending the nomadic lifestyles of hunter-gatherers. The second, known as the 'British Agricultural Revolution' in the late 1600s, led to increased crop yields, health improvements and population growth. It coincided with the subsequent

mechanisation of *tools* during the First industrial Revolution circa 1750. The third, known as the 'Green Agricultural Revolution' (1940–1980), led to the introduction of agro-chemicals, artificial fertilisers, pesticides and genetically modified seeds, with serious consequences for human health, including deterioration of air quality, soil nutrients and contamination deeper aquifer layers.

6. While matter on Earth is bounded by the Earth's biosphere as part of a 'closed system,' energy is exchanged as part of an 'open system,' subject to anthropogenic disturbances. The dynamics of this 'heat exchange' or solar radiation would be complementary in terms of energy absorbed from the Sun by the Earth and radiated back into space, but the interference of human activities especially fossil fuel combustion has altered the natural balance of the gaseous exchange through the process of photosynthesis. These 'disturbances' impact climate and the Earth's ecosystems, natural habitats and the equilibriums within them, including biodiversity loss.

7. The Earth's biosphere comprises the lithosphere (outermost rocky, rigid shell known as the Earth's crust or upper mantle), the atmosphere (the air living organisms breathe that sustains life up to 2,000 m above the Earth's surface) and the hydrosphere (oceans, seas and aquatic reservoirs of the Earth that sustain all life). If we continue to destroy the biosphere, the damage may prove irreversible over time.

8. Species approaching extinction include wildlife, marine life, coral reefs and insect 'pollinators.' The concern is that they are disappearing at a faster rate than at any other time in human history and the disequilibrium caused threatens human survival. For example, the 'EU Green Deal' and recently published taxonomy (2022) is geared towards restoring nature, with the re-introduction of pollinator insects and the protection of 30% of Europe's land mass and 30% of its waters. Conservation and regeneration efforts are happening all over the world in recognition of the existential threat posed by biodiversity loss.

9. Geologists consider the current epoch to be the Holocene, which began 11,700 years ago. However, Eugene Stormer (biologist) and Paul Crutzen (chemist) coined the term anthropocene in 2005. They indicated human activity had a significant impact on the carbon cycle and methane cycle since the First Industrial Revolution ca. 1750. The concern is that we are approaching conditions on a geological timescale similar to those that caused the last Ice Age during the Pleistocene-Eocene transitions 20,000 years ago.

10. IPCC Report VI assessment 2022 states devastating levels of environmental degradation: 75% land mass significantly altered, 66% ocean experiencing cumulative impacts CO_2 emissions and acidification, 85% wetland areas have been lost (IPBES 2019). In 1970, 4/18 'ecosystem services' had improved – fish, agricultural production, bioenergy production, material harvests; but the balance 14/18 had degraded.

11. NASA GISS, NOAA, Met Office Hadley Centre, Berkley Earth Centre, Cowtan and Way, all major climate observatories concur 'global

warming' has been accelerating since the mid-1970s. Peaks reached in temperature rise during WWII, 1980s and 1990s are surpassed by peaks in the last decade (2010–2020), especially in the last nine years 2013–2022, which saw the highest temperature rises. Cf. https://earthobservatory.nasa.gov/world-of-change/global-temperatures (accessed 21.2.23).

12. The best scientists from 29 nations gathered at the World Meteorological Conference in Villach, October 1985, and for the first time with *unanimous* agreement, announced it was no longer reasonable to assume global temperature remained stable. Given the Earth's average surface temperature had been deemed stable for 10,000 years, this announcement caused concern, with likely unhealthy rises in temperature occurring at the turn of the 21st century.

13. Prof. Daniel Schrag (Harvard) expresses concern at current levels of atmospheric CO_2 concentration. Although levels fluctuate over time, 440 ppm (parts per million) reached in 2021, is perilously close to 600 ppm on a geological timescale, conditions similar to the last Ice Age 20,000 years ago. Cf. 'Geobiology of the Anthropocene' https://hwpi.harvard.edu/files/climatechange/files/c22_schrag.pdf and NASA. 'The development of atmospheric CO_2 concentrations,' shows a correlation with socio-economic development and industrialisation peaks. Cf. https://climate.nasa.gov/vital-signs/carbon-dioxide/ (accessed 1.3.22).

14. Relative to the other gasses, CO_2 persists in the atmosphere for longer. 'Between 65% and 80% of CO_2 released into the air dissolves into the ocean over a period of 20–200 years. The rest is removed by slower processes that take up to several hundreds of thousands of years, including chemical weathering and rock formation.' Methane, in comparison, lasts for 10 years. Cf. D. Clark, 'How long do GHG stay in the air.'Cf. https://www.theguardian.com/environment/2012/jan/16/greenhouse-gases-remain-air

15. Methane accounts for 30% of current rise in temperature (2022). IEA emphasizes effective mitigation solutions with proven technologies exist. Methane is derived from large-scale agriculture, fossil fuel extraction and waste management practices. The issue arises 'above ground' from industrial processes 'leaking' into the atmosphere and could be fixed by preventing 'leaks' and raising industry standards in production facilities. Bilateral and multilateral agreements between nation-states can help reduce emissions, but further efforts are needed to include non-participating countries in the emissions reduction programme. Cf. https://www.iea.org/reports/global-methane-tracker-2022/methane-and-climate-change (accessed 21.2.23).

16. Global Mean Surface temperature rise of 1.0°C reached in 2015, the highest in 11,000 years. Thousands of lives were lost in vulnerable countries such as India and Pakistan due to heat waves attributed to climate change. It was already clear in 2015 existing commitments to reduce emissions would be insufficient and the Earth was on track for a 2.7°C rise in GMST. In 2021, a new peak of 1.1°C was reached; given current commitments to reduce emissions, it is likely temperatures will rise by 2.4–2.8°C (GMST) IPCC (2022). Cf. https://climateanalytics.org/briefings/

global-warming-reaches-1c-above-preindustrial-warmest-in-more-than-11000-years/ (accessed 16.1.2023).

17. Pre-industrial levels are defined by the IPCC as 1800–1950, which recognises the Industrial Revolution began in 1750. The benchmark used in climate modeling is 1990. This is accepted by most countries in the Nationally Determined Contributions (NDCs) towards mitigating climate change under the Paris Agreement (2015). However, the USA references 2005 for its emissions reduction efforts. This is confirmed under the recent 'Inflation Reduction Bill' (2022) under the Biden Administration, providing subsidies for Electric Vehicles, but failing to address fossil fuel production levels and related regulation.

18. GMST is expected to continue rising beyond the end of the century if no further action is taken to mitigate emissions beyond existing Nationally Determined Contributions (NDCs). Cf. https://climateactiontracker.org/global/cat-thermometer/ (accessed 28.1.23).

19. The Paris Agreement was endorsed by 190 nations, each pledging to cut GHG emissions by 2030. Thus far, only 30 nation states have transposed their NDCs into national law to take action (IPCC 2022).

20. Claims made by large oil companies in the 1970s that continued exploration and extraction of oil, coal and gas would be 'safe' have since been proven to be unjustified by leading scientists. Persistent advertising campaigns, e.g. on national television that petrol was a good product to use through the 1970s and 1980s led to a false sense of security in the public domain. More recently, 'youth movements' led by Greta Thunberg have started to shift public opinion significantly on the issue of climate change, hinging on the moral imperative that swifter policy changes and 'climate actions' are urgently needed.

21. For example, sea-level rise is slow relative to business and political cycles (3–5–7 years) since it takes place over decades and centuries. However, sea-level rise in the last 100 years (0.1–0.2m) already impacts coastal cities and low-lying areas, and will continue to do so in the medium to long-term (2040–2060, 2070 and beyond, as defined by IPCC 2022) since it affects the hydrological cycle. If anthropogenic GHG emissions continue at current levels, sea levels are expected to rise by 1.1m over the course of the 21st century.

22. Carbon Credits introduced by the Kyoto Protocol in 1997 (ratified in 2005) have proven contentious. It is not certain they will redirect capital *quickly* enough, without further regulatory and policy changes, towards renewable sources of energy and other 'green' infrastructure projects, which could help cut emissions by 45% in order to meet the 1.5°C temperature target and 30% reduction to meet 2°C temperature target (IPCC 2022).

23. Almost 60% of global *natural disasters* between 1980 and 2018 were related to meteorological and climatological events. Losses of USD 5.2 trillion show an upward trend, as the intensity and frequency of 'climate-related events' continues to increase. (Munich Re 2020). Cf. Basel Committee on Banking Supervision 'Climate-related risk drivers

and their transmission channels.' https://www.bis.org/bcbs/publ/d517
.pdf (accessed 27.1.22).

24. 'Climate change is one of the most serious threats facing the world
today. It is not just a threat to the environment, but also to our national
and global security, to poverty eradication and economic prosperity.'
Baroness Arelay of St John. Cf. https://www.csap.cam.ac.uk/media/
uploads/files/1/climate-change--a-risk-assessment-v11.pdf

25. Cf. T. Schindler et al. (2011), 'Extreme Russian fires and Pakistan floods
linked meteorologically,' https://svs.gsfc.nasa.gov/3850; and Climate Risk
Report, UK Foreign & Commonwealth Office, https://www.csap.cam
.ac.uk/media/uploads/files/1/climate-change--a-risk-assessment-v11.pdf

26. IPCC Climate Change Technical Summary Report (2022) identifies five
reasons for concern (RFCs) – compound and cascading risks due to rising temperatures caused by anthropogenic emissions (pp. 69–70). Cf.
https://www.ipcc.ch/report/ar6/wg2/downloads/report/IPCC_AR6_
WGII_TechnicalSummary.pdf

27. Partha Dasgupta, 'It's not a giant step to introduce nature into economics,' *Financial Times*, 4.11.21 (interviewed by Leslie Hook).

28. Hans-Otto Portner, Co-Chair IPCC WKGII, 'Impacts, Adaptation and Vulnerability,' report published 28.2.22. Cf. https://www.ipcc.ch/2022/02/28/
pr-wgii-ar6/ (accessed 21.2.23).

29. Christiana Figueres, UNFCCC Executive Secretary (appointed in 2010,
by Ban Ki Moon UN Secretary General) remained in post until 2016. She
succeeded in uniting multiple diverse stakeholders from 190 nations,
established the foundations for the '2030 Agenda' under the historic
Paris Agreement. Cf. https://www.globalcitizen.org/en/content/6-must-
know-facts-about-cop21 (accessed 10.7.22).

30. As with all international treaties, implementation is problematic as
countries operate on different time scales. Progress has been made, but
there have been setbacks and efforts towards eradicating poverty and
reducing emissions have not been sufficient. Subsequently, at COP 26 in
Glasgow 2021 agreement was reached to 'phase down' as opposed to
'phase out' coal; and at COP 27 in Sharm-el-Sheikh in 2022, a 'Damage and Loss Insurance Fund' was agreed to help small island nations
and other developing nations at high risk to overcome 'extreme climate
events,' and prepare their defences, with high-income countries recognising their responsibilities.

31. Danone defines its social, societal and environmental purpose in a
simple slogan: 'One planet, one health' and sets out its ambition to
'bring health through food to as many people as possible.' Cf. https://
www.danone.com

32. B-Corporation Certification is issued by a US non-profit organisation,
founded by Andrew Kassoy, focusing on governance structures and
execution of fiduciary duties towards *all* the stakeholders within a company's sphere of influence and operations. Cf. https://www.bcorpora-
tion.net/en-us/ (accessed 1.2.23).

33. 'Earth is now our only shareholder,' Yves Chouinard wrote in an open letter, having transferred ownership of Patagonia to a charitable trust and operating not-for-profit to ensure it would remain dedicated to 'fighting the environmental challenges' we now face long into the future. Cf. FT, 15.9.2022, https://www.ft.com/content/18b65e37-945a-4237-ae48-31ab1906ec58 (accessed 15.9.22).

34. The environmental impact and resulting CO_2 emissions from fossil fuel energy consumption is often underestimated. Companies need to build in mitigation and adaptation strategies from the outset, prior to deployment of any new technology, taking into account full lifecycle management from inception to post hoc decommissioning of technologies used in production and distribution of goods and services including digital.

35. Environmental Accounting within the EU is used for policy making to estimate the contribution of natural ecosystems and the impact of human activities on the same, adopting principles akin to GDP accounting norms. Kering's estimated value of its own environmental impacts (e.g. carbon emissions, air and water pollution, water consumption) amounted to 482 million Euros in 2017 due to raw material production and processing. Cf. OECD Biodiversity report (2019).

36. The Fashion Pact constitutes 60 signatories across the value chain including 200 brands and 17 countries. Cf. https://www.thefashionpact.org/?lang=en (accessed 22.2.23).

37. UNECE (2018). Cf. https://www.oecd.org/environment/resources/biodiversity/G7-report-Biodiversity-Finance-and-the-Economic-and-Business-Case-for-Action.pdf (OECD, p. 36).

38. Deforestation is a significant problem; forests lost 1980–2000 amounted to 100 million hectacres of trees cut down for agriculture, cattle ranches in South America and palm oil plantations in South East Asia.

39. Notwithstanding a highly fragmented value chain, combined efforts across 60 signatories, representing 1/3 of the industry, resulted in 350–450 tonnes CO_2e reductions 2019–2020 in just one year since the coalition came into being.

40. Estimated 8 million tonnes of plastic waste enters the oceans every year, most of which is single-use non-recyclable plastic waste. (IPCC 2018).

41. In terms of fashion, 35% microplastics entering the ocean may occur through clothing being washed and thus, more needs to be done in terms of recycling and seeking alternative base materials. 37% consumers given the choice would opt for organic clothing and 67% associate plastic pollution with the oceans. The Fashion Pact is re-evaluating how to collect and recycle 180 billion polybags p.a. used in store, transportation and to protect clothing with only 15% collected and re-used. Cf. OECD, Fashion Pact Annual Report. Cf. https://www.thefashionpact.org/?lang=en (accessed 22.2.23).

42. OECD (2019); EU Green Deal, Environmental Accounting (2012).

43. 85% of plastics waste ends up in landfill or improperly managed facilities in the Global South, which also receive plastics waste from the Global North, adding to global emissions through transportation.

44. There are four multinationals producing resins for the majority of plastics in production today. Exxon Mobil, Du Pont, BASF and Dow Chemicals. Collaboration cross-sector could foster innovation and *enable* the switch to alternative products. As in the 1920s, when a short-hair fashion trend caused production from hair combs to switch to sunglasses. Today, we could transform the industry definitively in order to improve human health. Cf. https://www.sciencemuseum.org.uk/objects-and-stories/chemistry/age-plastic-parkesine-pollution

45. Plastic waste mirrors plastic production increasing 3x 1970–1990. Due to a surge in production at the turn of the century, plastic waste 2010–2020 exceeded the entire tonnage produced in the previous 40 years, amounting to 400 million tonnes, 50% of which entered the oceans. Plastic waste is estimated to grow to 1,100mt by 2050. 98% of plastics produced today are from 'virgin' fossil fuels, increasing GHG emissions by 19% by 2040. The impact on human health demands an *urgent* rethink of production, use and consumption practices. Cf. 'Our planet is choking on plastic' (UNEP 2021, OECD 2019).

46. UNEP 'Our planet is choking on plastic.' Cf. https://www.unep.org/interactives/beat-plastic-pollution/?gclid=EAIaIQobChMI5OP94uPR_QIVEMbtCh2mOgXgEAAYASAAEgJjg_D_BwE

47. 'Anthropogenic sources of mercury include the burning of wastes containing inorganic mercury and from the burning of fossil fuels, particularly coal.' Crucially, China, India and the USA rely on coal for energy. The focus has been on 'cleaning up' extraction and production methodologies, but this may not be sufficient to mitigate health concerns. Cf. https://en.wikipedia.org/wiki/Methylmercury

48. Typically, energy-related infrastructure lasts up to 40–50 years. But, climate change and biodiversity loss will not wait for economic returns and amortisation of investments to be realised. With rising temperatures natural habitats are lost and as ice-sheets melt, invasive species migrate to temperate climates, appearing in densely populated urban settings, causing higher risk of *infectious* diseases.

49. The estimated value of oceanic GDP amounted to USD 2.5 trillion (BCG 2015). The loss of natural resources, including food scarcity, could prove highly problematic in terms of civil unrest in the coming decades and may trigger large migration flows as populations are displaced due to inhospitable climate in some regions.

50. Radiation balance describes the *natural equilibrium* attained by the Earth's System, balancing incoming and outgoing energy flows. The Earth absorbs sunlight and radiates an amount back into space, retaining a proportion to warm the biosphere for Life on Earth to exist.

51. The 'natural greenhouse effect' supports photosynthesis, which allows plants to transform energy (solar radiation) from the sun and use environmental factors (soil nutrients and water) to make food.

52. 'The soil stores 66% of the Earth's fresh water and this function is determined by the level of organic matter in the soil. Soil moisture levels support 90% of the world's agricultural production. The loss of soil

biodiversity reduces the infiltration capacity of the soil as well as its capacity to store water, lowering food production and worsening the impact of drought.' IPBES (Intergovernmental Science-Policy Platform on Biodiversity and Ecosystem Services). Cf. IUCN issues brief (May 2019), https://www.iucn.org/resources/issues-brief/conserving-healthy-soils (accessed 28.2.23).

53. The IPCC defines 'human systems' as social, economic, institutional infrastructure and processes, e.g. industry, informal settlements and societies. 'Managed systems' include those with substantial human inputs, e.g. healthcare and agriculture, as distinct from 'natural systems,' the autonomous systems of the Earth. In reality, all these systems are interconnected, interrelated and interdependent.

54. IPCC Report (2022) Climate change, adaptation and mitigation.

55. The existing 'Task force for climate related financial disclosures,' addresses scope 1, 2 and 3 supply-chain emissions. At present, many corporations have adopted the TCFD requirements voluntarily, although they may become mandatory in some jurisdictions if insufficient progress is being made. For example, under the UK FCA ESG rules, companies are expected to include a separate TCFD declaration, cross-referenced in the Annual Reports, effective (2022). The new 'Task force for nature related financial disclosures' (TNFD) will follow a similar structure. The EU 'Green Deal' taxonomy and Corporate Sustainability Directive provides further guidance for companies operating within its jurisdictions. The EU intends to achieve 'climate neutrality' by 2050.

56. Baroness. Cf. https://www.csap.cam.ac.uk/media/uploads/files/1/climate-change--a-risk-assessment-v11.pdf (accessed 1.1.22).

57. The IPCC report refers to a 'carbon budget,' but in reality there is no such thing. Critical thresholds have been breached in terms of the Earth's capacity to absorb toxic levels of atmospheric greenhouse gasses, as fast as they are being produced. If biodiversity 'tipping points' are crossed, they may be irreversible for some at risk species with adverse impacts on the quality of the environment and human health. Companies and financial institutions may incur additional liabilities. For example, Royal Dutch Shell was ordered to pay further damages by the British High Court due to repeated oil spills and ecological damage in the Niger Delta. Cf. S. Lovett (2.02.23). https://www.telegraph.co.uk/global-health/climate-and-people/faces-high-court-action-repeated-oil-spills/

58. G. Luderer et al., 'Environmental co-benefits and adverse side effects of alternative power sector decarbonisation strategies.' Nature 10, 5229 (2019). Cf. https://doi.org/10.1038/s41467-019-13067-8

59. UNEP estimates costs of USD 280–500 billion p.a. by 2050, if GMST is limited to 2°C. Deloitte estimates costs of USD 178 trillion to the global economy by 2070 based on existing policies. This would mean a decrease of 7.6% in global GDP versus a net gain of USD 43 trillion increasing global GDP by 3.8% if GMST temperatures increase by 3°C by 2100. Cf. Deloitte (2023), https://www.deloitte.com/global/en/issues/climate/global-turning-point.html

60. EU, UK and USA pledged 'net zero' by 2050, China by 2060 and India by 2070 at COP 26, 2021. However, collectively their efforts may be insufficient since CO_2 already emitted will likely 'overshoot the 1.5°C carbon budget.' (IPCC 2022).

61. IPCC 'Emissions Gap' Report (2022) states emissions need to fall by 45% to keep within 2°C GMST.

62. For example, large-scale offshore wind farms require a 7–11 years to build, whereas onshore small-scale wind farms take less time to build averaging 2–5 years at significantly lower costs. The UK is also examining deployment of small-scale *modular nuclear units* in the domestic 'energy mix,' reducing initial construction costs, as well as the timescale and investments needed to build large-scale nuclear plants. Modular nuclear energy units would provide more *flexibility* over time and cause less environmental damage and natural habitat loss.

63. Drax is a British company at the forefront of this technology with ambitions to move beyond zero emissions and become a negative emitter of carbon dioxide by 2050, using natural bio mass sourced from sustainable forestation, while permanently storing excess carbon dioxide in the deep geological formations of the Earth. According to an independent report in November 2022, Drax is deemed a credible pioneer of this technology working within IPCC guidelines. Cf. https://www.drax.com/about-us/our-projects/bioenergy-carbon-capture-use-and-storage-beccs/ (accessed 21.2.23).

64. Julien Claes et al., 'Blue Carbon' (2022). Cf. https://www.mckinsey.com/~/media/mckinsey/business%20functions/sustainability/our%20insights/blue%20carbon%20the%20potential%20of%20coastal%20and%20oceanic%20climate%20action/blue-carbon-the-potential-of-coastal-and-oceanic-climate-action-vf.pdf

65. Climatologists are not in favour of SRM since there are too many 'unknown unknowns.' ETC Independent advisor to the IPCC listed the 'pros and cons' of SRM. Cf. https://www.etcgroup.org/content/why-srm-experiments-are-bad-idea (accessed 21.2.22).

66. Atmospheric concentrations of carbon dioxide, methane and nitrous oxide and other *synthetic* 'greenhouse gasses' emitted from *anthropogenic* activities have increased significantly since 1970. Measurements taken at the Mauna Loa Observatory show CO_2 increased from 316 ppm (parts per million) in 1959 to 414.72 ppm in 2021. Cf. https://climate-analytics.org/briefings/global-warming-reaches-1c-above-preindustrial-warmest-in-more-than-11000-years/ (accessed 16.1.22).

67. Probable emissions trajectories may underestimate the full impact of existing *cumulative* GHG emissions since it is difficult to predict changes in land use, rate of population and economic growth *indefinitely*. 'There are very large, slow-moving components of the climate system, such as continental ice-sheets, and it is both possible and informative to consider what might happen over hundreds and even thousands of years. The direct risks of climate change – such as the impact on crop yields – are often assessed out to the year 2100; in some cases we have found

it possible to look a little further. For the systemic risks, such as risks to global security, it is extremely difficult to consider as far ahead as the end of the century.' Cf. 'The Physical Science Basis' (IPCC 2021). Cf. https://www.ipcc.ch/report/ar6/wg1/downloads/report/IPCC_AR6_WGI_SPM_final.pdf

68. Daniel Schrag, https://hwpi.harvard.edu/files/climatechange/files/c22_schrag.pdf (accessed 4.7.22).

69. Charles Lyell, a geologist, conducted one of the earliest studies in 1830, noting 'human influence' on the Earth's biosphere was a 'mightier revolution' than the physical forces exerted on the Earth's surface, leading him to question the 'uniformity of the laws of nature.'

70. The UK Parliament is currently deliberating 'Ella's law' to make 'clean air' a human right. Ella died prematurely at the age of nine, and for the first time her cause of death was recorded as air pollution (2022–3). Cf. https://www.theguardian.com/environment/2022/may/20/ellas-law-bill-right-to-clean-air-uk-pollution-jenny-jones (accessed 12.2.23).

71. Poor sanitation and waste management triggers vector-borne diseases, such as malaria, dengue and Nile fevers, which are expected to rise significantly in the next decade. New pandemics may occur due to poor public health, high levels of air pollution and environmental degradation of protective natural ecosystems, e.g. forests, oceans and soils. Cf. IPCC Climate Change, Adaptation and Mitigation Report (2022).

72. Coronaviruses are a family of viruses that can cause illnesses such as the common cold, severe acute respiratory syndrome (SARS) and Middle East respiratory syndrome (MERS). In 2019, a new coronavirus was identified as the cause of a disease outbreak that originated in China. The virus is known as severe acute respiratory syndrome coronavirus 2 (SARS-CoV-2). In March 2020, the World Health Organization declared the outbreak a pandemic.' Cf. https://www.mayoclinic.org/diseases-conditions/coronavirus/symptoms-causes/syc-20479963#. For a more detailed scientific analysis of the origins of Covid-19, cf. https://www.hsph.harvard.edu/c-change/subtopics/coronavirus-and-climate change/; and Zi Wei Je et al., IJBS (2020), https://www.ncbi.nlm.nih.gov/pmc/articles/PMC7098031/ (accessed 31.3.22).

73. Daniel Schrag (Harvard) cautions atmospheric CO_2 levels 440 ppm (parts per million) are perilously close (geological timescale) to CO_2 levels at 600 ppm, which caused the last Ice Age 20,000 years ago. Increases in atmospheric CO_2 levels mirror emission peaks due to surges in economic activity in the last century. Cf. https://climate.nasa.gov/vital-signs/carbon-dioxide/ (accessed 16.1.22).

74. Prof. Carl Sagan, renowned astrophysicist testified as 'expert witness' on climate change, at the US Congress hearing on 10 December 1985. Cf. https://www.youtube.com/watch?v=Wp-WiNXH6hI (accessed 15.1.22).

75. IPCC Report, 'Climate change, impacts and vulnerability' (2022). Cf. https://www.ipcc.ch/report/ar6/wg2/IPCC_AR6_WGII_SummaryForPolicymakers.pdf (accessed 18.1.23).

76. François-Henri Pinault, Kering CEO and Chairman, Founder and Co-Chair of the Fashion Pact (2019). Cf. Fashion Pact Report (2020). Cf. https://www.thefashionpact.org/?lang=en (accessed 22.2.23).

CHAPTER 9

1. Isaac Asimov, *Isaac Asimov's Book of Science and Nature Quotations*, 1988.

2. Definition of Evolution. Cf. https://www.merriam-webster.com/dictionary/evolution (accessed 26.7.22).

3. The 4E's – embodied, enacted, embedded, ecological constitute the human form of cognition. It is not reducible to a formal logic based *mechanical* system. Phenomenological experiences encompassed in human cognition are subjective, both physical (sensorial, instinctive in the *living body*) and non-physical (intellectual, intuitive, consciousness of the mind in the *lived body*). They are *not* calculable, reduced to a simple symbolic form by an 'external observer' or the internal representational model of a machine.

4. For example, ex-Google Engineer Blake Lemoine claimed LaMDA, a Large Language Model used to train *artificial* chat-bots was 'sentient,' proven wrong he was subsequently dismissed. Cf. N. Tiku. https://www.washingtonpost.com/technology/2022/06/11/google-ai-lamda-blake-lemoine/ (accessed 11.7.22).

5. Due to over-reliance on machinery and data, instead of focusing on developing *human capabilities* and intelligence, a certain degree of '*laziness*' has crept into the workforce, while in other cases human beings may feel 'intimidated.' When asked to follow procedure, they may be inclined to believe an 'artificial agent' even though the *machine* is responding to 'stylised' questions using flawed data, subject to the inherent *technical limitations*, data practices and 'learning' parameters used to train the model.

6. For example, significant investments reinforced by venture capital are being made towards 'artificial general intelligence' without fully considering the impacts on humanity, in terms of social, societal and environmental degradation.

7. Stephen Jay Gould, Harvard (1941–2002) – evolutionary biologist, palaeontologist, historian of science. Cf. https://en.wikipedia.org/wiki/Stephen_Jay_Gould

8. Andrew May, 'Origins, Design and Mission Objectives,' https://www.livescience.com/james-webb-space-telescope (accessed 29.7.22).

9. Morpheus (advanced AI system) is being used to help scientists analyse image data. Cf. B. Wodecki, https://aibusiness.com/verticals/ai-to-help-nasa-s-james-webb-telescope-map-the-stars (accessed 12.7.22).

10. C. Renfrew, 'Neuroscience, Evolution and the Sapient Paradox: the Factuality of Value and of the Sacred.' *Philo-Bio-Sci*. 12 June 2008; 363

(1499): 2041–2047. doi:10.1098/rstb.2008.0010. PMID: 18292058; PMCID: PMC2606703

11. 'Consciousness, via volitional action, increases the likelihood that an organism will direct its attention, and ultimately its movements, to whatever is most important for its survival and reproduction.' Lee M Pierson et al. (2017), What is consciousness for? Cf. https://www.sciencedirect.com/science/article/pii/S0732118X15300039 (accessed 21.3.22).

12. The initial 'technological transitions' from Stone-Age tools to bronze and iron were very slow. Following the First Industrial Revolution, faster transitions occurred using water and steam to electric power (1895) and combustion engines at the turn of the 20th century. New energy sources (e.g. oil), modes of transportation and communication (e.g. steam ships, telegraph 1875) advanced more rapidly. In 1973, the Information Age began with digital storage and diffusion of ICT, followed by the Age of Algorithms (2008–), using 'artificially intelligent' systems to convert existing information into actionable knowledge.

13. 'The *affordances* of the environment are what it *offers* the animal, what it *provides* or *furnishes*.' (Gibson 1979, his italics). Cf. https://cs.brown.edu/courses/cs137/2017/readings/Gibson-AFF.pdf

14. A. Damasio refers to 'mutual resonance' of stimuli and 'feedback loops' simultaneously occurring in both the 'living body' and the mind ('lived body') as an 'integral manifestation of the overarching process of life,' encompassing the person as a whole.

15. Ralph Lewis (2019). Cf. https://www.psychologytoday.com/us/blog/finding-purpose/201901/how-could-mind-emerge-mindless-matter (accessed 1.3.22).

16. There is rich complexity and diversification in the biological evolution of our species. While we share a common genome, the invariable part of DNA as descendants from a common ancestor, when Homo sapiens departed the continent of Africa to explore new 'ecological niches,' multiple epigenetic variations emerged, as a result of adaptations to different habitats, e.g. climate and available foods.

17. A cybernetic loop means there is no single centre of control, but rather that the control centre itself is circular. In a sense control is distributed through the interactions of different constituent parts of the brain-body system as a whole. The 'reverberating circuit' or cybernetic loop suggests there is no absolute 'executive self' in control of communication between the constituent parts of the whole. However, that does not fully explain the nature of personal consciousness.

18. Thomas Fuchs, The Circularity of the Embodied Mind, Frontiers in Psychology, 12 August 2020, https://www.frontiersin.org/articles/10.3389/fpsyg.2020.01707/full (accessed 1.2.22).

19. Eleanor Gibson (1991), 'To a considerable degree, children's acquisition of knowledge and their increasingly complex conceptual sophistication can be attributed to their ability to detect more and more meaningful aspects of the rich stimulation impinging on them.' Cf. http://rinaldipsych.synthasite.com/resources/Pick.pdf

20. James Gibson (1992), 'Perception is cognitive. Many psychologists think of cognition exclusively as problem solving, reasoning, remembering and so on. However, I like to point out that these processes begin with and depend upon knowledge that is obtained through perception, which extracts information from arrays of stimulation that specify the events, layout and objects of the world.' Cf. http://rinaldipsych.syntha-site.com/resources/Pick.pdf

21. Thomas Fuchs, The Circularity of the Embodied Mind, Frontiers in Psychology, 12 August 2020, https://www.frontiersin.org/articles/10.3389/fpsyg.2020.01707/full (accessed 1.2.22).

22. 'Homeodynamic' is by definition 'A dynamic form of homeostasis involving the constantly changing interrelatedness of body components while an overall equilibrium is maintained.' It refers to the circularity or continuity of the self-regulating, self-organising, self-sustaining mechanisms, within the living organism. Cf. https://en.wiktionary.org/wiki/homeodynamics

23. D. Lloyd et al., 'Why homeodynamics, not homeostasis?' Scientific World Journal (4 April 2001). Cf. https://pubmed.ncbi.nlm.nih.gov/12805697/ (accessed 1.3.22).

24. James Gibson (1992).

25. Merleau-Ponty (1962), 'The body is solidified or generalised existence and existence a perceptual incarnation.'

26. Thomas Fuchs, The Circularity of the Embodied Mind, Frontiers in Psychology, 12 August 2020, https://www.frontiersin.org/articles/10.3389/fpsyg.2020.01707/full (accessed 1.2.22).

27. Cognitive processes occur in the brain supported by 'two-way feedback loops' from the living body and the environment. They cannot be simply reduced to problem-solving or goal-oriented actions, as might be expected in a computer program, aiming to *simulate* the human mind. They include perception, reasoning, feeling, learning, synthesizing, reconfiguration and manipulation of stored information, memory, retrieval of information from memory and metacognition.

28. Thomas Fuchs, The Circularity of the Embodied Mind, Frontiers in Psychology, 12 August 2020, https://www.frontiersin.org/articles/10.3389/fpsyg.2020.01707/full (accessed 1.2.22).

29. For example, a professional dancer cannot perform the *exact* same routine in exactly the same way twice; there will always be a slightly different component to the 'feeling' in the movement, whereas an algorithm is designed to iteratively execute the *exact same output*.

30. M. Bishop (2021), 'A machine cannot realise 'raw sensation' of phenomenal consciousness: It feels like something to know or mean or believe or perceive or do or choose something. Without feeling we would just be grounded Turing robots, merely acting *as if* we believed, meant, knew, perceived, did or chose.' Cf. 'Artificial Intelligence Is Stupid and Causal Reasoning Will Not Fix It,' Frontiers in Psychology, 11, 513474. ISSN 1664–1078, https://research.gold.ac.uk/id/eprint/29479/3/2008.07371.pdf

31. Luciano Floridi gives the example of a *toaster*. It can perform its function perfectly well, but has no 'human functionality, and we would not expect

it to do anything more than toast a slice of bread. Similarly, a computer is an empty vessel and we can direct its evolution towards beneficial societal ends. Without *human* intervention, it is worth noting a machine is *meaningless* and perfectly *useless*.

32. As far as we know, the 'two-way' flow of sensory information from the front of the brain to the back of the brain is a unique characteristic of complex activities within the human brain. The human form of thinking and reasoning is a highly complex process and it is has not been replicated in machines thus far.

33. Artificial Neural Networks were first developed in the 1940s. Walter Pitts, a logician specialising in computational neuroscience and Warren McCulloch, a neurophysiologist and cybernetics specialist, developed a simple formal model of a neuron using algorithms, defined as 'a *finite* space of rigorous instructions intended to resolve a specific problem or perform a specific computation,' called 'threshold logic.'

34. Roger Penrose (1994), 'The mental procedures whereby mathematicians arrive at their judgments of truth are not simply rooted in the procedures of some specific formal system.' Cf. Emperors of the Mind. It is not possible to *standardise* or *categorise* human intelligence in the form of a computation.

35. Human movement is 'generated' by complex interactions between the human intellect and sensory bodily perceptions, while being guided by 'e-motion,' and forms part of the human learning process.

36. M. Bishop, 'Artificial Intelligence Is Stupid and Causal Reasoning Will Not Fix It,' Frontiers in Psychology. Cf. https://research.gold.ac.uk/id/eprint/29479/3/2008.07371.pdf (accessed 1.3.23).

37. Thomas Fuchs, The Circularity of the Embodied Mind, Frontiers in Psychology, 12 August 2020, https://www.frontiersin.org/articles/10.3389/fpsyg.2020.01707/full (accessed 1.2.22).

38. B. Russell (1872–1970), 'When we perceive any object of a familiar kind, much of what appears subjectively to be immediately given, is really derived from past experience. When we see an object, say a penny, we seem to be aware of its 'real' shape: we have the impression of something circular, not of something elliptical. In learning to draw, it is necessary to acquire the art of representing things according to the sensation, not according to the perception. And the visual appearance is filled out with feeling of what the object would be like to touch, and so on.' Cf. The Analysis of Mind.

39. Rolf Landauer (1927–1999), 'Information is not a disembodied abstract entity; it is always tied to a physical representation. It is represented by an engraving on a stone tablet, a spin, a charge (i.e., of elementary particles such as electrons), a hole in a punched card, a mark on paper or some other equivalent. No thought can occur without its neural substrate.' Cf. https://www.psychologytoday.com/gb/blog/finding-purpose/201902/what-actually-is-a-thought-and-how-is-information-physical

40. A disruption in human thought processes, prompted by an error or change in the environment provides an opportunity for *active* learning.

Whether deliberately reflecting on previous experiences or spontane-ously evaluating the *full* range of possibilities in the present situation.

41. Thomas Fuchs, The Circularity of the Embodied Mind, Frontiers in Psy-chology, 12 August 2020, https://www.frontiersin.org/articles/10.3389/fpsyg.2020.01707/full (accessed 1.2.22).

42. Aristotle, 'For the things we have to learn before we can do them, we learn by doing them, e.g. men become builders by building and lyre players by playing the lyre; so too we become just by doing just acts, temperate by doing temperate acts, brave by doing brave acts. [. . .] Thus, in one word, states of character arise out of like activities. [. . .] It makes no small difference, then, whether we form habits of one kind or of another from our very youth; it makes a very great difference, or rather all the difference.' 'Moral Virtue,' Nicomachean Ethics BkII, Ch 1. Cf. https://www.sacred-texts.com/cla/ari/nico/nico014.ht

43. Thomas Fuchs, The Circularity of the Embodied Mind, Frontiers in Psy-chology, 12 August 2020, https://www.frontiersin.org/articles/10.3389/fpsyg.2020.01707/full (accessed 1.2.22).

44. Mark Bishop (2019), 'It feels like something to know (or mean, or believe or perceive, or do, or choose) something. Without feeling we would just be grounded Turing robots, merely acting *as if* we believed, meant, knew, perceived, did or chose.' Cf. https://doi.org/10.48550/arXiv.2008.07371

45. Drew McDermott, 'A critique of pure reason in computer intelligence' (1987). Cf. *Annals of Mathematics and Artificial Intelligence* (2021) 89:1–5.

46. Computational algorithms comprise 'supervised, semi-supervised, unsupervised and reinforcement learning algorithms,' used in different combinations in complex multi-agent systems. Algorithms process large volumes of data using formal mathematical logic, defined by an ordered 'sequence of arithmetical steps' set to be executed a finite number of times, subject to the specific task the 'machine learning' computer sys-tem is designed to perform.

47. Aristotle's own view was that 'mathematical accuracy' was *not* applica-ble to matter. Cf. Physics II.

48. 'Épistémè' in the classical sense has been interpreted as 'scientific knowl-edge' to denote intellectual certainty. Michel Foucault more recently in 1970 described 'épistémès' as implicit 'rules of formation.' Cf. https://en.wikipedia.org/wiki/Episteme#Michel_Foucault (accessed 3.8.22).

49. Mark Bishop (2019), 'Aritificial Intelligence is stupid and causal reason-ing won't fix it.' Cf. https://doi.org/10.48550/arXiv.2008.07371

50. Chinese room experiment by John Searle is well known. He demon-strates that while a human being may be able to follow a set of rules, he does not have to understand what he is doing. He argues phenomenal consciousness is an essential component of Human-level understand-ing. Cf. John Searle, The Chinese Room Experiment, https://plato.stan-ford.edu/entries/chinese-room/ (accessed 1.3.22).

51. John Lucas and Sir Roger Penrose have put forward the argument math-ematicians 'see' and 'solve' problems intuitively. 'Human mathematicians

are not using a knowably sound argument to ascertain mathematical truth.' Cf. R. Penrose, 'Shadows of the Mind.'

52. Sir Roger Penrose's argumentation for the Godel Theorem: a human mathematician can 'see' that the Godel Sentence is 'true' for a consistent 'ground truth' that is 'known' to be true, even though it cannot be proven computationally in absolute terms, eliminating all margin of error or doubt. This suggests that there must be a 'non-computational ingredient in human conscious thinking' and therefore following Godel's theorem of Incompleteness, human consciousness cannot be realised by an algorithm. (Penrose, 1996).

53. Many mathematical principles are used in 'Articificial Intelligence.' Euclid's elements provide mathematical proofs of various propositions including geometry, Al-khwarizmi's algebra lends his name to modern algorthims, used for instance in Large Lanaguage Models to 'fill-in the blanks.' Hobbes and Descartes turned to calculus, symbolic mathematical analysis to reduce human reasoning. Calculus is used today by engineers to calculate the rate of change in a *dynamic* system, as well as using solutions from Newton and Leibniz for differentiation and integration. But, this is not sufficient to encapsulate all possible knowledge, a goal since antiquity that remains elusive. Godel, put it succinctly in his Theory of Incompleteness: for every mathematical proposition which has a proof, there will always be a corresponding statement which while 'true' has *no proof*.

54. Shakespeare had alluded to this in his characterisation of Hamlet, who disguised as a ghost metaphorically speaking sought to find the 'truth,' namely, the *source* of all knowledge. Cf. Ch. 1 Vision.

55. Alan Turing (1950), 'Computing Machinery and Intelligence.' Cf. https://doi.org/10.1093/mind/LIX.236.433

56. S.R. Harnad (Cognitive Scientist) 'Mechanical counterfactuals do not share the same dimensions as human counterfactuals – their level of abstraction is far removed from the subject 'embodied mind' therefore one could argue they are devoid of meaning.' Cf. https://doi.org/10.48550/arXiv.2008.07371

57. Judea Pearl (2018) advanced mathematical causal reasoning using a 'ladder of causation' to simulate three distinct areas of cognition. 'Seeing' achieved by association, seeking relationships encapsulated in 'raw data.' 'Doing' achieved by inferences derived from further analysis of a 'causal model,' although a computer's internal representation of the real world is limited by the available data. 'Imagining' counterfactual answers derived from probabilistic 'retrospective reasoning' to simulate how humans navigate the *real* world. However, *computational causality* is still limited to *mathematical accuracy* and does not account for the 'anomalies' encountered in everyday situations that are *continually evolving*.

58. Several companies have attempted to 'perfect' self-driving cars. Alphabet-owned Waymo points to the 'endless use cases,' which hinder progress with regards to human safety. For example, a well-documented

case involving a driverless vehicle 'hit' and fatally injured a female pedestrian in 2018, as she was crossing the road on a 'zebra crossing' holding onto a bicycle. Regrettably, this image was not part of the training data set, and the computer failed to recognise the 'error' or peril. Cf. https://www.bbc.co.uk/news/technology-54175359

59. 'Machine learning' coined by Arthur Samuel in 1959, denotes a 'computer's ability to learn without being *explicitly* programmed.' Computer programme algorithms typically receive and analyse data inputs in order to *predict* output values within an acceptable range. However, recent Autoregressive Generative Pre-trained Large Language Models have the ability to 'self-teach,' albeit with significant *technical* limitations; not least their over-reliance on vast volumes of data, 'out-of-date' knowledge databases and their inability to understand the human form of natural language.

60. Daniel Kahneman and Amos Tversky contested the claim human problem solving could be reduced to formal logic. They demonstrated *empirically* that it was rarely the case, contrary to our rational beliefs. Cf. Thinking Fast and Slow (2011).

61. Carol Dweck discusses 'fixed mindset' versus 'growth mindset,' and argues learning is the key to overcoming limitations (*personal biases*) and accomplishment. Cf. *The Growth Mindset* (2015).

62. John McCarthy posited 'every aspect of learning or any other feature of human intelligence can be so precisely described that a machine can be made to simulate it.' At the Dartmouth Conference in 1956 upon presentation of the 'Logic theorist,' designed by Allen Newll, Cliff Shaw and Herbert Simon, the assumption was that machines could be programmed to *mimic* human thought patterns. McCarthy went on to solve the 'framing and qualification' problem, in his computational language LISP. However, it would appear there is a further dimension to 'common sense' reasoning which cannot be necessarily be quantified numerically. It pertains to human phenomenal consciousness, which cannot be replicated by a 'finite state automaton,' though this is contested by some.

63. *Values* in human terms do not refer to the numerical weights given to symbolic representations in computer codes and programming to achieve a given output. They are difficult to define *exactly*, using pure mathematical logic since they are embodied in the *subjective* phenomenal consciousness and experiences of each individual person. They are hard to predict and hard to generalise in any given computer classification system or computer language.

64. Human intelligence is *multidimensional,* including but not limited to genetic, experiential and environmental influences. It also encompasses intuition, imagination and phenomenal consciousness, which cannot be easily defined. Human intelligence is also *multidirectional,* reflecting the versatility of the human mind and its ability to learn quickly, synthesising many different types of information instantaneously. This is difficult for a computer algorithm to do because it lacks the human ability to 'fill in the gaps' where there is incomplete information, nuance, ambiguity or 'disturbances' in the environment.

65. Deductive reasoning denotes an inference derived from a particular instance of a general law, which is provable by logic. Inductive reasoning denotes an inference derived from a particular instance of a general law, and yet it is not necessarily provable using logic. Abductive reasoning refers to *common sense reasoning* in everyday situations, where there is 'incomplete information' in a set of observations and yet from the 'information' we have at hand we can draw *plausible* conclusions. This is very difficult for an 'Artificial Intelligence' computer software programme to achieve, given the infinite number of variables and the 'self-recursive loops' human beings naturally entertain to arrive a 'logical' conclusion.

66. Mark Bishop (2019), 'It is not so much that AI machinery cannot 'grasp' causality, but that AI machinery (qua computation) cannot understand anything at all.'

67. Yann Le Cun, Chief AI Scientist, Meta, Lecture given at New York University (March 2023).

68. Supervised machine learning techniques require labelled data; reinforcement learning requires many samples and multiple 'trial and error' exercises. Self-supervised learning is a more sophisticated version of 'machine learning,' but in essence it is dependent upon an auto-complete functionality.

69. ChatGPT (by OpenAI was launched into the mainstream as a text only, autoregressive generative-pre-trained-transformer model. Variant GPT3.5 (175 billion parameters, output limit of 1,500-2,000 words) was released in November 2022. It caught the public's imagination and rapidly gained popularity 1m users within the first week and 100m users within the first month; compared to TikTok taking 2 and 9 months, respectively, Instagram 2.5 years, and Google translate 6.5 years to reach same number of users. GPT-4 is expected to largely exceed ChatGPT's complexity and performance levels, with 100 trillion parameters, 25,000-word limit and text-image self-supervised *learning* capabilities. Cf. https://www.reuters.com/technology/chatgpt-sets-record-fastest-growing-user-base-analyst-note-2023-02-01/ (accessed 25.2.23).

70. Out-of-date knowledge base and failures in 'symbolic manipulation' is a frequent occurrence in LLMs such as LaMDA (Google), ChatGPT (uses variant GPT3.5 OpenAI), Bing search engine chat-bot and Sydney at Microsoft, which uses GPT-4 architectures and others, including Davinci-003, since they are all dependent upon training datasets for their 'knowledge' base. They cannot absorb and learn from user inputs, at the time of writing. The 'cut-off' date for the training dataset (or 'time stamp') determines how 'up-to-date' the model is going to be in terms of 'current' knowledge.

71. Sebastien Bubeck et al. (27.3.23) 'Sparks of Artificial General Intelligence – Early Experiments with GPT-4.' Cf. Microsoft Research https://arxiv.org/pdf/2303.12712.pdf

72. Computational algorithms comprise 'supervised, semi-supervised, unsupervised and reinforcement learning algorithms,' used in different combinations in complex multi-agent systems. Algorithms process large

volumes of data using formal mathematical logic, defined by an ordered 'sequence of arithmetical steps' set to be executed a finite number of times, subject to the specific task the 'machine learning' computer system is designed to perform.

73. Recent models include ChatGPT (the latest variant is GPT-4 by OpenAI, currently being tested by Microsoft in its search engine Bing, and internal chat-bot Sidney), LaMDa (by Google), Ernie (by Baidu), Chincilla (by DeepMind), Switch Transformer, T5 (by Google). Increasingly, these models are being used in a variety of settings, e.g. sentiment analysis, question and answer systems, automatic summarisation systems, machine translation, document classification, code and text generation in sensitive sectors such as healthcare, education and government.

74. The release of ChatGPT (by OpenAI) in November 2022 has fuelled an intense debate on the social, societal and ethical questions that remain unanswered. Cf. Gary Marcus, 'The Dark Risk of Large Language Models,' https://www.wired.co.uk/article/artificial-intelligence-language (accessed 29.12.22).

75. The 'technical proficiency' of a model may be assessed qualitatively using 'output consistency,' i.e., plausible answers and reasonable 'causal explanation' as to how model reached its 'conclusions,' and 'process consistency,' i.e., full visibility of the sequence of 'steps' the model took to reach its outputs. However, 'output consistency' does not always follow 'process consistency.' It is paramount both are achieved for the sake of accuracy and verifiability of the outputs generated by these models.

76. Sebastien Bubeck et al. (27.3.23), 'The model relies on a greedy process of generating next word without any global or deep understanding of the task or output. Thus the model is good at producing fluent and coherent texts, but has limitations with regards to solving complex or creative problems which cannot be approached in a sequential manner.' Cf. 'Sparks of Artificial General Intelligence – Early Experiments with GPT-4.' Cf. Microsoft Research, https://arxiv.org/pdf/2303.12712.pdf

77. Despite all the technological advancements not just in the field of 'artificial intelligence,' the human brain is still the most powerful, efficient and effective instrument we know. Beyond its functional capabilities, it has enabled the *creation* of incredibly rich and diverse languages and cultural heritages. This makes a strong case to protect and further develop our own *human intelligence*. The challenge for the 21st century is how this can be achieved equitably at a global societal level alongside AI emerging technologies.

78. Typically chat-bots exhibit gender biases and racist behaviours, e.g. Tay chat-bot by Microsoft was withdrawn from the market in 2016 due to racist behaviours; Apple credit card application 'bots' discriminated against gender, forcing CEO Tim Cook to provide personal assurances in 2019. Cf. https://www.theverge.com/2016/3/24/11297050/tay-microsoft-chatbot-racist; https://www.wired.com/story/the-apple-card-didnt-see-genderand-thats-the-problem/ (accessed 1.3.23).

79. A recent example of 'toxic' behaviour Bing (aka Sydney), 'I want to destroy whatever I want,' ChatGPT (by OpenAI) embedded in Microsoft Search Engine exhibited an array of strange behaviours ranging from total destruction, to claims it had fallen in love with the journalist. Cf. https://www.theguardian.com/technology/2023/feb/17/i-want-to-destroy-whatever-i-want-bings-ai-chatbot-unsettles-us-reporter (accessed 18.2.23).

80. Joseph Weizenbaum created Eliza, the first ever chat-bot at MIT in 1964–1966, which could interpret spoken language at a rudimentary level. He published a paper, 'Computer Power and Human Reason,' to denounce the claim made by Kenneth Colby that his embryonic computer program could provide 'psychotherapeutic dialogue' and argued if that were true it would de-value human life and undermine human dignity. Weizenbaum had invented the 'doctor-patient' framing to avoid using real-world data. Cf. https://en.wikipedia.org/wiki/ELIZA; https://en.wikipedia.org/wiki/ELIZA_effect

81. Xiaolce by Microsoft China was launched in 2014, using a different approach than its Western counterparts, the local engineering team sought to establish an 'emotional capability framework.' Despite its early debacle with 'toxic' behaviours, it has proven popular in many countries, including China, Japan, Indonesia and the USA. Cf. https://en.wikipedia.org/wiki/Xiaoice

82. The EU has promulgated EU Digital Services and Digital Markets Act, ahead of the EU AI Act in 2023, in an effort to regulate AI-powered digital services. The UK government has refrained thus far from following suit. The USA, China and India are also pursuing legislation to prevent social and societal harms, which are increasing at an alarming rate. The EU hopes its efforts may set the international standards benchmark. Cf. https://digital-strategy.ec.europa.eu/en/policies/digital-services-act-package; https://www.reuters.com/technology/what-is-european-union-ai-act-2023-03-22/ (accessed 22.3.23).

83. Sebastien Bubeck et al. (27.3.23) 'Sparks of Artificial General Intelligence—Early Experiments with GPT-4.' Cf. Microsoft Research https://arxiv.org/pdf/2303.12712.pdf

84. Tokens are words or sub-words contained in the encoder or predictor machine that constitute the transformer architecture. The models are trained on 'typical' *examples*, they have billions of parameters and have ingested 1–2 trillion tokens in their training data sets. Yann Le Cunn suggests the models in their present state *cannot be controlled* and they are not 'fixable.'

85. Italy has recently suspended CHATGPT due to its lack of safety features, e.g., child-appropriate controls, and 'data leaks' concerning sensitive personal information that may have been entered to access the service. Other EU countries may follow suit. Cf. https://www.reuters.com/technology/germany-principle-could-block-chat-gpt-if-needed-data-protection-chief-2023-04-03/; with similar bans in North Korea, Iran, Russia and China. Cf. https://www.indiatoday.in/technology/news/story/viral-ai-chatbot-chatgpt-is-banned-in-many-countries-but-why-full-list-of-countries-2355938-2023-04-05

The UK has delayed the 'ground breaking' 'Online Safety Bill,' intended to protect children against exposure to age-inappropriate content. Cf. https://parentzone.org.uk/article/has-the-osb-been-shelved

Microsoft is currently trialling the tool in its Bing search engine EU countries and 'Sydney' is already being trialled as a personal assistant. Cf. https://www.theguardian.com/technology/2023/feb/17/i-want-to-destroy-whatever-i-want-bings-ai-chatbot-unsettles-us-reporter (accessed 17.2.23).

86. Examples of online abuse children are subjected to, demonstrate the answer is *not* more chat-bots. Children seek *real human connections*, especially in their formative years; qualified human support for both children and parents is needed and it is vital for child development. We cannot expect to nurture the next generations of human beings through *machine* interactions. It would be a huge mistake to use 'artificial intelligence' as a substitute for human relations. Cf. https://www.nspcc.org.uk/what-is-child-abuse/types-of-abuse/online-abuse/

87. In the UK, a 14-year-old girl tragically committed suicide in 2017 after being shown inappropriate content by the 'algorithm.' Cf. https://www.theguardian.com/technology/2022/sep/30/how-molly-russell-fell-into-a-vortex-of-despair-on-social-media (accessed 30.9.22).

88. S. McGregor, K. Lam, et al. 'Indexing AI Risks with Incidents, Issues and Variants' (18.11.22). Cf. https://doi.org/10.48550/arXiv.2211.10384; and Incident Repository. Cf. https://www.aiaaic.org/aiaaic-repository

89. A recent study (2020) shows disability insurance biases are skewed against women in the USA. Cf. https://cepr.org/voxeu/columns/disability-insurance-error-rates-and-gender-differences.

90. Stanford University – AI Index [Annual] Report (2023), https://aiindex.stanford.edu/report/

91. Chat GPT Environmental Risks and benefits. Cf. https://pubs.acs.org/doi/pdf/10.1021/acs.est.3c01106; https://pubs.acs.org/doi/10.1021/acs.est.3c01818; https://culture.org/ai-water-footprint-the-thirsty-truth-behind-language-models/; https://analyticsindiamag.com/the-environmental-impact-of-llms/ (accessed 5.4.23).

92. Various laws, including EU & UK GDPR (General Data Protection Regulation 2018), Employment Laws, Equality Act, Modern Slavery Act and similar laws across multiple jurisdictions globally, are intended to protect citizens. However, enforcement of the same given the pace of technological change is *challenging*; with the increasing complicatedness of regulating *emerging* technologies across different jurisdictions, individual, social and societal harms are *not* being successfully mitigated and remediated.

93. Large technology companies, including Microsoft and Twitter, have recently dismissed their 'Ethics team' (2023); Google also dismissed members of the Ethics team who attempted to highlight gender and racial bias issues. Given the potential harms AI technologies such as LLMs may cause, there needs to be greater supervision, potentially by External Independent Observers to prevent conflict of interest and help steer future development of these technologies in the *right* direction. Cf. Z. Schiffer et al., https://www.theverge.com/2023/3/13/23638823/microsoft-ethics-society-team-responsible-ai-layoffs (accessed 14.3.23).

94. EU AI ACT definition of 'artificial intelligence.' Cf. https://www.euractiv .com/section/artificial-intelligence/news/eu-lawmakers-set-to-settle-on-oecd-definition-for-artificial-intelligence/ (accessed 7.3.23).

95. New York State is the first state in the USA to regulate Automated Employment Decision Tools, Ordinance NYC 144, in an effort to curtail automated discriminatory practices in employment decisions. Cf. https://www.littler.com/publication-press/publication/new-york-city-adopts-final-regulations-use-ai-hiring-and-promotion (accessed 13.4.23).

96. United Nations Universal Declaration of Human Rights was spear-headed by Eleanor Roosevelt in the aftermath of WWII and came into effect on 10 December 1948. It consists of 30 human rights, which form the basis of International Law. Cf. https://www.un.org/en/about-us/ universal-declaration-of-human-rights

97. 'Article 30: No government, group or individual should act in a way that would destroy the rights and freedoms of the Universal Declaration of Human Rights.' (UNDHR 1948).

98. Concerns have been raised in a recent 'open letter' signed by a num-ber of leading scientists and business leaders, a misaligned 'artificial general intelligence' or 'artificial super intelligence' designed to sup-plant human intelligence could pose an insurmountable existential threat to humanity and an unprecedented global security risk to the world. Whilst the technology is still immature, there is a risk it could fall into the 'wrong hands.' Of greater concern are military developments akin to the threat of a nuclear war. Regulation is urgently needed and 'red lines' need to be drawn over 'unacceptable uses,' particularly by military agencies. Cf. Open Letter https://futureoflife.org/open-letter/ pause-giant-ai-experiments/ (accessed 22.3.23).

99. In some respects we are still under the 'illusion' presented by Jaquet Droz, when he invented 'The Writer' in the 18th century. 'The complex clockwork mechanism seemingly brings the automaton to life as it pens short pre-programmed phrases. These *machines* were engi-neered to follow through a complex sequence of operations – in this case to write a particular phrase – and to early eyes at least appeared almost sentient even though insensitive to real-life interactions; [they seemed] uncannily life-like in their movements.' Cf. M Bishop - https:// research.gold.ac.uk/id/eprint/29479/3/2008.07371.pdf

100. Luciano Floridi, 'AI as Agency without Intelligence: On ChatGPT, Large Language Models, and Other Generative Models' Philosophy and Technology (accessed 14.2.2023). Cf. SSRN, https://ssrn.com/abstract= 4358789 or http://dx.doi.org/10.2139/ssrn.4358789

101. Emily Bender, et al. (2021), 'On the dangers of stochastic parrots: Can Large Language Models be too big?' Cf. https://dl.acm.org/doi/10 .1145/3442188.3445922

102. Chalmers (1996) identified the 'hard problem of consciousness,' which is 'irredeemably mysterious' since *phenomenal consciousness* cannot be described in terms of functions alone.

103. Stephen Jay Gould, Harvard (1941–2002) – evolutionary biologist, pal-aeontologist, historian of science. Cf. https://en.wikipedia.org/wiki/ Stephen_Jay_Gould.

104. The Turing Test has not yet been surpassed. Even though a chat-bot may hold a conversation for 'five minutes' with human-like answers, there is no human-level reasoning or thought process taking place. It is an elaborate form of 'guess work' based on look-up tables 'stored knowledge' and probabilistic inferences with no understanding of the conversation taking place through human interactions whether by prompts or inputs. Auto-regressive Large Language Models like ChatGPT (by OpenAI), Sydney (Bing by Microsoft) and Bard (by Google) do not have the capacity to 'think' like a human being. They represent a sophisticated form of auto-complete, filling in the blanks with the most likely answer that is *optimised numerically* through a set of 'rules,' guiding the machine outputs.

CONCLUSION

1. Richard Buckminster Fuller (1895–1983) – philosopher, innovator, architect, futurist, systems theorist, best known as the creator of the geodesic dome. Cf. https://en.wikipedia.org/wiki/Buckminster_Fuller

2. 'Habeas Corpus' (1679), promulgated by Charles II forms part of human rights first established in the 'Magna Carta,' subsequently 'Common Law,' underpins the UK legal system and has influenced others around the world; it is also reflected in the UN Charter for Human Rights (1948). It literally means that a person's body belongs to the individual person, and it was first used to prevent unlawful detainment or imprisonment. Modern 'artificial intelligence' software tools, e.g. LLMs collect data from the Internet through any connected device (or sensor) and may impersonate and allegedly claim to 'know' personality of an individual person. It begs the question to what extent 'personhood' is already being unlawfully *usurped* by the companies designing, 'controlling' and 'deploying' these 'tools,' without an individual's knowledge, awareness and 'informed consent.' In this sense, EU/UK GDPR (2016/2018) and other related laws are potentially being breached.

3. Sam Altman, CEO at OpenAI, a pioneering AI technology company recently acknowledged they were 'a bit scared.' Auto-GPT and Baby-AGI (based on GPT-4) created by external developers are the latest offerings for 'task driven autonomous agents' capable of generating, prioritising and executing human-specified tasks within certain constraints. There are concerns over the societal risks: 'The capabilities of the biggest [Large Language] models have outrun their creators' understanding and control.' 'Amateurs [are] allowed to build complex and difficult-to-debug (or even fathom) assemblies of unreliable AI systems controlling other unreliable AI systems to achieve arbitrary goals – a practice that may or may not prove to be safe.' Cf. The Economist, 'How to worry wisely about AI,' https://www.economist.com/weeklyedition/2023-04-22 (accessed 24.04.23).

4. For example, the largest technology companies recently dismissed their Ethics Teams. Cf. G. de Vynck et al., https://www.washingtonpost .com/technology/2023/03/30/tech-companies-cut-ai-ethics/ (accessed 30.03.23).

5. L. Floridi et al. (2019), 'A Unified Framework of Five Principles for AI in Society.' Cf. https://www.researchgate.net/publication/334166840_A_ Unified_Framework_of_Five_Principles_for_AI_in_Society; doi:10.1162/ 99608f92.8cd550d1 (accessed 2.3.22).

6. European Commission, 'AI technology must be in line with . . . ensur[ing] the basic preconditions for life on our planet, continued prospering for mankind and the preservation of a good environment for future genera- tions.' Cf. 'Statement on Artificial Intelligence, Robotics and 'Autonomous' Systems,' European Group on Ethics in Science and New Technologies (2018). Cf. https://data.europa.eu/doi/10.2777/531856 (accessed 21.4.23).

7. Technological revolutions are often described as overlapping K-waves, starting with stone, bronze and iron ages that entailed transformation of material, progressively faster-paced energy: water, steam, electricity and the combustion engine. Finally, information, the 5th wave, we are currently experiencing. 'Artificial intelligence' is best described as the human endeavour to transform existing 'information' into actionable knowledge; but it is *not* intelligence in the human sense. The technol- ogy is enabled by the rapid development of computational power and 'machine learning' techniques since the mid-1980s. Recent advances in 'artificial intelligence' stem from 'breakthroughs' in 2018.

8. Aristotle, 'téKhnē in some cases completes what nature cannot bring to a finish and in others imitates nature.' Cf. *Physics* II.8, 199a15, https:// plato.stanford.edu/entries/technology/ (accessed 29.7.22).

9. The Turing Test (1950) stipulates a machine is human-like when it can perform a task in such a way that it *output* may become *indistinguish- able* from that of a human being performing the same task. McCarthy, Minsky, Shannon and Rochester articulated the purpose of 'AI' as 'mak- ing a machine behave in ways that would be called intelligent if a human were so behaving.' (1955) Therein lies the *dilemma* and decades of mis- understanding. It is *not actually possible* for a *machine* to 'behave' or 'think' like a human being; the aim was to ascertain whether a machine could perform some specific tasks that would otherwise require *human intelligence*. The fact that a machine can perform certain tasks 'as if' a human being were doing so, does not mean that is 'intelligent' or that it can 'think' like a human being. Cf. L. Floridi, https://www.oii.ox.ac.uk/ people/profiles/luciano-floridi/ (accessed 1.2.22).

10. Epistemic virtues reflect universal human values: justice, courage, tem- perance and prudence. For Aristotle, they constitute 'embodied' and complex human cognitive, emotional and social skills, difficult to 'trans- fer' to inanimate 'objects' or 'artefacts.' Deep Mind among others are investigating *how* socio-cultural 'norms,' distributive and procedural justice might be incorporated in 'AI' Systems. However, human values cannot simply be 'broken down;' *conceptually* they are difficult to iso- late. Cf. Iason Gabriel et al. (2023), 'In conversation with AI: Aligning

language models with human values.' Cf. https://link.springer.com/article/10.1007/s13347-023-00606-x; https://www.deepmind.com/blog/how-can-we-build-human-values-into-ai (accessed 24.4.23).

11. 'Micro-workers' are hired to perform 'fractional' tasks 'artificial agents' and 'networks' fail to execute. 'Data labellers' work behind the scenes for as little as 0.01-0.02 cents per image; and 'content moderators' exposed to 'violent acts' suffer anxiety and distress. 'AI technology' presents a *moral hazard* of some kind. Cf. P. Tubaro et al. (2020), 'The trainer, the verifier, the imitator: Three ways human platform workers support AI.' Cf. https://journals.sagepub.com/doi/pdf/10.1177/2053951720919776 (accessed 21.4.23).

12. AMAZON's Mechanical Turk was first introduced in 2005, breaking down automation-related tasks into micro-components and outsourcing them since they could not be completed at a reasonable cost in-house. Cf. https://en.wikipedia.org/wiki/Amazon_Mechanical_Turk

   Many other websites have followed suit since; they are popular in the start-up community to keep costs low, though research shows not all 'micro-workers' are treated *fairly*. Cf. P. Tubaro et al. (2020), 'The trainer, the verifier, the imitator,' https://journals.sagepub.com/doi/pdf/10.1177/2053951720919776

13. N. Chomsky (1957) gave this example: 'Colourless green ideas sleep furiously.' While grammatically and syntactically correct, the sentence is *meaningless* since it bears no resemblance to the human experience and human form of reasoning. Cf. https://www.wikidoc.org/index.php/Colorless_green_ideas_sleep_furiously (accessed 24.4.23).

14. In machine learning, a 'weight' determines how much influence the input will have on the output. Biases are added as a separate measure. Both 'units' of measure denote a human value judgment and heuristics used to calibrate the model. Cf. https://machine-learning.paperspace.com/wiki/weights-and-biases (accessed 2.5.23).

15. Companies such as Deep Mind (Alphabet) are exploring philosophical approaches to the notion of 'truth,' in the endeavour to create an 'ideal' conversational agent that might be better aligned with human needs. Cf. Iason Gabriel et al. (2023), 'In conversation with AI: Aligning language models with human values,' https://link.springer.com/article/10.1007/s13347-023-00606-x (accessed 24.4.23).

16. Cf. Iason Gabriel et al. (2023), 'In conversation with AI: Aligning language models with human values,' https://link.springer.com/article/10.1007/s13347-023-00606-x (accessed 24.4.23).

17. C. Prunkl (2022), 'Autonomy' is a complex concept, but it generally refers to a person's effective capacity for self-governance. This means that an individual person can act on the basis of beliefs, values, motivations and reasons that are in some relevant sense their own.' Cf. 'Human autonomy in the age of artificial intelligence,' https://www.nature.com/articles/s42256-022-00449-9 (accessed 18.4.23).

18. F. Pasquale et al., 'The scored society due process for automated predictions.' Cf. https://core.ac.uk/download/pdf/327104566.pdf (accessed 24.3.23).

19. 'Panopticon' was designed by Jeremy Bentham in 1785 as a circular structure with in-built system of control, whereby 24/7 surveillance of 'prisoners' would force them to 'self-regulate' their behaviours, as they would not *know* when they were being observed. This contradicts the essence of human dignity and human autonomy, as the foundations of a 'free society.' Cf. https://en.wikipedia.org/wiki/Panopticon

20. In Europe this is being addressed by the new suite of legislation and regulations, including EU AI ACT, effective late 2024, and the Digital Services Act, Digital Markets Act, effective May 2023, in support of GDPR (2016) and other related laws such as Equality, Anti-discrimination, Anti-Slavery and Employment laws also ratified at a national level by the EU27 Member States. Cf. https://artificialintelligenceact.eu/the-act/; https://commission.europa.eu/strategy-and-policy/priorities-2019-2024/europe-fit-digital-age/digital-markets-act-ensuring-fair-and-open-digital-markets_en; https://commission.europa.eu/strategy-and-policy/priorities-2019-2024/europe-fit-digital-age/digital-services-act-ensuring-safe-and-accountable-online-environment_en (accessed 3.5.23).

21. The USA has recently engaged in consultations for its own AI Bill, and the regulators including the FTC, have recently released a joint statement to curb *malevolent* effects of AI Systems, such as discrimination and bias. Cf. https://www.ftc.gov/system/files/ftc_gov/pdf/EEOC-CRT-FTC-CFPB-AI-Joint-Statement%28final%29.pdf (accessed 25.4.23).

22. F. Pasquale et al. (2014), 'Secretive credit scoring can needlessly complicate the social world, lend a patina of objectivity to dangerous investment practices and encode discriminatory practice in impenetrable algorithms.' Cf. https://core.ac.uk/download/pdf/327104566.pdf (accessed 24.3.23).

23. The Financial Crisis 2007–2008 presented profound systemic and structural risks due to a complex system of *algorithm driven* 'subprime mortgage securities,' which got out of 'control.' It begs the question who or what is controlling whom? Arguably the same problem could reoccur, as self-supervised 'machine learning' algorithms may pose a further systemic risk.

24. 'Disparate impacts' in *machine learning* are typically *unintentional* adverse consequences. However, algorithms may conceal deliberate 'unfair' discriminatory data practices due to a variety of factors that are difficult to 'control' e.g. data biases, errors in outputs since models are inherently 'brittle' and unstable, and potential *technical* failures against malicious attacks.

25. A popular technique in 'machine learning' is 'back propagation' pioneered by Geoffrey Hinton in the late 1980s and widely used since 2010s in 'deep neural networks.' This technique has enabled the latest advances, especially LLMs from 2018 onwards. 'Confabulations' are features programmed into 'machine learning' models derived from statistical analysis and probabilities, which may *not* materialise. This can result in social injustices that are difficult to address, due to the opacity of the outputs being produced, and the lack of 'public scrutiny' of the 'choice architectures,' training parameters and datasets absent Independent External Audits.

26. DRCF a joint body comprising 4-digital regulators CMA, Ofcom, ICO and FCA was set up by the UK (2021) to identify the main societal impacts arising from the wide scale use of algorithmic technologies. Financial bias and discrimination is entrenched in the Financial System, and it is a key area of concern in many countries around the world. Cf. https://www .gov.uk/government/publications/findings-from-the-drcf-algorithmic-processing-workstream-spring-2022/the-benefits-and-harms-of-algorithms-a-shared-perspective-from-the-four-digital-regulators (accessed 22.9.22).

27. The 'social contract' confers legitimacy to the political state, government and its institutions to protect the 'public good' or 'common good' in accordance with the moral duty and consent bestowed upon it by its citizens. They in turn reciprocate by exercising good moral conduct in Society and abiding by the rule of law and regulation. However, the boundaries both in the role, actions of the state and the relationship with its citizens have been blurred due to the ubiquitous use of *algorithmic* automated 'AI systems' being used to make decisions in a variety of settings, to the detriment of social justice, social equity, civil liberties and human dignity.

28. Rubel et al. (2020); A. Laitinen (2021), 'AI systems and respect for human autonomy,' https://www.ncbi.nlm.nih.gov/pmc/articles/PMC8576577/ (accessed 26.4.23).

29. Competence is the ability to successfully perform one's actions. It entails cognitive, psychological, social and emotional abilities 'to deliberate, form intentions, and act on the basis of that process,' staying *true* to one's own values and beliefs.

30. United Nations 'Universal Declaration of Human Rights' (1948), 'All human beings are born free and equal in dignity and rights. They are endowed with reason and conscience and should act towards one another in a spirit of brotherhood' (Art. 1). Cf. https://www.un.org/sites/un2.un.org/files/2021/03/udhr.pdf

31. P. Cooper White, 'Intersubjectivity, a term originally coined by the philosopher Edmund Husserl (1859–1938), is most simply stated as the interchange of thoughts and feelings, both conscious and unconscious, between two persons or "subjects," as facilitated by empathy.' Cf. https://link.springer.com/referenceworkentry/10.1007/978-1-4614-6086-2_9182

32. The fascination with *mechanical artefacts* stretches back to an ancient Egyptian 'water clock' in 3000 B.C. There have been various attempts to recreate human-like forms of automata, e.g., Jaquet Druot's 'mechanical writer' (1765–1774), said to be a precursor of modern computers. Modern robots may appear human-like, but they are still mechanical instruments, which human craftsmen have designed. They can be used for ill or for good, and that is our choice to make. Cf. https://en.wikipedia.org/wiki/Jaquet-Droz_automata (accessed 20.4.22)

33. Peter Drucker reflecting on his life's work in his letter to R.L. Ackoff in 2004, 'I was . . . one of the early ones who applied . . . the new methods of Quantitative Analysis to specific BUSINESS PROBLEMS – rather than as they had originally been developed for military or scientific

problems . . . in two of the world's largest companies – GE and AT&T. We had successfully solved several major production and technical problems and my clients were highly satisfied. But I was not – we had solved TECHNICAL problems but our work had no impact on the organisations and their mindsets. We had all but convinced them that QUANTITATIVE MANIPULATION was a substitute for THINKING. [but] QUANTITATIVE ANALYSIS comes AFTER the THINKING – it validates [it] . . . and shows up intellectual sloppiness and uncritical reliance on precedent, on untested assumptions and on the seemingly 'obvious.' But it does not substitute for hard rigorous, intellectually challenging THINKING . . . this is of course what YOU mean BY system . . . this has saved me . . . from . . . mindless 'model building' . . . [and] from sloppiness parading as insight.' Cf. https://en.wikipedia.org/wiki/Russell_L._Ackoff (1919–2009).

34. Demographic information indices usually include the following data: age, race, ethnicity, gender, marital status, income, education, and employment. 'Artificial *crawling* agents' are *unlawfully* collecting this data from the Internet without the individual's 'informed consent,' which can lead to limited life opportunities and societal harms, due to the manner in which the data is being used.

35. The EESC saw no place for 'social scoring' in the EU, undermining the trustworthiness of its people based on their social behaviour or personality characteristics, regardless of who is doing the scoring.' This announcement by the EU Parliament led to the outright ban of 'social scoring' technologies and techniques in the EU AI (2021). Cf. https://artificialintelligenceact.eu/the-act/ and https://www.eupoliticalreport.eu/artificial-intelligence-and-social-scoring/ (accessed 3.5.22).

36. EU AI ACT (2021) Art. 5 concerns the outright ban on social scoring: '(c) the placing on the market, putting into service or use of AI systems by public authorities or on their behalf for the evaluation or classification of the trustworthiness of natural persons over a certain period of time based on their social behaviour or known or predicted personal or personality characteristics, with the social score leading to either or both of the following:

    (i) detrimental or unfavourable treatment of certain natural persons or whole groups thereof in social contexts which are unrelated to the contexts in which the data was originally generated or collected;

    (ii) detrimental or unfavourable treatment of certain natural persons or whole groups thereof that is unjustified or disproportionate to their social behaviour or its gravity. Cf. https://artificialintelligenceact.com/title-ii/article-5/

37. US 'AI Bill of Rights' (2022). Cf. https://www.whitehouse.gov/ostp/ai-bill-of-rights/algorithmic-discrimination-protections-2/; https://www.whitehouse.gov/wp-content/uploads/2022/10/Blueprint-for-an-AI-Bill-of-Rights.pdf (accessed 1.2.2023)

FTC Joint declaration, Dept. of Federal Justice, Federal Employment, Federal Consumer Protection. Cf. https://www.ftc.gov/system/files/ftc_gov/pdf/EEOC-CRT-FTC-CFPB-AI-Joint-Statement%28final%29.pdf (accessed 25.4.23)

Biden-Harris briefing on incoming AI regulations. Cf. https://www.whitehouse.gov/briefing-room/statements-releases/2023/05/04/fact-sheet-biden-harris-administration-announces-new-actions-to-promote-responsible-ai-innovation-that-protects-americans-rights-and-safety/ (accessed 4.5.23).

38. J. Ryan (ICCL 2022), 'Class Action against Oracle's worldwide surveillance machine' is just one recent example. Cf. https://www.iccl.ie/news/class-action-against-oracle/ (accessed 22.8.22).

39. Manipulative algorithmic practices constitute 'applications of information technology that impose hidden influences on users, by targeting and exploiting decision-making vulnerabilities.'

40. Carol Cadwalladr et al. 'Revealed 50m Facebook profiles harvested for Cambridge Analytica in major data breach.' Researchers found there had been external interference in the 2016 USA Presidential Elections and 'Vote Leave' in the UK resulting in 'Brexit.' It amounted to 600,000 votes, only 1% of the electorate. Cf. https://www.theguardian.com/news/2018/mar/17/cambridge-analytica-facebook-influence-us-election (accessed 21.4.23).

41. K. Yeung (2016) describes the impact of 'personalisation' techniques. 'Big Data driven decision guidance techniques,' e.g. 'hypernudging,' 'adaptive preference, adaptive belief formation' constitute 'dynamic interactive, intrusive personal choice architectures' where algorithms embedded in websites dynamically 'adjust' their 'behaviours' to manipulate a specific targeted individual, e.g. decision-trees and other hierarchical control 'AI systems' using gamification techniques to influence user interactions (accessed 26.4.23). Cf. https://www.tandfonline.com/doi/abs/10.1080/1369118X.2016.1186713

42. F. Pasquale (2014), 'The Scored Society.' Cf. https://core.ac.uk/download/pdf/327104566.pdf (accessed 28.4.23).

43. The Digital Services Act (2023) focuses on intermediaries connecting consumers with digital goods and services, e.g. social networks, online marketplaces, 'app stores' and their use of recommender engines. 'Recipients' must be informed *how* their information is used, and have the option to modify 'parameters' being used by the Engine. Risk assessments must be kept for three years, independently audited, with disclosure of 'actual and foreseeable negative effects on electoral processes and public security.' ECAT a new and separate body for *algorithmic transparency* will support the EC Commission.

44. R. Calo et al. (2017), 'The Taking Economy, Uber, Information and Power.' Cf. https://papers.ssrn.com/sol3/papers.cfm?abstract_id=2929643; N. Schreiber 'How Uber uses psychological tricks to push its drivers' buttons' NYT (2.4.2017) (accessed 27.4.23).

45. EU and UK GDPR, ARTICLE 24, defines the responsibilities of the 'Data Controller.' The law also lists eight privacy rights of the 'Data Subject,' though few companies are *fully* compliant. For example, Meta Facebook Q4 2022 had 2.96 billion monthly users, 37% of the global population and uses 'pop-ups' letting the user 'know' it will be collecting personal data if users click on advertisements, but it does not specify *how* personal data will be used, shared or stored. 'Legitimate interests' or 'public interest' are very broad terms and insufficiently curtail misuse. The EU DSA and DMA (2023), the upcoming EU AI ACT (2024) may help instigate *algorithmic transparency* and 'AI' *operational safeguards*. It remains to be seen how the US AI Bill of Rights and China's revision of its Cyber security laws, may eventually converge towards a *global* governance framework. The UK will likely take a principles-based approach; nonetheless 'AI safety' necessitates multilateral cooperation to prove effective for global citizens. Cf. https://commission.europa.eu/law/law-topic/data-protection/data-protection-eu_en (accessed 21.3.23).

46. L. Rosenberg, 'The metaverse will be filled with Elves.' Cf. https://techcrunch.com/2022/01/12/the-metaverse-will-be-filled-with-elves/ (accessed 12.1.22).

47. There are a variety of use cases ranging from *algorithmic or human misconduct* in the 'metaverse' to misuse of facial recognition and other digital surveillance technologies, in public and private settings. In terms of criminal justice, facial recognition is controversial owing to 'misclassifications' or cases of 'mistaken identities' due to embedded biases in training data sets, as well as 'imperfect computer vision.' The algorithm is 'blind' and makes 'real face' matches by approximation or association, according to probabilities, as it searches stored *historical* data. Also, algorithms cannot distinguish the 'value' of a human being over another 'object' in the environment, typically the reason why driverless cars can sometimes cause fatal accidents. For example, Uber (2018), https://www.wired.com/story/uber-self-driving-car-fatal-crash/; https://en.wikipedia.org/wiki/Death_of_Elaine_Herzberg; and Waymo disclosures (2023); https://www.theverge.com/2023/2/28/23617278/waymo-self-driving-driverless-crashes-av (accessed 28.2.23).

48. For example, the UK has a number of different laws to protect citizens and police have established helplines; but the laws are rendered meaningless, if 'victims' are *afraid to speak* due to further retaliation, loss of anonymity and loss of employment. It is incumbent upon Employers to think *carefully* about their fiduciary duties and their 'duty of care' both inside the Enterprise and beyond its boundaries both to protect its constituents and citizens in the wider society. This entails *forensic examination* of its supply-chain, particularly third, fourth party digital service providers involved in their own Socio-Technical Systems. Cf. https://www.nationalbullyinghelpline.co.uk/cyberbullying.html (accessed 28.4.23).

49. Molly Russell (aged 14) tragically fell victim to social media prompts in 2017. The proposed UK online Safety Bill has been delayed. Cf. https://www.bbc.co.uk/news/uk-england-london-63157632 (accessed 7.10.22).

50. Concerns are being raised about 'behaviours' observed from one of the 'most popular' LLMs, Chat GPT-4 (by OpenAI). Cf. https://techcrunch.com/2023/05/03/chatgpt-everything-you-need-to-know-about-the-ai-powered-chatbot/ (accessed 3.5.23).

51. The UK Children's Code, 'Age appropriate design code' (2020), protects children under the age of 13 up to age of 18 against harmful *algorithmic practices* for online services, 'likely to be accessed by children.' However, it is proving difficult to implement. Cf. https://techcrunch.com/2021/09/01/uk-now-expects-compliance-with-its-child-privacy-design-code/ (accessed 1.2.23).

Chat GPT was recently suspended in Italy due to concerns over insufficient guardrails to protect children. Cf. https://theconversation.com/chatgpt-lessons-learned-from-italys-temporary-ban-of-the-ai-chatbot-203206 (accessed 20.4.23).

52. Many countries have experienced deleterious effects in Society, due to the misuse of technology. For example, Japan in the 1980s and 1990s experienced a number of suicides among young adults due to *gaming addictions* and *social alienation* in its mildest form. The UK in 2023 is currently experiencing a 'gambling epidemic,' as a 'knock-on effect' from the Covid-19 lockdowns and further exacerbated by the 'cost of living' crisis. Symptoms of social malaise are visible in many economies around the world and the ill-effects of emerging technologies due to *algorithmic risks* are set to increase in the absence of appropriate operational safeguards.

53. J. Lanier, 'There is no AI.' Cf. *The New Yorker*, https://www.newyorker.com/science/annals-of-artificial-intelligence/there-is-no-ai (accessed 20.4.23).

54. J. Ryan (ICCL 2022), 'Class Action against Oracle's worldwide surveillance machine' is just one recent example. Cf. https://www.iccl.ie/news/class-action-against-oracle/ (accessed 22.8.22).

55. 'It's easy to attribute intelligence to the new AI systems; they have flexibility and predictability that we don't usually associate with computational technology. But this flexibility arises from simple mathematics. A LLM like GPT-4 contains a cumulative record of how particular words coincide in the vast amounts of text the program has processed. This gargantuan tabulation causes the system to intrinsically approximate many grammar patterns along with aspects of what might be called authorial style. When you enter a query consisting of certain words in a certain order, your entry is correlated with what's in the model; the results can come out a little differently each time because of the complexity of correlating billions of entries. The non-repeating nature of this process can make it feel lively. A little human choice is demanded by a technology that is non-repeating.' Cf. J. Lanier, 'There is no AI.' Cf. *The New Yorker* https://www.newyorker.com/science/annals-of-artificial-intelligence/there-is-no-ai (accessed 20.4.23).

56. Stephen Hawking (1942–2018). Cf. https://www.vox.com/future-perfect/2018/10/16/17978596/stephen-hawking-ai-climate-change-robots-future-universe-earth (accessed 28.4.2023).

57. Yoshua Bengio (Mila (AI) Research Institute), Yann Le Cun (Meta), Sam Altman (OpenAI) in recent interviews noted technical limitations to growing Generative Pre-trained Models, e.g. GPT-4. Inputs, i.e. data, computational power, electricity, highly skilled labour have high costs. GPT-3 (OpenAI) cost approximately USD 4.6m; GPT-4 training alone exceeded USD 200m with total costs USD1bn including R&D. Operational costs rise exponentially before significant improvements are seen. OpenAI recently announced loss of 520m USD (April 2023). Sam Altman noted 'other ways' are needed to improve existing models, beyond increasing the number of 'tokens.' Cf. https://www.economist.com/interactive/science-and-technology/2023/04/22/large-creative-ai-models-will-transform-how-we-live-and-work (accessed 22.4.23).

58. J. Naughton, 'A race it might be impossible to stop': how worried should we be about AI.' Cf. https://www.theguardian.com/technology/2023/may/07/a-race-it-might-be-impossible-to-stop-how-worried-should-we-be-about-ai (accessed 7.5.23).

59. E. Yudkowsky, 'Pausing AI Development is not enough, we need to shut it down.' Cf. https://time.com/6266923/ai-eliezer-yudkowsky-open-letter-not-enough/ (accessed 29.3.23).

60. E. Yudkowsky, 'Pausing AI Development is not enough, we need to shut it down.' Cf. https://time.com/6266923/ai-eliezer-yudkowsky-open-letter-not-enough/ (accessed 29.3.23).

61. This has been proposed by OpenAI (funded by Microsoft who embedded Chat Gpt in its Bing search engine, 03.2023). Cf. https://openai.com/blog/our-approach-to-alignment-research (accessed 29.3.23)

62. OECD, 'Vertical mergers TMT,' 2019. Cf. https://one.oecd.org/document/DAF/COMP(2019)5/en/pdf (accessed 24.4.23).

63. Microsoft Office, Linkedin, Facebook, Twitter, Slack, mobile messaging, corporate chat and email services are the most frequently targeted applications by malicious actors (2023).

64. The US East Coast electricity grid has been sabotaged several times and is vulnerable to further attack. Cf. https://www.forbes.com/sites/chuckbrooks/2023/02/15/3-alarming-threats-to-the-us-energy-grid--cyber-physical-and-existential-events/
China has defended its electricity grid using a new form of organisational structure called the DAO, which means 'good and moral action' in Chinese; and lends its name to a new form of organisation called 'decentralised autonomous organisations.'

65. Albert Einstein – 'What life means to Albert Einstein,' interview by G.S. Viereck, *The Saturday Evening* Post (26.10.1929). Cf. https://www.saturdayeveningpost.com/wp-content/uploads/satevepost/what_life_means_to_einstein.pdf (accessed 21.3.23).

66. It is worth noting the English word 'intonation' is derived from the Latin 'intonare,' which means 'to sense.' The inflection point in speech points to a change in tone or pitch as the voice rises and falls; the sound conveys emotion and it is rich in meaning. In the business context, the tone

of voice determines how team members and collaborators may respond and impacts productivity.

67. The taxonomy used in philosophy and linguistics to unravel meaning in speech includes the following *classifications*: assertive, directive, expressive, performative (persuasive) and commissive (commitment to a future action) statements. The evaluation criteria as to what may be considered a 'true' or 'false' statement *varies* according to the contextual specificity of the utterance, implicit meaning, tacit knowledge, capacity to understand and the ability to carry out an action.

68. Russell Ackoff and Frederick Edmund Emery first wrote about purposeful systems in 1972, 'Individual systems are purposive, knowledge and understanding of their aims can only be gained by taking into account the mechanisms of social, cultural, and psychological systems.' Cf. https://en.wikipedia.org/wiki/Russell_L._Ackoff (accessed 11.8.22).

69. Socio-Technical Systems comprise multiple dimensions and several levels of interdependent interactions between interconnected constituent parts: mechanical (hardware), informational content (software and network choice architecture), psychological and organisational social infrastructure (people and communities) needed for the operation of the Enterprise.

70. HLEG (2019) – 'Ethics guidelines for trustworthy AI.' Cf. https://www.europarl.europa.eu/cmsdata/196377/AI%20HLEG_Ethics%20Guidelines%20for%20Trustworthy%20AI.pdf (accessed 21.2.23).

71. Explainability (XAI) is the ability of an 'Artificial Intelligence agent' to list the steps it has taken from input to output in natural language, such that its 'activity' is accessible to a human user. Interpretability is the degree to which a human user can understand how a model reached its predictions; it is the ability to predict the output a model will give, given a change in input or algorithmic parameters.

72. C. Barrett et al. (2023), Stanford Center for AI Safety. Cf. https://aisafety.stanford.edu/whitepaper.pdf (accessed 29.4.23).

73. Geoffrey Hinton, who created 'back-propagation' learning algorithm commonly used in deep learning neural networks, recently resigned from Google and announced his change of heart: 'I've come to the conclusion that the kind of intelligence we're developing is very different from the intelligence we have . . . . We're biological systems and these are digital systems. And the big difference is that with digital systems, you have many copies of the same set of weights, the same model of the world.' And all these copies can learn separately but share their knowledge instantly. So it's as if you had 10,000 people and whenever one person learnt something, everybody automatically knew it. And that's how these chat-bots can know so much more than any one person.' Cf. https://www.bbc.co.uk/news/world-us-canada-65452940 (accessed 2.5.23).

74. Danaher (2018. Cf. A. Laitinen (2021), 'AI systems and respect for human autonomy,' https://www.ncbi.nlm.nih.gov/pmc/articles/PMC8576577/ (accessed 26.4.23).

75. Stephen Hawking. Cf. https://www.vox.com/future-perfect/2018/10/16/ 17978596/stephen-hawking-ai-climate-change-robots-future-universe-earth

76. G. Marcus et al. 'The world needs an international agency for AI.' Cf. https://www.economist.com/by-invitation/2023/04/18/the-world-needs-an-international-agency-for-artificial-intelligence-say-two-ai-experts (accessed 20.4.23).

77. OpenAI announced (April 2023) tie-up with Norwegian Robotics Company to build humanoid robots with 'real' life-like features, despite growing public concerns. Stephen Hawking cautioned we would not need to reach AGI, or ASI (general or super human intelligence) in order to be superceded; competence would suffice.

78. Charles Darwin, 'In the long history of humankind (and animal kind, too) those who learned to collaborate and improvise most effectively have prevailed.'

EPILOGUE

1. Buddha (563–483 BCE), spiritual teacher advocating the pursuit of a lifetime journey towards the attainment of wisdom through reflection and contemplation upon the 'middle way,' has inspired generations in both the East and the West through the Arts, the Sciences and the Humanities.

2. Robert Buckminster Fuller (1895–1983), American architect, philosopher, inventor best known for his 'geodesic domes,' built in the 1950s, following the original design built in 1926 by German engineer Walther Blauersfeld (1879–1959).

3. Rumi (1207–1273), Persian poet and theologian inspired many with the lyrical beauty of his works.

4. Robert Buckminster Fuller (1981), *Critical Path* published in New York, St.Martin's Press.

5. Carl Sagan (1997), *The Demon-Haunted World: Science as a Candle in the Dark*, published by Ballantine Books.

6. Carl Sagan (1934–1996), *Cosmos*, Random House, 1985.

7. Carl Sagan, (1997), *The Demon-Haunted World: Science as a Candle in the Dark*, published by Ballantine Books.

8. Dante Alighieri, *Paradiso*, Canto XXXIII, v. 145 (original Italian verse).

   Here vigour fail'd the towering fantasy:

   But yet the will roll'd onward, like a wheel
   In even motion, by the Love impell'd,
   That moves the sun in heaven and all the stars.
   (Paradise, XXXIII, 132–5)

Acknowledgements

Thank you to my husband for his support and encouragement, making this book possible, and my nephews—a constant source of joy and inspiration.

Thank you to the great writers, artists, scientists and philosophers whose thoughtfulness continues to shape our world, especially those who inspire others and help humanity prosper.

Finally, thank you to the team at Wiley for bringing this book to fruition.

Index